INTERNATIONAL BUSINESS

THE ACADEMY OF INTERNATIONAL BUSINESS

Published in association with the UK Chapter of the Academy of International Business

Titles already published in this series:

INTERNATIONAL BUSINESS AND EUROPE IN TRANSITION (Volume 1)
Edited by Fred Burton, Mo Yamin and Stephen Young

INTERNATIONALISATION STRATEGIES (Volume 2)
Edited by George Chryssochoidis, Carla Millar and Jeremy Clegg

THE STRATEGY AND ORGANIZATION OF INTERNATIONAL BUSINESS (Volume 3)
Edited by Peter Buckley, Fred Burton and Hafiz Mirza

INTERNATIONALIZATION: PROCESS, CONTEXTS AND MARKETS (Volume 4)
Edited by Graham Hooley, Ray Loveridge and David Wilson

INTERNATIONAL BUSINESS ORGANIZATION (Volume 5)
Edited by Fred Burton, Malcolm Chapman and Adam Cross

International Business

Emerging Issues and Emerging Markets

Edited by

Carla C. J. M. Millar

Robert M. Grant

and

Chong Ju Choi

First published in Great Britain 2000 by

MACMILLAN PRESS LTD

Houndmills, Basingstoke, Hampshire RG21 6XS and London
Companies and representatives throughout the world

A catalogue record for this book is available from the British Library.

ISBN 0–333–77100–1

First published in the United States of America 2000 by

ST. MARTIN'S PRESS, INC.,

Scholarly and Reference Division,
175 Fifth Avenue, New York, N.Y. 10010

ISBN 0–312–22945–3

Library of Congress Cataloging-in-Publication Data
International business : emerging issues and emerging markets / edited by
Carla C. J. M. Millar, Robert M. Grant and Chong Ju Choi.
    p. cm.
Includes bibliographical references and index.
ISBN 0–312–22945–3
1. International economic relations.   2. International trade.   3. International
finance.   4.
Investment, Foreign.   5. International business enterprises.   I. Millar,
Carla C.J.M.   II. Grant, Robert M., 1948–   III. Choi, Chong Ju.
HF1359 .I568   1999
658'.049—dc21
                                                          99–049413

This book is printed on paper suitable for recycling and made from fully managed and
sustained forest sources.

10   9   8   7   6   5   4   3   2   1
09   08   07   06   05   04   03   02   01   00

Printed and bound in Great Britain by
Antony Rowe Ltd, Chippenham, Wiltshire

Contents

List of Figures

List of Tables

Foreword

On the brink of the new millennium **International Business** too is entering a new era.

This, the 6th volume in the Macmillan AIB Series covers a number of crucial research areas in the field: as editors we have addressed some major ones in Chapter 1 while all of the volume brings the reader the most recent conceptual and empirical research in International Business.

The volume consists of two parts. Part One is called 'Developments in international business' and covers advanced thinking in a number of important areas such as knowledge management, subsidiary management, small firm internationalisation and the impact of technological developments on international business.

It contains the UK AIB 25th Conference's Keynote Address by Professor Alan Rugman, on 'Multinational Enterprises and Public Policy'.

Part Two is a more direct reflection of the theme of the UK AIB's 25th conference 'International Business and Emerging Markets' and focuses on the impact of FDI in three specific regions: the European Union, Central and Eastern Europe and South East Asia.

As editors of the volume we would like to pay tribute to the dedication of all involved with the organisation of the 25th AIB Conference held at City University, the birthplace of this volume we arrived at through selection, rewriting and editing of some of its over 70 double blind refereed and accepted competitive papers.

We also are most grateful to all who worked so professionally and kindly with us in producing the book: Stephen Rutt and his team at the publishers, and Keith Povey, the copy-editor. Thanks to our colleagues who reviewed the papers, and to all authors who made the book such a special one.

Happy reading.

CARLA C.J.M. MILLAR
ROBERT M. GRANT
CHONG JU CHOI

List of Contributors

Paul Almeida
Georgetown University

Jim Bell
University of Otago

Mark E. Bleackley
London Business School

Robert Carty
University of Greenwich

Chong Ju Choi
The Judge Institute, Cambridge University

Jeremy Clegg
Centre for International Business, University of Leeds

Tony Cox
Aston Business School, Aston University

David Crick
DeMontfort University

John Fahy
Department of Marketing and Management, University of Limerick

David Floyd
University of Sunderland

Robert M. Grant
City University Business School and Georgetown University

Neil Hood
Strategic International Business Unit, University of Strathclyde

Graham Hooley
Aston Business School, Aston University

Lakis C. Kaounides
City University Business School

Carla C.J.M. Millar
City University Business School

Ram Mudambi
University of Reading and Case Western Reserve University

Alan M. Rugman
Templeton College, Oxford

Susan Scott-Green
Centre for International Business, University of Leeds

Boris Snoj
EPF, University of Maribor

Jaeyong Song
Columbia University

James H. Taggart
Strategic International Business Unit, University of Strathclyde

Yukio Takagaki
Department of Economics, Okinawa International University

Daniel van den Bulcke
RUCA, University of Antwerp

Alain Verbeke
Solvay Business School, University of Brussels

Peter J. Williamson
INSEAD

Stephen Young
Department of Marketing, University of Strathclyde

Haiyan Zhang
RUCA, University of Antwerp

Acknowledgements

The editors and publishers are grateful to the following for permission to reproduce copyright material: the *Journal of International Business Studies* for Alan M. Rugman and Alain Verbeke, 'Multinational Enterprises and Public Policy', 29(1), March 1998, pp. 115–36; and Elsevier Science for material from Ram Mudambi, 'MNE Internal Capital Markets and Subsidiary Strategic Independence', *International Business Review*, 8, 1999, pp. 197–211. Every effort has been made to contact all the copyright-holders, but if any have been inadvertently omitted the publishers will be pleased to make the necessary arrangement at the earliest opportunity.

1 Introduction – Current Issues in International Business Research

Carla C.J.M. Millar, Robert M. Grant and Chong Ju Choi

F23
014 047

THE FIELD OF INTERNATIONAL BUSINESS

The start of a new millennium has encouraged reflection upon the past and anticipation of the future across a wide range of human activities. This is certainly true of international business. The 1992 conference on 'International Business: An Emerging Vision' provided a forum for reviewing the state of international business (IB) and its future development, while the publication of the papers from the conference (Toyne and Nigh, 1997) offered a focal point for continuing debate. In this debate it is possible to identify two broad schools of thought concerning the field of IB: that which views IB essentially as a research context and set of issues, and that which views IB as a distinct area of study with its own theoretical basis.

The 'IB-as-context-and-issues' approach views IB as defined by a set of issues rising from cross-border aspects of business. These issues are inevitably broad since even the term 'international' is merely a proxy for a diversity of environmental factors relating to variations in location, political systems and institutions, social structures, cultures, languages, and economic institutions (including currencies). Researching these issues inevitably requires specialists from multiple disciplines. The challenge is to integrate the analytical power of these different disciplines. The implication is that, as a field of study, the primary role of IB is to provide international institutional contexts that support knowledge exchange among the various specialists.

The 'IB-as-discipline' approach places its emphasis upon multidisciplinary integration, leading to a body of IB literature. The proponents of this view recognise that IB will always draw concepts and theories from economics, political science, anthropology and other disciplines. However, the greatest contribution to knowledge will be in the integration of these disciplines and the subsequent development of a distinct body of IB theory. Within a business school setting, this approach would tend to be associated with the establishment of separate departments of IB.

1

As Stopford (1998) recognises, these different approaches yield different implications about the scope of IB research. The IB-as-issues approach encompasses a broad realm of topics ranging from national economic development to cross-cultural management. The risk, however, is that IB becomes 'no more than a kind of kitchen sink, full of interesting observations about the complexity of the world, but providing little insight into the essential choices policy makers and managers face' (Stopford, 1998, p. 636). If, on the other hand, IB is to develop a unifying theory, clearly its fields of interest must become more focussed.

Sullivan (1998) suggests that as far as IB's leading periodical, the *Journal of International Business Studies*, is concerned, the IB-as-discipline school may well have gained the upper hand. Classifying published papers by their 'schematic archetypes', Sullivan identified the increasing dominance of an 'analogue' paradigm in contrast to the richer, less linear 'composite' and 'prepositional' paradigms. This rise of 'narrow vision' in IB research runs the risks of imposing

> a constricting, almost Procrustean logic of interpretation. Analogue reasoning is prone to devolve into rigid, linear analysis that encourages consensus-building quantification as an end unto itself. Unchecked, the search for ultimate causes and effects can inspire an over-rationalised representation whose disregard for non-linear processes may lead to technically significant connections, but intellectually sterile findings. (Sullivan, 1998, p. 853)

Among those who argue for the development of a distinct body of IB theory, a central difficulty is that, after over half a century of development, there is still little to show in the way of a general theory of IB. The central areas of IB research – international trade and foreign direct investment – certainly do have well-developed core theories, but these theories have been taken directly from economics: in the case of international trade, theories of trade based upon comparative advantage, product differentiation, and strategic considerations, in the case of foreign direct investment, the analysis of economies of scale and scope, and transaction cost theory. Toyne and Nigh (Toyne, 1989; Toyne and Nigh, 1997, 1998) anticipate the shape and content of such a body of IB theory. They discern two existing paradigms of IB research, one that views international business activities as firms extending their activities beyond their own national borders (the 'extension paradigm') and one that explores cross-border flows of goods and services and the coordination and integration of operations and activities across borders (the 'cross-border management paradigm'). They then look forward to a broadening of the scope of IB theory through two avenues: first, a multi-level analysis of international phenomena that looks not only at the firm as the unit of analysis, but also, at a more aggregated level, the industry, the national state, and the 'supra-society'; and at a more disaggregated level, the group and the individual; second, the displacement of multidisciplinary IB research by interdisciplinary IB research.

Such projections of the development of an interdisciplinary, multilevel body of IB theory tend, so far, to be long on expectation and short on evidence. As we have already suggested, the IB field has made little progress towards developing a distinctive, interdisciplinary body of theory. Such integration that has occurred has tended to be within a narrow scope, e.g. attempts to integrate international business and international management streams (Buckley, 1996). However, in terms of multilevel research, progress can be discerned in research that links firm-level and national government-level behaviours (see, for example, Chapters 2 and 3 in this volume).

Certainly, the development of interdisciplinary and multilevel theories is much to be desired. However, the practicality of this goal is doubtful. As Stopford (1998) and others have recognised, the emergence of IB as a separate field of study was primarily a reaction by business scholars, especially in the US, to the US-centric view of business evident both in US corporations and US business schools during the 1950s. Now that 'teaching and theorising in the main business functions has become more international in scope', the question is: 'Does IB add anything to, say, finance that is not covered in the main finance courses or in the finance journals?' If the issues of IB, which range from global financial contagion, to cross-cultural business negotiations, and international transfers of best practices within multinational corporations, are characterised by their diversity and their complexity, two conclusions can be drawn. First, no single body of theory is applicable to more than a subset of IB issues. Second, in relation to each individual discipline, whether it is economics, organisational behaviour or accounting, and each individual function, whether it is finance, marketing, operations or strategy, IB issues are likely to be at the cutting edge of theory development. For example, in relation to organisation theory and design, it is the sheer complexity of multinational, multiproduct companies such as ABB, Corning, and Matsushita that has pushed organisational theory to consider three-way matrix structures, the principles of network structures, and the design of coordination and control systems. Similarly with strategy, it is the challenge of international issues, such as national competitiveness, that has captured the interest of leading strategy thinkers such as Michael Porter, and resulted in enrichment of the strategy field through the a better understanding of the evolution of firm capabilities and competitive advantage. Similarly, examples can be given for marketing, operations, information technology, etc.

Whichever view of IB one takes, IB as a context and a set of issues or IB as a discipline, the fundamental goals are the same. We are looking to build a body of knowledge that allows us to understand intentional business phenomena, to predict their emergence and evolution, and to manage them to improve firm performance and the welfare of mankind. Continuing progress in building such a body of knowledge is unlikely to result from focussing upon theory development. Theory is generated by grappling with real world issues. To this extent, the dynamism of IB is critically dependent upon the willingness and ability of IB scholars to recognise and address emerging issues in IB.

Is this happening? To some extent, yes. The work of Porter (1990, 1998), Krugman (1991a, b, 1995), the MIT Committee on International Competitiveness (Dertouzos *et al.*, 1989), and many others has encouraged an explosion of interest in national aspects of firm competitive advantage. In the structure and management of multinational corporations, the contributions of Bartlett and Ghoshal (1989), Doz (1980), and Hedlund (1986) represent important contributions. International joint ventures and strategic alliances are also a topic that has seen a surge of activity with important contributions by Contractor and Lorange (1988), Hagedoorn (1993), Hamel (1991), among others. At the same time, a look at any international business journal will confirm an enduring characteristic of the field: despite the rapid pace of change in the international business environment and the pace of innovation in international management practice, research in IB remains highly concentrated upon the two topics upon which IB was founded – international trade and foreign direct investment. What is being left out?

Rather than taking the functional area route, we proceed by discussing four topics that we believe have suffered from relative neglect by IB scholars:

- First, emerging and developing economies and economic growth. The majority of the research in international business is based on mature or developed economies, especially in North America and Western Europe; exceptions include Child (1994), Choi (1992, 1994) and Wade (1996). The research that is carried out in emerging and developing economies, tends to take the perspective of a corporation from a mature economy entering an emerging or developing economy, rather than the perspective of the organisations and institutions in the emerging or developing economy.
- Second, the financial systems, and the creation and allocation of capital by corporations in the international business environment have not been sufficiently researched. This strand of research has become an important one in the expanding field of comparative corporate governance, which shows the differences in financial systems across the world (Roe, 1994; Choi, 1992; Choi *et al.*, 1999a). In turn, these differences in financial systems are also closely influenced by the different legal systems across the world (La Porta *et al.*, 1996).
- Third, the nature of ideology and value systems (North, 1990), which have been seen as fundamental to successful economies, have not been

sufficiently studied in international business. Exceptions include Boddewyn (1988), Lenway and Murtha (1991), Choi (1992, 1998) and Murtha and Lenway (1994).

• Finally, the role of geography in business activitity, in particular, the patterns of specialisation by locality, and the processes that sustain these clusters. Porter's *Competitive Advantage of Nations* (1990) rekindled interest in the role of local industry clusters. Subsequently we have seen a convergence of interest among its scholars and geographers. The result has been a shifting of interest from the nation state to smaller geographical units.

EMERGING ECONOMIES AND ECONOMIC GROWTH

The events of June 1997 to December 1998 were salutary for scholars of international business and international economic development. The unravelling of the Asian 'miracle' economies (Krugman, 1999), the collapse of the Russian economy, and the currency crisis in Brazil dampened the euphoric predictions concerning the power of market capitalism to generate economic development in emerging markets. In spite of these developments, it is clear that, looking longer term, these markets offer major growth opportunities for multinationals. Compared to the low annual growth rates for most products in mature markets, sales in emerging markets have the potential to grow at an exponential rate for the indefinite future.

For corporations to make an informed judgement about investing in 'emerging markets' it is imperative that they appreciate both the common and the distinctive features of these markets. The term 'emerging markets' refers to certain regions of the world that seem rapidly to be entering the world business system; this includes most of the Asian countries, some Eastern European countries such as Hungary and the Czech Republic, and some Latin American countries such as Mexico, Chile and Brazil. Due to their phenomenal economic growth, large populations, and increasing corporate success in the global environment, the emerging markets have become a key focus for personal and institutional investors as well as for international corporations (Choi *et al.*, 1999a, 1999b).

At the same time, the nature of society, business exchange, legal systems, consumer demand and public policy in these emerging markets, which are often very different from the more mature economies, have provided difficult dilemmas for North American and Western European governments and corporations (Olson 1991, 1992). Even within emerging markets, of course, there can be substantial differences in regions such as Central and Eastern Europe, which are in transition, and in other parts of the world.

These changes suggest that there are two main strands to the study of the development of emerging markets. The first is the study of the emerging market business systems in the context of the political embeddedness of the institutions and organisations that impose constraints on the evolution of the business system (North 1990; Choi, 1992, 1994). This stream of research links to the next section in this chapter and incorporates differing patterns of corporate governance, the role of financial markets and the challenge posed by alliance capitalism to the predominant neo-liberal Anglo-Saxon capitalist orthodoxy. The second stream of research, covered in depth in the section thereafter, focuses on the role of knowledge in development – the relationship between the knowledge about technology and the knowledge about attributes, such as quality of a product, firm, etc. (World Bank, 1998), which impacts on the development of emerging markets.

Governments, Markets and Economic Development

> The fundamental distinction between domestic and international business is the existence of interventions by governments in inter-country business activity, which lead to business reactions. (Grosse and Behram, 1992, p. 94)

Thus, the study of international business has to focus primarily on firms that undertake business activities that cross national borders and on the policies of the host governments that regulate them. Avoiding the study of governmental policies and politics eliminates the *international* component of international business (Boddewyn, 1988). Of the factors that are transforming the global marketplace only some of them are directly influenced by the policy prescriptions of the host governments having an impact on international business. These influences include deregulation of economic and business activity, the decrease in protectionism and the emergence of trading blocs.

Although international business researchers have borrowed heavily from economic research in international trade (Dunning, 1996), they have neglected to take note of the research in development- and growth-based theories in economics. The debate about the role of the state lies at the heart of development economics. Until the early 1990s, this debate about the role of markets and governments in guiding the economy was conducted mainly along ideological lines. At one end of the ideological spectrum there were the advocates of the 'minimalist' state (Nozick, 1974) and at the other end were those who advocated the central role of the state in development. Much of this debate has been, and continues to be, dominated by the idea of 'market failure'. The early development theorists (Rosenstein-Rodan, 1943; Scitovsky, 1954; Hirschman, 1958) pointed to market failure as a reason for comprehensive planning. The actual experiences of the developing countries, in the context of problems associated with government intervention, and theoretical arguments against the role of the state, led to the recognition of 'government failure' as an impediment to development (von Hayek, 1967, 1986; Bauer, 1971, 1984; Little *et al.*, 1970). Increasing disenchantment about economic planning through the next three decades, formed a central part of what is referred to as the 'neo-classical resurgence'. The criticism about the deficiencies of planning focussed mainly on price distortions associated with the protectionist and import substitution policies that usually accompanied planning (Balassa, 1971; Kreuger, 1972; Dasgupta *et al.*, 1972; Little and Mirrlees, 1974). These traditional issues of economic and business development and growth are well within the research areas of international business; they have been relatively neglected by researchers, however.

This debate about the role of markets and governments was challenged from a different direction by the phenomenal growth in the East and South East Asian markets. For example, South Korea, whose economy had an outward orientation but with substantial government intervention in the investment process and import substitution, had registered phenomenal economic growth and went on to become a member of the Organisation for Economic Cooperation and Development (OECD) in quarter of a century (Wade, 1985; Jacobs, 1985; Kim and Yun, 1988). Over the last two decades, China has shown rapid growth through a number of different planning regimes, with no claims to being a free trading country with minimalist government (Riskin, 1987; Perkins, 1988).

Until very recently, straddling the development debate has been the World Bank, arguably one of the most powerful producers of international development knowledge. In the beginning, the Bank's main focus was on alleviation of poverty to stem the tide of communism with a firm belief in emulating the approach to economic modernisation believed to have been adopted by North America and Western Europe; the state was to play a significant role in poverty alleviation. In the early 1980s, the emergence of neo-liberal governments in a number of Western industrialised countries and changes in the overall context of the international political economy led to neo-liberalism emerging as the dominant narrative on development. This led to poverty alleviation being demoted as a priority for the Bank, with structural adjustment policies taking its place. The Bank had tried to depict the East Asian experience as essentially a normal part of capitalist development in accordance with neo-classical economics, marginalising the microeconomic industry and corporate factors as well as the role of legal systems and other institutional factors. It was only in 1993, in a Japanese government-funded study, that for the first time in a major World Bank publication it conceded that government intervention and other institutional and non-market factors had played some role in the economic development of most of East Asia (World Bank, 1993; Wade, 1996). In conceptual terms it throws up a range of options in terms of the role of government, banks, capital markets and other institutions in development, producing the differing business systems that compete in the global economy.

FINANCIAL SYSTEMS, CAPITAL AND GOVERNANCE

Although financial capital is fundamental to the success of corporations, industries and countries, the role of finance in international business has been a relatively neglected research topic. The issue of capital allocation and economic success has been one that has been argued by researchers and policymakers for at least most of the 20th century. Prominent economists such as John Hicks argued that the financial markets of the United Kingdom allowed rapid industrialisation in England through the mobilisation of capital and overcoming of risk for the development of immense, major industrial projects (Hicks, 1969). In contrast, Joseph Schumpeter argued that banks, rather than financial markets, were fundamental to economic success, because banks would identify and fund the key entrepreneurs to develop technological innovations (Schumpeter, 1934). The academic debate on the relationship between financial factors and economic growth has been discussed in detail recently by Levine (1997), King and Levine (1993), Shleifer and Vishny (1997) and Aoki and Dinc (1997). Empirical research has shown that although countries with larger banks and more active financial markets tend to also have higher economic growth rates, it is not certain which particular financial allocation mechanism or which mix of banks and financial markets helps to create the greater economic success (Levine, 1997; Albert, 1991; Choi, 1992).

The allocation of financial capital within the financial systems literature is an immense area covering international economics, economic development and corporate finance (La Porta *et al.*, 1996; Aoki and Dinc, 1997). Financial systems perform multiple functions including: allocating resources, monitoring management performance, mobilising savings, providing information about prices, and facilitating exchange in the economy (Lall, 1992, 1995; Levine, 1997). The effectiveness of financial systems in fostering economic success has been analysed in two major types of models. In the first type of economics and finance model, the financial system affects the rate of capital formation through savings rates changes and reallocations (Romer, 1986). In the second type of economics and finance model, the financial system helps to encourage new technology and production processes (Rodrik, 1997; Aghion and Bolton, 1997).

The comparative financial literature behind these two major models of economic success have not provided conclusive theoretical or empirical conclusions in three major areas, although differences in legal systems may be a crucial factor (La Porta *et al.* 1996). Firstly, there is very little research on the role played by institutional factors, such as legal traditions or political systems in influencing effective financial capital allocation; recent exceptions include La Porta *et al.* (1996); Choi *et al.*, (1999b). Secondly, although both effective banking and financial markets are seen to be crucial to economic success (Levine, 1997), there are few conclusions on which mix of these financial instruments, such as banking, insurance, equity markets and bond markets, is optimal for a particular economy or region. Thirdly, there is very little evidence on the linkage between financial capital allocation systems and the level of economic maturity (Demirguc-Kunt and Maksimovic, 1996). For example, it is not certain whether particular capital allocation mechanisms, such as banking, equity or bond markets, derivatives that may enhance economic success in mature economies such as the United States or United Kingdom, are appropriate for emerging or transition economies such as in regions of Asia, Latin America or Eastern Europe (Choi, 1992, 1994; Choi *et al.*, 1999a, 1999b).

Before the late 1990s, the majority of research in economics, finance and international business tended to study the financial capital allocation system common in the United States and United Kingdom. This system is based on a strong legal structure, along with external monitoring of economics, business and management performance through financial markets, especially equity markets (Jensen and Meckling, 1976). But the economic success throughout the 1980s of countries such as Japan, Germany and France where financial capital is fundamentally allocated through banking and insurance organisations raised fundamental questions (Albert, 1991; Choi, 1992). As mentioned earlier, this academic debate goes back at least as far as Schumpeter's (1934) belief in bank-driven capital allocation, versus Hick's (1969) belief in financial, equity-markets-driven capital allocation.

More recent research in economics and finance has begun to test empirically the differences between the financial-markets-driven capital allocation system of the United States and the United Kingdom, relative to the banking-driven capital allocation system of Japan and most continental European countries (in works such as Roe (1994, 1997); Choi *et al.* (1999b)). In countries such as Japan and Germany, and most of continental Europe, major banks and insurance companies act as external stakeholders by holding major shares in firms, exercising governance and control over internal management through a more informal, relationship-based exchange. Countries using this type of capital allocation mechanism have been broadly called 'stakeholder' economies, or social market economies (Albert, 1991; Choi, 1992; Choi *et al.*, 1999b). The complexity of applying this difference to Asia is that many Asian national business systems are still emerging and can often be a mix of both shareholder and stakeholder systems (Fruin, 1992).

IDEOLOGY, KNOWLEDGE AND CIVILIZATIONS

In spite of the dominant rhetoric of the global interlinked economy and the trend to homogenisation across countries, the compelling need to explain the differential rates of organisational performance on the basis of different modes of coordination and transaction governance over the past two decades has prompted many strands of international and comparative research on national business systems (Olson, 1991, 1992; Choi, 1994; North, 1990). According to Nelson (1992), there are three clusters of analysis concerning the determinants of 'national competitiveness'. First, viewing firms as the main competitive unit; second, microeconomic policies at the level of industries, and third, the macroeconomic performance of national economies. Research in international business needs, of course, to take into account all three levels of analysis and also include the importance of the interactions between institutions and organisations.

Dunning (1996), in his reexamination of the eclectic paradigm, recognises that the socio-institutional structure of market-based capitalism is undergoing changes, characterised principally by innovation-led growth, a 'voice' (Hirschman 1970) reaction to market failure, and cooperation as a competitiveness enhancing measure. These catalysts for the structural economic changes and the blurring of national boundaries, in addition to their various consequences on firm activities and performance, have led to an urgent need to reassess the traditional frameworks of international business and strategy for global competition. A key issue is the role of political, social and institutional factors driving today's successful business systems, and how such systems can be emulated by other countries. Choi (1992), Roe (1994, 1997), Choi *et al.* (1999a, 1999b), Boddewyn and Brewer (1994) and Kogut (1993) have analysed in depth the importance of the socio-economic home environments of the firm or the home market constraints on their competitiveness; other researchers have generally treated these as exogenous to the autonomous market system.

Knowledge

Knowledge has become an important topic of research in international business in the context of multinational enterprises and the transfer of knowledge across borders (Kogut and Zander 1993, 1995; Love 1995; McFetridge 1995; Grant and Spender, 1996; see also Chapter 6 in this volume). This past research has tended to define knowledge generically and to focus on the issue of how markets and organisations differ in their capabilities of transferring knowledge. Thus, the comparisons of markets versus organisations has been in a 'developed' country context. We postulate that the major questions of knowledge, multinational enterprise and efficiency of markets may change substantially in a transition or emerging market context, such as in Central/Eastern Europe or in parts of Asia (Choi, 1994). For example, investments in knowledge among North American multinational enterprises tend to focus on to research and development and original innovation; however, in the context of a less developed economy, investments in knowledge are more in the area of technology licensing, or in the establishment of institutions to protect intellectual property rights to knowledge.

There are two major issues concerning knowledge particularly relevant to the economic success of and the crisis in emerging markets. First, although there is a general interest in knowledge as a resource, there is a substantial gap in definitions between international business research and related areas of economics research. There is clear overlap in disciplines over some of the major issues, however, including multinational enterprise, management, global markets, knowledge transfer and public goods, just as a substantial part of international business research has relied on an international economics methodology (Grant and Spender, 1996; Dunning, 1996). We believe this gap has existed because although international business research has followed a relatively broad and interdisciplinary agenda within business and management research, international economics research has followed a narrower agenda of trade theory and exchange rates. In order to analyse knowledge as a resource there is thus a need to address the areas of diversion and overlap, and also to consider whether other areas of economics research have value in international business research. One area that especially warrants attention is the more recent research in economic development, which differentiates between knowledge about technology and knowledge about quality and attributes of goods and services, a type of knowledge that faces more general problems of imperfect information (Bowles and Gintis, 1996; Knack and Keefer, 1997; Levine, 1997; Choi, 1994; World Bank, 1998).

Second, international business research on knowledge has tended to analyse the specific situation of developed countries. For example, a typical starting point of analysis would be a North American multinational enterprise facing the issue of knowledge transfer through markets versus through its own subsidiaries (Kogut and Zander, 1993, 1995; Love, 1995; McFetridge, 1995) in a developed country business environment with relatively perfect information, effective institutions and intellectual property rights. The majority of business environments, however, are in a developing or emerging economy context, with imperfect information, institutions in transition and a lack of intellectual property rights. The value of knowledge in such an emerging economy context may be very different for multinational enterprises as well as for the overall economy and society. For example, the value of knowledge may be contained in the context of technology licensing, or in the development of certification agencies standardising quality and attributes of goods and services (Lall, 1992, 1995; Mody and Yilmaz, 1997; Amsden, 1989; Choi *et al.*, 1999a).

Ideologies and Civilisations

A highly interlinked new area of research would be to include the latest research developments in international relations and international political economy. Of course, researchers such as Boddewyn (1988) and Boddewyn and Brewer (1994) have shown the importance of such research for international business. However, the recent works of Huntington (1996), analysing global conflict in the post-war period as being driven by different civilisations, adds a different, more comprehensive paradigm to traditional concepts of 'culture' in international business (Hofstede, 1980).

Huntington's (1996) analysis of the world's civilisations, such as Western, Chinese, Islam, and Hindu, overlaps with North's (1990) analysis of ideology and value systems, and how they affect economic, industry and corporate performance, and not only in the extreme case of Islamic civilisation and religion and its values affecting the lending of money and interest rates. This grouping of countries and regions provides an alternative and in some respects a more realistic, system-based framework than the traditional culture literature (Hofstede, 1980) commonly used for analysis in management and international business.

ECONOMIC GEOGRAPHY, REGIONALISATION AND LOCAL ISSUES

A defining feature of the domain of IB has been the importance it has accorded to the nation state and its boundaries. Yet, the issues of IB are not restricted to business phenomena that occur across political boundaries. They are concerned with the much larger set of issues that arise when business transactions and business organisation cross cultures, institutional environments, and economic and social systems. Indeed, a major theme in economic geography, which has influenced international business, has been the focus on clusters of economic activity whose boundaries do not correspond to those of the nation state, or indeed to any other political or administrative boundaries. Interest in localised business development can be traced back to Alfred Marshall's analysis of 'industrial districts' (Marshall, 1920). Questions of economic development at the level of regions, cities, and otherwise-defined localities were taken up by economic geographers in the 1960s and 1970s, only to be reintroduced into international economics and international business by Krugman (1991a, 1991b, 1995) and Porter (1990, 1995, 1998), among others. Common to all these approaches is a focus upon external economies that produce 'agglomeration effects'. From the viewpoint of international business scholars, some of the key issues are the nature of inter-firm linkages that produce localised industry clusters and provide the dynamics to investment, innovation and economies of specialisation. Comparative research into the dynamics of these inter-firm linkages, such as the Saxenian's comparison of the microelectronics industry of Massachusetts and California's Silicon Valley (Saxenian, 1994) and Almeida's tracking of geographical paths of innovation using patent citation data (Almeida, 1996; Almcida and Kogut, 1999) indicate some of the progress that is being made in unravelling the links between inter-firm relations and economic development.

CONCLUSIONS

The next few years promise to be an exciting and productive period for research in IB. The recent debates over the scope and methodologies of IB are indicative of the diversity and dynamism of the field. Our own experiences and beliefs point us towards a broadening rather a narrowing of the field of IB. The issues confronting business managers and public policy decision-makers in the area of cross-border business activities extend well beyond the traditional topics of trade and direct investment. Issues concerning the internal management of multinational corporations, collaborative international relationships between firms, the links between firm strategy and national and local economic development, international issues regarding firm versus industry strategies, the interactions between corporate and government decision making are characterised by their diversity and their complexity. We have pointed to four areas where we consider there to be scope for further study by IB scholars. Progress in these areas is unlikely to involve a single discipline, nor is there as yet any interdisciplinary body of IB theory that provides tools powerful enough to explore these issues. For the medium term at least, progress in IB will be critically dependent on the ability of the field to attract the best minds in individual disciplines (whether economics, sociology, political science, or anthropology) and specific functional areas (ranging from technology to operations and marketing) to apply their toils and insights to the issues of international business. The potential for multilevel research (Toyne and Nigh, 1998) in the form of a simultaneous rather than separate analysis at the level of nations, industries and corporations may well offer greater richness even if it does introduce higher levels of complexity. Thus, rather than trying to apply ideas from corporations to countries, such as Porter (1990), the nature of competitiveness and success could be more closely in line with Nelson's three levels of analysis (Nelson, 1992).

In this sense, it seems highly unlikely that there is a 'universal' model of capitalism or a universal model of international prosperity for countries, industries or corporations. However, there could be a 'fit' across these three levels. For example, in bank-financed economies, such as those of continental Europe and Japan, the nature of industries and competition changes, just as the organisation or corporate structure may adjust to these different circumstances (Aoki and Dinc, 1997). This type of 'plurality' is the way forward for international business researchers.

References

Aghion, P. and Bolton, P. (1997) 'A theory of trickle-down growth and development', *Review of Economic Studies*, 64: pp. 151–172.

Albert, M. (1991) *Capitalism against Capitalism* (Paris: Centre for Economic Research).

Almeida, P. (1996) 'Knowledge sourcing by foreign multinationals: patent citation analysis in the US semiconductor industry', *Strategic Management Journal*, 17 (Winter special issue): pp. 155–165.

Almeida, P. and Kogut, B. (1999) 'Localization of knowledge and mobility of engineers in regional networks', *Management Science*, forthcoming.

Amsden, A. (1989) *Asia's Next Giant* (New York: Oxford University Press).

Aoki, M. and Dinc, S. (1997) 'Relational finance and its viability under competition', Stanford University, Graduate School of Business, mimeo.

Balassa, B. (1971) *The Structure of Protection in Developing Countries* (Baltimore: Johns Hopkins University Press).

Bartlett, C.A. and Ghoshal, S. (1989) *Managing Across Borders: The Transnational Solution* (Boston, MA: Harvard Business School Press).

Bauer, P.T. (1971) *Dissent on Development: Studies and Debates in Development Economics* (London: Weidenfeld & Nicolson).

Bauer, P.T. (1984) *Reality and Rhetoric* (London: Weidenfeld & Nicolson).

Boddewyn, J.J. (1988) Political aspects of MNE theory, *Journal of International Business Studies*. 13: pp. 341–363.

Boddewyn, J.J. and Brewer, T. (1994) 'International-business political behaviour: new theoretical directions', *Journal of International Business Studies*, 19: pp. 119–143.

Bowles, S. and Gintis, H. (1996) 'Efficient redistribution: new rules for markets, states and communities', *Politics and Society*, 24: pp. 307–342.

Buckley, P. (1996) 'The role of management in international business theory: a meta-analysis and integration of the literature on international business and international management', *Management International Review*, 36 (special issue): pp. 7–54.

Child, J. (1994) *Management in China During the Age of Reform* (Cambridge: Cambridge University Press).

Choi, C.J. (1992) 'Asian capitalism versus Western civilisation', Oxford University, mimeo.

Choi, C.J. (1994) 'Contract enforcement across cultures', *Organisation Studies*, 15: pp. 673–682.

Choi, C.J. (1998) 'Asian capitalism versus Western civilisation: further concepts', Cambridge University, mimeo.

Choi, C.J. and Lee, S.H. (1997) 'A knowledge-based view of co-operative interorganizational relationships', in P. Beamish and P. Killing (eds), *Co-operative Strategies: European Perspectives* (Massachusetts: Josey-Bass).

Choi, C.J., Lee, S.H. and Kim, J.B. (1999a) 'Countertrade and transaction governance in emerging economies', *Journal of International Business Studies*, 30: pp. 1–15.

Choi, C.J., Raman, M., Oussoltseva, O. and Lee, S.H. (1999b) 'Political embeddedness and institutional analysis in the new global triad', *Management International Review*, 45: pp. 30–48.

Contractor, F.J. and Lorange, P. (eds) (1988) *Cooperative Strategies in International Business* (Lexington, MA: Heath).

Dasgupta, P.S., Marglin, S. and Sen, A.K. (1972) *Guidelines for Project Evaluation* (New York: United Nations).

Demirgucs-Kunt, A. and Levine, R. (1996) 'Stock market development and financial intermediaries: stylized facts', *World Bank Economic Review*, 10: pp. 291–322.

Derouzos, M., Lester, R. and Solow, R. (1989) *Made in America* (Cambridge, MA: MIT Press).

Doz, Y.L. (1980) 'Strategic management in multinational companies', *Management Review*, 21(2): pp. 27–46.

Dunning, J. (1996) 'Reappraising the eclectic paradigm in an age of alliance capitalism', *Journal of International Business Studies*, 26: pp. 461–480.

Fruin, M. (1992) *The Japanese Enterprise System: Competitive Strategies and Co-operative Structures* (Oxford: Clarendon Press).

Grant, R. and Spender, J.-C. (1996) 'Knowledge and the firm: overview', *Strategic Management Journal*, 17 (Winter special issue): pp. 1–4.

Grosse, R. and Behram, J.N. (1992) 'Theory in international business', *Transnational Corporations*, 1 (February): p. 94.

Hagedoorn, J. (1993) 'Understanding the rationale for strategic technology partnering: Interorganizational models of cooperation and sectoral differences'. *Strategic Management Journal*, 14: 371–386.

Hamel, G. (1991) 'Competition for competence and inter-partner learning within international strategic alliances', *Strategic Management Journal*, 12 (Summer Special Issue): 83–103.

Hedlund, G. (1986) 'The hyermodern MNC – a heterarchy', *Human Resource Management*, 25: pp. 9–25.

Hicks, J. (1969) *A Theory of Economic History* (Oxford: Clarendon Press).

Hirschman, A.O. (1958) *The Strategy of Economic Development* (New Haven: Yale University Press).

Hirschman, A.O. (1970) *Exit, Voice and Loyalty* (Cambridge, MA: Harvard University Press).

Hofstede, G. (1980) *Culture's Consequences* (Beverly Hills: Sage).

Huntington, S. (1996) *The Clash of Civilisations* (New York: Simon and Schuster).

Jacobs, N. (1985) *The Korean Road to Modernization and Development* (Urbana: University of Illinois Press).

Jensen, M. and Meckling, W. (1976) 'Theory of the firm: managerial behaviour, agency costs, and ownership structure', *Journal of Financial Economics*, 3: pp. 305–360.

Kim, W.S. and Yun, K.Y. (1988) 'Fiscal policy and development in Korea', *World Development*, 16(1): pp. 65–83.

King, R. and Levine, R. (1993) 'Finance and growth: Schumpeter might be right', *Quarterly Journal of Economics*, 108: pp. 717–737.

Knack, S. and Keefer, P. (1997) 'Does social capital have an economic payoff? A cross-country investigation', *Quarterly Journal of Economics*, 122: pp. 1251–1288.

Kogut, B. (1993) *Country Competitiveness: Technology and the Organizing of Work* (Oxford: Oxford University Press).

Kogut, B. and Zander, U. (1993) 'Knowledge of the firm and the evolutionary theory of the multinational enterprise', *Journal of International Business Studies*, 24: pp. 625–645.

Kogut, B. and Zander, U. (1995) 'Knowledge, market failure and the multinational enterprise: a reply', *Journal of International Business Studies*, 26: pp. 417–426.

Krueger, A.O. (1972) 'Evaluating restrictionist trade regimes: theory and measurement', *Journal of Political Economy*, 80: pp. 48–62.

Krugman, P. (1991a) 'Increasing returns and economic geography', *Journal of Political Economy*, 99: pp. 483–499.

Krugman, P. (1991b) *Geography and Trade* (Cambridge, MA: MIT Press).

Krugman, P. (1995) *Development, Geography and Economic Theory* (Cambridge, MA: MIT Press).

Krugman, P. (1999) *The Return of Depression Economics* (New York: W.W. Norton & Co.).

Lall, S. (1992) 'Technological capabilities and industrialisation', *World Development*, 20: pp. 165–186.

Lall, S. (1995) 'Structural adjustment and African industry', *World Development*, 23: pp. 2019–2031.

La Porta, R., Lopez de Silanes, F., Shleifer, A. and Vishny, R. (1996) 'Law and finance', National Bureau of Economic Research Working Paper no. 5661, Cambridge, MA.

Lenway, S. and Murtha, T. (1991) 'The idea of the state in the international business literature', Division of Research, School of Business Administration, University of Michigan, Ann Arbor.

Levine, R. (1997) 'Financial development and economic growth: view and agenda', *Journal of Economic Literature*, 35: pp. 688–727.

Little, I.M.D. and Mirrlees, J.A. (1974) *Project Appraisal and Planning for Developing Countries* (London: Heinemann).

Little, I.M.D., Scitovsky, T. and Scott, M. (1970) *Industry and Trade in some Developing Countries* (New York: Oxford University Press).

Love, J. (1995) 'Knowledge, market failure and the multinational enterprise: A theoretical note', *Journal of International Business Studies*, 26: pp. 399–407.

McFetridge, D. (1995) 'Knowledge, market failure and the multinational enterprise: a comment', *Journal of International Business Studies*, 26: pp. 409–416.

Marshall, A. (1920) *Industry and Trade* (London: Macmillan).

Mody, A. and Yilmaz, K. (1997) 'Is there persistence in the growth of manufactured exports? Evidence from newly industrializing countries', *Journal of Development Economics*, 53: pp. 447–470.

Murtha, T. and Lenway, S. (1994) 'Country capabilities and the strategic state: how national political institutions affect multinational corporations' strategies', *Strategic Management Journal*, 15: pp. 120–141.

Nelson, R. (1992) 'Recent writings on competitiveness: boxing the compass', *California Management Review*, 34 (Summer): pp. 117–125.

North, D. (1990) *Institutions, Institutional Change and Economic Performance* (Cambridge: Cambridge University Press).

Nozick, R. (1974) *Anarchy, State and Utopia* (New York: Basic Books).

Olson, M. (1991) 'Autocracy, democracy, and prosperity', in R. Zeckhauser (ed.), *Strategy and Choice* (Cambridge, MA: MIT Press).

Olson, M. (1992) 'The hidden path to a successful economy', in C. Clague and G. Rausser (eds) *The Emergence of Market Economies in Eastern Europe* (Oxford: Blackwell Publishers).

Perkins, D.H. (1988) 'Reforming China's economic system', *Journal of Economic Literature*, 26(2): pp. 601–645.

Porter, M. (1990) *The Competitive Advantage of Nations* (New York: Free Press).

Porter, M. (1995) 'The competitive advantage of the inner city', *Harvard Business Review*, (May–June): pp. 41–60.

Porter, M. (1998) 'Clusters and the new economics of competition', *Harvard Business Review*, (November–December): pp. 50–64.

Riskin, C. (1987) *China's Political Economy: The Quest for Development since 1949* (Oxford: Oxford University Press).

Rodrik, D. (1997) *Has Globalization Gone Too Far?* (Washington, DC: Institute of International Economics).

Roe, M. (1994) *Strong Managers, Weak Owners: the Political Roots of American Corporate Finance* (Princeton: Princeton University Press).

Roe, M. (1997) 'The political roots of American corporate finance', *Journal of Applied Corporate Finance*, 9: pp. 8–22.

Romer, P.M. (1986) 'Increasing returns and long-run growth', *Journal of Political Economy*, 94(5): pp. 1002–1037.

Rosenstein-Rodan, P. (1943) 'Problems of industrialisation in Eastern and South-eastern Europe', *Economic Journal*, 53: pp. 202–212.

Saxenian, A. (1994) *Regional Advantage: Culture and Competition in Silicon Valley and Route 128* (Cambridge, MA: Harvard University Press).

Schumpeter, J. (1934) *The Theory of Economic Development* (Cambridge, MA: Harvard University Press).

Scitovsky, T. (1954) 'Two concepts of external economies', *Journal of Political Economy*, 52(2): pp. 143–151.

Shleifer, A. and Vishny, R. (1997) 'A survey of corporate governance', *Journal of Finance*, 25: pp. 737–784.

Stopford, J. M. (1998) Review of *International Business: An Emerging Vision, Journal of International Business Studies*, 29: pp. 635–637.

Sullivan, D. (1998) 'Cognitive tendencies in international business research: implications of a "narrow vision"', *Journal of International Business Studies*, 29: pp. 837–862.

Toyne, B. (1989) 'International exchange: a foundation for a theory of international business', *Journal of International Business Studies*, 20: pp. 1–17.

Toyne, B. and Nigh, D. (1997) *International Business: An Emerging Vision* (Columbia, SC: University of South Carolina Press).

Toyne, B. and Nigh, D. (1998) 'A more expansive view of international business', *Journal of International Business Studies*, 29: pp. 863–875.

Von Hayek, F.A. (1967) *Studies in Philosophy, Politics and Economics* (London: Routledge and Kegan Paul).

Von Hayek, F.A. (1986) *The Road to Serfdom* (London: Routledge and Kegan Paul).

Wade, R. (1985) 'The role of government in overcoming market failure: Taiwan, South Korea, and Japan', in H. Hughes (ed.), *Explaining the Success of East Asian Industrialisation* (Cambridge: Cambridge University Press).

Wade, R. (1996) 'Japan, the World Bank, and the art of paradigm maintenance: the East Asian miracle in proper perspective', *New Left Review*, 217 (May–June): pp. 18–29.

World Bank (1993) *The East Asian Miracle: Economic Growth and Public Policy* (Oxford: Oxford University Press).

World Bank (1998) *World Development Report: Knowledge for Development* (Oxford: Oxford University Press).

Part One

Developments in International Business

2 Multinational Enterprises and Public Policy

Alan M. Rugman and Alain Verbeke

In this chapter we attempt to review and integrate representative literature on the exceptionally broad topic of multinational enterprises (MNEs) and public policy towards them. To help us in this difficult task we build upon the insights offered by Richard Caves (1982) in Chapter 10 (on 'public policy') in his critically acclaimed advanced textbook, *Multinational Enterprise and Economic Analysis*. This book was first published in 1982 and substantially revised in a second edition in 1996. Our specific task is to consider the literature on MNEs and public policy as it has emerged since 1970 and make projections ahead to the relevance of this literature for the year 2020, which is the target date set by the 18 members of the Asia-Pacific Economic Cooperation Forum (APEC) for the realisation of full trade and foreign direct investment (FDI) liberalisation. Such liberalisation has already been implemented in the European Union (15 member states), and it will further expand as new countries are accepted as EU members in the 21st century.

In the first half of Chapter 10, Caves adopts a 'normative' approach, using neo-classical welfare economics to review the benefits and costs of national government policies. In the second half of that chapter, Caves considers some 'behavioural' approaches to public policy, based on the assumption that there are self-interested actors in the political domain who can influence the formation of public policy. While retaining these insights we introduce a third approach in this chapter. Using the resource-based theory of the firm, we develop an explicit 'strategic' perspective for MNEs interacting with governments. This provides insight into the managerial aspects of the firm-level strategy process, dealing with core competencies and dynamic capabilities, that need to be integrated into the MNE-government literature. Furthermore, we carefully differentiate the policies of home and host governments, and show how the institutional structures of both public policy and the MNE are relevant in the current international business literature.

The organisation of this chapter is as follows. First, we review the analytical and policy contributions of Caves on public policy and MNEs (and in the rest of his book where public policy issues are discussed.) Next, we develop an original analytical framework of our own to synthesise the literature on MNEs and public policy. Finally, we relate some of the key references in the literature on MNEs and public policy by Caves and others to our new analytical framework.

EFFICIENCY ASPECTS OF MNEs AND PUBLIC POLICY

The analytical approach adopted by Caves in Chapter 10 of *Multinational Enterprise and Economic Analysis* is that of a traditional economist, essentially concentrating on the efficiency aspects of MNE activities in a world where government regulations on MNEs are imposed for equity/distributional reasons. This distinction between efficiency and equity is extremely useful from the viewpoint of an economist, and it has been used by many writers on MNEs, e.g. Safarian (1966, 1993), Rugman (1980), Casson (1987) and Dunning (1993a).

Analysis of the efficiency aspects of MNEs builds upon the normative foundation of neo-classical welfare economics (in which distributional issues are assumed away). In Chapter 10, Caves carefully lays out all the assumptions required for neo-classical welfare economics to work, namely, that:

- each state attempts to maximise real national income
- distributional issues are entirely separate from efficiency ones
- each enterprise has a single 'home base' country to act as a numeraire
- each MNE and nation state operate in a competitive environment, with a downward-sloping demand curve for the proprietary assets of the MNE and an upward-sloping supply curve of MNE resource commitments for each nation
- policy making by governments can discriminate between foreign- and home-based MNEs.

Using this welfare economics framework, Caves is able in Chapter 10 to summarise the normative conclusions of earlier chapters as they apply to key issues, such as:

- taxation
- natural resource rents
- competition policy
- technology creation and transfer.

A flavour of the implications stemming from the welfare economics approach is given by the last issue of technology transfer. Many writers sympathetic to developing countries bemoan the perceived lack of technology transfer from the branch plant subsidiaries of foreign MNEs, and allege lower ratios of research and development (R&D) to sales by subsidiaries as evidence of this. Caves, however, makes the brilliant point that technology transfer takes place when the consumers in developing countries have access to the goods and services that embody the technology. Thus, the focus is not upon the domestic production of technology intensive goods and services in developing countries, but upon the end result of FDI, namely the consumption of technologically-intensive goods and services. Whether they are provided by foreign-owned or domestic firms is relatively unimportant.

In the second half of Chapter 10, Caves presents a behavioural approach to supplement the normative approach of the first half of the Chapter. In the behavioral approach, Caves allows for the self interest of agents in government policy making. He briefly reviews government policies that are aimed at regulating inward FDI, and then home government policy directed towards the promotion of FDI for reasons of market access. A first version of Caves' behavioural approach explains the actual focus of many governments on distributional issues and away from income maximisation. Utility-maximising electoral behaviour leads to redistribution at the expense of foreign MNEs because foreign equity holders cannot vote, and discrimination against foreigners may provide perceived utility to domestic citisens. In a second version, government policy is assumed to be the work of a coalition of government officials, who resent foreign MNEs mainly because of their ability to circumvent or avoid various types of regulation. In both versions of the behavioural approach, discriminatory measures are imposed on foreign MNEs. These behavioural models, however, do not appear very useful in explaining government support for domestic MNEs engaged in outward FDI. Finally, Caves discusses the role of multilateral agencies that attempt to regulate or facilitate FDI and MNE activity.

Caves' focus on the efficiency aspects of MNEs is fully consistent with the use of internalisation theory (explained earlier in his book) as the key theoretical explanation for the existence of MNEs. The early work on such a transactions-cost approach to the MNE was pioneered by Buckley and Casson (1976), Rugman (1981), Hennart (1982) and others. All of these writers considered the public policy implications of the MNE in a similar manner to that in Caves (1982). This body of work is, of course, a significant departure from the seminal work of Hymer (1976) based on his 1960 doctoral dissertation. Hymer and many political science-based writers on the MNE, such as Gilpin (1975,1987) and Grieco (1982), are not really interested in the efficiency aspects of MNEs; rather they wish to discuss such issues as the relative power of MNEs versus the nation state.

There is a rich tradition of work looking into the relative power of the MNE versus the nation state, with some of the more sensible observations being in Vernon (1971), Bergsten, Horst and Moran (1978) and Behrman and Grosse (1990). In this chapter we do not have space to review these arguments in detail, nor can we consider the relationship of this work on MNEs to the relevant literature in international political economy (IPE) generated by Susan Strange (1988, 1997) and Lorraine Eden (1991). In IPE, the focus is upon the interaction between MNEs and nation states, with emphasis upon the ability of MNEs to transcend the traditional authority of the nation state. Susan Strange alleges that the MNE has increased its power relative to the state in the areas of natural resources, finance and technology. In particular, US-based MNEs have developed control in these three 'market' areas, leading to an overall decline in the power of the 'state', but paradoxically to the reinforcement of US economic hegemony for most of the post-war period. Another relevant consideration is that non-governmental organisations (NGOs) and other sub-national groups are exercising an increasing amount of power in the Western democracies (Ostry, 1997). The role of NGOs is especially important in analysis of trade and environment issues (Vogel, 1995; Vogel and Rugman, 1997; Rugman and Verbeke, 1998).

In another advance on Caves' 'efficiency first' perspective on MNEs, Stopford and Strange (1991) have addressed the relationships between MNEs and states in an IPE triangular diplomacy framework in which there is a triad of bargaining relationships: state/state; state/firm; firm/firm. As other examples of IPE work, Milner (1988) and Goldstein (1993) built on Krasner (1978), Keohane (1984) and Keohane and Nye (1977) to describe the role of institutional factors in the administration of US trade policy. Goldstein found that the US Congress protects the US domestic market by a variety of protectionist trade laws, such as anti-dumping (AD) and counter-vailing duty (CVD) measures (Rugman and Anderson, 1987; Bhagwati, 1988; Rugman, 1996).

We do not devote any more attention to IPE, hegemonic stability theory and related theories of MNE-government conflict because today governments need to deal with both inward and outward FDI. We shall develop a framework that considers the symmetry between these two types of FDI. Our approach is consistent with that of Dunning (1993a, 1997) who traces the changing nature of interaction between MNEs and governments over the last 30 years. In particular, governments have switched attention from questions of the distribution of rents and structural issues of technology transfer and regulation towards policies aimed at attracting the knowledge-based mobile FDI taking place in a global system of alliance capitalism.

THE SIMPLE ANALYTICS OF MNEs AND PUBLIC POLICY

In this section we shall develop an analytical framework to incorporate the work synthesised by Caves with other, more recent literature in the field of international business. To do this we need to build a framework consisting of three sequential components, which we now describe. In this section we will position Caves' perspective within this new conceptual analytical framework. In the following sections we shall place the wider literature in this framework. The first component of the framework reflects the issue of consistency between MNE goals and government goals in both home and host countries. Most of the models of international economics on MNE–government relations build upon specific assumptions regarding this goal consistency, or lack thereof. Such assumptions determine both the substantive focus and the normative implications of these models. The four main possibilities in this area are shown in Figure 2.1.

In quadrant 1 of Figure 2.1, interactions between MNEs and both home and host governments are assumed to be driven by goal conflict. This reflects the tensions between the micro-efficiency-driven behaviour of MNEs and the macro-efficiency or distributional objectives of governments. The opposite situation arises in quadrant 4 of Figure 2.1 – here the goals of MNEs and both home and host governments are complementary. In quadrant 2 there is consistency between MNE and home country goals, but conflicts with host country goals. The reverse applies in quadrant 3. In the next section, we shall use this matrix to position a large part of the existing literature in international business and public policy.

Caves' perspective on the literature requires that each MNE has a clearly defined nationality, usually with a strong home base in which its Firm

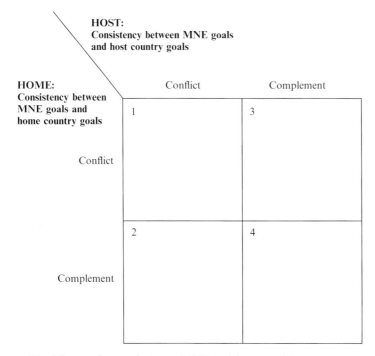

Figure 2.1 The consistency between MNE and home and host government goals

Specific Advantages (FSAs) are developed. The MNE has a centralised, hierarchical organisational structure to control the global production of each line of business. In terms of government regulation, Caves makes a clear distinction between home and host country interests. Given that the Caves perspective is primarily one of synthesis, it is hardly surprising that literature covering the various quadrants of Figure 2.1 is discussed in his book, albeit with a focus largely situated in quadrant 1. Caves concentrates his focus on research dealing with conflict issues between MNEs and governments, for example, taxation and competition policy, bargaining over natural resource rents and technology transfer issues.

The second component of the framework builds upon more recent insights in the international business field. There, it is recognised that the institutional characteristics of specific MNEs and specific countries largely determine MNE–government interactions. In contrast to the macro-analysis provided by the first component of our conceptual framework, which assumed a particular level of inherent goal congruence between firms and public agencies (largely based on ideological elements), this second component attempts to highlight the most important institutional elements determining MNE and government behaviour. These institutional elements are shown in Figure 2.2.

On the MNE axis, the key institutional issue for the firm is the dispersion of its FSAs across geographic borders. The FSAs of an MNE reflect its core competencies and dynamic capabilities (in terms of the resource-based theory of the firm). Incidentally, the FSA terminology precedes that of core competencies and dynamic capabilities (Rugman, 1980, 1981). A conventional ethnocentric MNE is characterised by a concentration of FSAs in the home country with a replication of home country production and managerial approaches in host nations. The product line manager in the home base controls the FSAs of the MNE. In contrast, a polycentric MNE is one with its FSAs dispersed into its various host nation subsidiaries. The country managers of the polycentric MNE develop and control the FSAs across whatever product markets they choose. Finally, a geocentric MNE attempts to develop a balance between the interests of product line and country managers. Here, some FSAs remain concentrated in the home base, whereas other FSAs are developed autonomously in the various host country subsidiaries. The Caves' perspective on the literature, with a focus on adversarial interactions, especially between the MNE and host nations, is justified only in the first case of an ethnocentric MNE. In both the latter two cases (of polycentric and geocentric MNEs), when FSAs are developed and controlled in several nations simultaneously, we need to build upon a richer framework that would allow us to explain the interaction between MNEs and governments.

On the government axis, the key parameter determining MNE–government relations is the symmetry between inward and outward FDI.

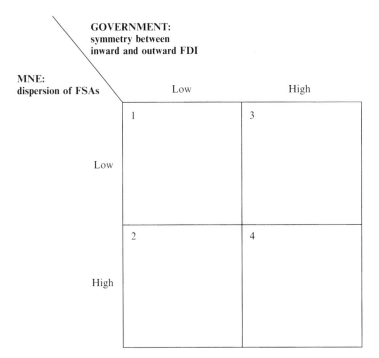

Figure 2.2   Institutional determinants of MNE–government interactions

In this chapter this parameter is viewed as an institutional element because a high symmetry represents an *ex post* reflection of the willingness of government to allow inward and outward FDI. A nation's policies towards MNEs will depend on whether it is (i) a net exporter of FDI (with MNEs using a strong home base); (ii) a net recipient of FDI (a typical host nation); or (iii) a 'dual' player with both outward and inward FDI. In each of these cases, the incentive structure facing governments in terms of regulating MNE behaviour is fundamentally different (Dunning, 1993b). In Figure 2.2, we relate these two determinants of MNE–government interactions. On the vertical axis for the MNE, we represent the dispersion of the MNE's FSAs as either low or high. On the horizontal axis for government, we place the symmetry between inward and outward FDI as either low or high. As regards this latter parameter, we assume a high absolute volume of FDI. If the FDI volume were low, the symmetry issue would obviously not be critical.

The Caves' perspective mainly describes one of the four cases in Figure 2.2; it is in quadrant 1. Here, there is no recognition of the dispersion of FSAs by the firm, and a low degree of symmetry between inward and outward FDI prevails. The view of MNEs as only demonstrating centralised structures (i.e., they only develop FSAs in their single home country base), and the view of governments as acting narrowly in accordance with either home or host nation perspectives allows for elegant, albeit often over-simplified, modelling by economists. In reality, three more complex cases may occur that do not lend themselves to simple modelling. In quadrant 2, firm-driven national responsiveness may induce governments to provide national treatment. This requires that governments understand the economic and strategic significance of MNEs operating a network with dispersed FSAs. Governments also need to be interested in the creation of sustainable value-added domestically, whether by domestic or foreign MNEs. In contrast, in quadrant 3, the symmetry between a country's inward FDI and outward FDI positions provides incentives for the non-discriminatory regulation of foreign MNEs, irrespective of their ethnocentric, polycentric or geocentric strategies. National treatment of foreign MNEs may then induce foreign MNEs to become more nationally responsive themselves. Finally, in quadrant 4, there is a government preference for global regulation and a firm preference for a 'supranational' approach to government policy. This is the opposite of Caves' view. The reason for such preferences is that with a symmetrical position of inward and outward FDI at the public policy level a dispersed FDI configuration at the firm level leads to complexities in terms of optimal business–government interactions that cannot be solved at the national level.

To summarise, in Caves' analysis the MNE is a centralised, hierarchical organisation that closely monitors and meters the use of its home-based FSAs. Government policy is systematically analysed from the viewpoint of either a host country (recipient of FDI), or a home country (exporter of FDI). Thus, Caves' perspective has a single (and simple) MNE–government context in quadrant 1 of Figure 2.2. However, the institutional determinants of MNE–government interaction are now recognised to be more complex than this, and so the other three quadrants of Figure 2.2 are necessary to properly explore the process of interactions between MNEs and home and host governments.

The third component of our new framework analyses the MNE's strategic approach to government policy in terms of strategic perspectives and desired outcomes. This is shown in Figure 2.3.

The strategic perspective on government policy reflects the extent to which it is viewed as either exogenous or endogenous by the managers of the MNE. If it is endogenous, this means that the MNE will attempt to alter the content and/or process of government policy in its favour. If it is exogenous, the MNE will work within the rules set by public agencies. Given this choice of interaction with governments, the MNE must design an appropriate strategy and structure to obtain either the benefits of integration or of national responsiveness when interacting with home and host governments. This leads to several complex situations in Figure 2.3, only one of which is discussed in depth by Caves. This is quadrant 1, where the MNE views

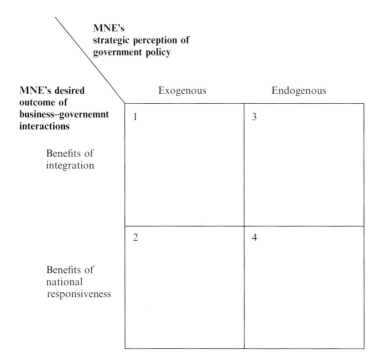

Figure 2.3 MNE's strategic approach to government policy

government policy as exogenous and its objective is to achieve the benefits of integration, i.e., conventional efficiency benefits in the area of scale economies, economies of scope and economies of exploiting national differences.

The other quadrants of Figure 2.3 represent the newer stream of international business literature. The four quadrants as a whole represent a 'transnational' approach to government policy. There the MNE has to make a strategic choice for each type of government regulation (or intervention) relevant to the firm. It does this within each region, for each SBU, and for each function and task. Each MNE has to decide two things. First, whether government policy will be viewed as an endogenous or exogenous variable; and second, whether benefits of national responsiveness versus integration will be pursued in its business–government interaction. The latter decision depends on the relative importance of the MNE's location-bound versus non-location-bound FSAs. The location-bound FSAs reflect proprietary competencies and capabilities which can be exploited in only a limited geographic region, e.g. an excellent local reputation, a well positioned retail network, privileged relationships with domestic economic actors, etc. If location-bound FSAs represent the key to competitive success, the MNE will focus on those areas of government regulation that constitute an opportunity or threat to developing and exploiting such FSAs. In contrast, if the MNE builds primarily on non-location-bound FSAs, such as global brand names and technologies that can easily be transferred internationally either as an intermediate good or embodied in a final product, then its focus in government relations will be on protecting and exploiting such FSAs.

There are four cases in Figure 2.3. In quadrant 1 government policy is used as a lever for global competitiveness. In quadrant 2 there is the good corporate citisen approach building upon a strategy of national responsiveness. In quadrant 4 the strategy of national responsiveness is extended to one of nation-bound bargaining, whereas in quadrant 3 the firm's interest will be in developing global bargaining strategies to be used when dealing with subnational, national and supranational public agencies. In fact, it could be argued that in quadrant 4, the MNE will develop location-bound FSAs in government relations in each country in which it operates, whereas in quadrant 3, the focus will be on non-location-bound-FSAs. This is a strategy of developing systemic advantages in dealing with public agencies across borders.

A NEW SYNTHESIS OF THE LITERATURE

Using Figure 2.4 we can appreciate the penetrating insights that Caves brings to our understanding of the relationship between MNEs and governments. At the time of the first edition (in 1982), Caves offered a state of the art approach that covered the great bulk of literature to that date. It is understandable, if unfortunate, that Caves chose not to update his approach in the 1996 second edition of his book. Later in this section we shall explore some of the limitations of Caves' approach, and how these can be overcome using our new analytical framework. At this stage, however, we explore the rich foundations provided by Caves.

In Figure 2.4, where most of the conventional economics literature can be positioned, all of which is covered by Caves, quadrants 1 and 4 are the polar extremes of the MNE–state debate. In quadrant 1 we have the Hymer (1976) quasi-Marxist view of the conflicts between MNEs and home and host governments. The focus is upon distributional issues and the power of the MNE versus the host nation state (Dunning and Rugman, 1985). We can also position the *Sovereignty at Bay* of Raymond Vernon (1971) in this quadrant. As Vernon (1991) himself states, the title of his book has been misinterpreted. He did not argue that the MNE would dominate the host nation state, but rather that there would be antagonistic relations between them, as we show in quadrant 1. Also in this quadrant can be placed the Kojima (1973, 1975, 1978, 1985) hypothesis to the effect that trade and FDI are substitutes in the US experience but complements in the Japanese case, i.e. that there are MNE–host and home government conflicts.

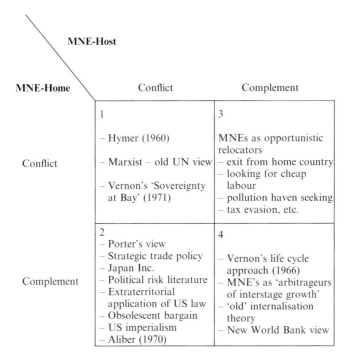

	Conflict	Complement
	MNE-Host	
MNE-Home		
Conflict	1 – Hymer (1960) – Marxist – old UN view – Vernon's 'Sovereignty at Bay' (1971)	3 MNEs as opportunistic relocators – exit from home country – looking for cheap labour – pollution haven seeking – tax evasion, etc.
Complement	2 – Porter's view – Strategic trade policy – Japan Inc. – Political risk literature – Extraterritorial application of US law – Obsolescent bargain – US imperialism – Aliber (1970)	4 – Vernon's life cycle approach (1966) – MNE's as 'arbitrageurs of interstage growth' – 'old' internalisation theory – New World Bank view

Figure 2.4   Examples of Figure 2.1

In contrast, in quadrant 4 of Figure 2.4 we position the complementary nature of MNE–home and host state relations. This is more consistent with Vernon (1966) and Knickerbocker (1973), according to which the MNE grows through a product life cycle of technology-intensive FSAs developed initially in a strong home base, then produced by wholly-owned subsidiaries in host economies and finally (when the product is mature) anywhere in the world with the lowest factor input costs. This is an efficiency-based view of the MNE–state relationship. This quadrant is also consistent with early views of internalisation theory in Buckley and Casson (1976), Rugman (1980, 1981), Dunning (1981) and Hennart (1982). The internalisation of technological and managerial know-how within the internal market of the MNE is a positive externality that overcomes the Coase (1937) problem of knowledge as a public good. Johnson (1970) and Magee (1977) explored how the MNE could 'appropriate', or own, firm-specific assets in know-how and in technology and thereby overcome the transaction cost of knowledge as a public good. The process of internalisation is efficiency based since the MNEs help both home and host nations to develop; indeed the MNE is the engine of economic development in quadrant 4 of Figure 2.4. To the extent that national governments understand the value to their country of access to the FSAs of MNEs, goal conflict can be largely avoided. Dunning (1994) has described why most governments are now 'acclaiming FDI as good news' after a period of hostility in the 1970s and early 1980s. In fact, this change in attitude reflects the understanding that the FSAs of MNEs cannot be simply unbundled or purchased as intermediate goods. This view has also been echoed in recent World Bank reports and it represents a welcome shift in the public policy perspective.

There are then two more complex cases in Figure 2.4. In quadrant 2 we place the Porter (1990) view of MNEs with a strong home base. There is a complementary relationship between the home government and its MNEs. In fact, appropriate government policy for each of the determinants of Porter's national diamond of competitiveness (i.e., factor conditions, demand conditions, related and supporting industries, the firms' strategy, structure and rivalry in a specific industry) will strengthen the domestic firms' home base and allow them to become successful internationally. However, Porter also argues that foreign-owned firms are not sources of competitive advantage for host nations, i.e. that the MNE is in conflict with the host nation. This quadrant 2 viewpoint of Porter is also representative of a large literature on strategic trade policy starting with Krugman (1986), Brander and Spencer (1985) and then misapplied to public policy by Tyson (1993) and Yoffie (1993), amongst others. Basically all of these writers develop cases in which the home government can subsidise its MNEs to develop first-mover advantages in a zero-sum game. Strategic trade policy has home states giving discriminatory subsidies to home-based MNEs, who then act as national champions to take global market shares away from MNEs based in host nations. In reality, such policies have mostly failed, as few governments have the necessary knowledge and the required implementing apparatus to catapult domestic firms into becoming globally competitive MNEs (Rugman and Verbeke, 1990). The earlier literature on Japan is also positioned in quadrant 2. Here the argument is that the Japanese keiretsus have developed in a strong and rivalrous home base and, helped by the Japanese government, have succeeded in global markets at the expense of host country firms (Ohmae, 1985; Gerlach, 1992; Nonaka and Takeuchi, 1995; Fruin, 1997). Aliber's (1970) theory of FDI is also in quadrant 2. He argues that a strong currency allows home-based MNEs to capitalise expected earnings at a higher rate than can host country firms.

Finally, the more conventional literature on political risk management by Kobrin (1982), Brewer (1983, 1985), Ghadar (1982), Nigh (1985), and others, is also in quadrant 2. The literature assumes that host governments should be able to regulate foreign MNEs, or otherwise change the political environmental parameters facing MNEs in the host nations. In this work, MNEs are often seen as a modern instruments of colonisation, bringing with them unwanted approaches (including managerial and labour practices) prevailing in their home nations. An extreme version of political risk is the obsolescing bargain hypothesis (Encarnation and Wells, 1985; Kobrin, 1984, 1987). This argues that the manufacturing or resource-based MNEs in host economies have sunk costs in the form of factories, mines and plantations, all of which could be nationalised by the host government and result in losses for the MNE. Here, the main point is that host government goals can only prevail at the expense of foreign MNE goals once the MNE has engaged in irreversible resource commitments and its bargaining position has weakened substantially. To help overcome this, there is still a US legal viewpoint that argues for extraterritorial application of its laws. The Helms-Burton Act on Cuba is the latest manifestation of this old-fashioned view that US MNEs can be used as complementary instruments of US foreign policy against the interests of the host governments.

In quadrant 3 we have the opposite situation. Here there is a conflict between MNEs and their home governments but a complementary relationship with host governments. An example of this is the argument over pollution havens whereby MNEs are alleged to flee tight home market regulations to go to lax host nation regimes. The cheap labour offshore assembly platform argument also fits here, as does the naive viewpoint that MNEs engage in transfer pricing and seek out tax havens at the expense of their governments. There has been less research on this quadrant than the literature in quadrant 2. What literature there is tends to refute the political science-led rationale for quadrant 3. For example, Eden (1985, 1997), building on earlier work, e.g. Copithorne (1971), Lall (1973), Nieckels (1976), Lessard (1979), Rugman and Eden (1985), finds no evidence for systematic transfer pricing by MNEs other than as a response to effective tax rate differentials and other exogenous market imperfections. The rationale for offshore assembly has been falling as most manufacturing sectors are reducing the labour content of their processes; there are some exceptions such as the offshore assembly of disc drives and other high technology commodity products. In NAFTA, the role of Mexico as a cheap labour and pollution haven for Asian and European MNEs was offset by rules of origin for automobiles and textiles which protect 'insider' North American MNEs (Rugman, 1994; Gestrin and Rugman, 1994; Eden and Molot, 1993; Hufbauer and Schott, 1992, 1993; Lustig, Bosworth and Lawrence, 1992). In more general terms, it would be incorrect to assume that MNEs, faced with excessive goal conflicts in their home countries, seek cooperation with mostly poorer host nations, where goal complementarity is prevailing. However, institutional competition among potential host countries to attract FDI can lead to generous investment promotion programs, even in the most developed economies, sometimes creating a situation of reverse discrimination.

Turning to Figure 2.5 we can see that, while the Caves material covers the four quadrants of Figure 2.4, it only fits into quadrant 1 of Figure 2.5. The

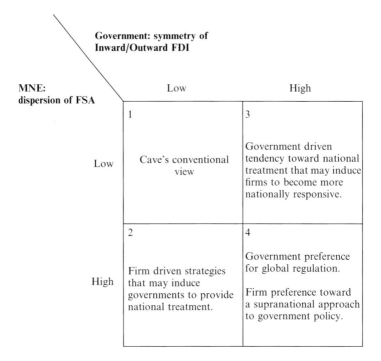

Figure 2.5   Examples of Figure 2.2

older literature in international business failed to address the ability of the MNE to disperse its FSAs globally, using its organisational structure and systems as a managerially based core competence. Indeed, the literature up to Caves (1982), including early internalisation theory, plus the Vernon (1966, 1971) and Porter (1990) work, all assume the creation of non-location-bound FSAs in the home country of the MNE that would lead to profits abroad through exports, licensing or FDI. Strategies for MNEs in quadrant 1 consist of replicating home country practices and are entirely dependent on decisions made in the home country concerning value chain configurations and coordination (Porter, 1990). There is no recognition of the need to develop location-bound FSAs in host countries that would lead to benefits of national responsiveness.

   The turning point in recognising the ability of the MNE to be nationally responsive can be traced to the neglected work of Doz (1986) and to the more influential book by Bartlett and Ghoshal (1989). These authors have added rigorous strategic modelling methods to the original insight by Perl-mutter (1969) into the decentralised role of polycentric managers. Bartlett and Ghoshal's work also demonstrates that when MNEs feel sufficiently confident about the economic and strategic potential of a specific foreign subsidiary or business unit abroad, then non-location-bound FSAs may actually be developed there. This gives the host nation a characteristic conventionally reserved to home nations, namely, to become a source country for new innovations. This leads to the situation shown in quadrant 2 of Figure 2.5 where firm driven strategies may induce governments to provide national treatment.

The conventional literature covered by Caves also assumes a low symmetry between inward and outward FDI, which is a key parameter determining government regulation of MNEs. The 'old' politics of international institutions, such as the General Agreement on Tariffs and Trade (GATT), concerned itself with tariff cuts and the negotiation of the removal of trade barriers. This was a focus on 'shallow integration' (Ostry, 1997; Brewer and Young, 1998). This shallow integration of successive GATT rounds assumed that little could be achieved on trade in services and in the FDI area because governments would be either a net exporter or a net recipient of FDI. The new agenda of the World Trade Organisation (WTO) and of the Organisation for Economic Cooperation and Development's (OECD) Multilateral Agreement on Investment (MAI) is to negotiate 'deep integration' and the removal of barriers to FDI. The objective of the MAI is to make domestic markets internationally contestable through the principle of national treatment – i.e. host governments are to treat MNEs in the same manner as domestic firms. Thus, in quadrant 3 of Figure 2.5, there is a new agenda for international relations that recognises the reality of a high symmetry between inward and outward FDI characterizing the government of many countries, including the United States, Canada, the EU, and Japan. This symmetry has led to the widespread adoption of the national treatment principle, i.e. it ends the discriminatory treatment of home and foreign firms by governments. This is consistent with Dunning (1994) who has suggested that inbound FDI may inject more market-orientated beliefs and practices in a domestic economic system and may alter the international competitiveness agenda of government.

The view that diverges the most sharply from Caves is found in quadrant 4 of Figure 2.5. Here, there is a mutual preference by both MNEs and governments for a 'supranational' approach to public policy. This will take into account the dispersion of the FSAs of MNEs and the high degree of symmetry of inward and outward FDI at the national level. Given the general institutional trend towards quadrant 4 in Figure 2.5, some possible MNE strategies towards MNE–government relations are analysed in Figure 2.6.

Figure 2.6 incorporates the resource-based view of the literature on MNE strategy and public policy developed in Rugman and Verbeke (1991). In this work, a vital distinction is drawn between location-bound FSAs and

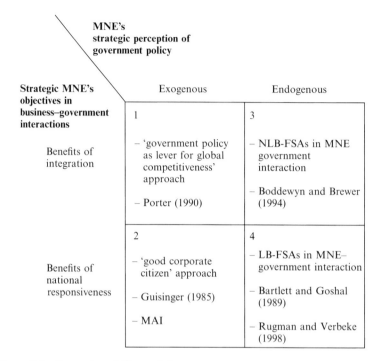

Figure 2.6   Examples of Figure 2.3

non-location-bound FSAs. Location-bound FSAs include those that lead to benefits of national responsiveness, whereas non-location-bound FSAs are those that lead to integration benefits of scale, scope and exploiting national differences. Application of this model to issues of strategic trade policy and shelter theory, competitiveness and NAFTA, can be found in Rugman and Verbeke (1990) and Rugman (1996).

The prevailing view on the impact of MNE–public policy linkages on international competitiveness is that of Porter (1990), which can be positioned in quadrant 1 of Figure 2.6. His use of the home base/cluster concept requires that the MNE adopts an integration strategy and regards the government policy as exogenous. The MNEs in the triad respond to, for example, home government subsidies and other policies strengthening the domestic 'diamond' (Porter, 1990) and use their large home base to become globally competitive. This is partly consistent with the resource-based view, but it limits the public-policy-induced development of managerially based FSAs to that generated by home government stimulus. There is no room in this work for subsidiary managers or foreign governments to contribute to the FSAs, except in the implementation stage of integration-based strategies. Applications of this thinking have been made to trade and environment issues by Porter and van der Linde (1995).

In quadrant 2 of Figure 2.6, government policy is still viewed as exogenous, but here MNEs develop strategies (building upon such policies) whose aim is to achieve benefits of national responsiveness in the various countries where the firm operates. Government policy is not viewed as a major determinant of international competitiveness. This view is consistent with the proposition that public policy should focus on providing a level playing field rather than creating an international competitive advantage. Issues of public policy that are relevant in quadrant 2 of Figure 2.6 include work on negotiation of a subsidies code for the GATT and WTO. Here the research of Guisinger *et al.* (1985), Hufbauer and Erb (1984) and Gladwin and Walter (1980) is relevant. The OECD's work on the MAI would occur in this quadrant.

In contrast, quadrant 4 reflects a proactive strategy of national responsiveness. The MNEs here have a decentralised or matrix organisational structure and they outperform average competitors through national responsiveness, as argued by Doz (1986), Prahalad and Doz (1987), and by Bartlett and Ghoshal (1989). An application of this has been made to corporate strategies and environmental regulations by Rugman and Verbeke (1998). In this work, government policy is viewed as a parameter that can be influenced (endogenised) through lobbying and negotiation. This is consistent with the conclusions of a body of political risk literature, which argues that such risk is largely determined by micro-environmental factors.

In quadrant 3 of Figure 2.6 it is also argued that government policy is endogenous, but this time the MNE aims to achieve the benefits of integration-based FSAs. These are non-location bound. The danger associated with active MNE strategies in this area is that they often represent a 'Trojan horse' approach. Firms themselves use strategic trade policy arguments to obtain government favours. First-mover advantages at the international level, strategic entry deterrence, technological spill-overs, learning curve effects, credible retaliation to foreign support programs, may be among the effects lobbied for by firms. The end result should be domestic MNEs with stronger non-location-bound FSAs. Unfortunately, such lobbying often disguises shelter-seeking strategies. These firms are unable to compete without artificial government support. Such behaviour has been variously defined as a political strategy by Boddewyn (1988) and by Boddewyn and Brewer (1994) or as a fourth generic strategy by Rugman and Verbeke (1990).

Perhaps the most interesting feature of the above analysis is that some firms are now adopting a 'transnational' strategy, in the spirit of Bartlett and Ghoshal (1989), that may cover each of the four quadrants in Figure 2.6, depending upon the area of regulation, the relevant country or the affected business unit.

CONCLUSIONS AND FUTURE RESEARCH

The conceptual framework described in this chapter suggests that there is more to the analysis of MNE–government relations than is described in Caves' synthesis of the conventional literature. Caves' work is useful when performing a general analysis of goal conflict between MNEs and governments in both home and host countries. The specific reasons for goal complementarity and conflict with particular governments can also be analysed using Caves' work.

However, the institutional reality driving much of today's business–government interactions is one whereby governments increasingly do not unambiguously represent either a home or a host country. The symmetrical status of countries both as source nations and as recipients of FDI makes it more difficult for governments to design specific incentive programmes and regulatory policies. At the country level, national treatment of FDI is often the appropriate policy. In addition, many large MNEs now have a dispersed structure of FSAs, which reduces their legal and strategic commitment to a single home base. Thus, national responsiveness has developed as the key strategy for many firms.

When the symmetry in FDI positions at the government level and the dispersion of FSAs at the firm level are taken into account simultaneously, both sets of actors have a keen interest in international and multilateral trade and investment liberalisation. Generally accepted rules need to guide MNE–government interactions. Finally, it is important to realise that the MNE's strategic approach to government policy is increasingly one in which choices tend to be made regarding the nature of the benefits sought (benefits of integration versus benefits of national responsiveness) and the extent to which actions will be undertaken to change or set the rules. This is the old issue of the extent to which government policy should be viewed as endogenous rather than exogenous to the firm. What is certain is that some MNEs have taken on board a broader spectrum of strategic alternatives in developing and exploiting their FSAs than was considered by Caves.

The next 20 years will see the development of an international business literature develop based much more of this new thinking than on the literature reviewed by Caves. The next round of the WTO will probably focus on further liberalisation of trade in services, issues of trade and the environment and issues of investment and competition policy. New work on the MAI at the OECD appears in Gestrin and Rugman (1995) and Brewer and Young (1998); this is consistent with earlier analysis of codes of conduct at the OECD by Safarian (1993) and Grosse (1980). The nature of networks and of R&D policy is also an area where our new framework provides guidance for future research. While the Japanese access Silicon Valley in the United States, US firms also draw R&D from Japan (Westney, 1993). Work on alliance capitalism, as discussed in papers in Dunning (1997) and on strategic alliances and cooperative strategies, as discussed in Contractor and Lorange (1988), D'Cruz and Rugman (1997), and in Beamish and Killing (1997), will grow in relevance. The alliance capitalism framework may well supplement the development and exploitation of FSAs by home-country-based MNEs as the focus of public policy.

The field of international business is expanding rapidly across these, and related, dimensions. Yet, in terms of analysis of the MNE and public policy, the analytical insights of Caves provide a solid foundation for present and future research. The 'multiple perspectives' approach now being used to bring disciplinary insights into the activities, operations and structures of MNEs is congruent with both the conventional static Caves economic efficiency analysis and also the current dynamic resource-based theory of the firm viewpoint incorporated into the new framework developed here. The interaction between MNEs and governments has been, and will remain in the future, a lively area of research activity for scholarship in the field of international business.

Acknowledgements

Helpful comments on this chapter were received from Mark Casson, John Dunning, Michael Gestrin, Steven Guisinger and an anonymous referee.

References

Aliber, R. Z. (1970) 'A theory of direct foreign investment', in C.P. Kindleberger (ed.) *The International Corporation* (Cambridge, MA: MIT Press) pp. 17–34.

Bartlett, C.A. and Ghoshal, S. (1989) *Managing Across Borders: The Transnational Solution* (Boston: Harvard Business School Press).

Beamish, P. and Killing, P. (1997) *Cooperative Strategies* (3 volumes) (San Francisco: The New Lexington Press).

Behrman, J.N. and Grosse, R.E. (1990) *International Business and Governments: Issues and Institutions* (Columbia, SC: University of South Carolina Press).

Bergsten, C.F., Horst, T. and Moran, T.H. (1978) *American Multinationals and American Interests* (Washington, DC: Brookings Institution).

Bhagwati, J. (1988) *Protectionism* (Cambridge, MA: MIT Press).

Boddewyn, J.J. (1988) 'Political aspects of MNE theory', *Journal of International Business Studies*, 19: 341–363.

Boddewyn, J.J. and Brewer, T. (1994) 'International business political behaviour: new theoretical directions', *Academy of Management Review*, 19(1): 119–143.

Brander, J., and Spencer, B. (1985) 'Export subsidies and international market share rivalry', *Journal of International Economics*, 18 (February): 85–100.

Brewer, T.L. (1983) 'The instability of controls on MNE's funds transfers and the instability of governments', *Journal of International Business Studies*, 14(3): 147–157.

Brewer, T.L. (ed.) (1985) *Political Risks in International Business: New Directions for Research, Management and Public Policy* (New York: Praeger Publishers).

Brewer, T.L. and Young, S. (1998) *The Multilateral Investment System and Multinational Enterprises* (Oxford: Oxford University Press).

Buckley, P.J. and Casson, M. (1976) *The Future of the Multinational Enterprise* (London: Macmillan).

Casson, M. (1987) *The Firm and the Market* (Cambridge, MA: MIT Press).

Caves, R.E. (1982) *Multinational Enterprise and Economic Analysis* (Cambridge: Cambridge University Press).

Coase, R.H. (1937) 'The nature of the firm', *Economica*, 4: 386–405.

Contractor, F. and Lorange, P. (eds) (1988) *Cooperative Strategies in International Business* (San Francisco: New Lexington Press).

Copithorne, L.W. (1971) 'International corporate transfer prices and government policy', *Canadian Journal of Economics*, 4: 324–341.

D'Cruz, J. and Rugman, A.M. (1997) 'The theory of the flagship firm', *European Management Journal*, 15(1): 403–411.

Doz, Y. (1986) *Strategic Management in Multinational Companies* (Oxford: Pergamon Press).

Dunning, J.H. (1981) *International Production and the Multinational Enterprise* (London: Allen and Unwin).

Dunning, J.H. (1993a) *Multinational Enterprises and the Global Economy* (New York: Addison-Wesley).

Dunning, J.H. (1993b) *The Globalisation of Business* (London: Routledge).

Dunning, J.H. (1994) 'Re-evaluating the benefits of foreign direct investment', *Transnational Corporations*, 3(1): 23–51.

Dunning, J.H. (ed.) (1997) *Governments, Globalisation and International Business* (Oxford: Oxford University Press).

Dunning, J.H. and Rugman, A.M. (1985). 'The influence of Hymer's dissertation on the theory of foreign direct investment', *American Economic Review*, papers and proceedings, 75: 228–232.

Eden, L. (1985) 'The micro-economics of transfer pricing', in A.M. Rugman and L. Eden (eds) *Multinationals and Transfer Pricing* (London: Croom-Helm) pp. 13–46.

Eden, L. (1991) 'Bringing the firm back in: multinationals in IPE', *Millennium Journal of International Studies*, 20(2): 197–224.

Eden, L. (1997) *Taxing Multinationals: Transfer Pricing and Corporate Income Taxation in North America* (Toronto: University of Toronto Press).

Eden, L. and Molot, M.A. (1993) 'Insiders and outsiders: defining "who is us" in the North American automobile industry', *Transnational Corporations*, 3(2) (December): 31–64.

Encarnation, D.J. and Wells, Jr, L.T. (1985) 'Sovereignty en garde: negotiating with foreign investors', *International Organisation* (Winter): 147–171.

Fruin, M. (1997) *Knowledge Works* (Oxford: Oxford University Press).

Gerlach, M. (1992) *Alliance Capitalism: The Social Organisation of Japanese Business* (Berkeley: University of California Press).

Gestrin, M. and Rugman, A.M. (1994) 'The North American Free Trade Agreement and foreign direct investment', *Transnational Corporations*, 3(1): 77–95.

Gestrin, M. and Rugman, A.M. (1995) 'The NAFTA investment provisions: prototype for multilateral investment rules, in Organisation for Economic Co-operation and Development', *Market Access After the Uruguay Round: Investment, Competition and Technology Perspectives* (Paris, OECD).

Ghadar, F. (1982) 'Political risk and the erosion of control: the case of the oil industry', *Columbia Journal of World Business*, 13(2): 47–51.

Gilpin, R. (1975) *US Power and the Multinational Corporation* (New York: Basic Books).

Gilpin, R. (1987) *The Political Economy of International Relations* (Princeton: Princeton University Press).

Gladwin, T.N. and Walter, I. (1980) *Multinationals under Fire: Lessons in the Management of Conflict* (New York: John Wiley).

Goldstein, J. (1993) *Ideas, Interests and American Trade Policy* (Ithaca: Cornell University Press).

Grieco, J.M. (1982) 'Between dependency and autonomy: India's experience with the international computer industry', *International Organisation*, 36(3): 609–632.

Grosse, R. (1980) *Foreign Investment Codes and the Location of Direct Investment* (New York: Praeger).

Guisinger, S.E. & Associates (1985) *Investment Incentives and Performance Requirements* (New York: Praeger).

Hennart, J.-F. (1982) *A Theory of Multinational Enterprise* (Ann Arbor, MI: University of Michigan Press).

Hufbauer, G.C. (1993) *NAFTA: An Assessment* (Washington, DC: Institute for International Economics).

Hufbauer, G.C. and Erb, J. (1984) *Subsidies in International Trade* (Washington, DC: Institute for International Economics).

Hufbauer, G.C. and Schott, J.J. (1992) *North American Free Trade Issues and Recommendations* (Washington, DC: Institute for International Economics).

Hymer, S.H. (1976) *The International Operations of National Firms: A Study of Direct Foreign Investment* (Cambridge, MA: MIT Press).

Johnson, H.G. (1970) 'The efficiency and welfare implications of the multinational corporation', in C.P. Kindleberger (ed.) *The International Corporation: A Symposium* (Cambridge, MA: MIT Press) pp. 33–56.

Keohane, R.O. (1984) *After Hegemony* (Princeton: Princeton University Press).

Keohane, R.O. and Nye, J. (1977) *Power and Interdependence* (Boston: Little Brown).

Knickerbocker, F.T. (1973) *Oligopolistic Reaction and Multinational Enterprise* (Boston: Harvard University Graduate School of Business Administration, Division of Research).

Kobrin, S.J. (1982) *Managing Political Risk Assessment* (Berkeley, CA: University of California Press).

Kobrin, S.J. (1984) 'Expropriation as an attempt to control foreign firms in LDCs: trends from 1960–79', *International Studies Quarterly*, 28(3): 329–348.

Kobrin, S.J. (1987) 'Testing the bargaining hypothesis in the manufacturing sector in developing countries', *International Organisation*, 41(4): 609–638.

Kojima, K. (1973) 'Macroeconomic approach to foreign direct investment', *Hitotsubashi Journal of Economics*, 14: 1–21.

Kojima, K. (1975) 'International trade and foreign investment – substitutes or complements?' *Hitotsubashi Journals of Economics*, 16: 1–12.

Kojima, K. (1978) *Direct foreign investment: a Japanese model of multinational business operations* (London: Croom Helm).

Kojima, K. (1985) 'Japanese and American direct investment in Asia – a comparative analysis', *Hitotsubashi Journal of Economics*, 26: 1–35.

Krasner, S. (1978) *Defending the National Interest* (Princeton: Princeton University Press).

Krugman, P.R. (ed.) (1986) *Strategic Trade Policy and the New International Economics* (Cambridge, MA: MIT Press).

Lall, S. (1973) 'Transfer pricing by multinational manufacturing firms', *Oxford Bulletin of Economics and Statistics*, 35: 173–195.

Lessard, D.R. (1979) 'Transfer prices, taxes, and financial markets: implications of internal financial transfers within the multinational corporation', in R.G. Hawkins (ed.) *The Economic Effect of Multinational Corporations* (Greenwich, CT: JAI Press) pp. 101–120.

Lustig, N., Bosworth, B.P. and Lawrence, R.Z. (1992) *Assessing the Impact of North American Free Trade* (Washington, DC: Brookings).

Magee, S.P. (1977) 'Information and multinational corporation: an appropriability theory of direct foreign investment', in J.N. Bhagwati (ed.) *The New International Economic Order* (Cambridge, MA: MIT Press) pp. 317–340.

Milner, H.V. (1988) *Resisting Protectionism: Global Industries and the Politics of International Trade* (Princeton NJ: Princeton University Press).

Nieckels, L. (1976) *Transfer Pricing in Multinational Firms* (Stockholm: Almqvist and Wiksell).

Nigh, D. (1985) 'The effect of political events on United States direct foreign investment', *Journal of International Business Studies*, 16: 1–17.

Nonaka, I. and Takeuchi, H. (1995) *The Knowledge-creating Company* (New York: Oxford University Press).

Ohmae, K. (1985) *Triad Power: The Coming Shape of Global Competition* (New York: The Free Press).

Ostry, S. (1997) *The Post Gold War Trading System: Who's on First?* (Chicago: University of Chicago Press).

Perlmutter, H. (1969) 'The tortuous evolution of the multilateral corporation', *Columbia Journal of World Business*, 4(1): 9–18.

Porter, M.G. (1990) *The Competitive Advantage of Nations* (New York: Free Press).

Porter, M.G. and van der Linde, C. (1995) 'Green and competitive', *Harvard Business Review*, 73(5): 120–134.

Prahalad, C.K. and Doz, Y.L. (1987) *The Multinational Mission* (New York: Free Press).

Rugman, A.M. (1980) *Multinationals in Canada: Theory, Performance and Economic Impact* (Boston: Martinus Nijhoff).

Rugman, A.M. (1981) *Inside the Multinationals: The Economics of Internal Markets* (New York: Columbia University Press).

Rugman, A.M. and Verbeke, A. (1991) 'Environmental change and global competitive strategy in Europe', in A.M. Rugman and A. Verbeke (eds) *Research in Global Strategic Management*, (Volume 2) *Global Competition and the European Community* (Greenwood CT: JAI Press Inc) pp. 3–28.

Rugman, A.M. (ed.) (1994) *Foreign Investment and NAFTA* (Columbia: University of South Carolina Press).

Rugman, A.M. (1996) *Multinational Enterprises and Trade Policy: Volume 2 of the Selected Scientific Papers of Alan M. Rugman* (Cheltenham: Elgar).

Rugman, A.M. and Verbeke, A. (1998) 'Corporate strategies and environmental regulations. An organizing framework', *Strategic Management Journal*, 19(3): 363–375.

Rugman, A.M. and Anderson, A. (1987) *Administered Protection in America* (London: Routledge).

Rugman, A.M. and Eden, L. (eds) (1985) *Multinationals and Transfer Pricing* (London: Croom-Helm).

Rugman, A.M. and Verbeke, A. (1990) *Global Corporate Strategy and Trade Policy* (London: Routledge).

Safarian, A.E. (1966) *Foreign Ownership of Canadian Industry* (Toronto: McGraw-Hill).

Safarian, A.E. (1993) *Multinational Enterprises and Public Policy* (Aldershot: Elgar).

Stopford, J. and Strange, S. (1991) *Rival States, Rival Firms: Competition for World Market Shares* (Cambridge: Cambridge University Press).

Strange, S. (1988) *States and Markets: An Introduction to International Political Economy* (London: Pinter).

Strange, S. (1997) *The Retreat of the State: The Diffusion of Power in the World Economy* (Cambridge: Cambridge University Press).

Tyson, L. D'A. (1993) *Who's Bashing Whom? Trade Conflict in High-Technology Industries* (Washington, DC: Institute for International Economics).

Vernon, R. (1966) 'International investment and international trade in the product cycle', *Quarterly Journal of Economics*, 80: 190–207.

Vernon, R. (1971) *Sovereignty at Bay: The Multinational Spread of US Enterprises* (New York: Basic Books).

Vernon, R. (1991) 'Sovereignty at Bay: Twenty Years After', *Millennium Journal of International Studies*, 20(2): 191–195.

Vogel, D. (1995) *Trading Up: Consumer and Environmental Regulations in a Global Economy* (Cambridge, MA: Harvard University Press).

Vogel, D. and Rugman, A.M. (1997) 'Environmentally related trade disputes between the United States and Canada', *American Review of Canadian Studies*, 27(4): 271–292.

Yoffie, D. (ed.) (1993) *Beyond Free Trade: Firms, Governments and Global Competition* (Boston: Harvard Business School Press).

3 Asian Economic Success and Crisis: Knowledge and Financial Capital

Chong Ju Choi and Carla C.J.M. Millar

INTRODUCTION

The Asian economic crisis of 1997 has become a widely debated topic in international business research and among policymakers. We believe that any framework for analysing the crisis needs to take into account the decades of success that preceded the crisis and that this can be done by incorporating 'knowledge' and 'capital' allocation in international business research. The purpose of this chapter is twofold: first, to provide an interdisciplinary analysis of the role of knowledge and financial capital allocation in international business and related disciplines such as international economics and development; and secondly, to analyse why the knowledge and financial capital allocation systems that were fundamental to the past economic success in Asia helped to create the present economic crisis.

Although many purely economic and market-based explanations and theories have been formulated about the Asian crisis, the non-economic, organisational and institutional factors in the crisis seem as important as the purely macroeconomic and market-driven fundamentals. The research of North (1990) and Olson (1982) on how organisations influence and change institutions is especially relevant for such analysis that takes into account economic as well as non-economic factors in business and economic performance. North's research showed how the combination of formal and informal constraints determines the rules of exchange and change in national economies (Hirsch and Lounsbury, 1996), combining the political, sociological, historical and ideological aspects of behavioural-based theories along with the rational theories of organisational economics. In analysing the economic crisis in Asia, we include the economic as well as the various non-market forces, such as institutional settings, that influence the nature of exchange and cooperation in emerging economy environments (Whitley, 1992; Boddewyn, 1988; Brewer, 1992). Thus, although global capital movements have been given as a primary economic reason for the Asian economic crisis, there is a need to analyse how capital was actually created, allocated and 'governed' through the institutional arrangements in Asia and why these arrangements became inappropriate in the crisis of the late 1990s.

Existing research in markets and capital allocation, especially from an international business perspective, does not take fully into account the different nature of costs in emerging economy business environments. Most Asian countries, including Indonesia, Thailand, Malaysia, Vietnam, and China, are emerging rather than mature business environments, and globalisation has further complicated the nature of their emergence (Rodrik, 1997; Hirschman, 1994). The importance of different costs, whether they be costs of monitoring and enforcement in exchange or general costs linked to product quality and obtaining information and knowledge, can be seen in the ongoing research and debate on transaction costs (Hirsch and Lounsbury, 1996; Choi, 1992; Choi, Lee and Kim, 1999), although the majority of this research has been in mature, developed, single country contexts. The academic debate on the relevance of transaction costs for market- and non-market-based exchange, for example, has continued in various works, such as Williamson (1996), Hill (1995), Nooteboom (1996), Ghoshal and Moran (1996) and Granovetter (1985), with the conclusion that both market- and non-market-based exchange within organisations are crucial for the success of any business environment. As discussed by North (1990) and Olson (1992), institutions have been developed by societies to create order and reduce uncertainty in exchange and cooperation. In Asia's emerging economies, such institutions have not been developed fully, magnifying the level of uncertainty – the globalisation of capital movements combined with the 'level' of the still developing financial institutions in Asia were key factors in the Asian economic crisis.

In this paper, we analyse the Asian economic crisis through the role played by two major factors: 'knowledge' and 'financial capital' allocation. We believe that an interdisciplinary framework, incorporating international business, international economics and economic development, can help to provide a more systematic understanding of not only past Asian economic success, but the present Asian economic crisis. The fundamental issue is that the national business systems (North, 1990; Olson, 1992) in Asia were phenomenally successful for decades and then dramatically problematical in 1997. There is a need to understand the factors for past success and to identify which of these factors, if any, were responsible for the crisis which began in 1997.

The approach in this chapter is twofold. First, we analyse the two systems of capital allocation and ownership that have proved to be successful in the mature economies of the world: shareholder and stakeholder systems (Roe, 1994; Hirschman, 1994; Freeman, 1984; Albert, 1991; Choi, 1992). Shareholder capital allocation systems, which characterise the business system in countries such as the United States and United Kingdom, are dominated by financial equity markets, strong legal systems and externally driven measurement of business and economic performance. In contrast, stakeholder capital allocation systems in countries such as Germany and Japan

are more internally organised around collaboration among banking, financial markets, government and employees (Gerlach, 1992; Fruin, 1992; Roe, 1994); banks and other non-institutional organisations play the crucial role in capital allocation. The Asian economic crisis was largely due to the fact that in many of the emerging countries of Asia,
including Thailand, Malaysia and Indonesia, neither system of external or internal financial capital allocation had been fully developed. Thus, the 'level' of financial institutions in the national business system (Levine, 1997; Demirguc-Kunt and Maksimovic, 1996; Boyd and Smith, 1996) is crucial to understanding the Asian crisis.

Secondly, we focus on the importance of taking into account the nature of 'knowledge' acquisition, diffusion and delivery in emerging economies. Despite the past economic success of emerging economies in Asia, Eastern Europe and Latin America, international business research has not sufficiently analysed how such emergent environments differ from the mature business environment of North America and the European Union; exceptions include Beamish and Banks (1957), Choi (1992), Inkpen and Beamish (1997) and Olson (1992). Emerging economies face a much higher level of uncertainty and change, therefore requiring additional factors in analysis relative to mature economies. In conditions of uncertainty, the traditional advantage of pure markets – the power to coordinate exchange partners – becomes considerably weakened.

The balance among the three major parts of knowledge – acquisition, diffusion and delivery – has changed. The strength of the collective, relationship- and trust-based national business systems in Asia was based on the 'diffusion' and dissemination of externally created knowledge, usually from areas such as North America and Western Europe (Grant, 1996; Grant and Baden-Fuller, 1995). However, as the global business environment becomes increasingly dependent on creativity, R&D, technology, and the so-called high-tech industrial milieu (Choi *et al.*, 1999a, b), global competitiveness in knowledge resources has become more dependent on acquisition and delivery, rather than diffusion. In this sense, the knowledge allocation mechanism in Asia, based primarily on past diffusion, is no longer appropriate in today's global business environment.

DOUBLE TRIAD: ASIA'S EMERGING MARKETS

According to North (1990), national institutions are formal and informal structures that mix with national organisations in determining the economic performance of a country. International business research in this area has focussed on the role of the state in affecting the success of national firms and has been analysed in various works: Rugman *et al.* (1997), Lenway and Murtha (1994), Murtha (1993), Murtha and Lenway (1994) on the role of the state; Kogut (1993) on country capabilities and technological innovations; Boddewyn (1988), Brewer (1992) on political risk and embeddedness. In reality, of course, firms take not only international market competition into account, but also the home market constraints or the role of national institutions. This is similar to the concept of two level games that has been widely researched in international relations and international political economy, which analyse simultaneously national institutions and international diplomacy (Putnam, 1988). According to Boddewyn (1988), firms compete in an environment that includes various non-market non-economic values such as the polity, the community and public opinion formers such as the media. North's (1990) structure of institutions and organisations helps to show the richness and realities of national business systems, much beyond the traditional, narrow neo-classical economic market paradigm. As discussed by Kogut (1993), countries' competitiveness can be attributed to the interaction of their particular organisational and institutional capabilities.

National Institutions versus International Markets

Recent research on multinational corporations originating from the United States, Germany and Japan shows the continuing importance and influence of national institutions on strategy, such as R&D, capital financing and direct investment (Pauly and Reich, 1997). This study has shown that, in terms of national institutions and their influence on multinational corporations, globalisation of international markets has had a smaller than expected effect (Pauly and Reich, 1997). This adds further impetus to our framework, which creates a double triad grouping of countries, one triad of international markets (Vernon, 1966) and the other triad of national institutions.

Firms face the constraints and advantages of national institutions. Dunning (1996) in a recent, comprehensive study of the factors that help firms to be competitive globally has discovered that firms from certain countries, such as the United States, find national institutions such as government regulation, subsidies and social practices, relatively less helpful for global competitiveness, whereas for European and Japanese companies, national institutions were seen to be an advantage and supportive of global competition (Pauly and Reich, 1997). The latter was also the case for emerging market economies.

Rugman (1997, and in Chapter 2 of this volume) helped to create the double diamond framework, taking into account international factors, and thus broadened the single diamond analysis of pure national competitiveness factors by Porter (1990). In a similar vein, our double triad framework (Figure 3.1) combines the existing, well-known, 'external'

External based Triad;   *Internal based Triad:*
trade flows, incomes   *domestic institutions*

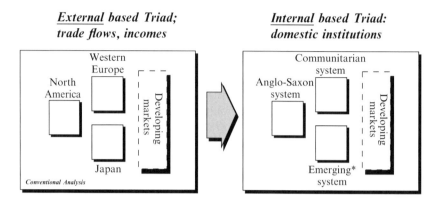

Figure 3.1 Double triad – external and internal

global economic triad, which is based on international markets, income levels and geography (Dunning, 1996; Vernon, 1966; Ohmae, 1985), with the realities of an 'internal' global triad taking national institutions into account (North, 1990).

The second component of the double triad is the domestic institutional factors, such as the roles of equity markets and banks in financing, the strength of legal systems and the collectivism or individualism of the societies. Under this type of grouping, we have the Anglo-Saxon business system (US, Canada, United Kingdom, Australia); a Communitarian business system (continental Europe) and an emerging business system grouping (parts of Asia, Eastern Europe, Latin America). This type of double triad framework is shown in Figure 3.1.

FACTOR I: FINANCIAL CAPITAL ALLOCATION

In terms of understanding emerging Asia from this new 'double triad' framework combining international markets and domestic institutional constraints, our analysis is based on the 'business system', or the various economic, political, social, and business issues that constrain and influence the behaviour of corporations from these systems (Olson, 1992; Kogut, 1991; Whitley, 1992). The first major factor that can help to frame the past economic success and present economic crisis in Asia is that of capital allocation. The issue of capital allocation and economic success has been argued for most of the 20th century. Prominent economists such as John Hicks argued that the financial markets of the United Kingdom allowed rapid industrialisation there, through the mobilisation of capital and the overcoming of risk for the development of major industrial projects (Hicks, 1969). In contrast, Joseph Schumpeter argued that banks rather than financial markets were fundamental to economic success because banks would identify and fund the key entrepreneurs to develop technological innovations (Schumpeter, 1934). The academic debate on the relationship between financial factors and economic growth has recently been discussed in detail by Levine (1997), King and Levine (1993) and Shleifer and Vishny (1997). Empirical research has shown that although countries with larger banks and more active financial markets tend also to have higher economic growth rates, it is not certain which particular financial allocation mechanism, or which mix of banks and financial markets helps to create the greater economic success (Levine, 1997; Albert, 1991; Stern, 1989).

The allocation of financial capital, is an immense area within the financial systems literature, covering international economics, economic development and corporate finance (Giovannini and Melo, 1993; Caprio *et al.*, 1994; Greenwood and Jovanovic, 1990; Fry, 1995). Fundamentally, financial systems serve major functions including: allocating resources; monitoring management performance; mobilising savings; providing information about prices; and facilitating exchange in the economy (Merton and Bodie, 1995; Levine, 1997). The effectiveness of financial systems in leading to economic success has been analysed in two major types of economic and finance models. In the first model, the financial system affects the rate of capital formation through savings rates changes and reallocations (Romer, 1986; Lucas, 1988; Rebelo, 1991). In the second model, the financial system helps to encourage new technology and production processes (Romer, 1990; Grossman and Helpman, 1991; Aghion and Howitt, 1992).

The economics and financial literature behind these two major models of economic success has failed to provide conclusive theoretical or empirical conclusions in a number of major areas. First, there is very little research on the role played by institutional factors such as legal traditions or political systems in influencing effective financial capital allocation; recent exceptions include LaPorta *et al.* (1996), Choi, Raman, Oussoltseva and Lee (1999) and Engerman and Sokoloff (1996). Secondly, although both effective banking and financial markets are seen to be crucial to economic success (Levine, 1997), there are few conclusions on the optimal mix of these financial instruments, such as banking, insurance, equity markets and bond markets, for a particular economy or region. Thirdly, there is very little evidence regarding the linkage between financial capital allocation systems and the level of economic maturity (Demirguc-Kunt and Maksimovic, 1996). For example, it is not certain whether particular capital allocation mechanisms, such as banking, equity or bond markets – derivatives which may enhance economic success in mature economies such as the United States or United Kingdom – are appropriate for more emerging economies such as in regions of Asia, Latin America or Eastern Europe.

Asia's Financial Capital System

Although some international economists, such as Paul Krugman, believe that the Asian economic miracle was exaggerated, it is difficult to deny the phenomenal economic growth throughout the Asian region over the last 30 years, which saw the increase in per capita income in countries such as South Korea increase over a hundred fold from US$100 to US$11 000. For the majority of the economies in Asia, capital allocation since the 1960s has tended to be closer to the model envisioned by Schumpeter (1934), where banks rather than financial markets play a major role in capital allocation decisions. The only exception to this system in Asia is Hong Kong, with its relatively service- and equity-market-driven systems (Choi, Lee and Kim, 1999; Amsden, 1989; Wade, 1990), which was modelled very much after the United States and United Kingdom. The unexpected Asian economic crisis of 1997 highlighted the need to research more fully the role of domestic and international institutions in the effectiveness of private sector organisations, such as banking, equity and bond markets. Even before the Asian economic crisis of 1997 and the more general emerging markets crises in Latin America and Russia in 1998, there had been a growing academic and policy debate on systems of capital allocation and their effects on national and regional economic success within the mature economies of North America and Western Europe. Before the 1990s, the majority of research in economics, finance and international business has tended to study the financial capital allocation system common in the United States and United Kingdom. This system is based on a strong legal structure, along with external monitoring of economics, business and management performance through financial markets, especially equity markets (Jensen and Meckling, 1976; Jensen and Murphy, 1990). But the economic success throughout the 1980s of countries such as Japan, Germany and France, where financial capital is mostly allocated through banking and insurance organisations raised fundamental questions of the two systems (Albert, 1991). As mentioned earlier, this academic debate goes back at least as far Schumpeter's (1934) belief in bank-driven capital allocation, versus Hicks' (1969) belief in financial, equity-markets-driven capital allocation.

The more recent research in economics and finance has begun to test empirically the differences between the financial-markets-driven capital allocation system of United States and United Kingdom, relative to the banking-driven capital allocation system of Japan and most of continental Europe (Choi, 1992; Franks and Mayer, 1997; Roe, 1994). In countries such as Japan and Germany, major banks and insurance companies act as external stakeholders by holding major shares in firms, exercising governance and control over internal management through a more informal, relationship-based exchange. Countries using this type of capital allocation mechanism have been broadly called 'stakeholder' or social market economies (Albert, 1991; Choi, 1992). The problem with applying this difference to Asia is that many Asian national business systems are still emerging and can often be a mix of both shareholder and stakeholder systems (Fruin, 1992; Gerlach, 1992).

Asia's Mixed Systems

As discussed by Simon (1991), the shareholder-based system of free market exchange assumes that exchange occurs with very little knowledge and identification of the other exchange partner, whereas, in reality, exchange needs to take into account such identification and shared values. We believe that in understanding Asia there is a need to appreciate that the difference between shareholder and stakeholders types of exchange can exist in 'mature' economies and is not an issue of mature versus emerging economies. Thus, the relatively less researched (Choi, 1992; Freeman, 1984) stakeholder systems that represent most continental European countries (Albert, 1991) have a far greater overlap in organisations and institutions, and exchange across organisations such as banking, government and financial markets resembles more the close exchange found within departments of an organisation in the more widely researched shareholder and financial-markets-driven system of capital allocation (North, 1990; Simon, 1991; Olson, 1992; Hirschman, 1994). The differences between shareholder and stakeholder systems of capital allocation are shown in Figure 3.2.

The acceptance of this diversity in relations among organisations and institutions (North, 1990; Simon, 1991) and between shareholder and stakeholder systems in mature economies helps to overcome the psychic distance and psychological uneasiness (Kogut and Singh, 1988; O'Grady and Lane, 1997; Johanson and Vahlne, 1977) towards emerging business systems such as

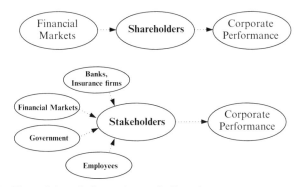

Figure 3.2 Financial capital creation and allocation

Asia. Our focus on comparative national systems, from the viewpoint of financial capital allocation systems has similarities to past research on institutional aspects of organisational analysis, such as Hirschman (1994).

The bank-driven financial capital allocation system envisioned by Schumpeter (1934) as the ideal system for economic success is a collective, relationship-based, stable national business system. Its fundamental strengths are long-run performance measures, relatively equal distribution of wealth and a broader inclusion of social issues such as the environment. Its fundamental weaknesses are its inability to change quickly and the fact that it is a system relatively closed to external influences, including foreign participation (Choi, 1992; Albert, 1991). As discussed earlier, most Asian countries adopted this system of financial capital allocation from the 1960s until the crisis of 1997, when two major changes, both internal and external to Asian national systems, occurred. The first was the general external change of globalisation, or the integration of goods, services and capital. As discussed in depth by Rodrik (1997), although there is a general consensus that globalisation of goods and services is economically positive, it is not certain that such benefits exist for globalisation of capital. Asian business systems, which experienced the volatility of global financial capital movements in 1997, did so from a stakeholder base or a system where financial capital was traditionally allocated through organisations such as banking, rather than financial equity and bond markets. As discussed earlier, the stakeholder system of Schumpeter (1934) is fundamentally a closed system of internal participants, such as banking, industry and government. This system is ill-equipped to deal with major external forces, such as deregulation in global financial capital movements. The increasing rates of uncertainty in the emerging business environments of much of Asia further increased the unstable impact of such global capital movements. The reason Asian business systems had originally adopted the more closed stakeholder system of financial capital allocated through banking was precisely linked to the very nature of uncertainty and change in the business environment of emerging economies such as those in Asia.

FACTOR II: KNOWLEDGE ALLOCATION

Knowledge has become an important topic of research in international business in the context of multinational enterprise and the transfer of knowledge across borders (Kogut and Zander, 1995; Love, 1995; Grant, 1996; Grant and Baden-Fuller, 1995; McFetridge, 1995). This research has tended to define knowledge generically and to focus on the issue of how markets and organisations differ in their capabilities to transfer knowledge. Thus, the comparisons between markets and organisations has been in a 'developed' country context, such as would face a North American multinational enterprise transferring knowledge across borders through its subsidiaries. The major questions of knowledge, multinational enterprise and efficient markets may change substantially in an emerging market context, such as in Eastern Europe or in parts of Asia (Choi, 1992). For example, the definition of knowledge in North American multinational enterprises may be defined as closer to research and development and original innovation. However, in an emerging economy context, knowledge's value may be in the context of technology licensing, or in the context of establishing institutions to protect intellectual property rights to knowledge.

There are two major issues concerning knowledge in the context of this chapter on Asian economic success and crisis. First, although there is a general interest in knowledge as a resource, there is a substantial gap in definitions between international business research and related areas of economics research. There is, however, clear overlap in disciplines over some of the major issues including multinational enterprise, global markets, knowledge transfer and public goods just as a substantial part of international business research has relied on an international economics methodology (Buckley and Casson, 1976; Dunning, 1996). We believe this gap has existed because although international business research has followed a relatively broad and interdisciplinary agenda within business and management research, international economics research has followed a more narrow agenda of trade theory and exchange rates. In order to analyse knowledge as resources there is thus a need to address the areas of diversion and overlap, and to consider whether other areas of economics research also have value in international business research. One area that especially warrants attention is the more recent research in economic development, which differentiates between knowledge about technology and knowledge about quality and attributes of goods and services, which face more general problems of imperfect information (Bowles and Gintis 1996; Knack and Keefer, 1997; Levine, 1997; Choi, 1992; Stiglitz, 1998).

Secondly, international business research on knowledge has tended to analyse the specific situation of developed countries. For example, a typical starting point of analysis would be a North American multinational enterprise facing the issue of knowledge transfer through markets or through its own subsidiaries (Kogut and Zander, 1993, 1995; Love, 1995; McFetridge, 1995) in a developed country business environment with relatively perfect information, effective institutions and intellectual property rights. The majority of business environments, however, are in a more developed or emerging economy context, with imperfect information, institutions in transition and lack of intellectual property rights. The value of knowledge in such an emerging economy context may be very different for multinational enterprises as well as for the overall economy and society. For example, the value of knowledge may be contained in the context of technology licensing, or in the development of certification agencies standardising quality and attributes of goods and services (Lall, 1992; Mody and Yilmaz, 1997; Wade, 1990; Amsden, 1989).

Definitions of Knowledge: Economics Research

In this section, we will briefly provide a summary of the broad economics literature and how past research can shed light on knowledge for international business research. The definition of knowledge in management or international business research has tended to rely on Polyani's (1944, 1966, 1971) distinctions between explicit or codifiable versus implicit or tacit characteristics (Nelson and Winter, 1982; Kogut and Zander, 1993, 1995). This led to the view that what could traditionally be seen as effective market mechanisms working under perfect information may be relatively ineffective in terms of knowledge transfer and exchange. Thus, alternative transfer mechanisms, such as the multinational enterprise and other interorganisational transfers, for example, strategic alliances, have been given as alternatives to the market (Choi and Lee, 1997; Beamish and Inkpen, 1997; Kogut and Zander, 1993). There is an implicit assumption made here that although markets are effective for non-knowledge assets such as capital, equipment, markets are ineffective for the exchange and transfer of intangible assets such as knowledge.

Past economics research on intangible resources have been in the context of the new economic growth theory (Romer, 1986; Krugman 1991). In this strand of literature, knowledge has been treated as an addition to the traditional economic resources of capital, land and labour; knowledge has tended to be seen in the context of human capital and education policies (Aghion and Bolton, 1997; Akerlof and Romer, 1993). Thus, this economics literature, based firmly in traditional neo-classical frameworks and assumptions, has not fully addressed the nature of knowledge and its implicit and intangible nature and has again used the effectiveness of market mechanisms for the creation and development of such human capital as a resource (Levine, 1997; Knack and Keefer, 1997; La Porta *et al.*, 1996; Stiglitz, 1998). This strand of economics literature, although addressing human capital and knowledge-like resources, has less relevance to international business research.

Although the economics of information has an extremely broad and deep literature starting from Schelling (1960) and Spence (1973), the focus of this research has been on the nature of markets under imperfect and asymmetric information. Issues such as moral hazard and adverse selection, along with the explosive growth in game theoretic models throughout the 1970s and 1980s, has permitted the analysis of market equilibrium under different assumptions concerning the availability of information. Like the more recent literature on economic growth mentioned earlier, the economics of information again has tangential linkages to knowledge research in international business but does overlap sufficiently to provide cross-fertilisation potential.

We believe the area of economics literature that has relevance for international business has occurred only in the mid-1990s with the increased interest in economic development, partly driven by the economies in transition in Central and Eastern Europe. The study of emerging economies in Eastern Europe, along with the numerous earlier studies of Asia (Amsden, 1989; Wade, 1990) helped to raise the following types of issues, that have especial relevance to future international business research. Firstly, that knowledge as a resource has to be analysed from the position of traditional economic growth theorists that have included it as part of human capital and seen education policy as the answer to its development (Romer, 1986). Secondly, fundamental questions of markets, institutions and orga-nisations have to be adjusted in the context of emerging economy environments (Lall, 1992; Choi, 1992). Thirdly, knowledge about generic technology, which tends to be standardised, needs to be separated from knowledge about the quality or attributes of goods and services. All these factors have fundamentally raised knowledge into a different context in economics research in the late 1990s, combining the analysis of develop-ment economics, economic growth and the earlier literature on economics of information.

Knowledge and the Asian Crisis

There are three aspects of knowledge that are relevant in terms of the Asian economic success and crisis: acquisition, dissemination and delivery (Stiglitz, 1998). Acquisition includes domestic creation as well as acquisition from foreign sources. Dissemination includes rapid diffusion within the domestic national business systems. Delivery is linked to the technological systems that allow effective delivery, such as the Internet and telecommunications systems. These distinctions are shown in Figure 3.3.

Traditionally, the relative strengths of the Asian national business systems (Choi, 1992) have been in the areas of dissemination and delivery; acquisition has been primarily borrowing from foreign sources through technology licensing (Amsden, 1989). The collective nature of Asian culture has allowed the rapid dissemination of knowledge acquired from the United States and Western Europe through trust-based networks and exchange (Choi, 1992). The fundamental problem that was arising even before the start of the 1997 Asian economic crisis was the problem of 'creativity', or the need for domestic creation of knowledge rather than dependence on foreign sources (Amsden, 1989; Wade, 1990). This became a special problem as the economies of United States and Western Europe became increasingly knowledge based, developing industries from computer software to biotechnology, media and entertainment.

Figure 3.3   National knowledge – acquisition, dissemination and delivery

Knowledge acquisition	Knowledge dissemination	Knowledge delivery
Acquisition primarily is from foreign sources or created domestically. Asian business systems primarily acquired their knowledge from the United States and Western Europe through technology licensing, with inadequate efforts towards domestic creativity (Amsden, 1989) and knowledge creation.	Effective dissemination or diffusion of knowledge is dependent on absorptive capacities (Cohen and Levinthal, 1990). The speed of such knowledge exchange and diffusion (Choi and Lee, 1997) is dependent on tacit, trust-based exchange, which is more common in collective societies such as in Asia.	The effectiveness of knowledge delivery to organisations and institutions in the national business system is dependent primarily on infrastructure such as telecommunications and IT systems. Asian economies successfully adopted such delivery systems primarily from the United States.

The key difference of these knowledge-based industries is their 'intangibility' in terms of quality attributes and success factors. The importance of intangibility of knowledge goes back at least as far as Polyani (1944) who differentiated between the informal, tacit aspects of knowledge versus the formal, explicit, codifiable aspects of information (Nelson and Winter, 1982). When economies become relatively more dependent on knowledge-based industries there is a shift in importance in the three aspects of knowledge: acquisition, dissemination, and delivery. Acquisition, especially domestic creation, becomes crucial to success. The Asian economic systems had learned only about the dissemination and delivery of tangible manufacturing industries and product attributes. The greater importance of intangibles and invisible assets (Itami and Roehl, 1987), including the value of financial assets and capital movements, were fundamentally new to the Asian business systems.

CONCLUSIONS

In this chapter, we have analysed the Asian economic crisis through the role played by two major factors: knowledge and financial capital allocation. We believe that an interdisciplinary framework incorporating international business, international economics and economic development can help to provide a more systematic understanding not only of past Asian economic success, but also the present Asian economic crisis. The fundamental issue is that the national business systems (North, 1990; Olson, 1992) in Asia were phenomenally success for decades and then dramatically problematic in 1997. There is a need to understand the factors for past success and which of these factors, if any, were responsible for the crisis that began in 1997. We developed a 'double triad' framework, including international markets and domestic institutions to better incorporate Asia's emerging economies into the global competition frameworks.

First, we analysed the two systems of capital allocation and ownership that have been proven widely successful in the mature economies of the world. These two major business systems can also be fundamentally divided into shareholder and stakeholder systems of capital allocation and ownership structures (Roe, 1994; Hirschman, 1994; Freeman, 1984; Albert, 1991). The Asian economic crisis was greatly due to the fact that in many of the more emerging countries of Asia, including Thailand, Malaysia and Indonesia, neither systems of external nor internal financial capital allocation had been fully developed. Thus, the 'level' of financial institutions in the national business system (Levine, 1997; Demirguc-Kunt and Maksimovic, 1996; Boyd and Smith, 1996) is crucial to understanding the Asian crisis.

Secondly, we focused on the importance of taking into account the nature of 'knowledge' acquisition, diffusion and delivery in emerging economies. Despite the past economic success of emerging economies in Asia, Eastern Europe and Latin America, international business research has not sufficiently analysed how such emerging environments differ from the mature business environment of North America and the European Union; exceptions include Choi (1992); Inkpen and Beamish (1997) and Olson (1992). The balance among the three major parts of knowledge – acquisition, diffusion and delivery – has changed. The strength of the collective, relationship- and trust-based national business systems in Asia was based on the diffusion and dissemination of externally created knowledge, usually from foreign countries such in North America and Western Europe. However, as the global business environment has become increasingly dependent on creativity, R&D, technology and the so-called, high-tech industrial milieu, global competitiveness in knowledge resources has become more dependent on acquisition and delivery, rather than diffusion. In this sense, the knowledge allocation mechanism in Asia, based primarily on past diffusion, has become no longer appropriate in today's global business environment.

Although the Asian economic crisis has been widely debated and researched, the analysis has tended to be dominated by purely neo-classical economic thought. This, however, does not take into account the undeniable phenomenal economic success from the 1960s until 1997. The approach in this chapter has been to follow a broader, interdisciplinary approach including economic as well as international business and management frameworks. The 'level' of emergence of the financial institutions in Asia and the ability to allocate or misallocate capital was a crucial factor in the crisis. A greater global dependence on knowledge creation and knowledge-based industries further added to the lack of maturity in Asian institutions.

At least two issues warrant further research. First, there is a need to compare the Asian business systems that are presently in crisis with those in less affected emerging business systems, such as in Eastern Europe, in order to compare and contrast the success and failure factors. Secondly, further empirical work and case studies on the nature of financial capital and knowledge creation and allocation in Asian business system is needed.

References

Aghion, P. and Bolton, P. (1997) 'A theory of trickle-down growth and development', *Review of Economic Studies*, 64: 151–172.
Aghion, P. and Howitt, P. (1992) 'A model of growth through creative destruction', *Econometrica*, 60: 323–351.
Akerlof, G. and Romer, P. (1993) 'Looting: the economic underworld of bankruptcy for profit', *Brookmgs Papers on Economic Activity*, 2: 2–60.
Albert, M. (1991) *Capitalisme contre capitalisme* (Paris: Seuil).
Amsden, A. (1989) *Asia's Next Giant* (Boston, MA: Harvard Business School Press).
Beamish, P. and Banks, J. (1987) 'Equity joint ventures and the theory of the multinational enterprise', *Journal of International Business Studies*, 18: 1–16.
Beamish, P. and Inkpen, A. (1997) 'Knowledge, bargaining power and international joint venture stability', *Academy of Management Review*, 22: 177–202.
Boddewyn, J. (1988) 'Political aspects of MNE theory', *Journal of International Business Studies*, 19: 341–365.
Bowles, S. and Gintis, H. (1996) 'Efficient redistribution: new rules for markets, states and communities', *Politics and Society*, 24: 307–342.
Boyd, J. and Smith, B. (1996) 'The co-evolution of the real and financial sectors in the growth process', *World Bank Economic Review*, 10: 371–396.
Brewer, T.L. (1992) 'An issue-area approach to the analysis of MNE–government relations', *Journal of International Business Studies*, 23: 295–310.
Buckley, P. and Casson, M. (1976) *The Future of Multinational Enterprise* (London: Macmillan).
Caprio, G., Atiyas I. and Hanson, J. (1994) *Financial Reform: Theory and Experience* (New York: Cambridge University Press).
Choi, C.J. (1992) 'Asian capitalism versus western civilization', Oxford University, mimeo.
Choi, C.J., Lee, S.H. and Kim, J.-B. (1999) 'Countertrade and transaction governance in emerging economies', *Journal of International Business Studies*, 21: 120–134.
Choi, C.J. and Lee, S.H. (1997) 'A knowledge-based view of co-operative interorganizational relationships', in P. Beamish and P. Killing (eds) *Co-operative Strategies: European Perspectives* (Massachusetts: Josey-Bass).
Choi, C.J., Raman, M., Oussoltseva, O. and Lee, S.H. (1999) 'Political embeddedness in the new global triad', *Management International Review*, 30: 27–45.
Cohen, W. and Levinthal, D. (1990) 'Absorptive capacity: a new perspective on learning and innovation', *Administrative Science Quarterly*, 35: 128–152.
Demirgucs-Kunt, A. and Levine, R. (1996) 'Stock market development and financial intermediaries: stylized facts', *World Bank Economic Review*, 10: 291–322.
Dunning, J. (1996) 'The geographical sources of the competitiveness of firms: some results of a new survey', *Transnational Corporations*, 5: 1–29.
Engerman, S. and Sokoloff, K. (1996) 'Factor endowments, institutions and differential paths of growth among new world economies: a view from economic

historians of the United States', in S. Haber (ed.) *How Latin American Fell Behind* (Stanford, CA: Stanford University Press) pp. 260–304.

Franks, J. and Mayer, C. (1997) 'Corporate ownership and control in the UK, Germany and France', *Journal of Applied Corporate, Finance*, 9: 30–45.

Freeman, S. (1984) *Strategic Management: a Stakeholder Approach* (Boston: Pitman Press).

Fruin, M. (1992) *The Japanese Enterprise System* (Oxford: Oxford University Press).

Fry, M. (1995) *Money, Interest and Banking in Economic Development* (Baltimore: John Hopkins University Press).

Gerlach, M. (1992) *Alliance Capitalism: The Social Organization of Japanese Business* (Berkeley: University of California Press).

Ghoshal, S. and Moran, J. (1996) 'Bad for practice: a critique of the transaction cost theory', *Academy of Management Review*, 212: 13–45.

Giovannini, A. and de Melo, M. (1993) 'Government revenue from financial repression', *American Economic Review*, 83: 953–963.

Granovetter, M. (1985) 'Economic action and social structure: the problem of embeddedness', *American Journal of Sociology*, 91: 481–510.

Grant, R. (1996) 'Prospering in dynamically competitive environments: organisational capability as knowledge integration', *Organization Science*, 7: 375–387.

Grant, R. and Baden-Fuller, C. (1995) 'A knowledge-based theory of inter-firm collaboration', *Academy of Management Best Paper Proceedings*.

Greenwood, J. and Jovanovic, B. (1990) 'Financial development, growth and the distribution of income', *Journal of Political Economy*, Oct., pp. 1076–1107.

Grossman, G. and Helpman, E. (1991) 'Quality ladders in the theory of growth', *Review of Economic Studies*, 58: 43–61.

Hicks, J. (1969) *A Theory of Economic History* (Oxford: Clarendon Press).

Hill, C. (1995) 'National institutional structures, transaction cost economizing and competitive advantage', *Organization Science*, 6: 119–131.

Hirsch, P. and Lounsbury, M. (1996) 'Rediscovering volition: the institutional economics of Douglass C. North', *Academy of Management Review*, book review essay, 21: 872–884.

Hirschman, A. (1994) 'Social conflict as pillar of democratic society', *Political Theory*, 22: 15–27.

Inkpen, A. and Beamish, P. (1997) 'Knowledge, bargaining power and international joint venture stability', *Academy of Management Review*, 22: 177–202.

Itami, H. and Roehl, T. (1987) *Mobilizing Invisible Assets* (Cambridge: Harvard University Press).

Jensen, M. and Meckling, W. (1976) 'Theory of the firm: managerial behavior, agency costs, and ownership structure', *Journal of Financial Economics*, 3: 305–360.

Jensen, M. and Murphy, K. (1990) 'Performance pay and top-management incentives', *Journal of Political Economy*, 98: 225–264.

Johanson, S. and Vahlne, J. (1977) 'The internationalisation process of the firm: a model of knowledge development and increasing foreign market commitments', *Journal of International Business Studies*, 8: 22–32.

King, R. and Levine, R. (1993) 'Finance and growth: Schumpeter might be right', *Quarterly Journal of Economics*, 108: 717–737.

Knack, S. and Keefer, P. (1997) 'Does social capital have an economic payoff? A cross-country investigation', *Quarterly Journal of Economics*, 122: 1251–1288.

Kogut, B. (1991) 'Country capabilities and the permeability of borders', *Strategic Management Journal* (summer special issue) 12: 33–47.

Kogut, B. (1993) *Country Competitiveness: Technology and the Organizing of Work* (Oxford: Oxford University Press).

Kogut, B. and Singh, H. (1988) 'The effect of national culture on the choice of entry mode', *Journal of International Business Studies*, 19: 411–432.

Kogut, B. and Zander, U. (1993) 'Knowledge of the firm and the evolutionary theory of the multinational enterprise', *Journal of International Business Studies*, 24: 625–645.

Kogut, B. and Zander, U. (1995) 'Knowledge, market failure and the multinational enterprise: a reply', *Journal of International Business Studies*, 26, pp. 417–426.

Krugman, P. (1991) *Geography and Trade* (Oxford: Oxford University Press).

La Porta, R. *et al.* (1996) 'Law and finance', National Bureau of Economic Research working paper no. 5661, Cambridge, MA.

Lall, S. (1992) 'Technological capacilities and industrialisation', *World Development*, 20: pp. 165–186.

Lenway, S. and Murtha, T. (1994) 'The state as strategist in international business research', *Jounal of International Business Studies*, 25: 513–535.

Levine, R. (1997) 'Financial development and economic growth: view and agenda', *Journal of Economic Literature*, 35: 688–727.

Love, J. (1995) 'Knowledge, market failure and the multinational enterprise: a theoretical note', *Journal of International Business Studies*, 26: 399–407.

Lucas, R. (1988) 'On the mechanics of economic development', *Journal of Monetary Economics*, 22: 3–42.

McFetridge, D.W. (1995) 'Knowledge, market failure and the multinational enterprise: a comment', *Journal of International Business Studies*, 26: 409–416.

Merton, R. and Bodie, Z. (1995) 'A conceptual framework for analyzing the financial environment', in B. Crane *et al.* (eds) *The Global Financial System: A Financial Perspective* (Boston, MA: Harvard Business School Press).

Mody, A. and Yilmaz, K. (1997) 'Is there persistence in the growth of manufactured exports? Evidence from newly industrialising countries', *Journal of Development Economics*, 53: 447–470.

Murtha, T. (1993) 'The state as strategic in international business research', University of Minnesota, Carleton School of Management, mimeo.

Murtha, T. and Lenway, S. (1994) 'Country capabilities and the strategic state: how national political institutions affect multinational corporations' strategies', *Strategic Management Journal*, 15: 120–141.

Nelson, R. and Winter, S. (1982) *An Evolutionary Theory of Economic Change* (Cambridge, MA: Belknap Press of Harvard University Press).

Nooteboom, B. (1996) 'Trust, opportunism and governance: a process and control model', *Organisation Studies*, 17: 985–1010.

North, D. (1990) *Institutions, Institutional Change and Economic Performance* (Cambridge, UK: Cambridge Umversity Press).

O'Grady, S. and Lane, H. (1997) 'The psychic distance paradox', *Journal of International Business Studies*, 27: 305–333.

Ohmae, K. (1985) *The Global Triad* (New York: Macmillan).

Olson, M. (1965) *The Loglc of Collective Aaction* (Cambridge, MA: Harvard University Press).

Olson, M. (1982) *The Rise and Decline of Nations* (New Haven, CT: Yale University Press).

Ostrom, E. (1990) *Governing the Common: The Evolution of Institutions for Collective Action* (Cambridge, UK: Cambridge University Press).

Pauly, L. and Reich, S. (1997) 'National structures and multinational corporate behavior: enduring differences in the age of globalisation', *International Organization*, 51: 1–30.

Polyani, K. (1944) *The Great Transformation* (New York: Rinehart and Company).

Polyani, K. (1966) *Dahoney and the Slave Trade* (Washington: University of Washington Press).

Polyani, K. (with Dalton, G.) (1971) *Primitive, Archaic and Modern Economies* (Boston, MA: Beacon Press).

Porter, M. (1990) *The Competitive Advantage of Nations* (New York: Macmillan).

Putnam, R. (1988) 'Diplomacy and domestic politics: the logic of two level games', *International Organization*, 42: 427–460.

Rebelo, S. (191) 'Long-run policy analysis and long-run growth', *Journal of Political Economy*, 99: 500–521.

Rodrik, D. (1997) *Has Globalisation Gone Too Far?* (Washington, DC: Institute of International Economies).

Roe, M. (1994) *Strong Managers, Weak Owners: the Political Roots of American Corporate Finance* (Princeton: Princeton University Press).

Romer, P.M. (1986) 'Increasing returns and long-run growth', *Journal of Political Economy*, 94: 1002–1037.

Romer, P.M. (1990) 'Endogenous technological change', *Journal of Political Economy*, 98: S71–102.

Rugman, A. (1997) *Multinational Enterprises and Trade Policy* (London: Edward Elgar).

Rugman, A., Kirtin, J. and Soloway, J. (1997) 'NAFTA, environmental regulations and Canadian competitiveness', *Journal of World Trade*, 31: 129–144.

Schelling, T. (1960) *The Strategy of Conflict* (Cambridge, MA: Harvard University Press).

Schumpeter, J. (1934) *The Theory of Economic Development* (Cambridge, MA: Harvard University Press).

Shleifer, A. and Vishny, R. (1997) 'A survey of corporate governance', *Journal of Finance*, 75: 110–147.

Simmel, G. (1978) *The Philosophy of Money* (London: Routledge).

Simon, H. (1991) 'Organizations and markets', *Journal of Ecogomic Perspectives*, 5: 25–44.

Spence, M. (1973) *Market Signalling* (Cambridge, MA: Harvard University Press).

Spender, J.-C. (1996) 'Making knowledge the basis of a dynamic theory of the firm', *Strategic Management Journal* (winter special issue) 17: 45–62.

Stern, N. (1989) 'The economics of development: a survey', *Economic Journal*, 99: 597–685.

Stiglitz, J. (1998) *World Bank Development Review* (Washington, DC: IBRD)

Vernon, R. (1966) 'International investment and international trade in the product cycle', *Quarterly Journal of Economics*, 90: 110–137.

Wade, R. (1990) *Governing the Market* (Princeton: Princeton University Press).

Whitley, R. (1992) *Asian Business Systems* (London: Sage).

Williamson, O. (1996) 'Economic organization: the case for candor', *Academy of Management Review*, 21: 48–57.

4 Internal Capital Markets in Multinational Firms: The Effects of Subsidiary Strategic Independence

Ram Mudambi

F23 L22 G32

The relationship between a firm's headquarters and its operating units has been the subject of considerable recent interest. One of the reasons for this interest has been the changing role of subsidiaries of multinational enterprises (MNEs). Subsidiaries of MNEs are expanding their role beyond traditional downstream activities like sales, service and assembly to encompass upstream activities like research and development (R&D), component production, strategic marketing and support activities (Bartlett and Ghoshal, 1989; Gupta and Govindrajan, 1991; Taggart, 1996a; Cantwell, 1997). In this context, MNEs have been consolidating their subsidiaries to give them geographic or product range responsibilities (Hood, Young and Lal, 1994; Birkinshaw, 1996).

The process of consolidation creates both winners and losers – some units receive broad mandates and responsibilities while others are slimmed down or closed altogether. These decisions are typically made at headquarters and often involve channelling resources within the firm. There is a recent body of literature suggesting that the primary function of the headquarters is to run this internal capital market, which effectively re-distributes resources within the firm (Shin and Stulz, 1996; Lamont, 1997; Stein, 1995, 1997).

Further, it is argued that the effectiveness of this internal capital market increases with the 'noise' in headquarters' information flows. Note that since the managers of various subsidiaries are in competition with each other for resources allocated by headquarters they have an incentive to overstate the value of their projects. As headquarters' ability to assess the true value of subsidiary projects declines, the value of the internal capital market as an allocation mechanism increases. Thus, internal capital markets are likely to be most effective in MNEs where geographical and cultural distances create the greatest chance that inaccuracies in information are difficult to pinpoint.

The question addressed in this chapter concerns the division of strategic decision-making authority between MNE headquarters and the subsidiaries. A major aspect of this is control over investment funds where headquarters control is indicated by the re-allocation of funds between subsidiaries. Thus, the chapter focuses on the relationship between the mandate of the subsidiary and the extent to which it is an active part of the internal capital market. In other words, does the acquisition of a broad mandate by a subsidiary reduce headquarters' control over its resources? The answer to this question has important implications for headquarters and subsidiary strategies within MNEs. If the breadth of the mandate of the subsidiary does not affect the ability of headquarters to control its resources, then the formation of strategically independent subsidiaries with global mandates is always beneficial for MNEs. The advantages of globalisation derived from headquarters are reinforced by the advantages of strategic decision making at the local and regional level. However, if increasing the scope of a subsidiary's mandate reduces headquarters' ability to control its resources, then the advantages of subsidiary strategic independence must be offset against the reduced efficiency of the MNE's internal capital market.

This view of headquarters–subsidiary financial relations is examined using a cross-sectional data set of MNEs operating in the UK. The empirical results offer considerable support for the proposed hypothesis. These results are of considerable importance to MNE managers since they suggest that the devolution of strategic responsibilities to subsidiaries must consider the impact on the firm's internal capital market. In particular, in situations where the internal capital market is most useful, strategic decision making is best retained at the firm's headquarters. It has been suggested that such situations are those where the external capital markets are relatively undeveloped so that information and agency problems are particularly pronounced (Stein, 1997). Conversely, where external markets are very well-developed, the additional gains from internal markets are likely to be small, so that strategic devolution is more likely to be a net benefit to the firm.

RESEARCH QUESTIONS AND METHODOLOGY

Research Questions

The basic research question concerns the relationship between a subsidiary's strategic independence and the MNE headquarters' control over its financial resources. The question of a subsidiary's strategic independence has been the subject of a large literature in international business, so a comprehensive literature survey will not be attempted here. Good reviews are available in Birkinshaw (1994) and Birkinshaw and Morrison (1995). In addition, a large and focused literature has been developed by Nordic scholars (see, for example, Andersson and Forsgren (1995), Forsgren, Holm and Johansen (1995), Forsgren and Johansen (1992), Holm (1992)). Many taxonomies

Figure 4.1   MNE subsidiary types

		Extent of strategic decision making	
		Low	*High*
Extent of responsibilities	*National*	Local assembly	National mandate
	Regional	Regionally rationalised assembly	Regional subsidiary mandate
	Global	World product mandate	Global subsidiary mandate

Adapted from D'Cruz (1986) and Moore (1995).

of subsidiary types are available in the literature. A taxonomy relevant for the current study is adapted from D'Cruz (1986) and Moore (1995) and presented as Figure 4.1. Note that this taxonomy relates only to the strategic independence of the subsidiary's operations and not to its participation in the internal capital market, i.e. it relates to operations and not to financial management. The descriptors specifically relate to manufacturing operations, as the study focuses on engineering and engineering-related firms.

A movement towards the bottom right cell in this simple taxonomy captures devolution of increasing strategic responsibilities. If such movement is accompanied by reduced headquarters control over subsidiary financial resources, then the devolution incurs costs in the form of reduced internal capital market efficiency. This reduced efficiency is likely to be a hindrance to the MNE if it has other subsidiaries with good strategic prospects, operating in locations where external capital markets are relatively poor. Its strategically independent subsidiaries will reduce its ability to channel aid to those subsidiaries through its internal capital market. In contrast, a negation of the above hypothesis implies that increasing the scope of the subsidiary's mandate can be one of the best ways to capture the MNE's inherent strategic advantages.

It is necessary at this point to address some important issues. First, it is important to make a distinction between the MNE's central treasury function and its internal capital market. Both are concerned with the management of the financial resources of the entire enterprise, but there is a difference in their decision horizons. The cash flows between a subsidiary and its parent are made up of three components:

(a) The pure day-to-day cash management function undertaken by the parent company's treasury department

(b) Remittances of funds (dividends, profits, royalties and other payments) from subsidiary to parent

(c) The allocation of capital budgets by the parent to the subsidiary.

The treasury department's focus is mainly on short-term cash management and on efficient financial structure and covers (a) above. Its concerns are more tactical and therefore short term. The internal capital market is the concern of (b) and (c). It is focused on long-term project finance and considerations of the MNE's geographic and product focus. It factors in the covariance of returns on different projects and takes into consideration the issues of capital budgeting and investment appraisal. All this requires taking a strategic and long-term view of the firm as a whole.

Second, we must consider whether weakened internal capital markets really matter that much. It may be argued that independent subsidiaries that act as profit centres can tap external capital markets (where they are well developed) so that the winning and losing subsidiaries within the MNE can be picked and monitored externally. Further, if such strategic independence makes subsidiaries more dynamic, then it is a net benefit for the MNE. There are two points that need to be made here.

(i) As pointed out by Stein (1997), the external capital market can only grant or not grant financial support to subsidiary projects. It can only 'pick winners' and cannot transfer funds across projects. The external capital market can only provide flows like (c) above. Thus, it serves to reinforce rather than alleviate the unit-focused biases of the subsidiary managers. The major role of the internal capital market is to overcome these biases, by combining flows (b) and (c). Thus, the internal capital market can both 'pick winners' and 'punish losers'. For instance, a subsidiary earning a large amount of current profit, but with weak future prospects would be 'harvested' by a smoothly functioning internal capital market. Outflows of profit and other remittances to the parent would exceed inflows of capital. However, if the subsidiary's strategic independence impeded the working of this market, *ceteris paribus*, outflows would be smaller as the subsidiary retained more of its earnings than would be optimal from the perspective of the firm as a whole.

(ii) Further, while it is possible that strategic independence *per se* makes subsidiaries more dynamic, the point of this chapter is that this may have some cost in terms of efficiency.

Third, the relationship between the internal capital market and the external capital market is an important one. It may be argued that it is the internal capital market, in which headquarters makes use of its specific competencies to direct the flow of resources, that differentiates the firm from a mere collection of financial assets. The insights of transaction cost economics imply that the firm is more than the sum of its parts and that the external capital market cannot duplicate it through piecemeal operation of its constituent units. Of course, the external capital market does function as a constraint on the internal capital market. Thus, if the market valuation of the firm's constituent parts diverges too far from the valuation of the firm as a whole, it is likely to become the target of a re-structuring bid like a takeover or a management buy-out.

Fourth, the issue of power, while not explicitly addressed in this chapter, is an important latent factor. Whether subsidiary mandates are granted or taken is an open question (Doz and Prahalad, 1981; Forsgren, Holm and Johansen, 1995). Headquarters may have little control of any kind over powerful subsidiaries, making the issue of control of their financial resources moot. This point is related to the second point above, for if subsidiaries operate with complete independence and the role of headquarters is limited, it is inevitable that a substantial portion of the benefits of globalisation will be lost. This is not to deny that there are strong forces pushing the MNE towards such a 'multi-domestic' strategy (Buckley and Carter, 1998; Casson, 1987, 1994).

Finally, the internal capital markets' approach to the MNE can be operationalised using a real options-based approach. An initial investment in a region or a technology can be viewed as creating a platform (or an option) for future expansion or development. Kogut and Kulatilaka (1994a, 1994b) note that a strategic business unit (SBU) structure leads to an underinvestment in projects with long-term growth potential and an underdevelopment of 'corporate assets'. This is because an SBU may view an investment as unattractive, even though it creates an option that may be valuable for other units. In this system, there is less incentive to invest if the value of the platform accrues to other SBUs. The value of the option (and of the internal capital market) increases with the level of uncertainty, the breadth of the opportunity set, the specificity of the assets created and the ability of the MNE to exercise the option.

Methodology

The MNE and its subsidiaries are engaged in a principal–agent relationship. Both the internal capital market and subsidiary strategic independence must be implemented through the incentives given to the local managers. It is therefore assumed that the incentive compatibility constraints emerging from the underlying principal–agent model are satisfied.

The relationship of interest, concerning the functioning of the MNE's internal capital market, can be thought of as a reduced form conditioned on the system of managerial incentives.[1] This reduced form can be represented by the relationship between the financial outflows from the subsidiary to its MNE parent and variables measuring the performance of the subsidiary relative to the MNE's other operations, as well as variables measuring the relative attractiveness of the subsidiary's location.

The objective of this paper is to test for the effect of subsidiary strategic independence on headquarters control of its financial resources. This is done by adding variables measuring subsidiary strategic independence to the above relationship. Denoting the net financial flows from the subsidiary to its MNE parent as NF, the relationship to be estimated is:

(1) $NF_t = f[$(Subsidiary performance measures)$_t$, (Location attractiveness)$_t$, (Subsidiary strategic independence)$_t]$

The two research hypotheses may be formally stated as follows:

H1: The headquarters of an MNE operates an internal capital market in which financial resources are transferred from one subsidiary to another on the basis of the overall strategic prospects and fit.
H2: Subsidiary strategic independence impedes the working of this internal capital market in the MNE.

The two hypotheses are nested, in the sense that H2 becomes relevant for testing only if H1 is not rejected. Statistical significance of the variables from the first two groups confirms the working of an internal capital market in MNEs (H1). A significant and negative impact of variables from the third group supports the hypothesis that increasing strategic independence of the subsidiary impedes the working of this internal capital market (H2).

DATA AND ESTIMATION

Data was obtained in two stages. In the first stage, a list of MNE engineering and engineering-related operations in the West Midlands region of England was compiled from business directories. All the firms were non-UK firms with subsidiaries operating in the UK. The region was chosen because it has been Britain's most successful region for attracting inward investment, with more than 900 companies investing over £3 billion and employing over 100 000 workers (Griffiths, 1993). After phone confirmations, a final list of 224 companies with personal contact names was assembled for the purpose of a directed mail survey.

The questionnaire was accompanied by a cover letter explaining the aims of the study, guaranteeing confidentiality and urging response. In order to improve the response rate, the questionnaire had to be short, concise and of current interest (salient) to the respondent (Heberlein and Baumgartner 1978). Ten days after the survey was mailed out, a reminder postcard was sent to all companies that had not yet responded.

Overall, 85 responses were received to the mail survey (37.9%). Of these, four were found to be national firms mistakenly identified as MNEs and seven were unusable for various other reasons, leaving 74 (33.0%) valid responses for evaluation. The response rate is well within the range expected for an unsolicited mail survey. The survey collected information on measures of strategic independence of MNE subsidiaries, net capital flows out of the UK subsidiary, the rate of return on corporate liquid funds and measures of corporate risk.

In the second stage, several international statistics were computed for the host countries of the MNEs in the sample. These statistics were obtained from *International Financial Statistics* published by the International Monetary Fund. In addition, country risk indices were drawn from the capital markets publication *Euromoney*.

Survey responses were cross-checked against company annual reports where possible. Some variables could be checked for the entire sample (global sales, employment, geographic and functional scope of the UK subsidiary's mandate and duration of UK operations). Others could only be checked for a majority of firms, while some very specific variables were not reported in published data. A high degree of correspondence between published data and survey responses was found, supporting the veracity of the survey responses. This is particularly important in the case of financial flow data between the subsidiary and its parent, since this can be subject to a number of distortions arising from transfer pricing. Published data is generally considered reliable since most MNEs minimise risks of being penalised by authorities by following a 'whiter than white' policy (Coates *et al.*, 1993).

Non-response bias was investigated with the widely used method suggested by Armstrong and Overton (1977). This involved comparing early and late respondents. Late respondents were defined to be those who responded after receiving the reminder postcard. Six sample measures were compared using a χ^2 test of independence. The responses from early and late respondents were virtually identical.

The variables assembled for use in the study correspond to the requirements of estimating equation (1). The dependent variable is the net financial outflow from the UK subsidiary to its overseas parent.

The first set of explanatory variables relates to subsidiary performance and location attractiveness. The variables were selected following the literature on international investment decision-making (Bettis and Hall, 1982; Bettis and Mahajan, 1985; Shapiro, 1986; Mudambi, 1995; Chenells and Griffith, 1997; Eun and Resnick, 1998). The variables relating to subsidiary performance measure the risk and return associated with the UK subsidiary's operations, relative to the MNE's overall operations. The variables relating to location attractiveness include an index of relative location risk (whose component parts include macroeconomic indicators and overall financial sector risks), exchange rate risks and relative tax rates. (See the Appendix for a detailed description of the variables.)

The second set of variables relates to subsidiary strategic independence. These variables were drawn from selected studies on MNE–subsidiary relationships (Rugman, 1981; D'Cruz, 1986; Prahalad and Doz, 1987; Roth and Morrison, 1992; Birkinshaw, 1996; Birkinshaw and Morrison, 1995; Moore, 1995; Taggart, 1996b; Mudambi and Mudambi, 1998). The variables measure the extent of local operation's R&D and exports, the extent of local decision making regarding suppliers, human resource management and process engineering, the functional and geographic scope of the subsidiary's output mandate and the duration of the subsidiary's operations in the UK.

The estimation of equation (1) is carried out using multiple regression analysis. The net flows from the subsidiary to its parent (NF94) is the dependent variable in the analysis, while the subsidiary relative performance measures, relative location attractiveness and subsidiary strategic independence measures are the explanatory variables.

The first set of variables, i.e. those relating to the relative performance of the subsidiary and the relative attractiveness of the UK as a location are metric and can be used directly in the estimation of equation (1). However, two problems arise in using the variables in the second set, i.e. those measuring the subsidiary's strategic independence. Firstly, several of them are categorical and/or ordinal. Secondly, several of them are highly correlated with each other. These reasons mean that they are unsuitable for direct use as regressors.

Factor Analysis

The problems are addressed by constructing statistical variables to summarise the information content along identifiable dimensions. This is done by running all the variables in the second set through principal component factor analysis. The latent root criterion is used to determine the number of factors (or summary variables) extracted. The rationale is that the variation in each variable is unity after the variable has been standardised. Thus, each factor should account for the variation in at least one variable if it is to be considered useful from a data summarisation perspective (Churchill, 1995).

The factor analysis results are presented in Table 4.1. There are three factors with eigenvalues greater than unity. The eigenvalue for the fourth factor is 0.6315. The three factors extracted may be termed 'strategic responsibilities' (STRAT), 'external orientation' (EXTERNAL) and 'process responsibilities' (PROCESS), on the basis of the varimax rotated factor loading matrix.

The first factor, 'strategic responsibilities', explains 33.2% of total variance. The extent to which supplier decisions are made by the subsidiary (SUPPLY), the amount of subsidiary R&D, the functional scope of the

Table 4.1   Factor analysis of subsidiary strategic independence–factor loadings and communalities (Varimax Rotation)

| Variable | Factor loadings | | | |
	Factor 1 STRAT	Factor 2 EXTERNAL	Factor 3 PROCESS	Communality
SUPPLY	**0.861**	0.237	0.017	0.798
R&D	**0.821**	0.064	0.150	0.701
FSCOPE	**0.893**	0.031	0.000	0.799
DT	**0.830**	0.227	0.190	0.777
GSCOPE	0.129	**0.845**	−0.192	0.768
EXPt	0.116	**0.857**	0.053	0.751
WEXPORT	0.111	**0.947**	0.047	0.912
PROC	0.213	−0.003	**0.810**	0.701
TRAIN	0.008	−0.056	**0.853**	0.731
Eigenvalue	3.5597	2.0970	1.2813	–
Variance	2.9908	2.4621	1.4851	6.9380
%Variance	0.332	0.274	0.165	0.771

Loadings of variables associated with particular factors are shown in bold.

subsidiary's activities (FSCOPE) and the experience of the subsidiary in the location (DT) all load heavily on this factor.

The second factor, 'external orientation', explains 27.4% of total variance. The geographic scope of the subsidiary's output mandate (GSCOPE), the percentage of its output that is exported (WEXPORT) and its export experience as a percentage of total tenure (EXPt) are the variables that load heavily on this factor.

The third factor, 'process responsibilities', explains another 16.5% of total variance. The subsidiary's responsibilities in process engineering (PROC) and training (TRAIN) are the variables that load heavily on this factor. In interviews with managers at several of the responding firms, it became clear that a considerable amount of training that occurred at these subsidiaries was of the operational or process type. This would explain the loading pattern that emerged.

Overall, the first three factors account for over 77% of the variance of all the underlying variables. The communalities of individual variables are very high as well, with the lowest value in excess of 70% and a high in excess of 90%.

Regression Analysis

The objective of this analysis is to estimate equation (1). The base-line estimation is carried out using ordinary least squares (OLS). These estimates

Table 4.2 Least squares estimates of the net financial flow equation (Dependent Variable: NF94)

Regressor	OLS Estimates	WLS Estimates (Wts. = EMPL)
Constant	−0.339 (1.19) *(1.23)*	0.393 (1.09)
ABROR	−3.262 (1.98) *(2.62)**	−3.003 (2.16)*
RISK	0.0960 (6.05)* *(5.25)**	0.0967 (6.98)*
RORFF	−12.264 (2.29)* *(2.35)**	−25.741 (3.92)*
RLOCRSK	0.00265 (2.53)* *(3.17)**	0.00190 (2.07)*
ΔEXRT	−2.307 (3.89)* *(5.21)**	−1.534 (2.47)*
TAX	0.250 (2.97)* *(3.10)**	0.184 (2.12)*
STRAT	−0.511 (5.65)* *(6.32*)*	−0.529 (5.96)*
EXTERNAL	−0.0956 (1.40) *(1.46)*	0.00979 (0.11)
PROCESS	−0.0278 (0.41) *(0.46)*	−0.194 (2.62)*
Diagnostics		
Adj.R^2	0.8456	0.8791
'F' Stat; (d.f.)	45.42; (9, 64)	59.97; (9,64)
Joint exclusion restriction on subsidiary strategic independence coefficients 'F' Stat; (d.f.)	13.981; (0.000)	14.737; (0.000)
Breusch-Pagan Test: $\chi^2(9)$; (p value)	29.724; (0.000)	8.108; (0.523)
Akaike IC	1.597	2.160

Notes:
(1) 't' statistics in brackets. Those calculated using White's heteroscedasticity–consistent variance–covariance matrix are shown in italics.
(2) Estimates significant at the 5% level are marked with an asterisk.

are presented in Table 4.2. However, as the subsidiaries varied considerably in terms of size, there was reason to suspect heteroscedasticity. This is because the net outflows of large subsidiaries have a much greater potential variation than the net outflows of smaller ones. This translates conditional variances that vary systematically with subsidiary size, which means that the OLS estimators are inefficient. This suspicion is confirmed by observing the results of the Breusch-Pagan test for heteroscedasticity, which is comprehensively failed (see Table 4.2).

This problem is addressed in three separate ways. First, the standard errors are re-estimated using White's heteroscedasticity–consistent variance-covariance matrix. This allows the estimated errors themselves to serve as scaling factors in adjusting the estimated conditional variances. The use of White's matrix generally results in improvements in the values of individual 't' statistics, as would be expected.

Second, weighted least squares (WLS) estimates are generated. These results are also presented in Table 4.2. The employment of the subsidiary (EMPL) is used as the proxy for size. The use of employment as the proxy for size is justified on the grounds that the firms are all in closely related lines of business, so that fundamental differences in the employment-size relationship are unlikely. The procedure is successful in correcting the heteroscedasticity problem, as the Breusch-Pagan test is now passed (see Table 4.2).

Third, maximum likelihood estimates are generated using a linear model of multiplicative heteroscedasticity, again using EMPL as the proxy for subsidiary size. These results are presented in Table 4.3. The estimates of the

Table 4.3 Maximum likelihood estimates of the net financial flow equation (Dependent Variable: NF94)

Regressor	Linear model with multiplicative heteroscedasticity (Wts. = EMPL)
Constant	−0.497 (2.00)*
ABROR	−3.161 (2.20)*
RISK	0.0983 (6.18)*
RORFF	−9.121 (1.94)
RLOCRSK	0.00280 (2.92)*
ΔEXRT	−2.494 (4.74)*
TAX	0.255 (3.38)*
STRAT	−0.508 (6.40)*
EXTERNAL	−0.121 (2.06)*
PROCESS	0.00878 (0.15)
Estimates of the (log-linear) variance process	
$(S_u)^2$	0.1464 (8.44)*
EMPL	0.0203 (2.08)*
Diagnostics	
Log-likelihood	−47.0518
Restricted log-likelihood	−49.0937
LR Test ^{2}(1); p value	4.0838; (0.0433)
Joint exclusion restriction on subsidiary strategic independence coefficients LR Test χ^2(3); p value	38.9328; (0.000)
Iterations	13

Notes:
(1) The estimated model sets the conditional variance as a log-linear function of subsidiary size as measured by employment (EMPL).
(2) 't' statistics in brackets. Estimates significant at the 5% level are marked with an asterisk.

variance process are found to fit extremely well, suggesting both the existence of and the successful correction for the heteroscedasticity problem.

RESULTS

Before considering the results in detail, two salient points are worth noting. First, examining the diagnostics, all the estimates provide very good fits to the data. Second, looking at the pattern of significance of parameter estimates, there is a remarkable degree of agreement. This is particularly notable when comparing the least squares and maximum likelihood estimates, which are generated through different estimating methodologies.

Two hypotheses are under test here. The internal capital markets hypothesis is examined first. Virtually all the variables relating to the firm's internal capital market emerge as statistically significant, the only exception being the rate of return on subsidiary free funds (RORFF) in the maximum likelihood estimation. (Even here, the acceptance of the null hypothesis of insignificance is marginal.) Further, the signs of the estimated coefficients are as predicted by theory.

As the excess return in the subsidiary (ABROR) decreases and its financial (RISK) and relative locational risks (RLOCRSK) increase, net outflows increase. As available local rate of return on liquid funds (RORFF) and the relative local tax advantage (TAX) increase, net outflows decline.

The effect of the exchange rate (DEXRT) on financial flows is likely to depend on a number of conflicting considerations. On cost considerations, net outflows will increase as the local currency appreciates (Stevens, 1993). However, the impact of currency appreciation is unclear when adding in the consideration of local production versus imports. Imports become cheaper and may substitute for local production, but profits from local production become higher when translated into home country currency. On balance, it is found that an increasing exchange rate is associated with lower outflows.

Thus, the evidence in favour of the internal capital markets hypothesis is quite convincing. The results do support the contention that MNE headquarters use their control to transfer financial resources into or away from subsidiaries depending on their relative performance within the group. Subsidiaries that are lagging the group as a whole display larger outflows of financial resources, suggesting that resources are being transferred away from them.

The second hypothesis under test is the relationship between the strategic independence of subsidiaries and the effectiveness of headquarters' control over their financial resources. Here the results are strong, but not as comprehensive. The level of subsidiary strategic responsibility (STRAT) appears significantly in all estimations and its influence is negative, as suggested by the hypothesis. As STRAT increases, the net outflows from the subsidiary to the parent, normalised for relative performance factors, declines. In other words, if the subsidiaries of two MNEs have the *same* level of relative performance within their groups, the one with the higher level of strategic responsibility experiences lower net outflows to its parent.

A second supporting test confirms this finding. An 'F' test is run on the least squares estimates to examine the exclusion restriction on the subsidiary strategic independence variables. An identical exclusion restriction is tested on the maximum likelihood estimates using a likelihood ratio test. In all cases the exclusion restriction is strongly rejected, supporting the contention that subsidiary strategic independence affects net outflows, even after normalising for relative performance.

The two other measures of subsidiary strategic independence do not appear as strongly in the estimates. The EXTERNAL variable exerts a significant negative effect in the maximum likelihood estimation and the PROCESS variable does the same in the WLS estimation. This is further evidence supporting the proposed hypothesis. The relatively weaker statistical performance of these variables may be ascribed to the fact that they are the second and third extracted factors respectively and consequently capture less of the variation of the underlying variables. This is particularly true in the case of the PROCESS variable.

CONCLUDING REMARKS

It has been recently suggested that the major role of headquarters in a multi-unit firm is to run an internal capital market, redistributing financial resources on the basis of its relatively unbiased evaluation of the various units' prospects. It is argued here that this role is particularly relevant to the headquarters of an MNE. In addition to the advantages available to a domestic multi-unit firm, an MNE can generate arbitrage profits through many other channels that derive from its operating in a number of different jurisdictions. These include re-invoicing centres, fee and royalty adjustments, leading and lagging, intra-corporate loans (back-to-back financing, currency swaps, etc.) shifting compensating balances, dividend adjustments and choice of invoicing currency (Lessard, 1979; Emmanuel and Mehafdi, 1994; Eun and Resnick, 1998).

While strategically independent subsidiaries are not new (Chapman, 1985), they were a declining organisational form for several decades after 1945. Over the last decade or so, there has been a resurgence of this organisational form as MNE managements seek to gain location specific and consolidation advantages. It is suggested here that such strategic independence may reduce MNE headquarters' control of their subsidiaries resources, reducing the efficiency of their internal capital markets.

In a large sample of engineering and engineering-related subsidiaries of non-UK parent MNEs, the working of the internal capital market is strongly supported. Further, and more importantly from the perspective of this study, subsidiary strategic independence appears to impede the working of this internal capital market.

In order to assess the managerial implications of these results, it is necessary to consider the advantages gained from the efficient working of the internal capital market in the MNE as a whole. It has been suggested that efficient internal capital markets are particularly valuable in environments where external capital markets are poor. Thus, while the external capital markets in the UK are good, an MNE will feel the ill-effects of the 'sand in the wheels' of its internal capital market so long as it has other subsidiaries in countries or regions where external capital markets are underdeveloped. This is because it will find that the strategic independence of one subsidiary will reduce its ability to take advantage of strategic opportunities in another.

Acknowledgement

I would like to thank John Cantwell and Mark Casson, as well as an anonymous referee for insightful comments that substantially improved the paper. I would also like to thank seminar participants at the University of Connecticut and the 25th AIB Conference at City University. I acknowledge the support of the School of Business at the University of Buckingham and the Economic Development Unit of the Milton Keynes Borough Council that made the survey possible. The usual disclaimer applies.

Note

Subsidiary strategic independence may create divided loyalties in managers, who may now have the opportunity to choose between the local operation and the MNE parent. The incentive structure is likely to influence the managers allegiance, supplementing the effects of culture. The possibilities based on cultural background can be summarised as follows:

		Allegiance to local operation	
		Low	*High*
Allegiance to MNE	Low	Free agents	Local managers
parent	High	Expatriate managers	Dual nationals

Adapted from Black *et al.* (1992)

The objective of the incentive structure is to influence managers' behaviour to mimic that of dual nationals.

Appendix 1: Variable Definitions

Subsidiary performance and location attractiveness

> RISK = Variance of UK subsidiary's rate of return on capital, 1986–1994.
>
> ABROR = Excess (or shortfall) of subsidiary's rate of return on capital relative to the MNE's overall rate of return on capital, 1994.
>
> RORFF = Rate of return on subsidiary liquid funds (free cash flows as defined by Jensen (1988)), 1994.
>
> RLOCRSK = Percentage differential in location risk (home country/host country (UK)); *Euromoney index*, 1994.
>
> ΔEXRT = Percentage change in exchange rate, risk (home country/host country (UK)), 1993–94.
>
> TAX = Percentage differential in corporation tax rate (home country/host country (UK)); 1994.
>
> NF94 = Net financial outflows from subsidiary to its MNE parent, i.e. all outflows of dividend payments, royalties, overhead charges, licence and management fees and miscellaneous transfers, less inflows of capital from the parent, but excluding capital raised directly by the subsidiary in the UK market, 1994.

Subsidiary strategic independence

> R&D = Local research and development spending as a percentage of subsidiary turnover, 1994.
>
> SUPPLY = Extent to which decisions on suppliers are made locally (7-point scale).
>
> FSCOPE = Functional scope of output mandate: 1 = sales and service, 2 = assembly, 3 = manufacturing, 4 = product development, 5 = international market development.
>
> DT = Duration of subsidiary operation in the UK in years, 1994.
>
> GSCOPE = Geographic scope of subsidiary's output mandate: 1 = UK only, 2 = Europe, 3 = worldwide.
>
> WEXPORT = Exports as a percentage of UK subsidiary turnover, 1994.
>
> EXPt = Duration of subsidiary export operations as a percentage of total duration of UK operations, 1994.
>
> PROC = Process engineering responsibilities (7-point scale).
>
> TRAIN = Extent to which subsidiary has responsibility for training.
>
> EMPL = Employment in UK subsidiary (thousands), 1994.

References

Andersson, U. and Forsgren, M. (1995) 'Using networks to determine multinational parental control of subsidiaries', in S.J. Paliwoda and J.K. Ryans Jr. (eds.) *International Marketing Reader* (London: Routledge).

Armstrong, J.S. and Overton, T. (1977) 'Estimating non-response bias in mail surveys', *Journal of Marketing Research*, 51(7): 71–86.

Bartlett, C.A. and Ghoshal, S. (1989) *Managing Across Borders: The Transnational Solution* (Boston: Harvard Business School Press).

Bettis, R.A. and Hall, W.K. (1982) 'Diversification strategy, accounting determined risk and accounting determined return', *Academy of Management Journal*, 25: 254–264.

Bettis, R.A. and Mahajan, V. (1985) 'Risk/return performance of diversified firms', *Management Science*, 31(7): 785–799.

Birkinshaw, J. (1994) 'Approaching hierarchy: a review of the literature on multinational strategy and structure', *Advances in Comparative Management*, 9: 111–144.

Birkinshaw, J. (1996) 'How multinational subsidiary mandates are gained and lost', *Journal of International Business Studies*, 27(3): 467–495.

Birkinshaw J. and Morrison, A.J. (1995) 'Configurations of strategy and structure in multinational subsidiaries', *Journal of International Business Studies*, 26(4): 729–753.

Black, J.S., Gregersen, H.B. and Mendenhall, M. (1992) *Global Assignments: Successfully Expatriating and Repatriating International Managers* (San Francisco: Jossey-Bass).

Buckley, P.J. and Carter, M. (1998) 'The economics of business process design in multinational firms', in R. Mudambi and M. Ricketts (eds) *The Organisation of the Firm: International Business Perspectives* (London: Routledge).

Cantwell, J. (1997) 'The globalisation of technology: what remains of the product cycle model?', in D. Archibugi and J. Michie (eds) *Technology, Globalisation and Economic Performance* (Cambridge: Cambridge University Press).

Casson, M. (1987) *The Firm and the Market: Studies in Multinational Enterprise and the Scope of the Firm* (Cambridge, MA: The MIT Press).

Casson, M. (1994) 'Why are firms hierarchical?' *International Journal of the Economics of Business*, 1(1): 47–76.

Chapman, S.D. (1985) 'British-based investment groups before 1914', *Economic History Review*, 2nd series, 38(2): 459–482.

Chenells, L. and Griffith, R. (1997) *Taxing Profits in a Changing World* (London: Institute for Fiscal Studies).

Churchill, G.A. Jr. (1995) *Marketing Research: Methodological Foundations* (Fort Worth, TX: The Dryden Press).

Coates, J.B. *et al.* (1993) *Corporate Performance Evaluation in Multinationals* (London: CIMA).

D'Cruz, J.R. (1986) 'Strategic management of subsidiaries', in H. Etemad and L.S. Dulude, (eds) *Managing the Multinational Subsidiary* (London: Croom Helm).

Doz, Y. and Prahalad, C.K. (1981) 'Headquarters influence and strategic control in MNCs', *Sloan Management Review*, Fall: 15–29.

Emmanuel, C. and Mehafdi, M. (1994) *Transfer Pricing* (London: Academic Press/CIMA).

Eun. C. and Resnick, B. (1998) *International Financial Management* (New York, NY and Burr Ridge, IL: Irwin-McGraw Hill).

Forsgren, M., Holm, U. and Johansen, J. (1995) 'Division headquarters go abroad – a step in the internationalization of the multinational corporation', *Journal of Management Studies*, 32(4): 475–491.

Forsgren, M. and Johansen, J. (1992) 'Managing in international multi-centre firms', in M. Forsgren and J. Johansen (eds), *Managing Networks in International Business* (Philadelphia: Gordon and Breach).

Griffiths, G. (1993) 'Powerful selling point', *Investors Chronicle*, 106(1349): 102.

Gupta, A. and Govindrajan, V. (1991) 'Knowledge flows and the structure of control within multinational corporations', *Academy of Management Review*, 16(4): 768–792.

Heberlein, T.A. and Baumgartner, R. (1978) 'Factors affecting response rates to mailed questionnaires: a quantitative analysis of the published literature', *American Sociological Review*, 43(4): 447–462.

Holm, U. (1992) *Internationalization of the Second Degree*. Published doctoral dissertation, Uppsala University.

Hood, N., Young, S. and Lal, D. (1994) 'Strategic evolution within Japanese manufacturing plants in Europe: UK evidence', *International Business Review*, 3(2), 3–26.

Jensen, M. (1988) 'Takeovers: their causes and consequences', *Journal of Economic Perspectives*, 2(1), 21–48.

Kogut, B. and Kulatilaka, N. (1994a). 'Operating flexibility, global manufacturing and the option value of a multinational network', *Management Science*, 40(1): 123–139.

Kogut, B. and Kulatilaka, N. (1994b). 'Options thinking and platform investments: investing in opportunity', *California Management Review*, 36(2): 52–71.

Lamont, O. (1997) 'Cash flow and investment: evidence from internal capital markets', *Journal of Finance*, 52(1): 83–109.

Lessard, D.R. (1979) 'Transfer prices taxes, and financial markets', in R.G. Hawkins (ed.) *The Economic Effect of Multinational Corporations* (Greenwich, CT: JAI Press).

Moore, K. (1995) 'A globalisation strategy for subsidiaries: subsidiary specific advantage', *Management Research Papers Series MRP 95/7*, Templeton College, Oxford University.

Mudambi, R. (1995) 'The MNE investment location decision: some empirical evidence', *Managerial and Decision Economics*, 16: 249–257.

Mudambi, R. and Mudambi, S. (1998) 'A model of buyer-supplier relations with implications for multinational firm', in R. Mudambi and M. Ricketts (eds) *The Organisation of the Firm: International Business Perspectives* (London: Routledge).

Prahalad, C.K. and Doz, Y.L. (1987) *The Multinational Mission: Balancing Local Demands and Global Vision* (New York: The Free Press).

Roth, K. and Morrison, A.J. (1992) 'Implementing global strategy: characteristics of global subsidiary mandates', *Journal of International Business Studies*, 23(4): 715–736.

Rugman, A. (1981) *Inside the Multinationals: The Economics of Internal Markets* (New York: Columbia University Press; London: Croom Helm).

Shapiro, A.C. (1986) *Multinational Financial Management*, 2nd edn (Boston: Allyn and Bacon).

Shin, H. and Stulz, R. (1996) 'An analysis of the divisional investment policies of diversified firms', NBER Working Paper No.5639, Cambridge, MA.

Stein, J.C. (1995) 'Internal capital markets and the competition for corporate resources', NBER Working Paper No.5101, Cambridge, MA.

Stein, J.C. (1997) 'Internal capital markets and the competition for corporate resources', *Journal of Finance*, 52(1): 111–133.

Stevens, G.V.G. (1993) 'Exchange rates and foreign direct investment: a note', *International Finance Discussion Papers* No.444 (April) (Washington DC: Board of Governors of the Federal Reserve System).

Taggart, J. (1996a) 'Strategic management of innovation in the multinational subsidiary', *Proceedings of the 23rd UK AIB Conference*, Aston University, Birmingham, 358–386.

Taggart, J. (1996b) 'Evolution of multinational strategy: evidence from Scottish manufacturing subsidiaries', *Journal of Marketing Management*, 12: 533–549.

5 The Resource-based Perspective and Small Firm Internationalisation: an Exploratory Approach

Stephen Young, Jim Bell and David Crick

The term 'internationalisation' is commonly used to describe 'the developmental process of increasing involvement in international business' by the firm (Young *et al.*, 1989). Despite this fairly broad definition, the emphasis in the literature has been on a narrow range of issues, particularly the mode of entry and country choice (although there has been increasing attention paid to inward–outward connections – see Welch and Luostarinen (1993)). There is, therefore, an interest in advancing the field of investigation beyond these limited confines to encompass a broader range of questions, as well as continuing to seek improved frameworks for explanation. This chapter pursues this line of enquiry, the two-fold objective being, first, to develop a framework derived from the resource-based view (RBV) of the firm; and, second, to evaluate its potential usefulness in understanding wider issues relating to the growth and internationalisation of smaller sized enterprises. By considering internationalisation within a strategic management context (see also Welch and Welch, 1996), the aim is to provide encouragement to take the debate forward and broaden the avenues of enquiry. Given the exploratory nature of the research, a case study approach is pursued. The topic of this chapter is particularly important today when a new breed of high growth, rapidly internationalising small firms is emerging, especially in knowledge-intensive sectors.

THE INTERNATIONALISATION PROCESS OF THE FIRM – AN EVALUATION OF THE LITERATURE

The standard works on the internationalisation of the firm are still those of Johanson and Wiedershein-Paul (1975) and Johanson and Vahlne (1977) who postulated that firms follow a slow, incremental process of internationalisation in terms of increasing knowledge, commitment and investment. This is a major point of controversy, which is not only of academic relevance but also has important policy implications for small-firm export and internationalisation advisory services. Criticisms were being made of the view of *incremental internationalisation* for both large and small firms as long ago as the late 1970s and early 1980s (e.g. Buckley *et al.*, 1978; Cannon and Willis, 1981; Reid, 1983), with insufficient attention being paid to the context of the industry, the company and the people involved. More fundamentally, however, recent work on 'international new ventures' (INVs) (McDougall *et al.*, 1994; Oviatt and McDougall, 1994), 'committed internationalists' (Sullivan and Bauerschmidt, 1990; Bonaccorsi, 1992) and 'high-technology and service-intensive' companies (Lindqvist, 1988; Bell, 1995) has shown rapid and dedicated internationalisation. Reviewing eight recent studies on small-firm internationalisation, Coviello and McAuley (1996) found results ranging from support for the traditional incremental internationalisation view (perhaps including inward internationalisation as a first step); to a redefinition of 'stages' in the context of industry and market characteristics, or non-linear relationships in terms of stages and mechanisms employed; and to challenges to the internationalisation process model.

These diverging results have led authors to seek alternative frameworks to the Johanson and Vahlne (1977, 1990) internationalisation process model or to extend the latter. The *internalisation/transaction* cost paradigm represents the most generally accepted model in the international business field. The substantial empirical support for the paradigm has, however, been generated primarily from studies of the one-off foreign direct investment (FDI) decisions of multinational enterprises (see, for example, Agarwal and Ramaswami (1992), Kim and Hwang (1992), Hennart and Park (1994)). The paradigm has been applied to the early internationalisation stages by Anderson and Coughlan (1987) who argued that integration of marketing and distribution functions may be preferred when the firm possesses specialised knowledge and when agents are difficult to find (see also Buckley *et al.*, 1990). McDougall *et al.* (1994), however, found that in some international new ventures, the entrepreneurial founders did not make internationalisation decisions on the basis of lowest cost locations; nor did they attempt to internalise activities to the point where the benefits of further internalisation were outweighed by the costs. Furthermore, strategic alliances were found to be common for international new ventures even though the firms ran the risk of losing proprietary know-how through opportunistic partner behaviour.

Increasing interest has been shown in n*etwork theory* and internationalisation (Sharma and Johanson, 1987; Johanson and Mattsson, 1988; Johanson and Vahlne, 1992; Benito and Welch, 1994). Based on detailed case studies of four software firms, Coviello and Munro (1997) conclude that: '... our understanding of the internationalisation process for small firms, at least small software firms, can be enhanced by integrating the models of incremental internationalisation with the network perspective'

(p. 379). The authors suggest that this externally driven view of internationalisation (the external web of formal and informal relationships) provides additional insights to the internally driven perspective of Johanson and Vahlne (1990); in this latter approach, the evolution of internationalisation is based on managers' cognitive learning and competency development, which gradually increases through experience. There is no question that network relationships with partners (both direct and indirect) provide helpful new insights and require to be incorporated into models or frameworks of small-firm internationalisation. However, the cause and effect relationships are not yet totally clear: for example, the Coviello and Munro (1997) results could be interpreted as meaning that networks represent a mechanism to overcome resource deficiencies, rather than being the driver of internationalisation *per se*. An interesting piece of work that incorporates networks within a strategic management perspective is that of Welch and Welch (1996).

Recognition that internationalisation is affected by multiple influences has led to growing interest in *contingency approaches*. Such a contingency view was articulated by Reid (1983), but did not attract much attention until recently. Woodcock *et al.* (1994), Yeoh and Jeong (1995), Kumar and Subramaniam (1997), amongst others, have developed contingency frameworks in the international business and exporting fields. Similarly, Bell and Young (1998) have argued that excessive attention has been paid to the merits of competing theories and models rather than to their potential complementarities. Their view is that both behaviouralist (internationalisation process and network models) and internalisation theories may be appropriate in different circumstances. Furthermore, it is postulated that the nature and pace of internationalisation is conditioned by product, industry and other external environmental variables, as well as by firm-specific factors and at any point of time, firms will be in a 'state' of internationalisation (which will be subject to both backward and forward momentum), rather than progressing through 'stages'. In justifying a contingency approach, Kumar and Subramaniam (1997) argue that the existing literature has not devoted much attention to evaluating market selection and mode of entry as interdependent decisions. One might go further to suggest that the range of the firm's internationalisation decisions, incorporating inward–outward connections as well as products, markets and entry modes, are made in a holistic way (a notion which was initially presented by Luostarinen (1979)).

What is clear from the above is that existing approaches do not satisfactorily explain internationalisation processes, especially the rapid internationalisation of high technology small firms. One promising avenue of enquiry lies in the *resource-based view* which has attracted considerable attention in the strategic management and organisational behaviour literature in the recent past. In international business, McDougall *et al.* (1994) have combined the resource-based view of the firm with the economic theory of entrepreneurship (Kirzner, 1973) to seek to explain the phenomenon of international new ventures (INVs – companies that are international/global from inception). The founders of INVs possess competencies, such as proprietary international networks, which they have developed from their earlier activities and these competencies facilitate an awareness of the potential for combining resources from different markets. In many enterprises, inertia acts as a barrier to internationalisation as it requires a change to routines,[1] whereas INV owners consider that ventures will not develop international competencies except by practicing international business. Additionally, INVs recognise the need to economise on scarce resources in their early growth phase, and hence they are unlikely to make costly investments in the ownership of assets when alternative governance structures (e.g. strategic alliances) are possible. For such INVs the costs of overseas investments may actually be less onerous than for many other firms due to micro-technologies and an emphasis on software and intellectual assets.

Aside from the above work of McDougall *et al.* (1994), and that of authors such as Madhok (1997), there have been few attempts to apply the RBV to small firm internationalisation, or to integrate the resource-based perspective with other models. Interestingly, the Johanson and Vahlne (1977, 1990) internationalisation process model has a similar theoretical base to the resource-based view, being rooted in the behavioural theory of the firm (Cyert and March, 1963; Aharoni, 1966) and Penrose's (1959) discourse on the growth of the firm. It is arguable, however, that too much attention has been paid by Johanson and Vahlne and other researchers testing the internationalisation process model, to the assumed outcomes (i.e. a firm's involvement in a specific foreign market develops according to an establishment chain and firms enter new markets with successively greater psychic distance) as opposed to the underlying explanation (Petersen and Pedersen, 1997). At a theoretical level, the models of causal cycles linking experiential market knowledge and operations, market commitment and the commitment of resources to foreign markets provide valuable insights into the internationalisation process. The notion that the firm will be expected to make stronger resource commitments incrementally as it gains experience from current activities in the market is an important one for the small enterprise.

There are still questions to be answered concerning the acquisition of resources. There is ample evidence to show that there are severe resource-based constraints on the strategic behaviour and growth of small companies (Barber *et al.*, 1989; Storey, 1994). These constraints may be internal and/or external: the former concern a lack of management and other personnel resources and the inability to manage resources effectively; the external environment is important because small firms survive by accessing resources from this environment, from such sources as customers, suppliers, competitors, governments, etc. However, the inability to manage the external environment may be another constraint inhibiting the search for, access to or use of the external resource. Gaining experiential knowledge may also be difficult for the small firm. Thus, many small companies operate through larger intermediary companies (agents or distributors), which are the only firms that have contact with end-user markets. Lack of contact with end users creates major barriers to the generation of market information (Stern and El-Ansary, 1992).

Initial enquiry thus suggests that the resource-based view may have a valuable contribution to make in assisting our understanding of small-firm internationalisation, especially in the present day environment; and in explaining internationalisation as part of the overall growth process in the firm. These issues are pursued in the remainder of this chapter.

THE RESOURCE-BASED VIEW OF THE FIRM

The RBV focusses upon the ability to acquire and maintain resources as the key to competitive advantage and organisational survival. Applied in the field of strategy in the seminal articles of Wernerfelt (1984) and Rumelt (1984), it highlights the importance of firm-specific factors in explaining performance and suggests a wide variety of ways in which an organisation can obtain the supply of resources critical to its survival and growth. Stemming from the work of Penrose (1959, p. 75), emphasis is placed upon '... the *heterogeneity* [italics added] ... of the productive services available or potentially available from its services that gives each firm its unique character'.

The RBV is not a single or integrated perspective, but rather a set of contributions published mainly since the early 1980s. As Foss (1997) points out, there is also considerable terminological confusion with theorists using concepts such as 'resources', 'competencies', 'capabilities', 'assets', etc., for what is essentially often the same thing. Nevertheless, the notions of 'core business' and 'core competencies' are important in highlighting critical capabilities and in providing a bridge between resources and strategies (Teece, 1987; Prahalad and Hamel, 1990; Lewis and Gregory, 1996). It is important, therefore, to distinguish between resources and capabilities. As Grant (1991, pp. 119–120) notes: 'While resources are the source of a firm's capabilities, capabilities are the main source of its competitive advantage' (see also Barney (1991)). Key characteristics of core competencies/capabilities include the fact that they span across businesses and products within a corporation, that they have temporal dominance over products and that they arise through the collective learning of the firm (Sanchez *et al.*, 1996, drawing on Rumelt, 1994).

One important feature of the RBV and competence-based competition that distinguishes it from earlier static approaches is its dynamic element. Stress is placed upon organisational learning and the learning organisation:

> Competence-based competition ... may therefore be likened to a state of *perpetual corporate entrepreneurialism* in which *continuous learning* about how to build new competencies and leverage existing competencies more effectively becomes a new dominant logic. (Sanchez *et al.*, 1996, p. 14)

A firm's resources and capabilities may derive from either inside or outside the firm. In respect of the latter, strategic alliances represent a way of competence leveraging or competence building through accessing the expertise or attributes possessed by partner enterprises, reducing risks or achieving economies of scale or learning through joint R&D and so on. Easton and Araujo (1996) have stressed the role of the industrial network approach in enriching the resource-based perspective. The former focusses upon the role of firms as one category of actor in an industrial system that comprises a network of actors, resources and activities. The industrial network approach is helpful in a consideration of new ways of building or leveraging resources and competencies and in recognising the blurred distinction between resources internal and external to the firm, although its fundamental approach is quite different.[2]

Reflecting the relative recency of most contributions to the RBV of the firm and the lack of integration among them, there are a number of problem areas in the perspective. One major issue is that 'there is no clear conceptual model of the endogenous creation of new resources' (Foss, 1997, p. 352; see also the critique by Porter, 1994). The nature of resources and especially competencies (and their differences) requires further investigation. In addition, the environment and environmental influences have not yet been treated in detail.

SOME IMPLICATIONS OF THE RESOURCE-BASED VIEW FOR THE INTERNATIONALISATION OF THE SMALL FIRM

There have been few applications of the RBV to either small-firm growth or to internationalisation; exceptions include the work of Oviatt and McDougall (1994), McDougall *et al.*, 1994 and Jensen (1996). However, the notions that diversification (including development from domestic into international markets) help in building new resources and that international contacts are a resource of value are presented in Wenerfelt's (1984) seminal treatise on the resource-based view.[3]

Derived from the literature review, the resource-based perspective suggests a number of issues that are relevant to the growth and internationalisation of the small firm.

First, firm survival and growth is achieved by the accumulation of resources and the utilisation of these to generate capabilities or competences.[4] Resources are packaged differently by firms to generate distinctive competencies, a notion that would readily explain variety in modes and markets. There is a close relationship with contingency approaches, since the contingencies represent the influences upon company behaviour; for example, firms may respond differently to the external environment in their efforts to build sustainable competencies. In an internationalisation context, the mode of entry chosen will be that which facilitates a competitive position in the particular overseas market, subject to the constraints imposed by resource shortages of various types. The mode of entry may be simply a mechanism by which to exploit the true competencies of the firm (e.g. unique products, brand names, market segmentation skills) or it may represent a competence in its own right. Lacking resources, small firms will be drawn to their external networks, which offer the opportunity of building or leveraging competencies through alliances; but since many small firms will have limited bargaining power in these alliances their behaviour is likely to be reactive. Although the basic emphasis on resources is similar to that of Johanson and Vahlne (1977, 1990) there are many differences. For example, since internationalisation is a requirement for success in many high-technology small firms (as the evidence reveals), then international operations become a source of resources and capabilities; shortages of resources do not inhibit internationalisation, rather they present a challenge which must be overcome.

Second, the resource-based perspective suggests a holistic view of the firm, with the coordinated deployment of assets and capabilities in creating, producing and marketing products. Technologies, product strategies, markets and marketing, and competitive environments are interdependent in this model and form a positive feedback system. This argues against consideration of national market choice or mode of entry as independent decisions as in existing models. The latter are integrated, not only within marketing strategies and operations, but also within other aspects of the firm's operations.

Third, the perspective views the firm as a learning organisation. This process of continuous learning may be described as 'iterative gap filling'. Key resources and capabilities quickly erode, and degenerate into resource/ capability gaps that require managerial attention. A learning process is foreseen in Johanson and Vahlne (1977, 1990), but it is specific to modes and markets.

Fourth, in respect of internationalisation specifically, there is a suggestion that initial decisions taken would on one hand be designed to exploit available competencies/resources; and on the other, aim to economise on scarce resources and overcome missing competencies. The subsequent internationalisation process will be influenced by the creation or leveraging of new generations of

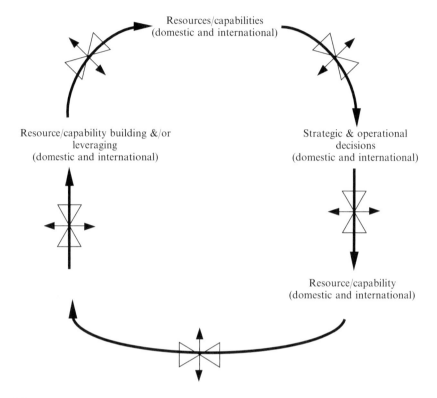

Notes:
1.   signals that the firm is an *open system* in terms of access to other firms and employees to provide resources (materials, skill knowledge) as inputs to its processes for developing, producing and marketing products, and access to markets to purchase its products in return for flows of resource market information, reputation, customer relationships.
2. There will be domestic and international links and transfers but these have been omitted in the figure.
3. The figure is presented as a *virtuous circle* of resource/capacity building and/or leveraging, but there is no inevitability in this process.

Source: Authors. See also Sanchez and Heene (1996); Lewis and Gregory (1996); Sanchez *et al.* (1996, p. 13).

Figure 5.1   Iterative learning and resource/capability building in firm growth

competencies within different value-adding areas of firm activities; and by building capabilities from international business operations specifically. The outcome of these various inter-relationships could be very different to the predictions of the 'internationalisation process' type models. For example, target markets internationally would be based on the firm's competencies, e.g. proprietary technology, niche products, access to customers. Methods of market entry and development would be chosen so as to access these target markets cost effectively, subject to the constraints of the nature of the product: for example, high cost, specialised products necessitating direct selling, niche markets suggesting the use of distributors. Moreover, there are likely to be crucial international marketing decisions not captured in the internationalisation stages models, such as pricing and advertising (including the role of exhibitions).

These proposed features of the RBV are incorporated into a framework for understanding this process of iterative learning and resource/capability building in firm growth illustrated in Figure 5.1. The framework is perhaps particularly useful for small firms where growth requires new resources and capabilities, but may be constrained at any time by resource/capability gaps. The key to success lies in a commitment to learning and the acquisition of knowledge. The complex interactions and influences between the firm and its environment are illustrated by presenting the firm as an open system.

The conceptual framework is still at an early stage. More work is required to begin to disentangle the complexities of international business decision making and the inter-relationships between different decision areas – product development, production and marketing – in international growth. With model building concerning the integration of firm growth and internationalisation processes as the objectives of this chapter, however, there is merit in testing the usefulness of the framework against company experience as a basis for further development.

METHOD

To explore the issues and conceptual framework presented above, the method employed is that of a single case study approach, supported by qualitative evidence from a wider sample of knowledge-intensive firms (15 companies in total).

The research was undertaken as part of a larger-scale research project being undertaken by the authors into the internationalisation of knowledge-intensive and traditional small firms in the UK. The purpose of this project is to provide a holistic perspective on small-firm growth and internationalisation. In this way the authors aim to identify new issues and perhaps to see the beginnings of a new research agenda.

This research involved 30 semi-structured, in-depth interviews, lasting two to three hours, with chief executives or export managers of small- to medium-sized internationalising companies. A matched sample of five high-tech and five low-tech firms was selected for investigation in each location (England, Scotland and Northern Ireland). The basic selection criteria were that firms should be current exporters, employ less than 200 staff and be independent and indigenous.

Avenues of enquiry included an exploration of:

- firms' initial business strategies, growth objectives and international orientation
- the background and motivation for exporting
- the rationale for the choice of export markets and initial market entry modes, and
- the firms' subsequent internationalisation activities

The interviews were semi-structured to allow interviewees scope to elaborate on each of these areas, yet permit each researcher to probe the important 'how' and 'why' questions. In order to facilitate full and free disclosure, interviews were not taped. However, information was subsequently recorded on a pre-designed template to ensure consistency between researchers. From the wider sample, a single case study, with supportive evidence from all knowledge-intensive sample enterprises, was developed for this chapter. This was considered to be the most appropriate method when seeking to explore a preliminary range of issues in depth and to build theory. According to Eisenhardt (1989), 'random selection (of cases) is neither necessary nor preferable'. Indeed, she further asserts that 'extreme examples' are most appropriate when seeking to extend theory. The case chosen was that of a small knowledge-intensive company based in Scotland. The company, Nautilus Ltd (the actual name of the firm has been disguised), was selected primarily because of the range and depth of information that was available on its evolution. There was also evidence of significant developments in its international business activities over a relatively short period of time. This research is limited to the knowledge-intensive sample companies only in order to eliminate some of the variability of experience which would otherwise be apparent in the results.

CASE EXAMPLE – NAUTILUS LTD

Nautilus, a UK company, was formed in 1986 to develop a small sub-sea remote-operated vehicle (ROV) around a patented viewport that would allow a camera to tilt and view through 360 degrees. Production commenced in November 1988, but the project required significant expertise in electronics and was regarded as non-core by its parent company and Nautilus was spun-off as a management buy-out (MBO) in May 1990. Targeting international markets first, export sales commenced in 1990 to Singapore, Australia and Sweden.

By 1995, company employment was 23 and annual turnover £2.5 million; projected sales for 1996 were £4.0 million. Nautilus had three product divisions, the first being the original small ROV (P1), developed organically,

Table 5.1 Nautilus – 1995 statistics

Product	Turnover	Export per cent	Major markets
P1	£0.75m	95	Worldwide
P2	£1.25m	40	UK, Norway, Brazil
P3	£0.50m	20	UK, Norway

and P2 (large ROVs) and P3 (ROV control systems) being developed through acquisition. Of the 1995 turnover, exports comprised approximately £1.3 million, broken down as shown in Table 5.1.

Tables 5.2 to 5.4 summarise the key corporate developments in the first ten years of the life of the company, product development and production evolution, and developments in marketing and markets respectively. When viewed from the perspective of the company as a whole, key corporate development 'stages', as identified by management, inevitably focus upon ownership and expansion-related events, namely the MBO and the subsequent acquisitions. These were the principal influence upon subsequent production and marketing decisions, etc. One important feature of the

Table 5.2 Nautilus – key corporate developments and strategies

Phase 1 (1986–1989)
- Development and launch of small remote-operated vehicle (ROV) (P1) based on patented technology, cost competitive production, targeted at new market segment.

Phase 2 (1990–1991)
- Management buy-out, including 25% equity funding from development agency. Acquired assets, patents and intellectual property rights to small ROV; development costs written off by former parent. ROV business non-core for former parent.
- Long-term strategy to widen base of company operations to cater for new market segments through acquisitions and organic development.

Phase 3 (1992–1994)
- Acquired assets and intellectual property rights of company in receivership. Provided access to offshore oil and gas market (P2). Funded entirely by new equity from development agency and venture capital company.
- Key employees recruited from acquired firm.
- Acquired intellectual property and manufacturing rights for large ROVs and power units (P2) as non-core business of another company. Aim to widen product offering to offshore oil and gas market.
- New version of original small ROV launched.

Phase 4 (1995–to date)
- Assets of control systems company acquired: latter manufactured products used in or on ROVs (P3).

Note: P1, P2, P3 refer to product ranges.

firm's development that emerges at this level of evaluation is the major role of the regional development agency and a national venture capital company. The provision of financial resources facilitated the strategy of acquisition-based growth; perhaps even more important was the director-level expertise the funding agencies brought to Nautilus, especially financial management skills and the disciplines of planning, forecasting and budgeting.

The resource-based view as expressed in Figure 5.1 suggests that successful growth is dependent upon recognising necessary resources and capabilities, and creating or acquiring these. Although Nautilus could draw initially upon the resources of its parent, the focus on internationalisation was very much a feature of the post-MBO period. International business know-how was not a core competence possessed by Nautilus in its early years. The export development literature suggests that entrepreneurs with greater exposure to the international environment are more likely to be

Table 5.3   Nautilus – product development and production

Major operational issues/objectives	*Key resources/capabilities*	*Resource/capability gaps*
Phase 1		
P1 • Cost-competitive manufacture. Production commenced Nov. 1988	• Patented technology • Tooling & design investment	• Limited electronics capabilities
Phase 2		
P1 • Product development, e.g. process distribution, video circuitry	• Industry expertise of new managing director (major shareholder) • Technical management (appointment of technical director)	
Phase 3		
P2 • Transfer of manufacture with acquisitions	• Quality management, etc. (recruitment of key employees from acquisitions)	• Dated product features (e.g. control electronics) • Product capabilities inadequate (e.g. power systems)
Phase 4		
P1 • Product development (e.g. increased vehicle power) and product relaunch	• Technical capabilities (e.g. control electronics, power systems)	
General		
• New factory established • Proposal to EU for R&D funding with university in Berlin		• Gaps in product range • No significant in-house R&D capability

Table 5.4 Nautilus – marketing and markets

Major operational issues/objectives	Key resources/capabilities	Resource/capability gaps
Phase 1		
P1 • Product launch • Focus on international markets	• High specification product, competitive price and potential new market segments	• No business/marketing plans
Phase 2		
P1 • Business/marketing plans • Market survey and identification of target markets (countries familiar with technology and with offshore oil and gas industry) • Exhibit at key trade shows in UK (because of costs), Asia and USA to identify distributors • By end 1989 distributors established in Sweden, Netherlands, USA, Australia, Singapore and S. Africa ('Scattergun policy')	• Committed distributors (achieved through incentivisation and company support, e.g. training in UK, sales leads from advertising)	• Many small niche markets (e.g. diving contractors, universities, hydro-electric companies) and lack of focus
Phase 3		
P1 • Establishment of additional overseas distributors		• Over-commitment of resources to incentivise distributors • Weak bargaining position with distributors
P2 • Acquisitions and decisions on geographical markets (as above, plus Brazil, Russia and UK) and market segments (unplanned) • Acquired 2 distributors from takeover. • Direct selling in UK	• Sales management (appointment of sales manager and 1 other salesman)	• Product weaknesses associated with acquisitions • Lack of market knowledge
Phase 4		
P2 • Decision on direct selling in USA (Houston) and Russia; 2 other distributors established in USA		
General		
• Increased level of advertising (trade magazines) • Widening of range of exhibitions	• Marketing manager appointed	• Gaps in product range • Additional sales staff required

receptive to stimuli and opportunities for outward business activities. Within Nautilus, the entrepreneur who led the MBO had spent 20 years in the Navy including diving experience. It may be speculated that although this entrepreneur had no direct exporting experience, his general understanding of the sub-sea industry created an awareness of international business.

An overview of Tables 5.3 and 5.4 does suggest a process of continuous learning within the organisation. This conclusion applies at all levels of firm operations. For example, at the time of start-up, patented technology was a key resource for Nautilus; ten years on, after various iterations, the lack of in-house R&D capabilities was a critical resource gap. Similarly, the choice of committed distributors provided a key resource initially; as the distributors themselves grew they did not devote the same time and resources to the products of Nautilus, and the latter did not have a strong enough bargaining position to dictate terms, except in Norway and Brazil, where Nautilus business represented a high proportion of the distributors' turnover.

The inter-relatedness of firm activities also emerges clearly from the tables. Issues of finance, human resources, product development, production and marketing may, on the one hand, provide reinforcement in the development of competencies and, on the other, act as constraints. For example, the appointment of personnel in technical and quality management had an important influence upon product capabilities and, therefore, upon marketing potential.

In respect of internationalisation specifically, the concept of iterative gap filling is also helpful in understanding the company's successful entry into overseas markets. At the initial stage of internationalisation, involving the small ROV (P1), a series of decision-making steps were in evidence, as follows:

• Understand the international market and the geographical location of customers and markets. Assisted by government export support in the form of marketing grants, a market survey was undertaken.
• Identify distributors. There was little option other than to use agents or distributors for P1 because of the requirement to tap small niche markets worldwide. Establishing distributors undoubtedly represented a finance-based barrier to internationalisation. The sub-optimal solution was to exhibit at key trade shows, initially in the UK for cost reasons and thereafter in Asia and the Americas; in order to reduce the costs of exhibiting overseas, the company tended to join trade missions organised by the UK Department of Trade and Industry (DTI).
• Incentivise distributors. Apart from financial rewards, incentives entailed training in the use of the equipment, assistance with initial demonstrations to customers, passing on sales leads generated by advertising in trade journals, and regular visits. Notwithstanding this commitment to distributor support, critical competence gaps were emerging by the end of the period:

first, there were concerns that the rewards and support offered to distributors were excessively generous; and, second, despite or because of this support, the distributors themselves had grown and were not devoting the time or resources to Nautilus products.

• Consider new entry modes. The acquisitions which took place between 1992 and 1994 provided access to the offshore oil and gas industry worldwide and introduced high value products with significant customisation requirements. The domestic and international marketing emphasis, therefore, changed to a mixture of distributors and direct selling. The latter approach was followed in the UK, and also in Houston (USA) and Moscow (Russia). A cost-minimising approach was pursued in the latter two markets from 1996 by the employment of salaried salespersons working from home. The appointments of a sales manager and one other salesperson were critical decisions at this time.

As the tables reveal, the resources and capabilities of the company had expanded significantly since start-up. However, in operating across a wider manufacturing, product and market spectrum, the resource/capability gaps were also substantial, encompassing:

• Finance: the custom-built factory was too large for existing activity levels and thus represented a significant overhead cost.
• Human resources: the company was deficient in sales and marketing personnel but recruitment was limited by financial constraints. The need for a change in company culture was also recognised as Nautilus expanded in the large ROV market.
• Product development: some of the products associated with the acquisitions were not state-of-the-art, so that urgent attention needed to be given to generating an in-house R&D capability. As Table 5.3 indicates, Nautilus had linked up with a German university to bid for EU funding for research into ROV control systems.
• Marketing and internationalisation: rapid expansion had left the company exposed in a variety of areas. These included deficiencies in market knowledge, especially for P2; the geographical and market diversity also meant that this small company was stretched thinly, particularly in the support (and policing) of distributors and in marketing support (press advertising, attendance at exhibitions, etc.).

OTHER CASE EXPERIENCES

It is accepted that the Nautilus case cannot be generalised; and the objective of the case was to illustrate linkages and processes that have not been explored to date rather than to generalise. At this preliminary stage of investigation, a single case was a useful tool to achieve this objective. However, the authors' research also investigated a larger number of knowledge-intensive firms, and this section aims to provide a wider perspective.

It should be noted initially that the internationalisation behaviour of the sample of knowledge-intensive firms was quite different to the relatively slow, incremental internationalisation postulated in the Johanson and Vahlne (1977) model. As evident in the Nautilus case, characteristics of internationalisation in the sample as a whole included: proactive motivations; concurrent domestic and international expansion (often no distinction was made between home and overseas markets); rapid internationalisation involving many markets simultaneously; strong evidence of networks (although these were not readily apparent in the Nautilus case); flexible methods of distribution, albeit with an initial emphasis on agents and distributors; and evidence of a planned approach to international expansion.

In terms of the resource-based view, the *need to accumulate* resources in knowledge-intensive sectors where product life cycles could be short *was* undoubtedly a *stimulus* to *rapid international expansion*. However, there were also other influences, such as changes of ownership or management since establishment through, for example, management buy-outs. The accumulation of resources and competencies was also associated in a number of cases with acquisitions, where the involvement of venture capitalists was commonly important. Perhaps the principal contribution of the RBV derives from its holistic perspective of firm behaviour. Thus *internationalisation* in the sample firms was *integrally bound up* with *overall business strategy* (including the relative emphasis on organic growth versus acquisitions), new product development (including develement of 'global' products) and/or new process development and marketing policy. Product strategy and the product range was a critical factor not only in influencing international expansion as a whole, but also in determining markets, methods of doing business and, associated with this, modes of distribution. The interdependence of technologies, business and product strategies, markets and marketing, and competitive environments have clearly been given too little consideration in much earlier work.

In respect of the view of *the firm as a learning organisation* engaged in a process of iterative gap filling, there is again supportive evidence in the sample (as in the Nautilus case). One company in noise instrumentation saw its strategy of a phased global product launch fail to sustain growth; the solution was to attempt to identify new products/services and/or new market segments through planned acquisitions in the USA and UK. Another company, which targeted the Asia Pacific markets with a lower specification product, found itself unable to compete in Europe and the USA; the solution in this case was internal R&D to develop leading-edge products for these sophisticated markets. This issue is particularly important with the rapid pace of change in knowledge-intensive industries, and a number of the sample companies while surviving and growing, were not significantly profitable.

DISCUSSION AND CONCLUSIONS

The purpose of this final section is to review the value of the resource-based view in facilitating a wider understanding of the internationalisation of small firms and its links to other conceptual approaches. It should be stressed initially that the approach adopted here is not designed to replace other models and frameworks. Rather, the intention is to take the debate forward and ask new questions. The outcomes of the resource-based perspective in terms of strategic behaviour and international decision-making are much less deterministic than those emanating from the internationalisation process models. Firms will have a different mix of resources/competencies and resource/competence gaps, and their strategic responses to these allow for the possibility of different paths to growth and internationalisation. In that sense, the resource-based approach has some similarities to contingency frameworks, since these are designed to show the influence of a range of internal and external variables. What this means, of course, is that it may be very difficult to generalise about patterns and processes of small-firm internationalisation. If resources are idiosyncratic and firms' resource bases vary, then the exploitation and augmentation of resources through internationalisation will also vary for each firm.

There is much to be learned from this business strategy approach to understanding the internationalisation of the small firm. At least in the knowledge-intensive companies studied here, internationalisation was a marketing decision to be made to support the volume and profit objectives of the company. It was not an activity that was necessarily separate or special in most of the sample enterprises. Problems of mode of entry, for example, were swamped by a range of other difficulties in finance, human resources, product development and marketing.

Supporting the exploratory work of McDougall *et al.* (1994) on international new ventures, internationalisation was shown in a number of companies to assist in the process of building and/or leveraging competencies. In most instances, there were no 'inertia barriers' to internationalisation: personnel within the enterprises recognised the need to satisfy widely scattered international customers; there was an awareness of differing cultures and business practices ('psychic distance' was not perceived as a major problem); and internationalisation was likely to enhance corporate flexibility and problem-solving capabilities.

Questions raised by this chapter to some extent mirror those identified by writers on the resource-based perspective as a whole: What are the differences between resources and competencies/capabilities? How does learning, both domestically and internationally, feed in to capability building? In what ways do environmental factors assist or hamper the generation of resources and competencies? The very notion of 'core competencies' is less relevant than in larger and established enterprises, as successful small firms must build such core capabilities. In order to manage the discussion, however, comment here is restricted to a number of key issues, particularly concerning the usefulness of the resource-based view as compared with other models and frameworks.

First, as noted earlier, the resource-based approach has similar roots to that of the Johanson and Vahlne (1977, 1990) internationalisation process model, although the fundamental approach is quite different. The emphasis in Johanson and Vahlne's work is upon the commitment of resources to foreign markets as the outcome of growing market commitment and market knowledge. From a resource-based perspective, a firm's commitment internationally is derived from a bundle of resources and capabilities; and its chosen form of international involvement is a mechanism to utilise these resources and capabilities to best effect. It was necessary in the research to impose a 'stages' approach for analytical purposes, but the stages of development as perceived by top management are quite different to internationalisation stages. Furthermore, the approach pursued here throws doubt on the notion that the market entry mode is the overwhelmingly important issue. Despite these comments, there are also similarities in the approaches – Johanson and Vahlne emphasise knowledge rooted in culture, while the RBV sees knowledge embedded in organisational routines: both regard knowledge as being generated and expanded by experience.

A second issue concerns the RBV and network theory. There was little evidence of a strong influence of network activity as a driving force in internationalisation in the Nautilus case. International networks and connections did, of course, exist through the international sourcing of components, and the firm's association with suppliers, through international R&D links with the German university, and through the international networks of the venture capital company.

Within the wider sample of knowledge-intensive firms, there was significant evidence of network influences in both initial internationalisation and international expansion. For example, the decision-maker's pre-existing contacts from prior employment led to the first export order in some companies, and in a number of cases client followership was an important factor in initial market selection. The RBV could encompass networking as a vehicle for complementing existing resources or circumventing resource gaps. Similarly, the role of international contacts as a potential resource was recognised in the early work of Wernerfelt (1984).

In recent work from a strategic management perspective, Welch and Welch (1996) regard networks as one of the 'strategic foundations' of the enterprise, alongside knowledge, skills and experience; and network development is viewed as an outcome of the internationalisation process. The thinking here is very similar to that of the RBV.

Further work is still necessary, however, particularly in clarifying what the term 'networks' actually means and what relationships would be included or excluded within 'networks' and also in establishing whether networking can be a planned as opposed to an inherently random activity. In one of the sample companies, the chief executive observed that he was a firm believer in talking to everyone he could, even his competitors (where the aim would be to persuade them that his company had a place in the market); it was on the basis of a contact made in 1991 in the USA, followed up every couple of years, that an acquisition was pending in 1998.

Third, there was evidence in the Nautilus case and other sample firms of key decisions in the process of internationalisation being principally designed to overcome financial constraints and minimise costs rather than to build upon competencies. This is evidenced by, for example, the use of exhibitions to identify potential distributors, distributor contracts or OEM agreements or the employment of 'associates' in overseas markets for cost-minimising purposes, and so on. This cost as opposed to value approach is supportive of a transaction cost view of internationalisation, as opposed to or alongside a resource-based view.

A fourth, and final issue concerns the critical role of the enterprise in the internationalisation of knowledge-intensive small firms. As noted earlier, McDougall *et al.* (1994) combined the RBV with the economic theory of entrepreneurship to explain the emergence of INVs, but this work is really in its infancy. The export literature has tended to emphasise language knowledge, experience of living and working abroad, and experiences of inward internationalisation through imports as factors encouraging inter-nationalisation; even recent research (Maignan and Lukas, 1997) has indicated that managers often have difficulties switching from practices in the domestic market to new conditions abroad. Confirming the research of McDougall *et al.* (1994), however, the entrepreneurs in the sample of knowledge-intensive firms mostly regarded international business as inevi-table. And because the sectors were international or global, business prac-tices were fairly common across frontiers. Entrepreneurial characteristics, too, were significant, such as the concepts of global vision and mind sets.

The conclusion of all of this is that the resource-based perspective alone is unlikely to have sufficient explanatory power. There is a requirement to examine more precisely the inter-relationships among models, including internationalisation process models, network theory, transaction cost theory and the resource-based approach.

This preliminary research has also highlighted the greater understanding that can be gained from considering internationalisation within the overall perspective of firms' strategies and growth. In pursuing this line of enquiry, more work is required in attempting to integrate insights from the small-firm literature with those from international business, and, especially perhaps investigating the growth of knowledge-intensive small enterprises.

This chapter has, thus, begun to raise new issues and identify new agendas in an area – the growth and internationalisation of knowledge-intensive firms – that will undoubtedly grow in importance in the next few years.

Acknowledgements

The authors would like to thank Marian Jones of Strathclyde International Business Unit, University of Strathclyde for her constructive comments and suggestions on an earlier draft of this chapter.

Notes

1. There have been a number of studies on barriers to exports e.g. Christensen *et al.* (1987), Yang *et al.* (1992), Ramaseshan and Soutar (1996).
2. Easton and Araujo (1996, p. 188) express this difference in perspective very clearly: 'The identity of the firm is not defined by the range of resources it has accumulated or the type of administrative framework it has chosen to coordinate activities and allocate resources. This identity is socially constructed and is a product of the firm's interaction with other actors'.
3. It is true that the notion of firm-specific advantages underlines much of the work on the theory of the multinational enterprise (see, for example, Caves, 1971). However, the approach taken by economists has tended to emphasis static, one-off decisions and also the investment decisions of multinational firms; and hence the dynamics of internationalisation and small firm processes have received much less attention.
4. The terms 'competencies' and 'capabilities' are used synonymously in this paper.

References

Agarwal, S. and Ramaswami, S.N. (1992) 'Choice of foreign market entry mode: impact of ownership, location and internalisation factors', *Journal of International Business Studies*, 23(1): 1–27.

Aharoni, Y. (1966) *The Foreign Investment Decision Process* (Boston, MA: Harvard University Press).

Anderson, E. and Coughlan, A.T. (1987) 'International market entry via independent or integrated channels of distribution', *Journal of Marketing*, 51 (January): 71–82.

Barber, J., Metcalfe, J.S. and Porteous, M. (1989) *Barriers to Growth in Small Firms* (London: Routledge).

Barney, J. (1991) 'Firm resources and sustained competitive advantage', *Journal of Management*, 17: 99–120.

Bell, J. (1995), 'The internationalisation of small computer software firms – a further challenge to 'stage' theories', *European Journal of Marketing*, 29(8): 60–75.

Bell, J. and Young, S. (1998) 'Towards an integrative framework of the internationalization of the firm', in G. Hooley, R. Loveridge and D. Wilson (eds) *Internationalization: Process, Context and Markets* (London: Macmillan; New York: St Martin's Press) pp. 5–28.

Benito, G.R.G. and Welch, L.S. (1994) 'Foreign market servicing: beyond choice of entry mode', *Journal of International Marketing*, 2(2): 7–27.

Bonaccorsi, A. (1992) 'On the relationship between firm size and export intensity', *Journal of International Business Studies*, 4(4): 605–635.

Buckley, P.J., Newbould, D. and Thurwell, J. (1978) *Going International – The Experience of Smaller Companies Overseas* (London: Associated Business Press).

Buckley, P.J., Pass, C.L. and Prescott, K. (1990) 'Foreign market servicing by multinationals: an integrated treatment', *International Marketing Review*, 7(4): 25–40.

Cannon, T. and Willis, M. (1981) 'The smaller firm in international trade', *European Small Business Journal*, 1(3): 45–55.

Caves, R.E. (1971) 'International corporations: the industrial economics of foreign investment', *Economica*, 38: 1–27.

Christensen, C.H., da Rocha, A. and Gertner, R.K. (1987) 'An empirical investigation on the factors influencing exporting success of Brazilian firms', *Journal of International Business Studies*, 18(3): 61–78.

Coviello, N.E. and McAuley, N.A. (1996) *Internationalisation Processes and the Smaller Firm: A Review of Contemporary Research*, Working Paper, Faculty of Management, University of Calgary, Canada.

Coviello, N.E. and Munro, H. (1997) 'Network relationships and the internationalisation process of small software firms', *International Business Review*, 6(4): 361–386.

Cyert, R.M. and March, J.G. (1963) *A Behavioural Theory of the Firm* (Englewood Cliffs, NJ: Prentice-Hall).

Dunning, J.H. (1993) *Multinational Enterprises and the Global Economy* (Wokingham, Berks: Addison-Wesley).

Easton, G. and Araujo, L. (1996) 'Characterising organizational competencies: an industrial networks approach', in R. Sanchez *et al.* (eds) *Dynamics of Competence-Based Competition* (Oxford: Pergamon), pp. 183–207.

Eisenhardt, K.M. (1989) 'Building theories from case study research', *Academy of Management Review*, 14(4): 532–550.

Foss, N.J. (ed.) (1997) *Resources, Firms, and Strategies. A Reader in the Resource-Based Perspective* (Oxford: Oxford University Press).

Grant, R.M. (1991) 'The resource-based theory of competitive advantage: implications for strategy formulation', *California Management Review*, Spring: 114–135.

Hennart, J.-F. and Park, Y.R. (1994) 'Location, governance and strategic determinants of Japanese manufacturing investment in the United States', *Strategic Management Journal*, 15: 419–436.

Jensen, Ø. (1996) 'Competence development by small firms in a vertically-constrained industry structure', in R. Sanchez, A. Heene and H. Thomas (eds) *Dynamics of Competence-Based Competition* (Oxford: Pergamon).

Johanson, J. and Mattsson, L.-G. (1988) 'Internationalization in industrial systems – a network approach', in N. Hood and J.-E. Vahlne (eds) *Strategies in Global Competition* (London: Croom Helm), pp. 287–314.

Johanson, J. and Vahlne, J.-E. (1977) 'The internationalization process of the firm – a model of knowledge development and increasing foreign market commitment', *Journal of International Business Studies*, Spring–Summer: 23–32.

Johanson, J. and Vahlne, J.-E. (1990) 'The mechanism of internationalization', *International Marketing Review*, 7(4): 11–24.

Johanson, J. and Vahlne, J.-E. (1992) 'Management of foreign market entry', *Scandinavian International Business Review*, 1(3): 9–27.

Johanson, J. and Wiedershein-Paul, F. (1975) 'The internationalization of the firm – four Swedish case studies', *Journal of Management Studies*, 12: 305–322.

Kim, W.C. and Hwang, P. (1992), 'Global strategy and multinational entry mode choice', *Journal of International Business Studies*, 23(1): 29–53.

Kirzner, I. (1973) *Competition and Entrepreneurship* (Chicago: University of Chicago Press).

Kumar, V. and Subramaniam, V. (1997) 'A contingency framework for the mode of entry decision', *Journal of World Business*, 32(1): 53–72.

Lewis, M.A. and Gregory, M.J. (1996) 'Developing and applying a process approach to competence analysis', in R. Sanchez *et al.* (eds) *Dynamics of Competence-Based Competition* (Oxford: Pergamon), pp. 141–164.

Lindqvist, M. (1988) *Internationalization of Small Technology Based Firms: Three Illustrative Case Studies on Swedish Firms*, Research Paper 88/15, Stockholm School of Economics, Sweden.

Luostarinen, R. (1979) *The Internationalization of the Firm* (Helsinki: Acta Academic Oeconomicae Helsingiensis).

McDougall, P.P., Shane, S. and Oviatt, B.M. (1994) 'Explaining the formation of international new ventures: the limits of theories from international business research', *Journal of Business Venturing*, 9: 469–487.

Madhok, A. (1997) 'Cost, value and foreign market entry mode: the transaction and the firm', *Strategic Management Journal*, 18: 39–61.

Maignan, I. and Lukas, B.A. (1997) 'Entry mode decisions: the role of managers' mental models', *Journal of Global Marketing*, 10(4): 7–22.

Oviatt, B.M. and McDougall, P.P. (1994) 'Toward a theory of international new ventures', *Journal of International Business Studies*, 25(1): 45–64.

Penrose, E. (1959) *The Theory of the Growth of the Firm* (London: John Wiley).

Petersen, P. and Pedersen, T. (1997) 'Twenty years after – support and critique of the Uppsala internationalisation model', in I. Björkman and M. Forsgren (eds) *The Nature of the International Firm* (Copenhagen: Copenhagen Business School Press), pp. 117–134.

Porter, M.E. (1994) 'Toward a dynamic theory of strategy', in R.P. Rumelt, D.E. Schendel and D.J. Teece (eds) *Fundamental Issues in Strategy* (Boston, MA: Harvard Business School Press).

Prahalad, C.K. and Hamel, G. (1990) 'The core competence of the corporation', *Harvard Business Review*, May–June: 79–91.

Ramaseshan, B. and Soutar, G.N. (1996) 'Combined effect of incentives and barriers on firms' export decisions', *International Business Review*, 5(1): 53–65.

Reid, S.D. (1983) 'Firm internationalization, transaction costs and strategic choice', *International Marketing Review*, 1(2): 45–55.

Rumelt, R.P. (1984) 'Towards a strategic theory of the firm', in R.B. Lamb (ed.) *Competitive Strategic Management* (Englewood Cliffs, NJ: Prentice-Hall) pp. 566–570.

Rumelt, R.P. (1994) 'Foreword', in G. Hamel and A. Heene (eds) *Competence Based Competition* (New York: Wiley), pp. xv–xix.

Sanchez, R. and Heene, A. (1996) 'A systems view of the firm in competence-based competition', In R. Sanchez *et al.* (eds) *Dynamics of Competence-Based Competition* (Oxford: Pergamon) pp. 39–62.

Sanchez, R. and Thomas, H. (1996) 'Strategic goals', in R. Sanchez *et al.* (eds) *Dynamics of Competence-Based Competition* (Oxford: Pergamon) pp. 63–84.

Sanchez, R., Heene, A. and Thomas, H. (1996) *Dynamics of Competence-Based Competition* (Oxford: Pergamon).

Sharma, D.D. and Johanson, J. (1987) 'Technical consultancy in internationalisation', *International Marketing Review*, Winter: 20–29.

Stern, L.W. and El-Ansary, A. (1992) M*arketing Channels* (Englewood Cliffs, NJ: Prentice-Hall).

Storey, D.J. (1994) *Understanding the Small Business Sector* (London: Routledge).

Sullivan, D. and Bauerschmidt, A. (1990) 'Incremental internationalization: a test of Johanson and Vahlne's thesis', *Management International Review*, 30: 19–30.

Teece, D.J. (1986) 'Profiting from technological innovation', in D.J. Teece (ed.) *The Competitive Challenge* (Cambridge, MA: Ballinger) pp. 185–220.

Welch, L.S. and Luostarinen, R. (1993) 'Inward–outward connections in internationalisation', *Journal of International Marketing*, 9(1): 44–56.

Welch, D.E. and Welch, L.S. (1996), 'The internationalization process and networks: a strategic management perspective', *Journal of International Marketing*, 4(3): 11–28.

Wernerfelt, B. (1984) 'A resource-based view of the firm', *Strategic Management Journal*, 5: 171–180.

Woodcock, P.C., Beamish, P.W. and Makino, S. (1994) 'Ownership-based entry mode strategies and international performance', *Journal of International Business Studies*, 25(2): 253–273.

Yang, Y.S., Leone, R.P. and Alden, D.L. (1992) 'A market expansion ability approach to identify potential exporters', *Journal of Marketing*, 56 (January): 84–96.

Yeoh, P.-L. and Jeong, I. (1995) 'Contingency relationships between entrepreneurship, export channel structure and environment', *European Journal of Marketing*, 29(8): 95–115.

Young, S., Hamill, J., Wheeler, C. and Davies, J.R. (1989) *International Market Entry and Development* (Hemel Hempstead: Harvester Wheatsheaf/Prentice-Hall).

6 Knowledge and the Multinational Enterprise

Robert M. Grant, Paul Almeida and Jaeyong Song

D21   F23   632   D83

The emerging knowledge-based view of the firm has revitalised interest in the theory of the firm. Conventional wisdom concerning the existence of the firm has centred around the Coase/Williamson view that firms exist to economise on the transaction costs of market contracting through substituting an administrative mechanism for decentralised market contracting. By focussing upon the role of knowledge in the production process, economists and management scholars have been able to provide a rationale for the firm that, although consistent with transaction cost explanations, offers much deeper insight into the organisational problem posed by the production of goods and services. Knowledge-based approaches to the theory of the firm also have the potential to yield richer implications (and, possibly, more readily testable predictions) with regard to firm's strategies and organisational structures than those offered by transaction cost analysis.

Scholars of international business (IB) are likely to experience a sense of *déjà vu* when confronted by the recent deluge of writings on knowledge management and the knowledge-based view of the firm. The theory of the multinational enterprise (MNE) has long viewed value creation through the exploitation of technology and other knowledge-based assets as central to the processes through which international firms create value. This chapter traces the history of knowledge-based approaches to the theory of the MNE. As we shall show, knowledge-based explanations of direct foreign investment have played a central role in analysis of the internationalisation of firms, and IB scholars have been at the forefront of the development of the so-called 'knowledge-based view of the firm'. Our primary focus will be to review the recent research concerning the role of knowledge in the structure, strategy, and performance of the MNE. We shall also consider recent contributions to the emerging knowledge-based view of the firm in order to identify potential implications for the theory of the MNE and practical issues concerning the management of MNEs. We conclude with two observations. First, that recent research into MNEs and international management is making a major contribution to the theory of the firm and management theory and practice in general. Second, that recent ideas concerning knowledge and its management can contribute to furthering our understanding of MNEs and the design of organisational processes which can allow MNEs to exploit more effectively their key knowledge resources.

THE 'KNOWLEDGE DIFFUSION' MODEL OF THE MNE

The idea that foreign direct investment is driven by firms' knowledge assets can be traced back to the earliest work on the theory of multinational enterprise, including the pioneering work of Stephen Hymer (1957). Analysis of the growing international dominance of US corporations in international business, and their expansion into Europe in particular, was attributed primarily to the technological advantages of these companies (Dunning, 1958; Servan-Schrieber, 1968). These technological advantages included not only technological innovations in products and processes but also superior management systems. The pattern of internationalisation associated with product innovation was linked by Ray Vernon (1955) to the product life cycle. This analysis of foreign direct investment being generated by home-based technological advantages was generalised by Caves (1971) who identified the exploitation of indivisible, firm-specific assets as the driving force of multinational expansion. Buckley and Casson (1976), Rugman (1981) and Teece (1986) added an important qualification to the analysis, noting that excess capacity in technology and other firm-specific resources was not a sufficient condition for foreign direct investment. For economies of scale and scope in these resources to be exploited internally within the firm depended upon the existence of transaction costs in the markets for these resources.

Implicit in this theory of the multinational corporation is a unidirectional view of knowledge flows. Knowledge is developed within the corporation's home base, primarily within its research labs, and is subsequently diffused world wide through a firm's subsidiaries (see Figure 6.1).

THE 'KNOWLEDGE LEVERAGING' VIEW OF THE MNE

During the past decade and a half, the knowledge diffusion view of foreign direct investment being pushed by the desire to exploit economies of scale and scope in firm-specific knowledge assets has given way to a broader, richer understanding of the processes through which MNEs create value from knowledge. What we term the 'knowledge leveraging' view of the MNE is the result of both empirical observations and developments in theory.

Empirical Studies of the Location of R&D by MNEs

Doubts over the knowledge diffusion view of the MNE were generated by evidence of the tendency for MNEs to disperse their R&D activities. Studies

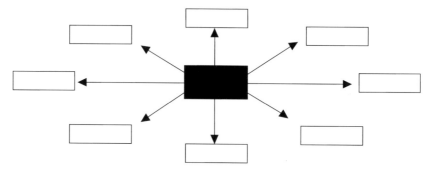

Key features:
1. Knowledge created at home base, then diffused globally.
2. Essential requirements:
   – economies of scale and scope in knowledge
   – market failure in knowledge transactions.

Figure 6.1   The knowledge diffusion view of the MNE

of the evolution of MNEs pointed to the tendency for local subsidiaries of MNEs, first, to undertake downstream functions such as sales, marketing, and customer support then to establish production facilities and, finally, in larger markets at least, to take on selective responsibilities for research and product development (Johanson and Vahlne, 1977). The establishment of overseas R&D facilities appears to be a critical stage in the development of MNEs' foreign subsidiaries (Hakanson, 1981). This dispersion of innovation activities by multinationals is further indicated by the tendency for companies to allocate an increasing proportion of their R&D budgets outside their home countries (Mansfield, Teece and Romero, 1979; Pearce, 1989; Florida, 1997).

The MNE as a Network

The tendency for MNEs to follow an evolutionary pattern where overseas subsidiaries became responsible for an increasing share of value chain activities was initially interpreted as MNEs establishing satellite R&D facilities in order to better serve the local market. Thus, a 1978 study of 53 US and European MNEs found that 184 out of the total 206 overseas R&D activities by the firms were orientated to serving the host market (Behrman and Fisher, 1980). Increasingly, the locational strategies and organisational structures of MNEs have been viewed as a compromise between two conflicting forces. First, the desire to locate production and R&D activities within overseas countries in order to promote adaptation to local conditions. Second, the desire to exploit the scale economies of global operation. Yves

Doz (1980) identified a number of MNEs, including Ericsson, Honeywell, Sperry Rand, Philips and Fairchild Semiconductor, that he identified as pursuing 'administrative coordination' strategies involving a 'constantly fluctuating balance between the imperatives' of worldwide integration and national responsiveness. While Doz viewed the attempt to reconcile global integration with national responsiveness as courting fragmentation and muddle, Bartlett and Ghoshal (1989) took a quite different view. They saw the 'transnational' corporation as adopting a strategy and structure that could successfully reconcile national adaptation with global integration. With this organisational form, production, research and product development activities could be globally dispersed, while simultaneously achieving a high level of global integration through closely coordinated flows of products, technologies and employees. Thus, while a individual country subsidiary has the role of serving its customer needs in its national market, it may also have a global mandate with regard to a particular product, component or technology.

Managing such a transnational firm is complex, requiring the meshing of carefully planned integration with flexibility and autonomy. Implementing such a strategy is likely to require that management has a strongly 'geocentric' orientation (Perlmutter, 1972). This view of the MNE as an integrated network involving a geographical distribution of assets, leadership roles and key strategic and knowledge-creating roles for foreign subsidiaries may require structures and management processes that are quite different from traditional hierarchies/structures or even the matrix structures of the 1970s. Hedlund's 'hypermodern heterarchy' is one conception of a globally networked organisation (Hedlund, 1986, 1994), while Birkinshaw has pointed to the key role of national subsidiaries in innovation and capability development (Birkinshaw *et al.*, 1998; Nobel and Birkinshaw, 1998).

Knowledge Accessing by the MNE

Underlying the knowledge diffusion view is a linear conception of technology development where new knowledge is created by the firm in its research lab, is embodied into product and process innovations within the home base and is then diffused to the world. In practice, however, knowledge generation within the MNE is more complex. Three considerations undermine the 'knowledge diffusion' view of the MNE:

• Technological knowledge is just one of many forms of productive knowledge. The firm's stock of knowledge comprises proprietary technologies and innovations, individual employee skills, market data and understanding, management capabilities (both functional and general management), external contacts, and a wide range of both factual and contextual knowledge relating to the external environment.

- Knowledge is acquired in different ways. Some knowledge is created within the firm through research, other forms of knowledge are created through learning-by-doing; a major part of the firm's stock of knowledge is acquired from outside the firm.
- Knowledge is generated in all parts of the firm. Knowledge-creating activities are not restricted to specific locations or specific functions of the firm.

Once we recognise that a major source of knowledge generation within the firm is accessing knowledge from outside the firm's boundaries, this suggests a further means by which MNEs can create value. The role of foreign direct investment in accessing immobile, country-specific resources has long been recognised. However, such resource-based international strategies have traditionally been associated with the quest for raw materials (oil, copper, and lumber) and low-cost labour, rather than knowledge.

Yet, like these other resources, knowledge too is only partially mobile. The idea that industry-specific knowledge tends to be geographically concentrated can be traced back to Alfred Marshall's (1920) 'industrial districts'. Marshall noted that economic activity was drawn to regions rich in the 'atmosphere of ideas'. Interest in localised industry 'clusters' was rekindled by Porter's *Competitive Advantage of Nations* (1990), which noted that competitive advantage tended to be located within groups of related and supported industries that were associated, not so much with countries, as with specific locations. These vibrant and innovative regions that produce knowledge externalities among firms, where the spillover effects are geographically limited have been carefully studied in California's Silicon Valley (Saxenian, 1990). In the US semiconductor industry, Almeida and Kogut (1994) use patent citation data to measure the extent to which technology flows tend to be localised within the 12 principal US clusters of semiconductor production. They link the inter-firm movements of technology within these local clusters to the inter-firm mobility of engineers.

The implication of this analysis is that MNEs are able to create value not only through exploiting economies of scale in knowledge through diffusing and utilizing knowledge assets on a global scale, but also from their ability to access knowledge in multiple geographical locations. This requires that they use their internal administrative mechanisms for knowledge transfer to overcome the geographical barriers responsible for the 'stickiness' of localised knowledge.

Evidence of this role of MNEs in using their global reach to access knowledge in multiple locations is evident from several studies. Pearce and Papanastassiou (1999) found that the UK R&D facilities of foreign MNEs had 'undergone a crucial metamorphosis from one of offering small-scale ad hoc support to individual local operations to that of playing a central role in global strategies that relate to both current market competition and technological evolution'. This evolution was driven, to a great extent, by the different technological inputs available in the UK compared to other countries: 'supply-side factors (the distinctiveness of a country's technological heritage and the strengths of its current scientific and research community) is now a crucial factor in attracting and motivating MNEs' R&D' (*ibid*, p. 39).

Almeida's (1996) study of patent citations among semiconductor MNEs provided strong support for the argument that a critical role of overseas subsidiaries is not just to exploit the parent company's knowledge assets but also to access knowledge in the overseas countries. Non-US semiconductor companies showed in their patenting behaviour a clear propensity to draw upon technologies developed in close proximity to their US subsidiaries: 'Foreign firms ... use local plants to upgrade their technological ability in fields which may be weak in their home countries'. (Almeida, p. 162). Almeida shows that foreign entrants may even be targeting the technology of specific local companies. For example, Siemen's in New Jersey appears to draw technology from the nearby Bell Laboratories; SGS-Thomson in Dallas, draws upon Texas Instruments' technology.

Rethinking Knowledge Diffusion: The Role of Absorptive Capacity

Fundamental to the knowledge diffusion view of value creation in the MNE is the idea that knowledge generation can be separated from knowledge application. Once created, knowledge can be embodied in product and process innovations and diffused throughout the overseas subsidiaries of the MNE. There are inherent inconsistencies in such a view. If new knowledge can be embodied in products and processes, especially those that are protected by patents, it is not apparent that a firm needs to use direct overseas investment in order to exploit its knowledge. Why cannot such knowledge be exploited through market transactions either in the form of direct exports or licensing the technology?

The failure of international markets in cross-national knowledge transfer reflects the problems of market contracts in knowledge transfers. As we shall explore in greater detail in the next section, exchange contracts for knowledge are only feasible in specific circumstances. These are, first, when intellectual property rights (e.g. the patent system) create a 'strong regime of appropriability' (Levin *et al.*, 1987) and, second, when knowledge can be embodied into products such that the user does not need access to the knowledge of the producer (Demsetz, 1991). In most circumstances, however, markets suffer from widespread failure in knowledge transactions.

We can establish the pervasiveness of market failure in knowledge transactions, but can the firm do a much better job of transferring knowledge between people, between units, and between locations? Some exploration of the organisational processes through which knowledge is transferred seems desirable.

Empirical evidence on international technology transfer points to two important features of the knowledge transfer process. First, it is neither a smooth nor easy process – it is often incomplete or unsuccessful. Second, the efficiency of technology transfer improves with experience. A detailed investigation into the composition of these transfer costs was undertaken by Teece (1977). Transfer costs comprised:

(a) pre-engineering technological exchanges
(b) engineering costs associated with transferring the product or process design
(c) R&D personnel costs associated with the transfer
(d) adaptation costs and costs of solving unexpected problems
(e) pre-start-up and start-up costs including the costs of training and debugging.

Teece also pointed out that the costs of these technology transfers varied with the capability of the firm (experience), the relationship between the transferor and recipient, home and host country factors, and the age of technology. It is interesting to note that the costs of transfer did not appear to be influenced substantially by whether or not the international transfer was within the same company or across separate firms (whether or not linked by joint venture agreements).

Teece's finding that the efficiency of technology transfer varied with the experience of the firm, pointed to the important role of existing knowledge base in assisting the acquisition of further knowledge. The idea that knowledge acquisition requires that new knowledge is linked to existing knowledge is fundamental to theories of learning. In their landmark paper, Cohen and Levinthal (1990) formalised and tested the complementarity between knowledge creation and knowledge transfer. If 'absorptive capacity' is a function of the recipient's knowledge base, then the use of knowledge cannot be separated from its creation. Hence, the ability of a MNE to transfer knowledge from its home base to its overseas subsidiaries depends, *inter alia*, upon the extent to which those overseas subsidiaries are themselves engaged in knowledge development.

Integrating the Different Knowledge Processes

The various contributions outlined above point to a more complex view of the means by which MNEs create value from knowledge than that offered by the knowledge diffusion model. In terms of knowledge generation, knowledge is created not only in the corporate research department of the company, it accumulates in all activities and results not only from explicit research activities but more importantly from learning-by-doing and everyday problem solving. Moreover, knowledge generation involves not

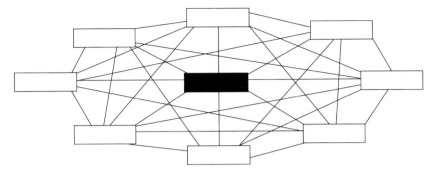

Key features:
1. Knowledge created in all parts of the organisation.
2. Knowledge accessed in multiple locations.
3. Knowledge creation and knowledge exploitation are joint activities (*absorptive capacity*)
5. Firm uses 'higher order organising principles' (Kogut and Zander, 1996)

Figure 6.2   The knowledge leveraging view of the MNE

only knowledge creation, but also the acquisition of knowledge from outside the firm's boundaries. A critical advantage of the MNE is its capacity to access knowledge in multiple locations. Knowledge application cannot be separated from knowledge generation. Hence, in order to exploit scale economies in knowledge use, through deploying it in multiple locations, the different geographical units must also be engaged in knowledge development. The result is a view of the MNE in which all organisational units, wherever they are located, are engaged to some extent in knowledge creation – all (whether deliberately or unconsciously) are engaged in accessing knowledge from their local environments. In order to create value from this knowledge accumulation, MNEs must both disseminate this knowledge in order exploit economies of scale and scope in its use, and integrate it such that different types of knowledge are combined in the production of goods and services. This multi-point process of creating, accessing, transferring and integrated knowledge we refer to as the 'knowledge leveraging' view of the MNE (see Figure 6.2).

KNOWLEDGE AND THE THEORY OF THE MNE

The view of the MNE as an international network that creates, accesses, integrates, and applies knowledge in multiple locations provides a much richer view of the processes through which MNEs create value from knowledge. In particular, it suggests a rationale for the MNE that extends beyond conventional transaction costs explanations for the superiority of direct investment over trade. To explore in greater detail the implications of knowledge for the theory and management of the MNE let us look a little further into the some key features of the emerging knowledge-based view of the firm.

The knowledge-based view of the firm represents the confluence of several streams of research. These include *organisational learning* (e.g. Levitt and March, 1988; Huber, 1991; Senge, 1990); *evolutionary economics* (Nelson and Winter, 1982); *organisational capabilities and competences* (Prahalad and Hamel, 1990; Leonard-Barton, 1992); and *innovation and new product development* (Teece, 1986; Nonaka, 1990; Henderson and Clark, 1990; Clark and Fujimoto, 1991). At its most general, the knowledge-based view of the firm may be seen as linking *resource-based theory* with *epistemology* (including influential contributions from Polanyi 1962, 1966; and Hayek, 1945). Attempts to synthesise these streams with regard to the theory of the firm include Kogut and Zander (1992), Nonaka (1994) Krogh, Roos and Slocum (1994), Spender (1994) and Grant (1996).

At the foundation of this knowledge-based view are assumptions concerning the nature of knowledge and its role in production. The fundamental precept of the knowledge-based view is that knowledge is the overwhelmingly important productive resource in terms of its contribution to value added and its strategic significance. If monopoly is a purely transitory phenomenon in an economy characterised by entrepreneurship and rapid technological change, then the primary source of profit is likely to be Ricardian rents rather than monopoly rents. If knowledge is the most important resource within the economy, then knowledge is the primary source of profit for firms. Indeed, knowledge possesses all the characteristics that resource-based theory suggests are critical to a resource's capacity to confer sustainable competitive advantage: scarcity, durability, and barriers to transfer and replication.

We have already made the distinction between the generation of knowledge and the application of knowledge. New knowledge is generated by individuals in specialist form: only by specialisation can individuals become masters of the existing stock of knowledge within their field and creators of new knowledge. However, the application of knowledge to the production of goods and services requires a broad range of different types of knowledge. Even a simple product such as a ceramic cup requires a wide range of technical and business skills for its production and sale. Hence, production requires the resolution of a fundamental organisational dilemma: if the creation of knowledge requires specialisation, while the application of knowledge requires assembling many different types of specialised knowledge, what organisational arrangements can reconcile the two? The problem of production is to establish mechanisms through which multiple individuals can coordinate their knowledge application, while preserving efficiencies of specialisation in knowledge acquisition. The solution lies in some process of *knowledge integration* which permits individuals to apply their specialised knowledge while obviating the need for individuals to acquire each other's specialist knowledge (Grant, 1996).

Central to the knowledge based view of the firm is the idea that the firm is a superior institution for governing the integration of knowledge necessary for producing goods and services. Because of its unusual properties, the inefficiencies of markets in transferring knowledge have long been recognised. In the case of information and other forms of explicit knowledge, the inefficiencies of market transactions are well known. The problem of private transactions in explicit knowledge have typically been attributed to the public good characteristics of such knowledge. In practice, the problems of knowledge are slightly different from typical public goods such as clean air and defence. Certainly, once created, explicit knowledge can be made available to others at very low marginal costs. However, the distinctive features of transactions in explicit knowledge are, first, that in selling knowledge the seller does not give up possession of it and, second, that knowledge cannot be sold without the seller first revealing it to the potential buyer (Arrow, 1962). The problems of tacit knowledge are somewhat different. Because tacit knowledge is embodied within its possessor it cannot be traded only as part of the labour services of its possessor. Hence, the general problem for both tacit and explicit knowledge is that of *inalienability* (Choi *et al.*, 1998) – with the exception of those forms of intellectual property where legislation has created enforceable property rights, ownership of knowledge cannot be transferred by means of contracts.

Central to the knowledge-based view of the firm is the idea that the rationale for the firm as an institution for organising transactions extends beyond the mere avoidance of the transaction costs of markets to take account of the positive benefits associated with the internalisation of knowledge transactions. Hence, the knowledge-based view goes some way to meeting Zajac and Olsen's (1993) call to take account of transaction value as well as transaction cost, and Ghoshal and Moran's (1996) plea for an approach to economic organisation that was not founded on the opportunistic behaviour of human beings.

The essence of the knowledge-based rationale for the firm is that the firm exists as an institution for the production of goods and services. The central problem of the firm from a management viewpoint is that of coordination. If there are efficiencies from specialisation, how are the different specialists to be coordinated in order to produce something? This is different from the central problem of economics, which is the allocation of scarce resources to competing uses. Allocation problems are solved through exchange contracts. However, once resources have been allocated, whether by voluntaristic exchange, or by administrative fiat, there is still the issue of how they are to work together. Thus, Kogut and Zander (1992) argue that the central role of the firm is not so much to economise on the transaction cost of markets, as to provide a set of 'higher level organising principles' to support sophisticated processes of knowledge creation and integration. Grant (1996) suggests that these organising principles comprise the following: rules and directives, the structuring of economic activity in order to sequence the activities of different workers, organisational routines, and group problem solving and decision making. In implementing these mechanisms for integrating different types of knowledge, firms are assisted by the base of *common knowledge* provided by language and shared meaning. Kogut and Zander (1996) suggest that the critical advantage of the firm over alternative institutions is that the firm provides a rich social context for collaborative economic activity. However, none of this means that the tasks of creating, transferring or integrating knowledge are easy.

Applying these ideas to the theory of the MNE, Kogut and Zander (1993) develop a knowledge-based rationale for the MNE whose basis is not the transaction costs of the markets for knowledge, but the superior efficiency of the MNE as a vehicle for knowledge transfer across borders. The essence of this efficiency is the nature of the firm as a social community in which knowledge can be understood and shared. They argue that the more tacit is the knowledge base of a company, then the greater the advantage of internalisation over licensing in exploiting that knowledge. Using data on innovations by Swedish companies, they (1993), found that the more complex, the less codifiable, and the less teachable the knowledge embodied in an innovation, the more likely that the firm would choose direct investment over licensing to exploit that innovation overseas.

It can be argued (and has been – see Foss, 1996a), that a knowledge-based analysis adds little value to a transaction cost analysis of the advantages of firms over markets. Although the gains from 'higher order organising principles' may be necessary to explain the existence of the firm, they are not sufficient. According to Foss,

> Agents (human resources) could simply meet under the same factory roof, own their own capital equipment or rent it to each other, and develop value-enhancing higher-order organising principles among themselves (as a team).

The problem, however, is that too narrow a focus upon transaction costs may cause us to lose focus upon what it is that firms do; once we accept the argument that the arrangements that we normally see within a firm can be created by independent contractors, we are faced with the problem of what the firm really is. Thus, the debate between Foss (1996b), Kogut and Zander (1996), and Connor and Prahalad (1996) over knowledge-based approaches to the theory of the firm ended up with the recognition that the critical differences between the participants stemmed from different conceptions of the nature of the firm. Because of the ambiguity of defining the firm in precise terms, Demsetz has chosen to refer to 'firm-like institutions' (Demsetz, 1995).

The argument that internalisation within the firm is the result of market failure is weakened by the observation that markets and firms are not the only institutions for organising economic activity. Collaborative inter-firm relationships, whether viewed as market hierarchy hybrids or as a distinct organisational form based upon relational contract, have been recognised as avoiding many of the transactions costs associated with market contracts for knowledge. In addition, because alliances do not involve irreversible investments in routines, institutional structures and other organisationally specific competencies, they may also be able to achieve much greater flexibility than is available to the firm. However, from a knowledge integration perspective, it is the very absence of investment in common language, social norms, organisational routines, and institutionalised modes of decision making that limits their capacity to conduct the low-cost knowledge integration activities that characterise firms. Alliances are likely to be superior to markets in terms of their ability to provide a framework for multi-period rather than single-period games and their capacity to overcome problems of opportunism through investments in trust and mutual 'exchanges of hostages'. However, in supporting 'higher organising principles,' alliances are inevitable inferior to firms.

This does not imply that direct investment will always be preferred to international strategic alliances in exploiting knowledge assets. As Grant and Baden-Fuller (1995) show, when excess capacity in knowledge resources arises because of a mismatch between a firm's knowledge domain and its product domain, when uncertainty exists as to the future input-output relationships between knowledge and products, and when early-mover advantage is present, then advantages of alliances are likely to offset their disadvantages

Further evidence of the role of efficiency of the MNE in the cross-border transfer of knowledge is found in current research that we are undertaking (see Almeida, Grant and Song, 1999 for a recent report). Using a matched sample of 148 patents filed by the US subsidiaries of non-US semiconductor companies, 148 patents filed by the US alliance partners of non-US semiconductor companies, and 148 patents filed by US companies with no alliance or ownership links to the non-US semiconductor companies, we compared patent citations to each of these patents in the home country of the non-US semiconductor company. The greater frequency of citations to the patents filed by overseas subsidiaries we interpreted as evidence of the greater efficiency of the MNE in transferring technology overseas than either alliances or pure market relationships.

KNOWLEDGE MANAGEMENT PROCESSES WITHIN THE MNE

Distinguishing Different Knowledge Management Processes

To go further in developing insight into the relative efficiencies of alternative institutional forms, we need to understand more fully how knowledge creates value within the economic system. So far we have focussed upon knowledge transfer, but why is knowledge transferred, to whom, and for what purposes?

As we have already observed, the knowledge-based literature distinguishes two broad categories of knowledge activities: those that involve increasing the organisation's stock of knowledge – Spender (1992) refers to these as *knowledge generation* – and those that involve the utilisation of that stock of knowledge – Spender refers to these as *knowledge application*. This distinction corresponds closely to James March's (1991) distinction between *exploration* and *exploitation* in organisational learn-ing. The knowledge diffusion model of the MNE adopts a simplified view of both knowledge generation and knowledge application: knowledge generation is equated with *knowledge creation* through R&D and other internal knowledge generating processes; knowledge application is equated with knowledge diffusion – the international transfer of technology and know-how. The knowledge leveraging model of the MNE implies a more complex view of knowledge management processes within the firm. Not only do each of these categories (knowledge generation and knowledge application) involve a number of different types of activity, but the two categories are linked. Building upon the concept of absorptive capacity, Almeida (1996) argues that the primary mechanism through which the MNE creates value is through *knowledge building* – the combined processes of knowledge transfer and knowledge creation.

Linkage between knowledge generation and knowledge application is apparent in much of the recent work on knowledge management. As we have noted, the dominant economics-based approach to knowledge envisaged a linear development process that went from scientific discovery to the embodiment of science in inventions, to the commercialisation of invention through innovation, and the subsequent diffusion of the innovation. The role of the organisation became more central in the work on organisational learning. A major emphasis of this literature was upon the acquisition and processing of information in order to reduce uncertainty (Levitt and March, 1988; March, 1991), and cognitive processes within organisations (Argyris and Schon, 1978). Nonaka (1994) has taken a broader view of knowledge creation. Knowledge is accumulated through a dynamic process of transformation through which knowledge is converted from tacit to explicit and from explicit to tacit, and moves between individual, group, organisational, and inter-organisational levels. Thus, Nonaka's 'SECI' spiral of knowledge creation comprises:

- Socialisation – the transfer of tacit knowledge between individuals and from the individual to the group and organisational level
- Externalisation – the conversion of tacit into explicit knowledge
- Combination – the combining of explicit knowledge between individuals
- Internalisation – the conversion of explicit into tacit knowledge.

A key aspect of this knowledge accumulation process concerns the central role played by tacit knowledge within the firm. This centrality of tacit knowledge marks a clear departure of the Nonaka model from the well-established information processing view of the firm. In particular, it direct attention towards the problems of communicating and sharing deeply personal knowledge (Nonaka emphasises the role of metaphor in this process), the role of *redundancy* in supporting the knowledge spiral, and the need for physical, psychological and philosophical space (what Nonaka, 1998, terms *ba*) for knowledge creation. As Hedlund and Nonaka (1993) point out, the processes of knowledge creation in firms are culturally embedded. Thus, Western firms place their primary emphasis on knowledge creation at the individual level and upon the management of explicit knowledge at the group and organisational levels. Japanese firms, by contrast, are far more committed to the movement of knowledge between the individual, group, organisational, and inter-organisational levels, and with a much stronger orientation around the management of tacit knowledge.

Despite the emphasis that much of the recent knowledge management literature has placed upon knowledge creation, most companies recognise that the greatest potential for value creation, whether measured by revenues or market capitalisation, is offered, not from the generation of new knowledge, but from the better utilisation of the knowledge that already exists within the boundaries of the firm. Indeed, many of the activities that involve the utilisation of existing knowledge through its transfer and integration are what Nonaka refers to as knowledge creation – reinforcing the arguments of Cohen and Levinthal, Almeida, and others of the complementarity, possibly even the inseparability, of the processes of knowledge generation and knowledge application.

Mechanisms of Knowledge Transfer

From the standpoint of the MNE, whether we adopt conventional ideas of knowledge diffusion, or Nonaka's notion that transferring knowledge between individuals and groups involves knowledge creation, it is clear that the movement of knowledge between different geographical locations is central to the process through which MNEs add value. Once we recognise the distinctive characteristics of different types of knowledge, in particular the distinction between tacit and explicit knowledge, then internal knowledge transfer becomes a complex management issue. In the burgeoning area of knowledge management, the most intense activity among both corporations and consulting firms has been in the development and implementations of mechanisms for increasing knowledge transfer in the firm. This activity extends from the use of shared databases to the transfer of best practices.

How knowledge is transferred across geographical distance and across the boundaries of nations and organisational units is highly dependent on the characteristics of the knowledge involved – we have already identified the critical distinction between tacit and explicit knowledge. Differences in types of knowledge imply differences not only in knowledge transfer mechanisms but also in the strategies of firms. Within the management consulting industry, firms can be classified into two main groups on the basis of their knowledge management strategies. *Codifiers*, such as Andersen Consulting, pursue the economics of knowledge reuse with a heavy emphasis on using IT to generate value through the reuse of explicit, codified knowledge. *Personalisers*, such as McKinsey & Company, provide customised expertise with a heavy reliance upon tacit knowledge (Hansen *et al.*, 1999).

Figure 6.3 classifies a number of knowledge transfer modes and mechanisms according to two characteristics: their suitability for transferring knowledge of different degrees of codifiability and their capacity for disseminating knowledge to multiple individuals.

In terms of codifiability, at one end of the scale is explicit, full-codifiable knowledge such as quantifiable data that can be transferred through electronic data exchange and stored in electronic databases. At the other end of the scale is deeply embedded tacit knowledge, which, at the far left-hand end of the scale, cannot be transferred between individuals. In this case, knowledge transfer is only possible through transferring the individuals who possess the knowledge. Consider, for example, the skills of a fragrance expert. The skills are partly learned and partly genetic, the key factor is that they are virtually unteachable. Hence, MNEs such as Unilever and Procter and Gamble will gain maximum utilisation from their fragrance experts through using them as mobile consultants. Where tacit skills become more capable of transfer through training, then knowledge transfer can be achieved through some combination of personnel transfer, on-the-job training and perhaps more formalised training sessions.

For most MNEs, computer-based information systems for transferring electronic data have been seen as the backbone of the knowledge management system. Such a view takes a narrow approach to knowledge management: for most companies it is reckoned that tacit knowledge is quantitatively more important as a source of value. While electronic

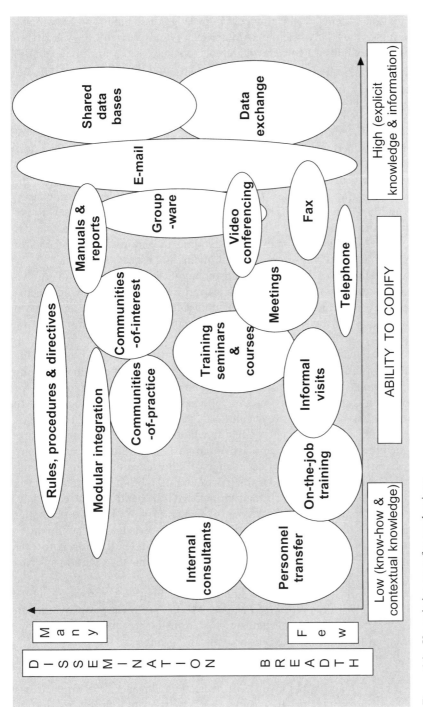

Figure 6.3 Knowledge transfer mechanisms

information systems permit low-cost knowledge dissemination across many individuals, they lack 'richness' in terms of limits to the complexity of language, flexibility of format, degree of personalisation, and the extent of interactivity they permit (Weick, 1979; Daft and Lengl, 1986; Daft and Wiginton, 1979). These 'lean' communication mechanisms are suited to the transfer of highly codifiable knowledge, but become less efficient as knowledge becomes less codifiable, more tacit and more complex.

In the intermediate range of tacitness is the variety of knowledge types for which richer media, such as face-to-face conversations, allow clarification, questioning, and a deeper exchange of knowledge. These media are especially useful when the context of the knowledge transfer in unclear or the knowledge matter is complex. Leaner media like letters, telephone conversations and faxes are perhaps cheaper and less time consuming but they do not facilitate the same level of knowledge exchange. Thus, for the transfer of complex knowledge, for example, relating to new product concepts or complex manufacturing processes, rich media are especially useful.

Most instances of knowledge transfer involve multiple types of knowledge. In these cases, richer communication media, including voice media (telephone), combined video–voice media (video-conferencing), and written media (fax, paper reports) are important in supporting and complementing computer-based information systems. For example, telephone communication is used widely as a highly interactive bilateral medium permitting clarification and interpretation of electronic data and problem-solving activity. Similarly, video conferencing is used within MNEs, not so much for information transmission as much as a decision-making tool that helps to build consensus and convey emotion. Faxes permit easy and quick communication of graphical sketches, while written memos and reports provided authority and authenticity to support electronic communication.

Probably the greatest single challenge of knowledge management facing the MNE is achieving the widespread dissemination of knowledge that has a substantial tacit dimension. If tacit knowledge is to be disseminated widely, then it must somehow be converted into explicit form. As Kogut and Zander (1992, p. 390) observe, unless individuals' tacit knowledge can be taught to others or transformed into organising principles, 'the craft shop is forever simply a shop'. In recent years, the ability of electronic information systems to capture richer, less codifiable forms of knowledge has grown with the development of more communication and documentation software such as groupware (e.g. Lotus Notes). For many MNEs, groupware is providing an increasingly important mechanism for transferring project-based and experiential learning between individuals and groups.

Codifying more deeply tacit knowledge has proved a more difficult challenge for firms. Despite the high expectations that were held out for expert systems and other forms of artificial intelligence, the applications have been limited so far. In recent years, attention has shifted to sharing tacit knowledge between smaller groups where a high level of common knowledge makes possible the rich interchange of embedded knowledge. An important finding of Brown and Duguid (1991) was the existence of informal networks of knowledge sharing among workers with common interest built around networks of personal acquaintances. These communities of practice not only foster learning through the sharing of experiential knowledge through stories and metaphors, but also promote innovation. Increasingly, firms have sought to build bridges between the formal and informal processes of knowledge transfer through recognising the significance of these informal 'communities of practice' and 'communities of interest' and to provide support to their continued existence as well as fostering the emergence of new knowledge-sharing networks.

Increasing the Effectiveness of Knowledge Management within the MNE

Given the great diversity of processes through which companies manage knowledge, the problem of knowledge management is clearly not one of scarcity of tools, ideas and techniques. Rather it is the reverse. The plethora of weapons in the arsenal of knowledge management is likely to confuse rather than promote the pursuit of innovation and productivity. Effective management of knowledge requires clarity over two key issues:

• the goals of knowledge management
• the characteristics of the knowledge being managed.

In terms of the goals of knowledge management we have already distinguished between knowledge generation and knowledge application. Table 6.1 goes further and provides a more detailed analysis of the knowledge management activities that comprise knowledge generation and knowledge application.

Identifying and Storing Knowledge

The primary thrust of knowledge management initiatives within firms has been directed towards basic activities such as the identification and archiving of knowledge within the company. Many companies have echoed the plea of Lew Platt of Hewlett Packard that if only HP knew what HP knows it would be three times more profitable. The result has been a surge of interest among large corporation in creating systems to document individual expertise and collective experiences. Because of their geographical diversity and the national and cultural barriers that impede knowledge flows between organisational units, MNEs have been especially prominent in this area.

The major interest and major problems are not in the identification and accessing of information and other forms of explicit knowledge. In general, IT systems do a good job in this area, although integrating different national

Table 1   Knowledge management processes within the firm

Knowledge generation:	
• Knowledge creation	Creating new (mainly technical and scientific) knowledge through research
• Learning-by-doing	Accumulating know-how (especially that relating to processes) through the accumulation of experience ('moving down the learning curve')
• External learning	The transfer of both explicit and tacit knowledge from outside the firm's boundaries
Knowledge application:	
• Knowledge replication	Duplicating existing organisational knowledge (typically in a different location) in order to exploit economies of scale and scale in knowledge utilisation
• Knowledge integration	Combining different types of knowledge to transform inputs into outputs

Adapted from Cusumano (1997).

systems remains a problem for many MNEs, especially those that have grown through acquisition. The primary challenges are in distilling, archiving and transferring experiential knowledge. The management consulting companies have been leaders in efforts to develop resources that capture expertise and experience in the form of databases and libraries that can be readily accessed by project teams and individuals. Thus, Arthur Andersen developed a series of 'convergent knowledge bases' designed to help practitioners sell and perform engagements. These included a repository of tools and methodologies, an engagement information system, and its 'Global Best Practices' database of 'highly distilled research concerning the most effective ways of performing particular processes' (HBS, 1998). This Global Best Practices database uses a classification system for business processes developed in collaboration with the American Productivity and Quality Center that is now used by the International Benchmarking Clearinghouse. Ernst & Young's Center for Business Knowledge has two major knowledge management groups: the Repository Management Group, which organises document repositories and databases, and the Knowledge Web Group, which designs and manages the firm's knowledge management architecture, applications, navigational tools and taxonomies. These systems developed by the consulting companies have provided the models for knowledge archiving systems developed by leading MNEs including companies such as DuPont, Dow Chemical, Unilever and General Motors.

Knowledge Replication

Looking beyond the collection and storage of knowledge, the next stage is the replication of knowledge held in one place or by a few people.

Knowledge replication creates value primarily because it exploits economics of scale in knowledge. These economies of scale derive from two key properties of knowledge: first, it is not exclusionary in use, it can transferred to another person without its possessor being deprived of it, second, it can be transferred at a lower cost than the original cost of creating it. Economies of scale are especially important in information and scientific knowledge, which can typically be transferred at a very low cost. In the case of know-how, transfer costs are much higher, since tacit knowledge transfer requires learning-by-doing. Hence, exploiting economies of scale and scope in tacit knowledge normally requires that it can be converted into some form of explicit knowledge that can then be more readily disseminated throughout the organisation (Nonaka and Takeuchi, 1995). One reason why craft industries are dominated by small firms is that the firm cannot easily replicate the tacit knowledge of individual craftsmen. The central feature of industrialisation is the systematisation of such knowledge, making it both replicable and permitting the application of machines to undertake an increasing number of operations. If knowledge cannot be converted into explicit form, then its transfer is much more complex and difficult. Replication requires comparatively long periods of training and learning-by-doing, which normally involves the transfer of personnel. Either moving the learners to the experts or transferring the experts to coach and develop the learners. The extent to which management consulting firms seek to exploit tacit knowledge through codifying it and replicating it many times over, as opposed to directly applying 'deep knowledge' to complex, high-level problems, distinguishes a strategy of 'codification' from one of 'personalisation' (Hansen *et al.*, 1999).

In terms of transferring and replicating complex, organisationally embedded knowledge, interest has focussed upon the area called 'transfer of best practices' – essentially, the replication of superior organisational processes. Research by Szulanski (1996) identified three major barriers to the transfer of best practices within firms: limited absorptive capacity of the recipient, uncertainty over cause-effect relationships ('causal ambiguity'), and poor communication and lack of intimacy in the relationship between the source and the recipient ('arduous relationship'). The critical features of organisational processes is that they involve organisationally embedded tacit knowledge that is exercised through organisational routines. The knowledge cannot be divorced from the practice, hence the transfer of documented, explicit knowledge about the practice will not transfer the practice itself. A study of a transfer of a major cost-saving innovation among Mobil's different oil fields noted the complete failure of a transfer strategy based upon documentation and a video. A second initiative which involved a case study that was taught at a training seminar for production managers resulted in 31% adoption. To achieve a higher level of adoption however, required the co-location of personnel, i.e. visits by other production managers to the innovating oil field, and secondment of personnel from the innovating oil field to other production units (Prusak, 1998).

Replication of organisational capabilities is fundamental to the processes through which MNEs extend national competitive advantages into the international competitive advantages. The internationalisation process of companies as diverse as Ford Motor Company, McDonalds Restaurants, Dell Computer, Marriott International and UPS is based upon taking a set of business processes that were developed within the home market and transferring these to overseas markets. A key element of such replication is the ability to distill a major part of the tacit knowledge embodied in these capabilities into more explicit form. Thus, McDonalds' processes for the operation of its fast-food restaurants is documented in a multitude of operating manuals. However, the primary mechanism for the transfer of McDonalds' processes from the US to each overseas markets is primarily through training of restaurant managers and assistant managers in programmes at Hamburger University and the on-site supervision and training given by McDonald's consultants at the new location. Because so much of the relevant knowledge embodied in organisational routines is tacit and cannot be readily systematised into explicit form, replication of business practices and processes presents a huge challenge. Polanyi's (1962) observation of the failure of a Hungarian light bulb plant, using standard Western technology and equipment, to produce a single flawless bulb is apposite in this regard.

The replication of existing knowledge in different geographical locations is the essence of the knowledge dissemination process in the MNE. The international expansion of US industrial corporations such as Singer, International Harvester, Ford and DuPont during the early decades of the 20th century was driven by the desire to replicate product and process technologies and management capabilities in multiple markets. Expansion through geographical replication is the fundamental feature of McDonalds' strategy. Within semiconductors, knowledge replication is especially important in disseminating process technology across multiple plants.

Knowledge Integration

At the same time, international exploitation of knowledge is not simply about replication, it is also about bringing together different types of knowledge from different locations. As we have already noted, a fundamental dilemma for economic organisation is the reconciliation of the efficiencies of specialisation in knowledge creation with the need to combine many different types of knowledge in order to produce goods and services. The solution lies in some process of *knowledge integration* that permits individuals to apply their specialised knowledge to the production of goods and services, while preserving the efficiencies of specialisation in knowledge acquisition. Hence, if the MNE is accessing knowledge in different locations, efficiency in knowledge integration requires mechanisms for bringing together different knowledge bases while avoiding the heavy costs of every national unit absorbing the knowledge that is possessed by every other unit.

Thus, in the semiconductor industry, the increased complexity and sophistication of design and fabrication permits an increasing proportion of the functionality of final products, whether computers or mobile telephones, to be embodied within integrated circuits. Increasingly, individual semi-conductors, especially application-specific integrated circuits (ASICs) are becoming multifunctional. Designing such multifunctional ICs requires the bringing together of expertise from different parts, and different locations, of the corporation. The basic principle of product design for achieving knowledge integration while economising upon cross-learning is *modularity*. The basic idea is that product design is based upon modules organised as subsystems and components, with standardised interfaces between them. The result is to greatly facilitate integration, since development in any single module does not require constant coordination with every other part of the design. As far as company organisation is concerned, the main idea is that the design and development process is organised in modular form to parallel the modular design of the product (Sanchez and Mahoney, 1996; Bayliss and Clark, 1997).

Thus, in relation to computer software, Cusumano shows how Micro-soft's leadership in operating system and applications software has been supported by a product development system based around modular design of the product and modular organisation of the product development effort around small teams, even though the entire product development teams for Windows NT, Windows 95 or Internet Explorer each comprised over 450 people (Cusumano, 1997). Microsoft's browser required a team of about 300, with several hundred more working on add-on features such as Internet mail. The essential requirement for such modularisation is the establishment of interfaces that permit the modules to work together. Key features of Microsoft's 'synch and stabilise' approach are the imposition of rules that permit flexibility and innovation within teams, but ensure coordination of the project as a whole. Critical aspects of interface management include common development languages, clearly defined goals for each module in terms of features and functions, daily and weekly builds, which occur at fixed times (either 2 pm or 5 pm) when the software is complied and tested, and periodic stabilisations when the features of each component are fixed and then provide a common basis from which each modular team can move on to the next set of design milestones.

The advantages of such a modular approach in permitting flexibility in terms of innovation and adjustment are apparent in the tortuous evolu-tion of Netscape's Navigator browser. The tightly coupled structure of Netscape's initial version of Navigator and the frequency of 'spaghetti code' handicapped Netscape's ability to upgrade and extend the product. The resulting rewriting of Navigator around a modular architecture delayed upgrading the product allowing Microsoft to gain leadership in the market for browsers (Cusumano and Yoffie, 1998).

These issues of achieving knowledge integration in new product development through the modularisation of design is especially important to MNEs where the coordination problems of internationally dispersed product development activities are particularly acute. However, the modularity issue is relevant to the design of MNEs themselves. If the essence of production is the integration of the knowledge of many different individuals, then modular organisational designs may be viewed as efficient responses to the costs of knowledge integration. If the greater part of the knowledge used by firms is tacit, then it can be transferred only at high cost. Modularity is a means of achieving integration across a broad range of different knowledge bases while minimising the costs of knowledge transfer. The essence of the efficiency benefits of modular structures is that each unit is capable of integrating knowledge among the individuals within the unit, while avoiding the need continuously to transfer knowledge between units. The critical issues for organisational design are, then, the organisation of the activities of the firm into modules and the definition of interfaces between the modules. The establishment of interfaces is critical. It is the interfaces that provide the basis for knowledge integration between modules. Within organisations, the 'standardised interfaces' between organisational units are the standardised control systems through which overall coordination is achieved. In the case of a classical conglomerate, such as the former Hanson group, the main interface linking the modules was Hanson's financial management system. Because each business was deemed to be technologically and strategically independent of every other, the operation of each division as an independent entity with very little inter-divisional knowledge integration was highly feasible. Where higher levels of knowledge integration are required between modules, then interfaces need to be more complex and less standardised. Typically, the more closely related the businesses of a corporation then the greater the requirements for knowledge integration and the more complex are the integration mechanisms. In the typical MNE, integration is achieved through a financial control system, a strategic planning system and a human resource planning and appraisal system. In addition, a common corporate culture provides the basis for an informal system of knowledge integration.

CONCLUSION

The theory of foreign direct investment has long recognised the potential for value creation through exploiting economies of scale and scope in knowledge deployment and avoiding the costs associated in knowledge transactions. To this extent, international business scholars have been at the forefront of developments in the emerging knowledge-based view of the firm. However, during recent years, the surge of interest in theoretical and practical issues of knowledge management offer the potential to extend and enrich our understanding of MNEs and their management.

This chapter has addressed two main sets of issues. The first has been the processes through which MNEs can use value in order to create value. We have observed that the MNE is engaged in multiple processes through which knowledge is generated and applied, and that these processes are closely linked. Recognising the central role of knowledge and the means by which it is integrated into goods and services, gives us further insight into the existence of the MNE and its advantages over alternative institutional forms (namely, markets and interfirm alliances) than is offered by transaction cost economics alone. In particular, identifying the processes and mechanisms through which knowledge generation and application occur within the firm offers us considerable insight into the challenges of organising the MNE.

The second set of issues concerns knowledge management within the MNE. If knowledge is the overwhelmingly important asset of the firm, and if the potential of the MNE to create value depends upon the firm's effectiveness in creating, accessing, and deploying knowledge, then knowledge management is the central task of executives. Amid the huge volume of prescription and advice on knowledge management, we argue that there are two factors that are fundamental to effective knowledge management. First, recognition of the characteristics of the knowledge being management, especially with regard to its tacitness and its potential for codification. Second, recognition of the processes through which knowledge is creating value. MNEs achieve efficiency in creating value from knowledge through using rules to standardise procedures and formats, directives to administer coordination between national units, interpersonal relationships between employees, organisational routines to permit coordination and integration between specialists with very different skill bases, and a common culture to facilitate communication and cooperation. The design and choice of different organisational mechanisms must take careful account of the nature of the knowledge management process (e.g. the extent to which it seeks to replicate knowledge, to combine knowledge, or to create new knowledge through problem solving), and the types of knowledge being transferred (in particular, the less codifiable the knowledge, the richer the communication medium needs to be). Although the need to relate control systems to knowledge strategies has been recognised (Gupta and Govindarajan, 1991), little explicit attention has been given to the implication of different knowledge management processes. In the area of management practice, firms have made huge strides in the use of IT to transfer information and support communication worldwide. The next level of knowledge management lies in the design and operation of organisational structures, management systems, and shared values and behavioural norms that can facilitate the movement of complementary knowledge types and link together the different modes of communication and knowledge transfer.

As business globalises, firm advantages arising from traditional sources such as the unique access to capital, labour or markets can be expected to decline. Correspondingly, a company's ability to develop, access, integrate and deploy knowledge across its worldwide system is likely to grow ever more critical. We have identified the overall advantages in building and deploying knowledge across borders. There is substantial scope for future research to investigate in detail the design and performance of international knowledge management practices ranging from the transfer of manufacturing best practices to international new product development. A key element of such research is likely to be the relative effectiveness of different communication media, not only IT, audio and video communication, but to include a better understanding of the nature of interpersonal relationships and the role of mixed-mode communication is supporting rich knowledge transfer.

References

Almeida, P. (1996) 'Knowledge sourcing by foreign multinationals: patent citation analysis in the us semiconductor industry', *Strategic Management Journal* (Special Issue on 'Knowledge and the Firm') 7: 155–165.
Almeida, P., Grant, R.M. and Song, J. (1999) 'Firms, alliances, and markets in cross-border knowledge building', Discussion Paper, McDonough School of Business, Georgetown University, Washington, DC.
Almeida, P. and Kogut, B. (1994) 'Technology and geography: the localization of knowledge and the mobility of patent holders', Working Paper, The Huntsman Center for Global Competition and Innovation, The Wharton School, Philadelphia, PA.
Argyris, C. and Schon, D.A. (1978) *Organizational Learning* (Reading, MA: Addison-Wesley).
Arrow, K. (1962) 'Economic welfare and the allocation of resources for invention', in National Bureau of Economic Research, *The Rate and Direction of Inventive Activity* (Princeton: Princeton University Press) pp. 609–625.
Bartlett, C.A. and Ghoshal, S. (1989) *Managing Across Borders: The Transnational Solution* (Boston, MA: Harvard Business School Press).
Bayliss, C.Y. and Clark, K.B. (1997) 'Managing in an age of modularity', *Harvard Business Review* (September–October): 46–58.
Behrman, J.N. and Fisher, W.A. (1980) 'Transnational corporations: market orientations and R&D abroad', *Columbia Journal of World Business*, Fall: pp. 55–60.
Birkinshaw, J., Hood, N. and Jonsson, S. (1998) 'Building Firm Specific Advantages in Multinational Corporations: the role of subsidiary initiative', *Strategic Management Journal*, 19: pp. 221–242.

Brown, J.S. and Duguid, P. (1991) 'Organizational learning and communities-of-practice: toward a unified view of working, learning and innovation', *Organization Science*, 2: pp. 40–57.

Buckley, P. and Casson, M. (1976) *Alternatives to the Multinational Enterprise* (London: Macmillan).

Caves, R.E. (1971) 'International corporations: the industrial economics of foreign investment', *Economica*, 38: pp. 1–27.

Choi, C.J., Raman, M. and Ussoltseva, O. (1998) 'Knowledge-based exchange: inalienability and reciprocity', Discussion Paper, City University Business School, London, August.

Clark, K. and Fujimoto, T. (1991) *Product Development Performance* (Boston, MA: Harvard Business School Press).

Cohen, W. and Levinthal, D. (1990) 'Absorptive capacity: a new perspective on learning and innovation', *Administrative Science Quarterly*, 35: pp. 128–152.

Connor, K. and Prahalad, C.K. (1996) 'A resource-based theory of the firm: knowledge versus opportunism', *Organization Science*, 7: 477–501.

Cusumano, M.A. (1997) 'How Microsoft makes large teams work like small teams', *Sloan Management Review*, Fall: pp. 9–20.

Cusumano, M.A. and Yoffie, D.B. (1998) *Competing on Internet Time: Lessons from Netscape and its Battle with Microsoft* (New York: Free Press).

Daft, R.L. and Wiginton, J.C. (1979) 'Language and organization', *Academy of Management Review*, 4: pp. 179–191.

Daft, R.L. and Lengl, R.H. (1986) 'Organizational information requirements, media richness and structural design', *Management Science*, 32: pp. 554–571.

Demsetz, H. (1991) 'The theory of the firm revisited', in O.E. Williamson and S.G. Winter (eds) *The Nature of the Firm* (New York: Oxford University Press): pp. 159–178.

Demsetz, H. (1995) *The Economics of the Business Firm: Seven Critical Commentaries* (Cambridge: Cambridge University Press).

Doz, Y.L. (1980) 'Strategic management in multinational companies', *Sloan Management Review*, 21(2): pp. 27–46.

Dunning, J.H. (1958) *American Investment in British Manufacturing Industry* (London: George Allen and Unwin).

Florida, R. (1997) 'The globalization of R&D: results of a survey of foreign-affiliated R&D laboratories in the USA', *Research Policy*, 26: pp. 85–103.

Foss, N.J. (1996a) 'Knowledge-based approaches to the theory of the firm: some critical comments', *Organization Science*, 7(5) September–October: pp. 471–480.

Foss, N.J. (1996b) 'More critical comments on knowledge-based theories of the firm', *Organization Science*, 7(5) September–October: pp. 519–523.

Ghoshal, S. and Moran, P. (1996) 'Bad for practice: a critique of transaction cost theory', *Academy of Management Review*, 21: pp. 13–47.

Grant, R.M. (1996) 'Prospering in dynamically competitive environments: organizational capability as knowledge integration', *Organization Science*, 7: pp. 375–387.

Grant, R.M. and Baden-Fuller, C. (1995) 'A knowledge-based theory of inter-firm collaboration', *Academy of Management Best Papers Conference Proceedings*.

Gupta, A.K. and Govindarajan, V. (1991) 'Knowledge flows and the structure of control within multinational corporations', *Academy of Management Review*, 16: pp. 768–792.

Hakanson, L. (1981) 'Organization and evolution of foreign R&D in Swedish MNCs', *Geografiska Annaler*, 63B: pp. 47–56.

Hansen, M.T., Nohria, N. and Tierney, T. (1999) 'What's your strategy for managing knowledge?', *Harvard Business Review*, 77 (March–April): pp. 106–118.

Hayek, F.A. (1945) 'The use of knowledge in society', *American Economic Review*, 35 (September): 1–18.

HBS (1998) *A Note on Knowledge Management*, Case number 9-398-031, Harvard Business School, Boston, MA.

Hedlund, G. (1986) 'The hypermodern MNC – a heterarchy', *Human Resource Management*, 25: pp. 9–25.

Hedlund, G. (1994) 'A model of knowledge management and the N-form corporation', *Strategic Management Journal*, 15 (Special Issue), Summer: pp. 73–90.

Hedlund, G. and Nonaka, I. (1993) 'Models of knowledge management in the West and Japan', in P. Lorange, B. Chakravarty, J. Roos and A. Van de Van (eds) *Implementing Strategic Processes* (Oxford: Blackwell): pp. 117–144.

Henderson, R. and Clark, K. (1990) 'Architectural innovation: the reconfiguration of existing product technologies and the failure of established firms', *Administrative Science Quarterly*, 35: pp. 9–31.

Huber, G.P. (1991) 'Organizational learning: the contributing processes and literatures', *Organization Science*, 2: pp. 88–115.

Hymer, S. (1957) *The International Operations of National Firms: A Study of Direct Investment*, Ph.D. Dissertation, Massachusetts Institute of Technology.

Johanson, J. and Vahlne, J.E. (1977) 'The internationalization process of the firm: a model of knowledge development and increasing foreign commitment', *Journal of International Business Studies*, 8(2): pp. 23–32.

Kogut, B. and Zander, U. (1992) 'Knowledge of the firm, combinative capabilities, and the replication of technology', *Organization Science*, 3: pp. 383–397.

Kogut, B. and Zander, U. (1993) 'Knowledge of the firm and the evolutionary theory of the multinational corporation', *Journal of International Business Studies*, 24: pp. 625–645.

Kogut, B. and Zander, U. (1996) 'What firms do: coordination, identity, and learning', *Organization Science*, 7: 502–518.

Krogh, G. von, Roos, J. and Slocum, K. (1994) 'An essay on corporate epistemology', *Strategic Management Journal*, 15 (Special Issue): 53–72.

Leonard-Barton, D. (1992) 'Core capabilities and core rigidities: a paradox in managing new product development', *Strategic Management Journal*, 13 (Summer Special Issue): 111–125.

Levin, R. *et al.* (1987) 'Appropriating the returns from industrial research and development', *Brookings Papers on Economic Activity*, 3: pp. 783–820.

Levitt, B and March, J.G. (1988) 'Organizational learning', *Annual Review of Sociology*, 14: pp. 319–340.

Mansfield, E., Teece, D.J. and Romero, A. (1979) 'Overseas R&D by US-based firms', *Economica*, 46: pp. 187–196.

March, J.G. (1991) 'Exploration and exploitation in organizational learning', *Organization Science*, 2: pp. 71–87.

Marshall, A. (1920) *Industry and Trade* (London: Macmillan).

Nelson, R. and Winter, S. (1992) *An Evolutionary Theory of Economic Change* (Cambridge: Belknap).

Nobel, R. and Birkinshaw, J. (1998) 'Innovation in multinational corporations: control and communication patterns in international R&D operations', *Strategic Management Journal*, 19: pp. 479–496.

Nonaka, I. (1994) 'A dynamic theory of organizational knowledge creation', *Organization Science*, 5: 14–37.

Nonaka, I. (1998) 'The concept of *ba*: building a foundation for knowledge creation', *California Management Review*, 40(3) (Spring): pp. 40–54.

Nonaka, I. (1990) 'Redundant, overlapping organization: a Japanese approach to managing the innovation process', *California Management Review*, Spring: 27–38.

Nonaka, I. and Takeuchi, H. (1995) *The Knowledge Creating Firm* (New York: Oxford University Press).

Pearce, R.D. (1989) *The Internationalization of R&D by Multinational Enterprises* (London: St. Martin's Press).

Pearce, R.D. and Papanastassiou, M. (1999) 'Overseas R&D and the strategic evolution of MNEs: evidence from labs in the UK', *Research Policy*, 28: 23–41.

Perlmutter, H.V. (1972) 'The multinational firm and the future', *Annals of the American Academy of Political and Social Science*, September: 139–152.

Polanyi, M. (1962) *Personal Knowledge* (Chicago: University of Chicago Press).

Polanyi, M. (1966) *The Taint Dimension* (New York: Anchor Day).

Porter, M. (1990) 'The competitive advantage of nations', *Harvard Business Review*, March–April: 73–100.

Prahalad, C.K. and Hamel, G. (1990) 'The core competence of the corporation', *Harvard Business Review*, 68 (May–June): pp. 79–91.

Prusak, L. (1998) Presentation to Second Annual Berkeley Forum on Knowledge and the Firm, University of California, Berkeley, September 24.

Rugman, A. (1981) *Inside the Multinationals: The Economics of Internal Markets* (New York: Columbia University Press).

Sanchez, R. and Mahoney, T. (1996) 'Modularity, flexibility and knowledge management in product and organization design', *Strategic Management Journal*, 17 (Winter Special Issue): 63–76.

Saxenian, A. (1990) 'Regional networks and the resurgence of Silicon Valley', *California Management Review*, 33 (Fall): 39–112.

Senge, P. (1990) *The Fifth Dimension* (London: Century Business).

Servan-Schrieber, J. (1968) *The American Challenge* (New York: Athenaeum).

Spender, J.C. (1992) 'Limits to learning from the West', *International Executive*, 34: 389–410.

Spender J.-C. (1994) 'Organizational knowledge, collective practices and Penrose rents', *International Business Review*, 3: 353–367.

Szulanski, G. (1996) 'Exploring internal stickiness: impediments to the transfer of best practice within the firm', *Strategic Management Journal* 17 (Winter Special Issue): 27–44.

Teece, D.J. (1977) 'Technology transfer by multinational firms: the resource costs of transferring technological know-how', *Economic Journal*, 87: 242–261.

Teece, D.J. (1986) 'Transaction cost economics and multinational enterprise', *Journal of Economic Behavior and Organisation*, 7: 21–45.

Vernon, R. (1955) 'International investment and international trade in the product life cycle', *Quarterly Journal of Economics*, May: 190–207.

Weick, K. (1979) *The Social Psychology of Organizing*, 2nd edn (Reading, MA: Addison-Wesley).

Zajac, E.J. and Olsen, C.P. (1993) 'From transaction cost to transactional value analysis: implications for the study of interorganizational strategies', *Journal of Management Studies*, 30: 131–145.

130-55

(US, UK, Germany
Japan)

L65 L61
L63 L62

F23 L24

032

7 New Technologies and International Business in the 21st Century: Technological Convergence, Networks and Global Competition

Lakis C. Kaounides

Specialisation by the national affiliates of multinational enterprises (MNEs) on the basis of locational advantage (UNCTAD, 1993, 1997, 1998) requires increasingly complex coordination through intricate webs of dynamic networks of internal and external relationships (Dicken, 1998). The outcome is new locational patterns for production and R&D activities in international business. These developments form part of a general tend towards increased global integration,[1] which is moving beyond trade-based integration to more complex integration of MNE's research, production and product development activities. Such strategies are predicated on the continuing liberalisation of world trade in goods and services. This liberalisation already includes: the 1997 agreements on basic telecommunications, financial services and information technology (WTO, 1998); the protection of trade-related aspects of intellectual property rights (TRIPs); multilateral rules on the environment, labour standards and investment (UNCTAD, 1998); and the harmonisation of national competition policies. The advent of major scientific, engineering and technological revolutions, however, ushers in new questions in international business for corporations and nations and their reciprocal relation in the next century.

In this paper we explore four questions:

1. What are the new science-based generic technologies that will transform industrial products and processes, shift industry boundaries, and provide the basis for international competitive advantage in the coming years?
2. What are the implications of new technologies for internationalisation strategies in general and strategic alliances in particular?
3. What is the appropriate role for government policy towards science, technology and innovation? The literature on national systems of innovation (Freeman, 1987, 1997; Lundvall, 1992; Nelson, 1993) ascribes a strong role to national historical and institutional influences in shaping and

130

conditioning firms' abilities to invent, innovate and commercialise new technologies and compete in the world market. On the other hand, there is the tendency for globalisation to undermine the significance of the nation state in technological advance (Chesnais, 1988). In this view national technology policies would be of questionable effectiveness or desirability if new knowledge disseminates fast over national boundaries.

4. Is the Anglo-American model of innovation and technology management, which emphasises opportunism and global spread, superior to the 'Rhine'[2] model (in its German and Japanese variants), which emphasises national systems of innovation (NSI) (Kogut, 1999; Doremus *et al.*, 1998)? Does this place German and Japanese MNEs at a disadvantage in terms of speed, agility and entrepreneurship in responding to emerging technologies or in engaging in international mergers and acquisitions?

SCIENTIFIC AND TECHNOLOGICAL REVOLUTIONS IN THE EARLY 21st CENTURY

A key feature of current developments in technology is increasing technological interdependence. For example, advances in IT, computers and communications depend on advances in materials (Kaounides, 1995b). In turn, advances in materials crucially depend on advances in computing power and mathematical modelling and simulations. Convergence of previously separate scientific and technological fields is occurring not only *within* the three main generic sciences – physics, chemistry and biology – but also *across* them, as exemplified by the scientific and technological convergence within nanotechnology (Kaounides, 1997b, 1999). These developments herald major changes in international business, the organisation and conduct of R&D globally, and the core capabilities of corporations and their strategic deployment across blurred industrial boundaries in complex webs and alliances.

The Revolution in Materials Science and Engineering

Since the mid-1980s we have witnessed a quiet, but far-reaching, revolution in the science and engineering foundations of all classes of materials (metals, polymers, ceramics and composites). We are increasingly able to design materials on the basis of a fundamental and quantitative understanding of their structure and its relation to resultant properties (Kaounides, 1995b, 1996a, b). This facilitates incremental improvement of existing, conventional materials up to their theoretical limits and the development of entirely new materials, which go beyond such performance limits and are tailored to meet the requirements of a specific application. This reverses the experience and design practices of the last two centuries of industrial capitalism, in that we can now start from a desirable configuration of properties and design and fabricate a material to meet these needs. Material scientists *and* engineers can now begin to intervene, reorder and remix the atomic and molecular structure of matter, and control its structure, properties and performance in use.

This, however, is not an easy undertaking and necessitates a close understanding of the relationship among a material's microstructure, its synthesis and processing path, and the resulting properties in use. This complex task requires the cumulative building of in-house generic knowledge and skills in several materials science and engineering disciplines, mathematical modelling and simulation techniques and advanced testing, measurement and characterisation capabilities. These are in addition to the required competences in specific materials, components, and devices and in systems integration (Chelsom and Kaounides, 1995). Those corporations that control materials technologies and have acquired the requisite skills over time will dominate relevant technologies and their performance in the 21st century. This observation acquires added significance with the beginnings of nanotechnology and the design and production of materials molecule by molecule, including the use of biological and self-assembly processes. Moreover, these developments indicate that materials producers must get close to customers (and vice versa) in formal or informal long-term alliances in order to design, fabricate and supply materials, components and systems that meet the performance, manufacturing or assembly needs of customers. The following case studies illustrate this.

Case Study 1 – The Alcoa–Audi Strategic R&D Alliance in Advanced Materials Technologies

Alcoa, the world's largest aluminium company, has been building up its in-house materials science and engineering core capabilities since the early to mid-1980s. The company believes that in order for suppliers and materials producers in particular, to be able to compete effectively in the materials markets of the next century, they must meet the prerequisites of an emerging technical paradigm. That is, companies must possess an increasing ability to define in quantitative terms, fundamentally understand and control a material's internal micro-structure, the processing path it goes through and its resulting properties and performance in specific application. They must then be able to apply this knowledge base to integrate the design of the material, the design of the product or component and the design of the manufacturing process. This must be accompanied by considerable skills in testing, evaluation and characterisation of the material embodied in such components and sub-assemblies whether they be for automotive, aerospace or other applications. The totality of these skills and knowledge is indispensable if companies are to be able to, as they are increasingly called upon to do, provide high performance net shape structural materials system solutions that are environmentally friendly and meet the needs of user industries. This also means that materials producers must get close to customers and understand these needs in terms of performance requirements and manufacturing and assembly of sub-assemblies and the final product. This requirement is exacerbated today as vehicle manufacturers increasingly concentrate on their core skills (e.g. design and assembly of passenger cell, engine, power train, suspension and car body) and require their first tier selected suppliers to provide even more complex sub-systems (which may include electronic systems) in the form of package solutions easily integrated into the assembly of the final product. Alcoa is of the view that suppliers that are unable to provide such tailored, high performance and ecologically sustainable materials systems solutions will be eliminated in a few years (Kaounides 1995b, 1996a, 1996b). It is important to note that Alcoa is also preparing for the arrival of physics-based nanophase materials design and nano-fabrication technologies, which will dramatically cut the R&D cycle in existing materials and will create entirely new materials in the first decade of the 21st century and beyond.

The future evolution of supplier–vehicle manufacturer relations in the global car industry can be illustrated by the far sighted Alcoa–Audi R&D alliance for the development of a new lightweight aluminium car body structure, which began in 1982 and persisted in its endeavours even when commercialisation was a technically difficult, distant and risky prospect. Environmental considerations, in the form of stricter emission regulations and the needs to reduce fuel consumption, hence reduce weight, led Audi to a search for a material lighter than steel and a partnership with Alcoa. The first commercial result of this long-run collaboration was a quantum leap in weight reduction technology and automotive structural manufacturing, embodied in the development of the aluminium space frame (ASF). The aluminium-intensive vehicle introduced by Audi in 1994 is a significant first step towards a 'green' car which is cost effective, high performance, low emission and recyclable.

Alcoa was able to apply its accumulated knowledge base in materials science and engineering to develop next generation advanced aluminium alloys and fabrication processes to deliver systems package solution that met the performance, manufacturing and assembly needs of Audi. Second and third generation advanced alloy systems are now under development. Whether aluminium can make inroads into the mass automotive markets by the early years of the next century, however, also depends on the response of steel producers who can also deploy the advances in materials science and engineering to improve performance. The aluminium intensive car has served as a 'wake up' call for steel producers who have formed international collaborative alliances with vehicle manufacturers to develop new genera-tions of advanced steels and car body structures to meet the challenge from aluminium.

Case Study 2 – Rolls-Royce: Core Materials Competences and External Partnerships

Rolls-Royce is putting a major emphasis on building its understanding of the science base and processing of materials in order to push incremental development of existing traditional materials (e.g. titanium and nickel) and to apply powerful computers and mathematical modelling techniques to assist the utilisation of new materials. Existing materials can be improved and new ones created through the use of computer modelling and materials science and engineering. This flexibility is essential for an aerospace company operating at the limits of materials. For Rolls-Royce, its future differentiation does not lie in the ability to invent and develop new materials. Rather it is focusing on two core competencies, *fundamental understanding* and the *application of materials*. This approach is consequently reshaping its R&D focus. Rolls-Royce collaborates across Europe, the US and Japan. Moreover it collaborates with universities in fundamental research (Figure 7.1) as, for example, the new technology centre at Cambridge University in mathematical modelling and simulation and in next generation nickel-based materials and future high temperature materials.

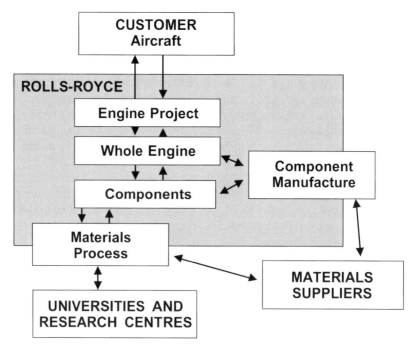

Figure 7.1 Integrated materials processes at Rolls-Royce. *Source*: Adapted by author from information provided by Rolls-Royce (Kaounides, 1995b).

Although alliances and partnerships are likely to prove essential in acquiring the range of technological competences required for effective innovation, central to the firm's ability to exploit the potential of new materials technology is the need to integrate effectively multiple sources and types of knowledge. In an area such as optoelectronics this implies substantial investment in developing in-house multidisciplinary knowledge, skills and competences in order to innovate and differentiate. These developments suggest that effective global technology strategies require, first, strategic alliances and global networks between materials producers and users and, second, coordination between firms and national governments.

The Life Sciences Revolution

It is claimed that biology has emerged as the dominant science of the 21st century (UK Office of Science and Technology, 1995b). Powerful new research tools and the deeper understanding in areas such as molecular and cell biology, genetics and advanced instrumentation techniques are now making it possible to resolve biological questions (e.g. the functioning of the brain or of the immune system) that would have been intractable even a few years ago. These scientific advances are also leading to important improvements in molecular and bioprocess design, and the production of food, chemicals and materials through biological systems. Moreover, the application of advanced information technology to the life sciences together with the deciphering of the human, plant and animal genome (likely to be completed by the early years of the century) will lead to significant new advances and applications in the life sciences.

These rapid advances in generic biological technologies are creating opportunities both in existing industries and for the creation of entirely new industries, across health care, medicine, food and nutrition, environmental management, chemical synthesis and manufacture, and agriculture and non-food agricultural products. In environmental technologies, for example, it may be possible to solve existing problems using genetically modified micro-organisms and plants in bioremediation or to provide biological manufacture in plants and animals as a more environmentally friendly approach than current production methods.

The innovation process in the health and life sciences industries involves far stronger linkages to basic research than most other high technology industries, including electronics. Discoveries in basic medical research, for example, have a direct and immediate relevance for diagnostics and therapeutics. New biotechnology and bioengineering companies tend, therefore, to cluster in close proximity to academic centres of excellence in basic research, and, moreover, maintain strong links with university departments and centres. Furthermore, a common mechanism by which small startups and large companies acquire new skills and competences is the transfer of key academic researchers from universities. Anderson *et al.* (1996) point out that patents taken out in the UK tend to refer to UK-based scientific publications and this strong and direct link between the domestic science base and domestic patenting activity has empirical support for several other countries.

Biotechnology advances and strategic alliances
A mere four or five years ago, the US drugs industry was bracing itself for a scarcity of new targets, the need for differentiated drugs, containment of escalating R&D costs, the need to exploit economies of scale, and the growth of managed care. The prospects for the drug companies were transformed by the arrival of a large number of late-stage innovative drugs available from biotechnology firms and from medium-sized companies, which could not market on their own. This coincided with the explosion in new targets and compound diversity ushered in by combinatorial chemistry and genomics. As a result, the industry refocussed on enhancing R&D productivity, plugging product gaps and marketing innovative branded products, including those aimed at niche rather than large markets. The result has been an upsurge in the number and value of strategic alliances between biotechnology and pharmaceutical companies. These have involved upfront and milestone research payments, licensing deals, and the sale of marketing rights, especially for Phase III drugs. Technological tools and platforms, many of which did not exist even six years ago, include genomics, combinatorial chemistry, high throughput screening and bioinformatics. These developments have tended to increase the critical mass of the R&D effort (at present around $2 billion) encouraging the globalisation of the R&D process, the consolidation in the life sciences industry, and the formation of strategic alliances between the large pharmaceutical companies and small biotech start-ups (see Figures 7.2 and 7.3, and Kaounides, 1997b).

Advances in Optoelectronics, Computers and Communications

Advances in computers and communications 1990s–2010s
In recent years a convergence has been underway between the previously discreet fields of computers, electronics and optoelectronics, communications (fixed wireline, optical and radio, mobile, computer and telecoms networking) and media and content technology. This process has been pushed forward by continuous advances in the technologies underpinning these converging fields, namely microelectronics, photonics and radio (UK Office of Science and Technology, 1995a). These rapid developments are accompanied by technological discontinuities in several areas including the arrival of multimedia, the creation of networks and interconnectivity

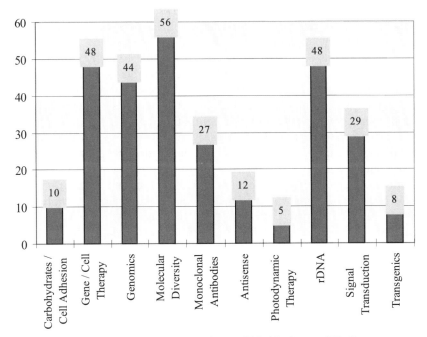

Figure 7.2 Biotech alliances by technology, 1995–98. *Source*: Windhover Information Inc. (Norwalk, CT) in Ernst & Young (1996).

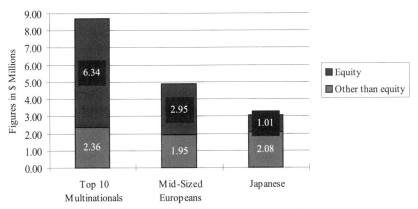

Figure 7.3 Upfront alliance payments. (Includes deals in which there was a known upfront payment.) *Source*: Windhover Information Inc. (Norwalk, CT) in Ernst & Young (1996).

on a global scale, and the advent of low-cost portable computers and cellular phones facilitating access to information from almost anywhere, at any time. In an overview of the sector, the UK Technology Foresight Programme identified the main deliverables of the sector as being software systems (e.g. applications, frameworks, generics and basics), electronic systems (e.g. sensors, processors, memories) and, increasingly, content, that is packages of interactive media information.

The value chains of these deliverables are complex, but they share many common supporting technologies and components. Software developed for specific applications (e.g. word processing) becomes more generic, and is increasingly incorporated within the computer's systems software (assisted by the continuous increase of the computing hardware). Underpinning developments in software and electronic systems (e.g. networks; applications technologies including robotics, computer-aided design (CAD), computer-assisted engineering (CAE) and computer-integrated manufacture (CIM), systems management; human–computer interaction; and production technology) are fundamental innovations such as technologies of compression, storage, sensing, displays, devices (e.g. Si (silicon) or GaAs (gallium arsenide)), radio, radar and power sources. These depend upon a multidisciplinary science base comprising computer science, mathematics, materials science, microelectronics, photonics, control, instrumentation and communications. It is notable that advances in the capacity to process, transmit and store information, as well as recent developments in multimedia and the Internet, are to a large degree materials-dependent.

The convergence of previously separate fields and the consequent discontinuities in digital communication networks, portability and mobility and in media technology, are creating the conditions for a new growth spurt in these markets. This will be based on a transition from the professional to the consumer mass market, the advent of electronic commerce on a global scale and the massive expansion of digital media content. The globally interconnected economy is at hand with predictions of one billion interconnected computers in the near future and a billion transistors on each computer after 2010!

The information technology, electronics/optoelectronics and communication sector is a global business dominated by large corporations possessing substantial financial, technological and organisational capabilities. At the same time, the challenges of developing new technologies, fusing existing technological streams, and operating at the interface of previously discrete industries pose huge challenges, particularly regarding the choice between in-house versus outsourced and networked skills and resources. The challenges of technology-based industries also present key issues at the national level in terms of maintaining a strong national presence. The UK is the fifth largest electronics producer in the world, largely based on its ability to attract inward investment by technology-based MNEs, including those originating from newly industrialising economies such as Taiwan and the Republic of Korea. However, the fragility of a strategy that has emphasised the inflow of FDI in specific sectors has been underscored by the project cancellations and plant closures in the wake of the 1998 banking crisis in the Far East.

Nanotechnology

All technologies at present use large aggregations of atoms. Using advanced processing technologies we can create materials atomic layer by atomic layer. The era of nanotechnology has come first to electronics and opto-electronics but we can anticipate by the early 2010s a more widespread ability to build matter atom by atom and molecule by molecule. Despite the difficulties in building machines and devices at that level, enthusiasts predict a multi-billion dollar industry that will revolutionise all known technologies, products and manufacturing processes (Kaounides, 1995b, 1996a, 1996b).

Managing Convergent Technologies: the Japanese Model

Japanese companies have been leaders in managing technological conver-gence, especially in the fields of optoelectonics, computing and commu-nication. This leadership has been most apparent in consumer electronics and office equipment. Traditionally, this management of convergence has been through the integration of existing technologies. More recently a new paradigm of Japanese technology management has emerged with increased emphasis on knowledge creation through R&D (Kodama, 1995). This para-digm involves the articulation of future market requirements into the conceptualisation of concrete products and the identification of the mate-rials, components and technologies required for such products. This drives technological diversification, technology sourcing through alliances, the creation of hybrid technologies such as optoelectronics and mechatronics, and the 'parallel sequencing' of product families and technologies.

The outcome may be discernible differences in the organisation and horizontal co-ordination of R&D management within Japanese firms as compared to their American and European counterparts. Japanese managers appear not to allow financial returns and sophisticated tools to dictate R&D decisions. Rather, a careful consideration is given to the technological requirements that are necessary to remain competitive in the world market. However, the crisis following 1997 has placed great strain on Japanese companies' relations with banks and threatened the entire stability of the keiretsu system.

A consequence of technological concergence is that competition in Japan is inter-industry as opposed to inter-firm. In optical fibres, for example, technological leadership in Japan has switched from industry to industry, from glass manufacturers to communication device manufacturers and from communication enterprises to cable manufacturers. The leading innovations at each stage originated from different industries and as this occurred, dramatic technological developments ensued. Moreover, joint research projects undertaken spanned the boundaries of the different indus-trial sectors. The innovation cycle here is a multi-layered spiral with R&D

carried on simultaneously in several industries, and the leaders in each cycle solving technological problems by using competences accumulated in their own sector.

In microelectronics, metal oxide semiconductor DRAM devices have, on average, followed a 3-year innovation cycle since 1972, so that when a new product is introduced the production of the previous one declines dramatically even as its price falls. Firms cannot survive unless they invest in R&D for the development of next generation products. Here, Kodama (1995) argues that investment decisions cannot be made on the basis of the rate of return but rather on the 'principle of surf riding': either a company invests in successive waves of innovations or they sink as competitors surge ahead riding next generation products. The following case study offers some examples of these approaches to technology management and product development.

Case Study 3 – Toshiba's R&D Organisation and Strategy

'Parallel sequencing' involves the overlapped development of sequential generations of a product line and its associated technologies. This strategy is supported at Toshiba by its widely imitated three-tier R&D organisation. Central corporate laboratories at Tier 1 conduct basic research with a 5–10 year (or more) time horizon, in such fields as information processing, new materials and hardware and software technologies. Toshiba's Cambridge research centre in the UK also conducts fundamental research into the physics of semiconductor materials and collaborates with the R&D centre in Tokyo. Tier 2 development laboratories belong to the individual business groups or divisions (e.g. Information and Communications, Multimedia, Microelectronics, New Materials) and conduct research on product-orientated next-generation technologies that would be commercialised within a 3–5-year time span. The development results in Tier 2 are eventually incorporated into current products and new models at the Tier 3 engineering departments of business groups or divisions dispersed throughout Toshiba's manufacturing facilities. The time frame here is up to three years. This innovation process clearly illustrates the importance of intra- and inter-organisational teamwork and routines in learning, knowledge creation and application, further elaborated below.

'Parallel Sequencing' of Semiconductor Memory Devices
The three tier R&D system can be illustrated in the case of the development of successive generations of memory devices. (Kaounides, 1995b). The corporate R&D centre is engaged in research on new materials, devices and process technologies with five years or more to commercialisation, and is currently involved in R&D on 256M bit DRAM's and beyond. The Tier 2 Semiconductor Device Engineering Laboratory (SDEL) is carrying out

research on next generation products to be commercialised within 3–5 years. The engineering departments are involved in current generation 16M bit DRAM families and are continually improving production methods, costs and yields.

Each generation of DRAM R&D is transferred between the three layers or tiers. Each tier is responsible for developing the requisite technologies, that would be transferred to the next tier. As the R&D programme of the corporate laboratory for a certain DRAM generation nears its end, the SDEL allocates R&D resources to form a joint project and receives the research results and working samples from the corporate laboratory. As R&D progresses on this generation of DRAM in the SDEL, the engineering department joins the joint project, enabling its engineers to master the technologies transferred from Tier 1 and Tier 2 by the time the SDEL has completed its working sample. The engineering department develops the latter into complete DRAM samples and supports its commercialisation and volume production at factory level. Successive generations of technology become increasingly complex, difficult and costly, hence Toshiba seeks alliances in complementary technologies, in moving for example from 256M bit to 1G bit technologies. One such alliance is that formed recently between Toshiba, IBM and Siemens (Kaounides, 1995b). Strategic technology alliances are central to Toshiba's technology and business strategy.

Focus on Electronics and Energy (E&E) Related Businesses
The overlapped development approach must, however, be taken in context. Toshibas's strategic focus in the longrun is on electronics and energy (E&E) related businesses, including information/communications systems and electronics devices, heavy electrical apparatus and consumer products (including HDTV's, multimedia, air conditioners and refrigerators). Speed is of the essence for Toshiba and this has underpinned its efforts for several years now to restructure and reshape its global operations. Since 1994, the urgent priority has become the speed with which the company can direct resources to promising new market opportunities. Hence the launching of the Advanced-I project, in order to enable the company *to draw upon its vast global resources* in order to achieve leadership in products and systems that fuse information, communications and visual technologies. This project eliminates barriers across the company and business groups, facilitates the sharing of technologies and provides speed and autonomy in decision making in commercialising new products that are not related to existing business lines. The aim is to place the company at the forefront of multimedia developments, given that it already possesses leadership positions in technologies that are essential in portable multimedia products (e.g. components such as semiconductors, LCD's, rechargeable batteries, portable PC's and digital video disk).

In 1992, Toshiba implemented a fundamental reorganisation of its corporate research, in order to facilitate cross-fertilisation and exchange of information, ideas and people across the laboratories, while integrating R&D activities horizontally across business groups and divisions. This was done in order to meet the requirements for successful R&D in the 1990s and beyond. The key requirement today is that R&D must generate innovative and breakthrough technologies, as compared to more predictable developments in the 1980s (illustrated by memory devices above).

THE INTERNATIONALISATION OF R&D AND THE ROLE OF STRATEGIC ALLIANCES IN CORE TECHNOLOGIES

International Strategic Alliances

In the 1980s and 1990s there was an increasing trend towards the internationalisation of industry's R&D and technology sourcing and location activities (OECD, 1991a, 1992; Hagedoorn, 1995; Hagedoorn and Schakenraad, 1990, 1992, 1993; US National Science Board, 1996). In academia, there has been a large increase in cross-country collaborative research in the form of co-authorships in the last ten years. Moreover, in some countries, international collaboration in research in the public sector as a whole now accounts for up to 10% of government R&D spend. International collaboration by western countries includes bilateral collaboration with other countries and 'megascience' programmes, whose size and scope necessitate multinational participation (e.g. global climate change).

In the private sector, R&D collaboration across national borders through inter-firm collaboration has been increasing sharply, especially in core generic technologies such as information technology, biotechnology and new materials. In the period 1977–1980 there were 177 known technology alliances created, in 1981–1984 there were 509, and in 1985–1988 these increased sharply to 988. Although the formation of such strategic inter-firm, cross-border alliances in high technology slowed down somewhat in the 1990–1994 period, according to the most recently available data (US National Science Foundation, 1996) these were comparable to those entered into in the mid-1980's.

This overall rise in international R&D collaboration in industry has been accompanied by a change in the nature of these partnerships. In the 1970s the main form was that of joint ventures and research corporations where a new entity was formed with each of the equity partners sharing the profit or losses generated proportionately. However as the 1980s progressed and into the 1990s, the most prevalent form of partnerships was that of the non-equity R&D agreement in which partners pursued similar innovations and shared in the technologies so generated while reducing the cost and risk of

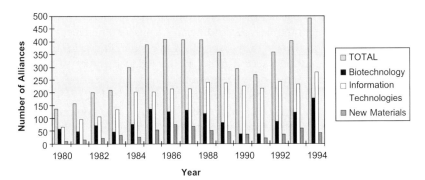

Figure 7.4 Number of strategic technology alliances by selected technology, 1980–94.
Source: J. Hagedoorn, Cooperative agreements and technology indicators data base in
Science & Engineering indicators, NRC 1996

doing so. Both non-equity and equity partnerships are prevalent in the core
generic technologies, as shown in Figure 7.4.

Internationalisation of R&D

An increasing proportion of companies' R&D is performed outside of their
home countries. The expansion of overseas R&D facilities has followed the
needs for overseas production facilities to adapt products to local markets
and to utilise local technology. In the US, between 1980 and 1993, industry's
offshore R&D investment increased three times faster than the increase in
domestically performed R&D, and now counts for over 10% of the total.
The largest percentage share and rate of growth of overseas R&D by
US companies was the R&D investment in chemicals companies and their
subsidiaries including pharmaceutical and industrial chemicals. In fact,
pharmaceuticals accounted for about 30% of total overseas R&D invest-
ment in 1993 or equivalent to 17% of domestically performed R&D by
US pharmaceuticals companies. Although the greater part of US overseas
R&D is directed towards Europe (about 76%), there has been a trend by
US corporations to increase R&D spending in Asia (US National Science
Foundation, 1995).

At the same time, there has been an expansion of R&D spending by
foreign-owned companies in the US. Between 1980 and 1993, R&D activities by foreign firms in the US grew by more than three times the rate of
growth of R&D performed domestically by US firms. Four-fifths of this rise
originated from just five countries: Japan, Switzerland, the UK, Germany
and France, and of these, the most rapid increase is attributable to Japan
and Switzerland. The expansion in foreign R&D expenditures in the US has

been accompanied by acceleration in the establishment of R&D facilities in the US by foreign companies. According to an important recent study of 635 US R&D facilities owned by over 300 European, Japanese and South Korean companies in 1994 (see Table 7.1) the R&D facilities of Japanese firms far outnumber those of other nations. The concentration of foreign R&D facilities by industry is as follows: biotechnology (111), chemicals and rubber (109), automotive (52), computer software (41), commuters (39), and semiconductors. The selected localities in the US were: Silicon Valley, Los Angeles, Detroit, Boston, Princeton NJ and North Carolina's Research Triangle Park. Japanese companies identified the acquisition of technology, keeping in touch with technological advances and assisting the parent corporation in meeting US customers' needs as key reasons for the location of R&D in the US. Much of the basic research conducted in the US by foreign companies is in pharmaceuticals and biotechnology, enabling them to reach into and participate in formal and informal local networks in the generation and distribution of scientific knowledge in the biosciences and chemistry.

This trend is also reflected in foreign R&D conducted in other economies with the largest R&D activities, except Japan (where it has remained at 0.1% of domestic industrial R&D between 1981–1993). The proportion of foreign R&D to total domestic R&D in France, the UK and Canada ranges between 12 and 18%, and between 3 and 6% for Italy and Germany in 1992. For the 12 members of the then European Community this proportion rose from 5.5% in 1981 to over 7% in 1992.

'TECHNO-GLOBALISM' VERSUS 'TECHNO-NATIONALISM'

In a globalised world economy where technology, finance, goods and information flow relatively unhindered across national boundaries have national technology policies become obsolete? Even if successful in boosting the a technological edge of domestic firms, government-induced knowledge creation is likely to offer only short-lived advantages as technology seeps across national borders to overseas competitors. Here, cross-border alliances and networks could act as mechanisms for the diffusion of scientific and technology-based knowledge across national frontiers. Another mechanism could be the domestic location of laboratories and design centres belonging to foreign MNE's, and/or links and networks between academic institutions globally. The key questions here are (i) whether these very same mechanisms, which could lead to leakages and de-skilling, are essential today for the *inflow* of complementary scientific expertise in the generation of local knowledge and dynamic spillover effects in cumulative virtuous circles, and (ii) whether home MNEs and their national system

Table 7.1 Foreign-owned R&D facilities in the US, 1994

	Total	Japan	UK	Germany	France	Switzerland	South Korea	Netherlands	Sweden	Other
Total	635	219	109	95	52	45	26	26	22	41
Computers	39	22	0	4	0	0	7	3	0	3
Software	41	25	6	4	3	0	1	1	0	1
Semiconductors	35	19	0	3	0	0	10	3	0	0
Telecommunications	29	14	2	4	2	1	1	0	2	3
Opto-electronics	20	11	2	3	0	0	0	0	1	3
HDTV, other electronics	71	33	10	9	4	5	3	4	0	3
Drugs, biotechnology	111	22	23	18	11	17	1	5	5	9
Chemicals, rubber, materials	109	23	19	28	17	10	0	4	0	8
Metals	15	5	3	1	4	1	0	0	1	0
Automotive	53	34	1	11	2	0	3	0	2	0
Machinery	22	7	4	2	3	0	0	0	6	0
Instrumentation, controls	40	1	23	3	5	4	0	3	1	0
Foods, consumer goods, misc.	53	7	7	6	2	6	0	5	1	7

Note: The sums by industry may not add to the country totals because of cross-industry R&D facilities.
Source: D.H. Dalton and M.G. Sherapio, Jr. U.S. Research Facilities of Foreign Companies (Washington, DC: Department of Commerce, Technology Administration/Japan Technology Program, 1995).

of innovation (NSI) can, in isolation, operate on the frontier of research excellence. The potential redundancy of national technology policies results from convergence of the economies of the major industrialised economies, resulting in speedier imitation of competitive advantages.

National Technology Policies in East Asia

Despite acceleration in the rates of global diffusion of new technologies, governments in a number of East Asian countries have increased their emphasis on national innovation policies. For example:

• In Japan, technology promotion has its legal foundation in the Science and Technology Fundamental Law of November 1995). The Basic Plan specified a sum of 17 billion yen over the 5-year period 1996–2001, providing a boost to basic research, and identified the need for Japan to pursue more original scientific and technological research in several fundamental fields of seminal importance to Japanese society and industry. In early 1999 spending was according to plan. Given the constraints of an ageing population and very high public sector deficits (100% of GDP at present), science and technology are seen as the key instruments enabling Japan to achieve the necessary productivity and growth in the next century, without 'hollowing out'. Fransman (1999) showed that Japan responded to the globalisation of science and technology by internationalising its national R&D programmes and by creating new international scientific projects, both of which were still designed to meet national objectives.

• Taiwan's White Paper on Science and Technology charts a blueprint for science and technology development in the next century. The Paper points to the 'ambitious government sponsored high-tech development plans' of Singapore, the Republic of Korea and Malaysia and the need for increasing emphasis on basic research with close collaboration between university researchers and industry. Taiwan expanded its R&D spending from US$ 0.81 billion in 1986 to US$ 4.58 billion in 1995 (1.81% of GDP) in 1995. Taiwan now has the world's third largest information industry, and fourth largest semiconductor industry. Building on the existing industrial infrastructure and human capital in science and technology, the Paper sets out several strategic objectives, including improvements in institutional coordination and inter-organisational information flows and linkages. R&D expenditure is planned to increase to 2.5% of GDP by the year 2000 and to 3.0% of GDP by 2005, with frontier research comprising of 15% of total R&D. National science and technology programmes include telecoms, disaster prevention, human genome and agricultural biotechnology. Taiwan intends to become a 'high-tech island' in the early years of this century, with the creation of more science parks in order to accelerate this shift. Each new science park is expected to contain around 200 high tech firms with an annual turnover of NT$ 400 billion. Around the core science parks, public/ private high-tech parks, research parks and software parks will be established. These high-tech industrial parks will serve as nuclei for the development of 'science cities', which will be linked by the National Information Infrastructure Programme now being implemented.

• Singapore is also strengthening its technology and human resource base by building world class research facilities, tertiary institutions and physical infrastructure at the science parks, with the government allocating US$ 2 billion in the early 1990s to an R&D fund in order to develop skills, manpower and technologies required by industry. The government has been recruiting 200 foreign research scientists and engineers annually over a five-year period. Singapore poses the location issue in its most clear form: government policy attempts to keep the infrastructure sufficiently attractive to retain the thousands of footloose MNEs comprising its economy and to attract new ones, including R&D and design centres.

• The Republic of Korea began implementing an ambitious 'Highly Advanced National Project' between 1992 and 2001, where the public sector will spend US$ 3 billion over the period with matching funds from the private sector. It aims to establish Korea as a major scientific and technological power to challenge Japan and Western economies in the 21st century. Seven new market technologies (next generation integrated semi-conductors; integrated services and data network; HDTV; electric vehicle; intelligent computers; antibiotics and chemicals for agriculture; advanced manufacturing systems) and seven fundamental or basic technologies (advanced materials; next generation transport systems; biotechnology; environmental technologies; new energy resources; new atomic reactor; human interface technology) have been selected for government-industry-academia long run collaborative R&D. The project has passed its half-way mark and the indications are that significant progress has been made. In 1998 the government began to emphasise basic research, along the Japanese example.

National Innovation Systems and Knowledge-based Economies

The OECD (1996a–d) has focussed attention on the growing investment in high technology, the employment of high-skilled labour and the associated rise of 'knowledge-based' economies, which are increasingly based on the creation, diffusion and use of information and knowledge. Here, knowledge and technology are the key drivers of economic growth and productivity, and knowledge-generating investments in R&D, education and training programmes and new management structures play a central role in the dynamics of growth in an economy. Moreover, the distribution of knowledge through both formal and informal mechanisms and networks is an essential determinant of economic performance at the micro- and macro-economic level. Codified knowledge is transmitted through computer and communications networks within the firm, across firms and across institutions and nations. Tacit knowledge, which contains the ability to understand, modify, adapt and utilise codified knowledge, is also, therefore, an essential component of innovation and economic performance, and highlights the need for, and critical importance of, continuous learning by individuals, firms and institutions in an economy. Innovation in the knowledge-based economy is an interactive process involving cooperation and communication between different agents (firms, universities, laboratories and individuals) and the transfer and exchange of codified and tacit knowledge.

The innovative performance of an economy can therefore be conceptualised to be a result of the networks and interactions between different economic agents and institutions comprising the national system of innovation, which is now reaching out and forming links internationally, engaged in the creation, distribution and application of knowledge (Kaounides, 1999). Consequently, these interactions and flows between industry, academia and the government in a NSI strongly affect the innovative performance of firms, industries and economies. In this framework, the ability of a NSI to ensure timely access to the necessary stocks of knowledge, the efficiency with which knowledge is distributed and utilised along country-specific diffusion paths and technology trajectories will have a determining impact on the innovative performance of individual firms as well as on the economy as a whole. The concept of the knowledge-driven economy fully underpins the current UK industrial policy and is diffusing in other OECD economies.

Government intervention therefore plays a key role in the provision of education and training programmes for highly skilled human capital, the formation of collaborative programmes, the distribution of knowledge and the diffusion of technology, and the promotion of organisational change at the firm level. The policies can maximise gains from advances in scientific knowledge and technology. Government research laboratories and universities comprise the core of the science base of an economy, historically performing the role of scientific knowledge creation through basic research and the education of scientists and engineers. This *remains of paramount importance* given the science-based generic technologies discussed above. Increasingly, however, in the networked knowledge economy, the science system must also play a new role in terms of industry collaboration for the diffusion and transfer of knowledge and technology. At the centre of these global multi-polar knowledge creating activities and networks will increasingly be MNE's developing and implementing integrated production and research strategies which take advantage of the benefits of different locations and NSI in order to achieve global corporate strategic objectives. Effectively integrating R&D organisations across cultures and nations is, however, a complex managerial task.

The diffusion of information technologies in knowledge-based economies and the rapid growth in the availability of low-cost information are inexorably leading to the need for the acquisition and continuous upgrading of the requisite skills and competencies to understand, select, and use codified knowledge. Hence, efforts to learn skills, and other forms of tacit knowledge to obtain and apply new codified knowledge and theoretical and analytical research findings, become critical factors in the innovation process. In a knowledge-based economy education, training and learning skills in both codified and tacit knowledge become primary determinants of the advancement, performance and employment opportunities at the level of the individual, the firm and the national economy (OECD, 1996d). An essential component of this process is 'learning by doing', which facilitates the cumulative and iterative transformation of tacit into codified knowledge, and through practical experience, back into new forms of tacit knowledge, and so on.

The firm, therefore, must itself become a continuously learning organisation, right across its managerial, organisational and skills base in order to be able to access and apply new scientific and technological information and knowledge. This internal learning process is complemented and enhanced through the formation of inter-organisational networks engaged in interactive learning and skill acquisition. This conforms to the rising importance of not only the creation of knowledge but also its dissemination, transfer and application. In this context, where know-how and skills are of importance, strategic skills and competencies are developed and shared interactively within networks of firms and other institutions within national systems of innovation. Consequently, the ability to access such networks and join interactive learning processes determines the economic influence of individuals and firms (David and Foray, 1995). This fits in with the now prevalent view of the innovation process as involving several actors (e.g. universities, firms and the market) and feedback relations across *several* points in the knowledge and information process, that is between scientific research, engineering, product development and marketing.

In this view, firms form external alliances, linkages and networks in order to promote inter-organisational learning and access complementary assets, technologies and skills. Besides pooling costs and risks in product and process innovation, sharing manufacturing, distribution and marketing costs, collaborative alliances and partnerships also enable firms to gain access to new research results and complementary technologies in product development. Here firms need to identify in-house skills, those that are to be developed in alliance with outside partners, and those activities that are to be outsourced.

CONCLUSIONS

Science-based Generic Technological Revolutions

In this chapter, we examined the nature of the revolutions in the scientific and engineering foundations of several frontier technologies underpinning existing industries and the creation of new industries in the 21st century. These advances range across materials science, the biosciences and IT/electronics/communications (including the underlying sciences of photonics and electronics. These advances are characterised by:

- global competition from research clusters in geographically dispersed locations
- complementary and convergence between scientific disciplines and technologies such that products and services combine previously discreet technologies and are therefore becoming dependent upon the *fusion* of once separate technologies
- such technological convergence and fusion requires the building of interfirm networks which span national borders and drive the internationalisation of scientific and technological activities by both private and public sector organisations and institutions.

Management Tasks

Management tasks for the 21st century include the organisation and management of the R&D and innovation process in conditions of increasing complexity, rapid change, eroding boundaries, scientific and technological convergence and consequent discontinuities, and the use of in-house and externally sourced knowledge to fuse related and converging technologies into new products and processes to be exploited worldwide. It is clear that firms must also develop skills for managing continuous and, in many cases, unanticipated change, the creation of change as a competitive weapon, and in predicting the arrival of new, possibly disruptive (Christensen, 1998), technologies and products creating major shifts in their markets.

Managing Technology and Strategic Alliances Across Different National Systems of Innovation

The local clusters of scientific knowledge production are embedded into national systems of innovation, with different historical and cultural backgrounds and different mechanisms through which information and knowledge is distributed and applied. Here the role of national governments becomes critical in not merely correcting for market failure in knowledge generation, but also in guiding the creation and development of local clusters through investment incentives, establishing the necessary infrastructure of information and scientific research and training, and standards and regulation (Tassey, 1992).

The multidisciplinary, multi-polar and multi-nodal nature of scientific and technological advance necessitates that firms form linkages to access knowledge from academia and government laboratories and other firms. This necessitates the formation and implementation of global R&D and production location strategies that are strongly integrated with corporate strategic objectives at senior management level. In the same way that the knowledge creation capabilities and performance of a nation will depend on the nature of its global scientific linkages and alliances, corporate R&D performance will increasingly depend on the quality and in-house management of scientific and technology-based knowledge generation alliances and networks that span the globe. Toshiba's ability to develop next generation semiconductor devices at the atomic scale (Kaounides, 1995b) depended not only on the accumulated knowledge base of its central laboratories in Japan and their networks within the Japanese NSI but also on the location of a basic research laboratory in Cambridge Science Park, UK, and its alliance with renowned scientists in physics at Cambridge University. In short, Toshiba needed to participate in the UK's national system of innovation.

Internationalisation and Location of R&D Facilities Abroad

Historically, firms have located development facilities close to manufacuring plants in order to assist the development and commercialisation of increasingly complex products (Kuemmerle, 1997). However, given the rapid advance of multidisciplinary scientific knowledge at several focal points internationally (in the same and other related and complementary fields) MNEs have no choice but to form deep linkages with such sources, engage actively in the process of information gathering, knowledge creation and learning, and to deploy this within corporate-wide networks and research programmes aimed at meeting corporate strategic objectives.

There is therefore an increasing need for companies to locate R&D facilities abroad, not simply to find out what research is being done (this does not necessitate location abroad today) but also to recruit local scientists and researchers, and to form links with local science, university and industry networks embedded in national systems of innovation. That is companies need to *participate* in local networks and information flows and manage the two-way flows of tacit and codified knowledge, create new knowledge and integrate it into globally located R&D facilities and strategies.

Is the Japanese and/or the Asian Capitalist Model Fatally Wounded?

The ability of MNEs to respond to the scientific and technological imperatives outlined above depends to a great extent on their historical origins and roots within their own NSI. Here we distinguish between the Anglo-American system and the Rhineland system (Albert, 1993; OECD, 1995). Japan's move to the technology frontier in several fields has created the need to change its system of innovation from that it pursued during its catch-up phase (Okimoto,1989; Kaounides, 1995a, 1996b, 1999b). The Japanese NSI increasingly focuses upon building capabilities in basic research, invention and creativity, where the Anglo-American system excels. Japan and other Asian economies have placed greater emphasis on the promotion of science and technology as the key to productivity and growth in the next century. We should expect that the Asian financial crisis will lead to an even *greater* emphasis on and promotion of science and technology in the future. Given the historically and institutionally accumulated strengths of the Japanese corporate and national mechanisms for innovation in recognising, systematically pursuing and and fusing emerging technologies, we should expect these strengths and capabilities to reassert themselves again in the next decade. Indeed, Japanese MNEs may emerge stronger from the current recession and financial crisis. The restructuring announced by Sony and Nissan in 1999, involving large job cuts and reorganisation in order to take advantage of Internet technologies may herald a sea change in Japanese corporate attitudes producing greater flexibility and agility with greater attention to shareholder value and rates of return.

Notes

1. This process is questioned by Kozul-Wright and Rowthorn (1998) who focus on the regional nature of FDI activities by MNEs.
2. Albert (1993) examines the characteristics and performance of the neo-liberal, market-orientated, entrepreneurial Anglo-American capitalist model (see also Thurow, 1993; OECD, 1995), which competes against the more financially cautious, communitarian, socially responsible and long-run orientated Rhine model, which stretches from northern Europe via post-war Germany to Switzerland in continental Europe and encompassing, in part, Japan. Germany encapsulates a liberal economic regime where the state plays a strong but limited role ('ordo-liberalism') while sharing with other Rhine model economies the values of an egalitarian society, and where the interests of the group take precedence over the interests of the individual: companies, trade unions and other organisations to which individuals belong are regarded as communities providing protection and a social structure making for stability. Within companies, the Rhine model emphasises mutuality and shared responsibility. In Germany, joint management or 'co-responsibility' ('Mitbestimmung') in decision making brings together shareholders, employees, executives and trade unions in a community of interests around a long-run view of investment and growth. This 'stakeholder' form of organisation differs from the 'stockholder' model, which concentrates exclusively on who owns shares in a business. A somewhat different set of concepts and institutions in Japan (e.g. 'amae' and 'iemoto') and the characteristics of Japanese corporate life (e.g. life-time employment, seniority-based payments systems, group incentive schemes and the keiretsu system) result in the same collective

feeling of belonging to a community. The OECD (1995) provides a distinction between two major archetypal financial systems and their implications for the financing of innovation: *market-based systems* (USA, UK) characterised by reliance, in the main, on financial securities in obtaining external capital and which have a clear separation between ownership and control, and *credit-based systems* (Japan, Germany, France, Sweden, developing countries), where banks play a key role in the supply of external finance and in corporate governance as partners in corporate management. The latter system makes for more stable, long-run relations between finance and industry within NSI and a focus on the deployment of funds in projects of a longer run nature. The OECD finds no evidence that the internationalisation of finance has led to the predominance of the Anglo-American model over the credit-based system. Rather, both systems seem to be retaining the most relevant and beneficial characteristics of their systems while adapting to the changes ushered in by globalisation.

References

Albert, M. (1993) *Capitalism Versus Capitalism* (New York: Four Walls Eight Windows).

Anderson, J. *et al.* (1996) 'Human genetic technology: exploring the links between science and innovation', *Technological Analysis and Strategic Management*, 8(2): 106–126.

Chelsom, J. and Kaounides, L. (1995) 'The materials revolution', in D. Bennett and F. Stewart (eds) *Technological Innovation and Global Challenges*, Proceedings of the European Conference on the Management of Technology, Aston University, Birmingham, 5th–7th July.

Christensen, C.M. (1998) *The Innovator's Dilemma: When New Technologies Cause Great Firms to Fail* (Boston, MA: Harvard Business School Press).

David, P. and Foray, D. (1995) 'Accessing and expanding the science and technology knowledge-base', *OECD STI Review*, 16: 16–21.

Dicken, P. (1998) *Global Shift*, 3rd edn (London: Macmillan).

Doremus, P.N. *et al.* (1998) *The Myth of the Global Corporation* (Princeton, NJ: Princeton University Press).

Ernst & Young (1996) *Biotech 97: Alignment, An Industry Annual Report* (Palo Alto, CA: Ernst & Young LLP).

Fransman, M. (1999) *Visions of Innovation: The Firm and Japan* (New York: Oxford University Press).

Freeman, C. (1987) *Technology Policy and Economic Performance: Lessons from Japan* (London: Pinter).

Freeman, C. (1997) 'National systems of innovation', in D. Archibugi and J. Michie (eds) *Technology, Globalisation and Economic Performance* (Cambridge: Cambridge University Press).

Hagedoorn, J. (ed.) (1995) *Technical Change and the World Economy* (Aldershot: Edward Elgar).

Hagedoorn, J. and Schakenraad, J. (1990) 'Inter-firm partnerships and cooperative strategies in core technologies', in C. Freeman, and L. Soete (eds) *New Explorations in the Economic of Technological Change* (London: Pinter).

Hagedoorn, J. and Schakenraad, J. (1992) 'Leading companies and networks of strategic alliance in information technologies', *Research Policy*, 12: 163–190.

Hagedoorn, J and Schakenraad J. (1994) 'The effect of strategic technology alliances on company performance', *Strategic Management Journal*, 17: 291–309.

Kaounides, L. (1995a) 'Advanced materials in high technology and world class manufacturing', *Advanced Materials Technology Series*, Series 1 (Vienna: UNIDO), March.

Kaounides, L. (1995b) 'Advanced materials: corporate strategies for competitive advantage, Management Report' (London: Financial Times), December.

Kaounides, L. (1996a) 'New materials and simultaneous engineering in the car industry: the Alcoa–Audi alliance in lightweight aluminium body structures', in *Manufacturing Technology* (London: Institution of Mechanical Engineers Publications) pp. 157–169.

Kaounides, L. (1996b) 'Materials science and engineering', in *World Science Report* (Paris: UNESCO) pp. 260–281.

Kaounides, L. (1997b) 'The core technical competencies of the corporation in the 21st century', 7th International Forum on Technology Management, 5th–7th November (Kyoto, Japan).

Kaounides, L. (1999) 'Science, technology and global competitive advantage: the strategic implications of emerging technologies for corporations and nations', *International Studies in Management and Organisation*, 29(1) pp. 53–79.

Kodama, F. (1995) *Emerging Patterns of Innovation: Sources of Japan's Technological Edge* (Boston, MA: Harvard Business School Press).

Kogut, B. (1999) 'What makes a company global?', *Harvard Business Review*, 77 (January–February): 84–98.

Kozul-Wright, R. and Rowthorn, R. (1998) 'Spoilt for choice? Multinational corporations and the geography of international production', *Oxford Review of Economic Policy*, 14(1): 1–27.

Kuemmerle, W. (1997) 'Building effective R&D capabilities abroad', *Harvard Business Review*, 75 (March–April): 61–70

Lundvall, B.A. (1992) *National Systems of Innovation – Toward a Theory of Innovation and Interactive Learning* (London: Pinter).

Nelson, R.R. (ed.) (1993) *National Systems of Innovation: A Comparative Analysis* (Oxford: Oxford University Press).

OECD (1991a) *Technology and Productivity: The Challenge for Economic Policy* (Paris: OECD).

OECD (1991b) *Strategic Industries in a Global Economy: Policy Issues for the 1990's* (Paris: OECD).

OECD (1991c) *Technology in a Changing World (Analytical Report by L. Soete)* (Paris: OECD).

OECD (1992) *Technology and the Economy: The Key Relationships* (Paris: OECD).

OECD (1995) *National Systems for the Financing of Innovation* (Paris: OECD).

OECD (1996a) *Employment and Growth in a Knowledge-Based Economy* (Paris: OECD).

OECD (1996b) *Technology, Productivity and Job Creation* (Paris: OECD).

OECD (1996c) *Transitions to Learning Economies and Societies* (Paris: OECD).

OECD (1996d) 'The knowledge-based economy', in *Science, Technology and Industry Outlook, 1996* (Paris: OECD).

Okimoto, D. (1989) *Between MITI and the Market: Japanese Industrial Policy in High Technology* (Stanford: Stanford University Press).

Tassey, G. (1992) *Technology Infrastructure and Competitive Position* (Norwell, MA: Kluwer Academic Publishers).

Thurow, L. (1993) *Head to Head* (New York: Warner Books).

UK Office of Science and Technology (1995a) *Progress through Partnership: Information Technology, Electronics and Communications*, Panel Report (London: HMSO).

UK Office of Science and Technology (1995b) *Progress through Partnership: Health and the Life Sciences*, Panel Report (London: HMSO).

UNCTAD (1993) *Integrated International Production*, World Investment Report (Geneva: UNCTAD).

UNCTAD (1997) *World Investment Report* (Geneva: UNCTAD).

UNCTAD (1998) *FDI: Trends and Determinants*, World Investment Report (Geneva: UNCTAD).

US National Science Foundation (1995) *Asia's New High-Tech Competition*, Science Resources Studies Division (Arlington, VA: NSF): pp. 95–309.

US National Science Board (1996) *Science and Engineering Indicators 1996* (Washington, DC: Government Printing Office).

World Trade Organisation (WTO) (1998) *Annual Report* (Geneva: WTO).

Part Two

The Impact of Foreign Direct Investment in the European Union, Central and Eastern Europe, and South East Asia

8 The Determinants of New Foreign Direct Investment Capital Flows into Europe: The US and Japan Compared

Jeremy Clegg and Susan Scott-Green

F21
F23
F13
G32

INTRODUCTION

This chapter concerns the developments in the European Community[1] (EC) in the 1980s, and links these to the literature on the determinants of foreign direct investment (FDI) in the EC. It is argued that the economic institutional developments of the EC, which involve integration in one form or another, function in two important ways. One is the conventional quest for internal market efficiency, and the second is the creation of an implicit set of incentives for firms to invest within the EC. For foreign firms, these incentives centre on the issue of being an insider firm or an outsider firm, and the expectations about future income streams attaching to the alternatives.

The effect of the development of the EC in respect of increased integration and enlargement can only be properly assessed in the context of a comprehensive model, which this chapter sets out to build. The leading hypotheses on the determinants of FDI into the EC are examined and a model is constructed for data covering the period 1984–1989. The data are for new FDI capital flows (excluding reinvested earnings) from the US and Japan to the EC when it had 12 members (EC12). In contrast to much earlier empirical work, the host countries of the EC are clustered into three groups, in order to explore structural differences in the model. The regression equations encompass both real and financial variables in order to capture faithfully the character of FDI flows.

The key results are that the models found for the US and Japan contrast considerably, and this is attributed to the different degrees of establishment of US and Japanese affiliates in the EC. While the real variables assume the greatest importance, financial variables do appear significant. The pattern of findings suggests that the growth of FDI into the EC is linked to host characteristics, and to perceptions of the Single Market Programme (SMP).

159

For Japanese firms, as comparative outsiders, the impact of the announcement of the SMP appears to have been particularly great. The results for the US give some support to the relative tariff discrimination hypothesis in respect of the accession of Greece, Portugal and Spain. However, the tariff variable is likely to capture other more diffuse factors. The pure role of tariffs is a diminishing one, as tariff levels now lie at the lowest historical levels between the developed countries. On the evidence from findings on the SMP, the main impact of accession on FDI behaviour is likely to have pre-dated the period 1984–1989.

The chapter concludes that the recent evolution of the EC can be understood, at least in part, as a mission to secure a maximum share of world investment. Accordingly, the EC is involved in a process of competitive integration in the face of market opening and regional integration elsewhere in the world, notably in East Asia, China and North America. The implications of this research are that economic integration initiatives can have a significant effect on FDI inflows. This relationship is very likely to become more prominent as an underlying motivation for continued European economic integration.

BACKGROUND

The development of the European Community in the 1980s had a profound effect on domestic, intra-European and extra-European trade and investment. This chapter focuses on one aspect of economic development during 1984–1989: inward FDI from Japan and the US, comparing the determinants of these two flows, including the impact of the development of the EC.

During 1980–1990, the inward FDI stock in Europe (EC12) rose by 380% in nominal terms (UNCTAD, 1996). The US and Japan continued to dominate as sources, but their relative flows manifested very different trends; Japanese FDI into the EC increased over ten-fold in nominal terms from 1984–1989, while flows out of the US grew more slowly, at around three-fold. Within this overall rise, there was a proportionately greater increase in intra-European FDI, which accounted for 53.3% of total inflows in 1989, compared with 41.4% in 1984 (Eurostat, 1992). Clearly, the developments in the Community made FDI into Europe more attractive, commanding an average of 59.4% of world FDI flows in 1991–1993, compared with 45% in 1984–1987 (OECD, 1995).

THE DEVELOPMENT OF THE EC: INSTITUTIONAL CONSIDERATIONS

The European Community has steadily been broadened and deepened, as it has progressed towards the creation of an integrated Europe. Multinational enterprises from outside the EC have responded to the EC's institutional changes via trade and, more particularly, through FDI. These outsider firms, anticipating a deterioration in their competitive position, seek to offset their disadvantages by becoming insider firms (Almor and Hirsch, 1995). This institutional dimension bolsters the magnetic power of internal market size – the single most important attractant of FDI, and the leading economic motive for regional integration and EC enlargement.

The period 1984–1989 saw major steps to closer integration: EC membership increased from 10 to 12 with the accession of Spain and Portugal in 1986, exchange rate instability was reduced by European monetary arrangements, and the Single Market Programme (SMP) was announced. Although mandated in 1987 via the Single European Act (SEA), the SMP, which took effect in 1993, was outlined in 1985 as a White Paper, thus influencing business decisions throughout the period of the chapter. The SEA created further impetus for FDI inflows in anticipation not only of market enlargement, but more specifically of the smoothing of trade arrangements among the member states. Indeed, a surge in FDI inflows did occur in the 1987–1989 period, compared with inward FDI growth in 1985–1987.

RESEARCH ON THE DETERMINANTS OF INWARD FDI INTO THE EC

Since the initial statistical work of Scaperlanda (1967) on US FDI in the EC, researchers have placed great reliance on neo-classical investment models. Using these, a growing list of hypotheses has been tested, including the four core hypotheses of market size and growth, tariff discrimination, and the impact of EC market integration.

The Effects of Market-related Factors on FDI

The level of FDI has been shown to be theoretically positively related to the absolute size of foreign market, through the reduction in the burden of transaction costs and the spatial economies of a foreign production location. Empirical work has extensively corroborated the role of demand conditions in determining FDI flows, with the market size hypothesis tending to be supported most strongly. The implication is that the market size *per se* dominates in the FDI decision, and this suggests *prima facie* justification for the emphasis on enlargement throughout the history of the EC.

Aristotelous and Fountas (1996) discovered that market size was significant in the 1980s and early 1990s for US and Japanese inward FDI, but found no support for the market growth variable in either country's FDI flows. The performance of variables to test the market growth hypothesis has very much fallen behind that of market size. Theoretically it should be more strongly related to expansionary investment, which is itself in turn associated with reinvested earnings (by mature existing affiliates). The conclusion is that market size is the paramount variable in promoting FDI, especially around the time of the creation of the European Economic Community (EEC) and during later economic integration. Another important finding in the empirical literature is the existence of an investment lag, which is often captured by the lagging of the market size variable by one period.

The Trade Policy of the EC, Internal Market Integration and FDI

The tariff discrimination hypothesis does generally appear to be upheld (for instance, Lunn, 1980; Scaperlanda and Balough, 1983; Culem, 1988, Clegg and Scott-Green, 1998); however, the construction of the variables capturing this is often controversial. The proxy variables employed are recognised as likely to capture non-tariff barriers (NTBs) as well.[2] In addition, there are two variants of the hypothesis: the absolute 'tariff wall' hypothesis, and the relative discrimination hypothesis (see Clegg, 1995).

The countries of the EC operated throughout 1984–1989 under a tariff-free code, with the exception of Spain, Portugal and Greece, which, as recent joiners of the community, were phasing out tariffs on intra-EC trade under an agreed schedule. However, as the EC has matured it has cultivated its own EC-wide discrimination against foreign imports through the use of NTBs, exerting an incentive to produce within the EC.

Altogether, statistical evidence for the European Community suggests a net substitution of FDI inflows for imports at the national level, particularly inward FDI organised on a regional, pan-EC, basis. Market integration enables the unified market to be served internally from fewer locations. This promotes the attainment of scale economies, both for indigenous and incoming firms. Import-substituting FDI from long-term investors, e.g., US firms, has been progressively replaced by investment to rationalise the existing stock of FDI that primarily served individual European markets. New investors, such as Japanese firms, should therefore invest in integrated production from the start.

Aristotelous and Fountas (1996) found strong support for a significant inflow of FDI in anticipation of a barriers-free Europe. They estimated the increase in FDI from the US attributable to the 'single market effect' to be $713 million between 1987 and 1992. On the contrary, Nicolaides and Thomsen (1991) argue that the SMP has only affected the timing of the Japanese FDI boom in the EC and not its overall long-run level. However, the data suggest that Japanese FDI has been positively affected by the SMP, and Dunning (1997, p. 209) argues that 'it is difficult to perceive how globalisation could have had the consequences it has in Europe if the (SMP) programme (or something like it) had not come about'.

Balasubramanyam and Greenaway (1992) suggest that the fear of Fortress Europe, rather than the lure of a large and integrated market, has been a factor in the sudden surge of Japanese FDI, as a means of becoming an insider firm (Almor and Hirsch, 1995). However, they conclude that there are additional locational advantages to the existence of the more integrated European market.

The Exchange Rate Mechanism (ERM) has been a significant statement of the importance attached to monetary stabilisation within the EC. As discussed above, the ERM operated relatively well during the period under study. It is clear that greater exchange rate certainty should promote FDI, and MNEs, unlike the governments, welcome market integration in all its respects within the EC. This is largely because they have the capacity to benefit, through investment in the most advantageous locations. Firms are likely to increase intra-EC FDI, as a result of integration as individual countries no longer exist as economically segmented markets.

The Impact of Exchange Rate Effects on FDI

To date the statistical literature relating to FDI into the EC as a unit has not included any hypotheses on exchange rates, although Scaperlanda and Balough (1983) and Lunn (1983) have advocated that this be done. The underlying problem in predicting the impact on FDI flows is that the outcome is net of several influences, which work in opposition to each other. In addition, there are dynamic elements in the impact of exchange rate effects on FDI. For this reason, it is important to include a variable to capture expected changes in the exchange rate. Empirical work on this topic has focused on the US (Cushman, 1985). Stevens (1993) concludes that host currency appreciation reduces FDI inflows.

Most recently, Aristotelous and Fountas (1996) have argued that a real depreciation of the host country's currency will lead to an increase in capital flows as foreign countries try to take advantage of relatively cheaper domestic labour. Also a real depreciation would lead to an increase in the relative wealth of foreign firms and to an increase in foreign purchases of domestic assets. Their statistical analysis supports this predicted increase in FDI from an increase in real exchange rates (i.e. a real depreciation of a host country's currency) for both Japanese and US FDI in the 1980s.

Incorporating expected exchange rate changes, Logue and Willet (1977) and Kohlhagen (1977) believe that an expected increase in the effective exchange rate will increase FDI (that is because firms would invest in real assets denominated in a foreign currency that is expected to appreciate). Cushman (1985, p. 302) infers that the effect of expectations is most likely to be negative. Cushman's (1985) estimates for pooled bilateral US FDI outflows to five developed countries shows significant reductions in US FDI associated with increases in the current effective value of foreign exchange, and very significant reductions in FDI associated with the expected appreciation of foreign currency. A criticism of these finance-based approaches is that they assume that the objective of foreign operations is the repatriation of returns. This is rarely the case, especially with mature multinationals.

Balasubramanyam and Greenaway (1992) point out that the sudden surge in Japanese FDI in the EC complicates the issues of assessing its determinants. The rise in Japanese FDI into the US and the EC coincided with Japan's balance of payments surplus and FDI could be seen as a vent for that surplus, when accompanied by an exchange rate misalignment. In addition, Dunning has argued that the main impact of the SMP has been through its effects on other variables influencing FDI (Dunning, 1997), rather than as a clearly observable direct effect.

Multinationals and the Relative International Cost of Borrowing

How the MNE chooses to finance foreign operations has been rather overlooked by mainstream research (see, however, Gilman (1981)). Just one study by Culem (1988) has included a financing variable, yet the precise source of international finance is central to determining the value that FDI will assume as a financial variable. If the home country cost of borrowing rises relative to that in the host, foreign affiliates would tend to increase their local borrowing. This refinancing of debt would generate a once-and-for-all reduction in net FDI outflows at the country level. Culem (1988) found the effect of relative interest rates to be insignificant for US FDI in the EC, but the most comprehensive study of the financing decision is that of Boatwright and Renton (1975) for the UK. This latter study clearly found in favour of the hypothesis aided by data on a quarterly basis, which reveal interest rate impacts far better than annual data. By analogy to the argument put forward for exchange rate effects, it is important to include a variable for the impact of expected changes in the relative interest rates.

Wage Costs and Labour Variables

Theory suggests that wage costs should exert a discernible effect on the location of production. Many studies specify wage costs, though few record significance for this variable. For instance, Culem (1988) found that both the absolute and differential (host-home) labour cost variables were insignificant in explaining US FDI in selected EC countries (and for EC FDI in the US). This evidence suggests that horizontal (market-orientated) FDI between developed trade blocs is not significantly motivated by labour costs, and that the location of production is mainly dictated by transport costs, and the need for proximity to the market, including the effect of Non-Trade Barriers (NTBs).

Conclusions on Existing Empirical Work

In any single- or multi-country study using aggregate FDI data, it is beneficial to keep in mind the multinational enterprises that are responsible. The theory of the MNE stresses that the characteristics of the individual firms influence FDI strategy. For instance, the existing degree of internationalisation and local servicing by multinationals in the EC will be important. The market position in home and target markets as well as corporate objectives and strategies are further factors. In aggregate data the industry composition of FDI will generate structural differences in equations between different countries.

THE MODEL

This chapter attempts to draw together the strands of existing research on US and Japanese FDI in order to construct a coherent and inclusive model of FDI inflows from outside the EC for the period 1984–1989. The data covers the EC(12). In contrast to most of the studies reviewed above, systematic differences in the model between EC host countries are explored. The only limitation is that of the number of observations per country (just 6 years). As a compromise, the countries are clustered into three groups. Initially arrived at through grouping by income per capita, maturity as a foreign investing and host nation, these clusters (see Tables 8.1 and 8.2) were subsequently confirmed by clustering the countries' data. The data for all countries are also pooled in order to establish the nature of any overall model and to ease comparison with the body of existing empirical research.

Dependent Variable Definition and Construction

The dependent variable is constructed from annual estimates of aggregate FDI inflows from the US and Japan into the member countries of the EC(12) between 1984 and 1989. The data cover only new capital flows, that is, net equity capital inflows, and exclude reinvested earnings. The proportion of reinvested earnings varies over time, and is linked to the business cycle of the investing country and the host.[3]

The Structure of the Model

The basic full formulation of the equation to be tested is as follows:

$$\Delta \text{FDI}_{ijt} = \alpha_0 + \alpha_1 RDI_{ijt} + \alpha_2 M_{ijt-1} + \alpha_3 \Delta M_{ijt} + \alpha_4 AVWS_{ijt}$$
$$+ \alpha_5 \text{GFCF}_{ijt} + \alpha_6 \text{XR}_{ijt} + \alpha_7 \text{EXP.XR}_{ijt} + \alpha_8 \text{IR}_{ijt}$$
$$+ \alpha_9 \text{EXP.IR}_{ijt} + \alpha_{10} \text{TAR}_{ijt} + \alpha_{11} \text{EC92}_{ijt} + \alpha_{12} \text{TAX}_{ijt} + u_{ijt}$$

Where $i = 1$ is the US and $i = 2$ is Japan. EC(12) is the specification of the EC over the period, with data for 11 EC host countries (Belgium and Luxembourg are combined as a single entity known here as 'Bleu') arranged in $j = 1, 2, 3, 4$ EC host country groups, and time, $t = 1, 2, \ldots, 6$. In the equations and the tabulated results, $j = 1$ represents the pooled equations, in which the regressions are run on the natural scale data for all the host countries. Table 8.1 summarises the expected signs of the independent variables.

STATISTICAL FINDINGS

Tables 8.2 and 8.3 present the regression results for the US and Japan, respectively. The findings for the two countries differ sufficiently that the discussions of the results are conducted separately for each, and cross-referenced where appropriate.

The US Equations

The pooled regressions for the US are only modestly successful. The most likely reason for this is the partial nature of the data, limiting the equations' ability to describe the FDI behaviour of US multinationals. Most US affiliates in the EC are well established. Given that 85% of the European market for US goods and services is catered for by affiliate sales, and just 15% by exports (Clegg, 1995), it is likely that US MNEs rely more heavily upon reinvested earnings than do Japanese firms.

The Group 2 countries are especially interesting as they are the latest entrants to the EC. The negative sign on the market size and growth variables for the countries of Group 2 (Greece, Portugal and Spain) may arise because the link between local market conditions and inward FDI, typical of segmented national markets before European integration, has been superseded by the use of these countries as production bases for the wider European market. The positive relationship of FDI and host research intensity suggests that the more research-intensive is the host industry, then the greater will be the FDI inflow. This finding obtains for both the pooled and the Group 2 equations.

The divergent results between the pooled equation for the labour costs variable and the other equations are resonant of the findings of Culem (1988). The labour cost variable is clearly behaving according to expectation in the pooled equation, i.e. FDI is being attracted to the countries in the EC with lower labour costs.

Both policy variables expected to have an impact on FDI fail to perform uniformly according to theory in the US equations. The tariff reduction variable has a positive sign, significant at 10%, in the pooled equation. This is probably a fair reflection of the moderate importance of tariff barriers

Table 8.1 The definitions of variables and the expected directions of the relationships between the dependent and independent variables

Real variables	Sign	Description and outline definition
δFDI	..	Annual extra-EC FDI net capital inflow
RDI	+	Technology intensity: current research and development expenditure divided by aggregate gross value added
M	+	Market size of each state: measured by GNP lagged one period
ΔM	+	Annual change in market size of each state: proportionate change in GNP
AVWS	−	Labour cost variable: average wages and salaries per employee
GFCF	+	Physical capital intensity: gross fixed capital formation per employee
TAR	+	EC internal tariff dismantlement: relative tariff discrimination against non-EC countries
EC92	+	EC internal non-tariff barrier elimination programme: proxied by a dummy variable scheme

Financial variables	Sign	Description and outline definition
XR		Exchange rate level: bilateral exchange rate of the host against the home currency
EXP.XR	+	Expected exchange rate: expectations about the value of the bilateral exchange rate of the host against the home currency
IR	+	Relative interest rate: relative cost of borrowing of the host to the home country
EXP.IR	−	Expected relative interest rate: expectations about changes in the value of the relative interest rate of the host to the home country
TAX	−	Host corporate taxation: disincentive effect of high corporate taxation on affiliates (FDI) in the host EC country

when at historically low levels. It should be said that this significance is likely to capture more widespread factors to do with US firms' investment strategies on the accession of the Group 2 countries. The absence of a positive impact for the variable EC92 in all the equations is probably a result of US firms being largely fully indigenised by the time of the announcement and early stages of the SMP. New investment by US MNEs in the form of new capital outflows has not been imperative, as existing US multinationals have been able to call on reinvested earnings to realise their investment plans.

The exchange rate variable is significant only in the pooled equation, but is positive and so counter to expectation. This demonstrates that inward FDI from the US increases as host currencies' exchange values rise – a feature

Table 8.2 Multiple regression results for the determinants of US FDI in the EC(12) 1984–89

	RDI	M	ΔM	AVWS	GFCF	TAR	EC92	XR	EXP.XR	IR	EXP.IR	TAX	Constant	R^2	Adj. R^2	F. Stat.	DW	DF
Pooled	0.105369 (1.655c)	−1.17E-11 (−.340)	−0.00143 (−.372)	−6.24E-06 (−2.287b)	−4.92E-05 (−.230)	0.001325 (1.589c)	3.88E-04 (.406)	2.39E-06 (3.500a)	0.001569 (.987)	0.002896 (1.708b)	−0.00154 (−.665)	1.21E-05 (.059)	−0.00286 (−.856)	0.4621	0.3403	3.7940a	2.5436	53
Group 1 (UK,Fr,G,N)	−0.34959 (−1.066)	−9.59E-09 (−1.323)	0.002489 (.390)	1.32E-05 (.831)	−7.41E-04 (−.950)	n.a.	−2.63E-04 (−.240)	4.26E-04 (1.307)	0.006722 (2.259b)	−0.0238 (−2.623b)	−0.0288 (−2.696a)	0.00993 (3.413a)	−9.44E-04 (−.152)	0.8482	0.7090	6.0943a	2.8969	12
Group 2 (Gr,P,Sp)	3.246757 (2.970b)	−3.20E-10 (−1.982c)	−0.01089 (−1.934c)	−1.34E-04 (−.201)	−5.22E-04 (−.428)	0.003593 (1.193)	0.002645 (.781)	−3.81E-05 (−.688)	−0.00926 (−1.043)	−0.04109 (−4.083a)	−0.02435 (−3.887c)	−0.00844 (−2.457b)	0.119682 (2.570b)	0.9550	0.8471	8.8485b	3.0238	5
Group 3 (Bleu,Ir,It,Dk)	−0.83062 (−.423)	−2.53E-08 (−.475)	0.002745 (.122)	4.12E-05 (.335)	5.27E-04 (.452)	n.a.	−8.76E-04 (−.248)	−2.28E-06 (−.359)	−0.00225 (−.465)	0.038553 (.737)	0.024235 (.559)	0.001265 (.428)	−0.05963 (−.655)	0.3146	−0.3137	0.5007	2.9848	12

Notes:
Figures in parenthesis are the t statistics
Significance levels are denoted: a (1%), b (5%) and c (10%)
n.a. denotes not applicable
Pooled consists of entire EC(12)
Group 1 consists of UK, France, Germany and The Netherlands
Group 2 consists of Spain, Portugal and Greece
Group 3 consists of Italy, Ireland, Bleu and Denmark

Table 8.3 Multiple Regression results for the determinants of Japanese FDI in the EC(12) 1984–89

	RDI	M	ΔM	AVWS	GFCF	TAR	EC92	XR	EXP.XR	IR	EXP.IR	TAX	Constant	R²	Adj. R²	F. Stat.	DW	DF
Pooled	0.318547 (3.288[a])	8.59E-11 (1.815[b])	-0.01284 (-2.404[b])	2.62E-05 (6.964[a])	0.001243 (1.028)	n.a.	6.45E-05 (.111)	-8.06E-04 (-5.394[a])	-0.001618 (-.491)	-0.015278 (-3.935[a])	-0.008035 (-2.963[a])	-1.52E-05 (-.045)	0.007664 (1.278)	0.7408	0.6822	12.656[a]	1.0800	53
Group 1 (UK,Fr,G,N)	0.842788 (1.152)	-1.41E-08 (-.922)	-0.001437 (-.096)	2.60E-05 (.924)	-0.002424 (-1.140)	n.a.	0.008486 (2.034[b])	0.415146 (1.405)	0.007466 (.723)	0.006964 (.459)	0.005476 (.484)	0.00155 (.184)	-0.026545 (-.462)	0.8650	0.7412	6.9870[a]	1.2124	12
Group 2 (Gr,P,Sp)	-0.91924 (-.725)	3.02E-10 (1.734[c])	-0.008065 (-1.371)	-2.67E-04 (-.437)	0.00204 (1.410)	0.001284 (.534)	-0.005891 (-1.635[c])	0.015674 (1.826[c])	0.01091 (1.610[c])	0.008863 (.976)	0.001344 (.409)	0.006014 (1.645[c])	-0.07945 (-1.711[c])	0.8190	0.3843	1.8841	2.8797	5
Group 3 (Bleu,Ir,It,Dk)	0.046167 (.053)	5.67E-10 (.015)	-0.023512 (-1.056)	2.65E-05 (.456)	0.001809 (1.772[c])	n.a.	-1.12E-04 (-.035)	-9.34E-04 (-.384)	0.002589 (.174)	0.020355 (.509)	0.009057 (.449)	3.11E-04 (.283)	-0.035985 (-.895)	0.6204	0.2724	1.7829	1.8095	12

Notes:
Figures in parenthesis are the t statistics
Significance levels are denoted: a (1%), b (5%) and c (10%)
n.a. denotes not applicable
Pooled consists of entire EC(12)
Group 1 consists of UK, France, Germany and The Netherlands
Group 2 consists of Spain, Portugal and Greece
Group 3 consists of Italy, Ireland, Bleu and Denmark

that may be correlated with the underlying fortunes of the host economies. The expected exchange rate variable performs as expected in the Group 1 equation, but nowhere else. The variable is expressed as the ratio of the trend value to the actual value, so a positive result indicates that expected rises in the host currency lead to inflows of US FDI, and vice versa.

The relative interest rate variable – the ratio of the nominal host domestic interest rate to the home interest rate – is significantly positive (as expected) in the pooled equations for the US, but is of contrary sign in the equations for Groups 1 and 2. This suggests that the expected variation in the variable occurs between the Groups of countries rather than within them, but that within each group of countries increased FDI has been associated with decreases in the host relative interest rates. The expected interest rate variable returns a significant negative sign, as hypothesised, for the Group 1 and Group 2 countries. This perhaps indicates that macroeconomic financial conditions in these countries are an issue for corporate treasurers, and expectations do influence capital outflows.

The corporate taxation variable should, in theory, impact negatively on inward FDI. However a significant negative sign is found only for Group 2, while a significant positive sign is found for Group 1. It may be that the sensitivity of investors to high host tax rates is greater in the newer host countries, where ways of accommodating these (e.g. via transfer price manipulation) have not yet been put in place.

The overriding comment on Group 3 – which consists of Bleu, Denmark, Ireland and Italy – must be that there is no significance. The fact that the model varies to such a strong degree in its appropriateness between the groups supports the clustering procedure. However, in the case of these countries the absence of findings may be the outcome of heterogeneity between the countries in the group, despite the general success of the clustering procedure.

The F statistics identify those equations that were significant overall. These are the pooled equations for Groups 1 and 2. The diagnostic statistics, the DW, appears not to suggest serious autocorrelation in general except for Group 3 – for which the results themselves were unsatisfactory. A formal test of structural difference (a chow test) on the unrestricted model (the equations for Groups 1, 2 and 3) versus the restricted model (the pooled equation) produces a F statistic of 1.618, which is not significantly different from zero. Therefore, the US equations are not distinct in their ability to explain US FDI, a result that partly derives from the low levels of underlying significance.

Japanese Equations

The overall impression given by the Japanese equations is that, unlike their better-established US counterparts, Japanese multinationals have reacted more strongly to European integration, by building up their FDI in the EC through new capital inflows. This is consistent with both a defensive and offensive strategy. In view of the significant positive (as expected) EC92 result in the equation for Group 1, Japanese MNEs appear to be reacting strongly to perceived EC barriers as well as to the scale of the market. This is indicated by a strong positive finding for market size in the pooled equation. However, the negative sign on the market growth variable, also in the pooled equation, is the hallmark of pan-EC integrated FDI, which occurs when the host economy is used to service the EC market as a whole. Accordingly, any faster growth outside the economy in which the investment is made results in a negative sign. This was also encountered for Group 2 for the USA, where a similar argument appears to apply.

Looking across the variables, research intensity is positive in the pooled equation. This testifies to the country composition of Japanese FDI flows to the EC favouring the higher technology intensity countries. The fact that this result does not apply to the separate country groups suggests that the main part of the variance is between the groups rather than within them.

The labour cost variable comes out positive in the pooled equation, perhaps suggesting that Japanese MNEs had sought the most productive and skilled locations. This is quite contrary to the US finding. It indicates that Japanese FDI in these countries is orientated towards EC countries at the higher end of the range of labour costs. This may reflect the preference for Japanese firms to locate in their largest markets, at a time when their operations had their primary rationale in circumventing trade barriers.

Variables that behave as expected in the pooled equation include capital intensity, the exchange rate and the expected interest rate, where the standard hypothesised explanations apply. The negative relative interest rate result for Japan in the pooled equation suggests that Japanese FDI has been expanded in those hosts where the host interest rate has been highest relative to Japan, and vice versa. Because Japanese FDI is recorded as gross (rather than net) outflows, this defect probably interferes in particular with the ability of the data to capture current financial factors (as opposed to real factors, which are, in comparison, relatively stable).

The Group 1 equation has just one significant result, the EC92 variable; everything else pales into insignificance. The countries concerned – the UK, France, Germany and the Netherlands – are precisely those in which Japanese firms would seek to build up their presence in the approach to the single European market. The fact that no other variables are significant is surprising, and it may once more indicate the defective nature of the Japanese FDI data.

There is some doubt over the equation for Group 2 (Greece, Portugal and Spain), which fails to gain overall significance despite significant coefficients on certain variables. This is probably because the absolute level of Japanese FDI in this group is low and a clear model has not yet emerged. Market size performs as expected, reflecting the importance of local market growth in Group 2 for Japanese firms, a feature that does not apply to US firms, possibly on account of the fact that Japanese firms are newly established by comparison. The EC92 variable records a negative sign. This may be reflecting the other side of the coin of Japanese multinationals' investment strategies in the Group 1 countries, that is to focus on the core markets of the EC when circumventing discrimination against outsider firms.

Also in the Group 2 equation, the exchange rate variable performs contrary to expectations. By analogy to the US finding, this may be a feature that correlates with the Japanese firms' estimation of the underlying fortunes of the host economies. The expected exchange rate variable finding is, however, positive as hypothesised. The corporate tax variable is positive, against expectations. Here the argument made out for the contrary US result cannot apply, as Japan is a new investor in the Group 2 countries. Again, it may be too much to ask of the Japanese data, which are more insensitive to financial factors than the US data, to produce the expected result. It is, however, possible that tax may be only a part of the fiscal package in these countries, which are favoured locations in EC regional policy – a feature that may outweigh tax in the Japanese investment decision.

The Japanese equation for Group 3 is insignificant overall, with only capital intensity explaining inward Japanese FDI flows, with the expected sign. It is not readily apparent why only this variable should perform as expected in this equation. However, the gross nature of the Japanese data may well stand in the way of an accurate estimation of the important variables for these countries. In summary, the overall level of significance in the Japanese equations is superior to that in the US equations, notwithstanding the fact that the incidence of contrary signs is greater.

Finally, a chow test of structural difference yields a F statistic of 1.937, which is significant at the 10% level. This shows that the Japanese equations do differ significantly in their ability to describe Japanese FDI flows, and that the underlying model is distinct between the groups of countries. The fact that the motivation for Japanese FDI differs by host country supports the procedure of grouping the countries employed in this chapter.

CONCLUSIONS

This chapter started with the premise that institutional developments are important in the investment location decisions of multinational firms. The evidence of our statistical research gives some support for this. The performance of the variable designed to capture the announcement impact of the SMP has indicated that the behaviour of MNEs is responsive to major institutional European changes. The hypothesised effect of the EC92 variable is seen for new capital inflows from Japan, to the group consisting of the UK, France, Germany and the Netherlands.

It is especially interesting that the announcement in the mid- to late-1980s of institutional changes under the SMP impacted so early on investment behaviour, i.e. exerting an effect well in advance of the actual changes themselves. This demonstrates the weight that firms put on expectations that are essentially unquantifiable – explaining why researchers are so frequently obliged to employ dummy variables. This weight derives from firms' views on their prospective future income streams arising from deeper involvement in the EC (and in the key EC countries) versus the alternatives. These expectations concern competitors' actions, those of the Commission, and of the future importance of the EC as a market in the world economy. To make progress in modelling FDI flows, it will be necessary to employ improved variables that better capture firms' perspectives.

The conventional variable to measure discrimination against third countries – tariffs – records a modest level of significance for the USA. This degree of significance is limited because tariff rates are already at historically low levels between the developed countries, and because the impact of joining the EC is felt several years before the actual accession takes place, in a way somewhat analogous to the SMP effect. In the case of the US firms, already with so much in the way of established operations in the EC by the start of the 1980s, most investment plans were probably well in place, and funds raised through reinvested earnings within Europe were understandably often the primary source of finance for strategic EC investment in the period 1984–1989. The tariff variable probably also correlates with other factors that favoured increased FDI, such as US firms' improving view of business prospects in the acceding countries.

The marked contrasts between the USA and Japan that have emerged have been explained as the outcome of the different degrees of establishment in Europe by multinationals from the two countries. The exclusion of reinvested earnings is clearly a weakness in some respects, but in this chapter we have put a premium on ensuring compatibility between the US data and the Japanese data, in order to draw out the maximum meaning from the equations.

Looking to the next major initiative of an institutional nature in the European Union (EU), namely Economic and Monetary Union (EMU), the indications from our research are that the impact of this will largely come from firms' perceptions of the benefits versus the costs to them of investing in locations either inside or outside the countries to be encompassed (at least in the first wave) of EMU. It is the likely reactions of firms that in turn will condition the remaining member states' positions on whether, and when, to join EMU. The indications from our analysis of EC92 are that the effects via FDI can be significant.

The institutional measures of the EC all involve the reduction of internal barriers of one type or another, in an attempt by EC members collectively to increase their share of world investment. This chapter has been concerned with the estimation of a model of new capital inflows, but the circumstantial evidence does suggest that the EC as a whole, as a result of the announcement of the SMP initiative, did become a more attractive location, as witnessed by the turnaround in its share of world FDI since the late 1980s (Clegg, 1996). This indicates that increased economic integration is positively evaluated by enterprises. We do appear to be in a world where competitive integration is one of the key policy tools that groups of small- and medium-sized contiguous countries (as in the EC) can employ. By using this tool, they may maintain their share of world investment, when confronted by fast economic growth and market opening in locations such as East Asia and China, and in the face of competing North American integration.

Overviewing the methodological approach of the chapter, it is possible to say that the specification of a comprehensive model, embracing both real and financial variables has been supported. The back catalogue of research on the determinants of FDI and FDI flows is relatively weak in respect of the financial determinants. However, FDI is a financial as well as a real phenomenon, and neither aspect of its character can be ignored. The inclusion of both real and financial variables has certainly contributed to the degree of success, and future statistical work will almost certainly not ignore financial variables to the same extent as much of the empirical work to date.

Notes

1. We refer throughout to the European Community (EC), which was renamed as the European Union (EU) in 1992.
2. For a more detailed discussion of the research on US FDI in the EC, see Clegg (1995).
3. The relationship between the business cycle and FDI is explored in Clegg (1996).

References

Almor, T. and Hirsch, S. (1995) 'Outsiders' response to Europe 1992: theoretical considerations and empirical evidence', *Journal of International Business Studies*, 26(2): 223–237.

Aristotelous, K. and Fountas, S. (1996) 'An empirical analysis of inward foreign direct investment flows in the EU with emphasis on the market enlargement hypothesis', *Journal of Common Market Studies*, 34(4): 571–583.

Balasubramanyan, V.N. and Greenaway, D. (1992) 'Economic integration and FDI: Japanese investment in the EC', *Journal of International Business Studies*, 30(2): 175–193.

Boatwright, B.D. and Renton, G.A. (1975) 'An analysis of United Kingdom inflows and outflows of direct foreign investment', *Review of Economics and Statistics*, 57(4): 478–86.

Clegg, J. (1995) 'United States foreign direct investment in the European Community: The effects of market integration in perspective', in F. Burton, M. Yamin and S. Young (eds) *The Changing European Environment* (London: Macmillan).

Clegg, J. (1996) 'The development of multinational enterprises', in P.W. Daniels and W.F. Lever (eds) *The Global Economy in Transition* (London: Longman).

Clegg, J. and Scott-Green, S. (1998) 'The determinants of Japanese foreign direct investment flows to the European Community, 1963–1990', in J.-L. Mucchielli (ed.) *Multinational Location Strategy* (London: JAI Press).

Culem, C.G. (1988) 'The locational determinants of direct investments among industrialised countries', *European Economic Review*, 32(4): 885–904.

Cushman, D.O. (1985) 'Real exchange rate risk, expectations, and the level of direct investment', *Review of Economics and Statistics*, 67: 297–308.

Dunning, J.H. (1997) 'The European internal market programme and inbound foreign direct investment – Part II', *Journal of Common Market Studies*, 35(2): 189–223.

Eurostat (1992) *European Community Direct Investment 1984–89* (Luxembourg: Office for Official Publications of the European Communities).

Gilman, M.G. (1981) *The Financing of Foreign Direct Investment: A Study of the Determinants of Capital Flows in Multinational Enterprises* (London: Frances Pinter).

Kohlhagen, S.W. (1977) 'The effects of exchange-rate adjustments on international investment: A further comment', in P.B. Clark, D. Logue and R. Sweeney (eds) *The Effects of Exchange Rate Adjustments* (Washington, DC: US Government Printing Office).

Logue, D.E. and Willet, T.D. (1977) 'The effect of exchange-rate adjustments on international investment', in P.B. Clark, D. Logue and R. Sweeney (eds) *The Effects of Exchange Rate Adjustments* (Washington, DC: US Government Printing Office).

Lunn, J. (1980) 'Determinants of US direct investment in the EEC: further evidence', *European Economic Review*, 13(1): 93–101.

Lunn, J. (1983) 'Determinants of US direct investment in the EEC: revisited again', *European Economic Review*, 21(3): 391–3.

Nicolaides, P. and Thomsen, S. (1991) 'Can protectionism explain direct investment?', *Journal of Common Market Studies*, 29(6): 635–643.

OECD (1995) *International Direct Investment Statistics Yearbook 1995* (Paris: OECD).

Scaperlanda, A.E. (1967) 'The EEC and US foreign investment: some empirical evidence', *Economic Journal*, 77: 22–6.

Scaperlanda, A.E. and Balough, R.S. (1983) 'Determinants of US direct investment in the EEC: revisited', *European Economic Review*, 21(3): 381–90.

Stevens, G.V.G. (1993) 'Exchange rates and foreign direct investment: a note', *International Finance Discussion Papers*, No. 444. April (Washington, DC: Federal Reserve).

UNCTAD (1996) *World Investment Report 1996: Investment Trade and International Policy Arrangements* (New York: UN).

F23 G34
L22 032
M31

9 European Integration and the Restructuring of Multinational Enterprise Operations

Mark E. Bleackley and Peter J. Williamson

INTRODUCTION

At both the corporate and political level there has been a widespread recognition that the fragmented nature of the European market, resulting from differing national rules and regulations, was impeding the ability of Europe's leading companies to achieve economies that would improve the competitiveness of their operations and thereby assist in the global corporate battle with their non-European competitors (Dekker, 1985).

Political efforts to provide a legislative foundation for a more unified European marketplace received a significant boost with the introduction of the 1985 White Paper on Completing the Internal Market. Momentum was maintained with the passing of the Single European Act in 1987, which was a concerted attempt by the EC heads of state to adopt a series of directives aimed at abolishing technical and non-tariff barriers and harmonising rules that had acted to separate the national markets of Europe. Both sets of legislation called for completion of a pan-European internal market by 31 December 1992.

In order to capture the proposed benefits and respond to the threats associated with the development of this 'Single European Market', many companies were expected to restructure significantly their European operations and organisational strategies. Indeed, during the late 1980s and early 1990s the words 'Single Europe 1992' were never out of the business press and frequently used to justify a wide variety of corporate initiatives.

Ultimately, it would be this corporate restructuring that would determine the true extent of European integration, rather than the political initiatives that open the way for, or react to, the various economic and competitive forces. In this sense MNEs play a critical role in fashioning, as well as responding to regional economic integration (Dunning, 1993).

The marketing hype has now died down and yet the true extent of corporate restructuring in Europe is unknown. This chapter draws on a study that was undertaken on behalf of The Conference Board Europe. The research was commissioned with a view to gaining a better understanding of the corporate restructuring activity that has taken place among European-based companies over the last few years. This chapter reports on one element of the research project, namely that dealing with the extent and nature of this restructuring activity.[1]

The next section describes the different dimensions of corporate restructuring that were examined in the study. This is followed by a brief analysis of the existing literature on corporate restructuring activity specifically as it relates to the European Single Market. The next section describes the main features of the research methodology and companies surveyed. We then report on the results of the survey followed by an analysis of the patterns of restructuring activity observed. We conclude with a commentary on the emerging forces shaping European corporate development.

THE MEANING OF CORPORATE RESTRUCTURNG

There is no generally accepted definition in the academic literature of corporate restructuring. In the context of this study, we chose a number of different dimensions of the way in which companies might reconfigure their European-based operations in the light of changes in their competitive environment. Three specific dimensions of corporate restructuring were adopted: expansion and rationalisation, geographic scope, and the organisational locus of managerial responsibility.

Expansion or Rationalisation

One of the economic benefits put forward for the creation of a larger, more unified European market is that it would enable companies to capture greater scale economies, by producing a larger amount of each product range at any one site, thereby bringing about a fall in unit costs. These scale benefits are expected to be available not only in manufacturing, but also in such activities as procurement, distribution and marketing. The likely outcome is that the European market will be served by a reduced number of facilities. Restructuring under this scenario represents a consolidation of the company's operations, which might include the closure of a number of existing (sub-scale) facilities or the elimination of certain duplicate activities, such as product development, which were previously carried out in a number of protected national markets.

Increasing the size of the potential market by removing trade barriers, also serves to raise the degree of competition in each national market (Geroski, 1989). Thus, incumbent firms might be expected to enhance their marketing and sales activities in order to protect their national markets from foreign competition. At the same time, opportunities to capture a share of other European markets might necessitate an expansion of activities designed to serve these new markets. For example, companies that previously had a strong presence in only their home market and were now looking to develop a sales strategy for the broader European market were expected to establish partnerships with existing channels as well as to increase their investment in locally-based distribution, sales and service subsidiaries (Williamson, 1992).

Consequently, we have chosen to capture this change in a company's network of European activities by focussing on the expansion-rationalisation dimension of restructuring. Specifically, we examine whether the resources committed to each value-added activity or function have been either increased (expansion) or reduced (rationalisation).

Geographic Scope

Despite the political rhetoric and the economic logic underpinning the Single Market, a pan-European scope is only one of several organising frameworks for the European corporation. Some companies see themselves operating in what are distinct national territories, while other firms view their pan-European operations as an integral piece of the global organisation. This dimension, therefore, measures the extent to which the geographical scope of a company's activities has changed towards a more national, pan-European or global operation.

Broadly, this refers to the geographical positioning and organisation of an activity. Under this definition we are trying to capture more than just the number and location of the sites where each activity in the value chain is performed, what Porter (1986) referred to as the configuration of a company's activities.[2] We also take account of the related elements of scale of the particular activity and the geographic markets served. For example, a company's R&D activities may operate under a global mandate, drawing on worldwide resources and technological capabilities, while the actual operations may be situated in only one or two locations around the world.

Organisational Locus of Managerial Responsibility

Under this dimension we address the changes that have occurred in the hierarchical location of decision-making responsibility for each major activity within the organisation. This is taken to lie somewhere between central authority (centralisation) at one extreme and local autonomy (decentralisation) at the other.

Along with formalisation and specialisation, the 'centralisation' dimension has received considerable attention as a structural mechanism (Pugh *et al.*, 1968). It has been shown to be directly correlated to the extent of global integration (Garnier, 1982) and closely associated with a concentrated configuration of activities (Morrison and Roth, 1993).

It has been suggested that the requirement to centralise or decentralise decision-making responsibility within an organisation varies according to the specific activity or function (Turner and Henry, 1994, summarising Bartlett and Ghoshal, 1989, pp. 60–62) with activities such as manufacturing, basic research, finance and treasury management tending to be centralised, while development, sourcing, marketing and sales are decentralised. Similarly, Shetty (1979) found that the degree of decentralisation was highest in marketing and production, and lowest in finance and R&D.

It should be noted that these three dimensions – expansion-rationalisation, geographic scope, organisational locus of managerial responsibility – are not mutually exclusive in that a particular restructuring initiative might involve changes in more than one area. Thus, for example, a company may have reduced its number of factories in Europe while reconfiguring the remaining plants to manufacture on a pan-European rather than a national scale. Furthermore, over the six year reporting timescale of this survey, any companies undergoing a prolonged period of restructuring could be expected to report changes in a number of dimensions and across a range of activities.

Corporate restructuring in this context is therefore a much broader definition than the delayering of management or large-scale redundancies that have occurred in many companies (although these may result from a particular restructuring programme). For instance, companies might choose to restructure in the pursuit of new growth opportunities. Furthermore, restructuring is more than just the reconfiguration of physical assets; it might also involve changing employee's attitudes and mind set.

CORPORATE RESTRUCTURING IN EUROPE

Examining the Evidence

There has been a steady stream of commentary on corporate restructuring activity in the context of the Single European Market. This has looked at the restructuring of specific activities within the value chain, such as manufacturing (Bartmess and Cerny, 1993; Collins and Schmenner, 1995), research and development (Conference Board, 1995) and sales and service (Williamson, 1992); it has analysed the effects on particular industries (Atamer, 1991) and has detailed the restructuring activities of individual firms (Tilles, 1992).

In this chapter, we make three distinct contributions to the existing work. Firstly, not only are we seeking to provide a more comprehensive review of restructuring among European-based firms, we also aim to gather the data that will enable us to draw comparisons concerning the relative incidence of restructuring across both activity and industry sector.

We can illustrate the potential variation in restructuring patterns across activities in the context of one dimension of restructuring; that is changes in the organisational locus of managerial responsibility. There is evidence to suggest that the move towards greater economic and political integration in Europe has caused some companies to rethink the loci of their decision-making responsibilities. For example, both Ford of Europe and General Motors have raised the degree of centralisation of their R&D, purchasing and product planning activities (Turner and Henry, 1994). More broadly, one study analysing changes in European sales and marketing structures in the late 1980s found that half the sample of firms had devolved more power to the local operations, while another quarter had set out to strengthen centralised control (Lester, 1990). While this supports Bartlett and Ghoshal's (1989) contention that restructuring patterns vary according to the specific activity, it also suggests that within a particular value-added activity or function the pattern is a great deal more complex.

The second contribution of this work is to introduce a more structured approach to the concept of corporate restructuring. When corporate restructuring has been mentioned in the context of an evolving Single European Market, it has often been associated with a rationalisation of activities in terms of cost cutting and asset divestment, and an increased centralisation of operating responsibilities within the company. It is anticipated that the use of three related but contrasting dimensions by which we can gauge the incidence of restructuring among the companies surveyed will contribute to a more detailed understanding of the restructuring phenomenon.

It has already been noted that companies restructure in different ways, even when the focus is on just one particular area of a company's operations, such as sales and marketing. While the existing literature sees the European Single Market as a major stimulus for this restructuring activity, it offers little explanation for the reason why the pattern might vary from one company to another.

The third and final contribution thus concentrates on the factors that might account for these differences between companies. In particular we suggest that there are two factors that strongly influence the nature and extent of a company's restructuring activity, namely the dynamics of the industry in which it operates and its existing stage of organisational development across Europe.

Factors Influencing the Pattern of European Restructuring

Industry dynamics

The first factor is the dynamics operating within a company's particular industry. This draws on the industrial organisation (IO) perspective on competition and suggests that the pressures operating within a particular industry have a major impact on the strategic responses of business (Doz, Bartlett and Prahalad, 1981). For example, some industries (such as media and telecommunication) are experiencing growing demand and major firms are attempting to establish dominant global positions. Such industry dynamics might be associated with expansion and a broadening of geographical scope. Other industries (such as automotive and cement) face stagnant demand and overcapacity, and companies operating in these industries are more likely to restructure through a number of cost cutting and efficiency measures.

More specifically, one study (Hill and Still, 1990) found that industry factors were a major influence on the sales structures of US multinationals' foreign subsidiaries. They noted that industrial goods and Electronic Data Processing (EDP) companies were more likely (than consumer goods companies) to group national markets in their sales coverage. Language commonalities, market size and geographic proximity were said to be key factors in identifying which markets to combine.

Organisational development

The second factor that is expected to have a major influence on a company's restructuring activity is its existing stage of organisational development. The underlying concept is that companies are assisted or constrained in what they can do and their ability to change by their existing organisational configuration and capabilities, which in turn is a function of the nature of the company's historical evolution; often termed its administrative or organisational heritage. Consequently, differences in the patterns of restructuring observed, as well as management's ability to implement the desired changes, could reflect different development histories.

Let us consider the ways in which a company's existing stage of development in Europe might influence its restructuring options. Firstly, relatively new entrants into the European marketplace might be better placed to take advantage of falling entry barriers within Europe by establishing European-scale operations in the most favourable European location. Eastman Chemical, the US chemical concern, was one firm that believed it could benefit from its relatively late arrival into Europe. According to its President of EMEA (Europe, Middle East and Africa) operations: 'Others operate like multinational companies with assets in every country. We can manufacture in large volumes in one place and ship all over Europe' (Kemezis, 1992).

Those companies that have maintained facilities in several European locations over a number of years, could argue that they benefit from the cumulative experience gained from operating in a number of distinct European markets where they have been able to take account of different cultures, tastes and languages.

Other European companies are emerging from a relatively sheltered competitive environment in their home markets, within which they built a dominant position. With their home market under threat, these 'national champions' are looking to take advantage of opportunities opening up in other European markets by leveraging their domestic capabilities. However, at the same time it is conceivable that the attitudes, systems and vested interests that served them well in their home market might also constrain their development into a fully fledged pan-European organisation.

Finally, there are those non-European firms that have been operating on a pan-European basis for some time. Many US-based multinationals, which set up operations in Europe prior to World War II, established a European regional office during the 1970s and early 1980s. These offices housed staff specialists at the regional level in such functions as human resources, finance, engineering and production (Daniels, 1986). The European headquarters of Ford was formed even earlier, in 1967, from the integration of Ford's British and German subsidiaries (Financial Times, 1994: 31).

Consequently, in the context of corporate restructuring in Europe, we expect that a company's founding or initial entry position into the European market, as well as its existing organisational configuration of activities, are key structural determinants of a company's restructuring pattern over the last few years. Based on these two dimensions we have identified four different representations for a company's organisational development position in Europe, namely those:

- companies that already operate on a pan-European basis (pan-European)
- domestic companies that have only recently begun moving into other European markets (national champions)
- companies that are organised primarily around self-contained businesses in a number of European countries (multi-domestic)
- non-European companies that have only recently established operations in Europe (new entrant)

In summary, to examine the true extent of corporate restructuring activity among European-based companies we shall adopt an analytical framework, which comprises three distinct components: a restructuring matrix where the extent of restructuring can be measured across a range of value-added activities and a number of dimensions of restructuring;[3] the stage of organisational development and the industry sector in which the company operates.

METHODOLOGY

Anecdotal evidence suggests that corporate restructuring activity is often incremental in nature. It might take the form of detailed and often subtle changes, such as an extension of the company's sales and service network, a centralisation of its basic research activity or the adoption of a new pattern of logistics and plant specialisation. These changes can seldom be identified and examined purely on the basis of publicly available information. A detailed questionnaire-based survey was considered to be an appropriate methodology for piecing together this jigsaw of individual moves.

The survey was undertaken among member companies of The Conference Board's European Council on Corporate Strategy, complemented by a select number of companies either from other Councils or from outside the Conference Board membership. In each case the respondent was a director of strategy or planning.

In total, 41 companies participated in the survey, many of which rank amongst the world's leading international firms.[4] Each company is present in a number of European markets, other than its own home country. Some of the companies have their headquarters outside Europe but have substantial operations within. The survey companies employ between 500 and 140 000 people in their European operations (a combined workforce of over 1.1 million employees) and represent a broad range of industry sectors (see Table 9.1).

Table 9.1 Sample characteristics

Geographical origin	No. of companies	Industry sector	No of companies
Europe	29	Computers and electronics	9
US	10	Commercial services	7
Japan	1	Energy	7
Other (Australia)	1	Financial services	7
		Construction materials	4
		Consumer products	4
		Other*	3

* Pharmaceuticals, construction equipment and diversified industrial.

The first part of the questionnaire asked for a brief description of the participating company and the completion of the 'restructuring matrix'. Each respondent was asked to indicate in the matrix those value-added activities that had undergone significant restructuring between 1988–1994[5] and the particular nature of this change. The second part of the questionnaire was a structured interview carried out either in person or on the telephone. The questions were designed to elicit more information on the nature of the restructuring programme and its implementation.

RESULTS

This section investigates the extent of corporate restructuring among the companies surveyed and is based on the responses to the first part of the questionnaire. These results are presented in four stages. The first stage looks at the total amount of restructuring activity. The second stage addresses the nature of restructuring undertaken across the value added activities, by focussing on the three dimensions of restructuring (expansion-rationalisation, geographic scope, organisational locus of managerial responsibility). In the third stage we report on variations observed in the patterns of restructuring by industry sector and, in the final stage, on how the pattern of restructuring might vary depending on the company's current stage of organisational development.

The Amount of Restructuring

A significant amount of restructuring has taken place among the companies surveyed (see Table 9.2). On average each firm has undertaken changes in at least two of the three restructuring dimensions, for each *value-added activity*. So, for example, over the last few years a firm might have undertaken a significant rationalisation of its manufacturing base and moved to establish a more centralised operation within, whilst making little change in its geographic scope.

No category of activity has been left unaffected. Among the activities, the IT infrastructure has seen the most change, accounting for almost 15% of all restructuring activity, while a significant change has also taken place in the downstream activities of marketing, sales and service, and distribution.

When the companies are grouped by their major *industry sector* (38 of the 41 companies can be classified into six broad sectors) it is apparent that all industries have been affected by the restructuring trend, although there are noticeable differences between them.

The greatest incidence of change took place among the consumer products firms, represented by such companies as BAT Industries, CPC International and Unilever. The sectors in which companies experienced the

Table 9.2   Amount of restructuring

Amount of restructuring by:					
Value-added activity/function	*Count**	*Industry sector*	*Count***	*Stage of organisational development*	*Count***
IT infrastructure	103	Consumer products	20.3	Multi-domestic	19.2
Marketing	93	Computers and	18.6	Pan-European	15.7
Sales and service	90	electronics		National champion	15.1
Distribution	86	Financial services	18.0		
Manufacturing	81	Commercial services	17.4		
Supply	81	Energy	13.6		
European management team	80	Construction materials	12.0		
R&D	79				

* Total count of occasions where major change reported by each company.
** Incidence of change per category representative.

least amount of change were energy and construction materials. One possible explanation for the relatively low count in the energy sector is that one or two of the constituent firms, such as British Gas and National Power might have had less incentive to restructure during the time that they were under state control and operating in a more regulated environment (they were privatised in 1986 and 1990, respectively).

Further, the incidence of restructuring activity is considerable, regardless of the particular *stage of organisational development* the firms have adopted.[6] However, the greatest amount of change was undertaken by those firms restructuring around a multi-domestic configuration.

The Different Dimensions of Restructuring[7]

Expansion or rationalisation
The extent to which companies have either expanded or rationalised their operations varies by type of activity. Around two-thirds of the companies rationalised their manufacturing and physical distribution operations in the last few years, while only a few companies decided to expand. The reduced costs of transportation and lowering of fiscal barriers, combined with the pressure to increase the efficiency of existing operations, has enabled companies to eliminate duplicate operations that served only national markets.

In contrast, we found that in the marketing function in particular, and to a lesser extent in sales and service, more companies expanded rather than rationalised their operations. This is noticeable in a number of ways. For example, some companies have been allocating more corporate resources to such marketing activities as product development and promotion, while others have been expanding their sales networks with the aim of providing a more localised service.

Finally, when looking at the extent to which the IT function has changed, it appears that a similar number of companies have rationalised as have expanded the activity. In fact, four companies indicated that they had both expanded and rationalised their IT infrastructure. Within its fertiliser business, the Norwegian firm Norsk Hydro expanded the use of IT by installing on-truck computers, at the same time it reduced the number of systems and staff employed in its IT department. The former was designed to improve the quality and speed of customer delivery, while the latter enabled the firm to make significant savings while up-grading its software systems.

Geographic scope
We now address the second dimension of restructuring, examining the extent to which the geographic scope of corporate activities has changed in the last few years. Without exception, the results demonstrate that there has been a strong push towards a pan-European focus for each major activity in the value chain. One indication of this is that during the survey period, 25 of the 41 companies created a management team with specific responsibility for pan-European matters. Notwithstanding the strong pan-European bias, the pattern does vary between activities.

(i) The pan-Europeanisation of R&D, marketing and IT. The R&D, IT infrastructure and marketing functions have generally moved to being organised on a pan-European basis, although in each case a number of companies have adopted either a national or global focus.

The potential benefits of adopting a pan-European scope can be seen in the case of the marketing function. Prior to the launch of a major restructuring programme in Europe in 1989, the US company Tambrands was organised on a country-by-country basis such that each country office conducted its own marketing programme, for example, by designing the product packaging and selecting its own advertising agency. As part of the restructuring, a European marketing group was set up in the UK with responsibility for advertising, packaging, new product development and some pricing and promotion decisions across Europe. Some promotion activity and other below-the-line programmes remained the responsibility of the country offices. This led to Tambrands using only one agency for Europe and the development of a single campaign with only 10–20% of the individual copy elements being customised for each European market. Economies were also achieved through a reduction in the varieties of packaging for all European markets from 200 to two. Local differences were accommodated with instructions being printed on the packages in multiple languages (Tully, 1992).

In contrast, the restructuring activities of another US consumer products firm show that this trend towards the pan-Europeanisation of the marketing function is not universal. This company's restructuring programme, which began in 1993, in fact represented a partial move away from an earlier attempt to establish a pan-European organisation for its apparel business. The poor performance of new product introductions under the earlier set-up was said to be the result of a failure properly to understand prevailing national differences in marketing channels and consumer tastes. Although some activities, such as manufacturing, continue to be organised on a pan-European basis with headquarters in Paris, responsibility for the marketing activity has subsequently been transferred back to the national offices. Furthermore, the predominantly expatriate workforce responsible for marketing in the European office was replaced by nationals working out of their own country offices. Since the introduction of these changes, performance indicators for the business have improved.

(ii) The shift to global supply networks. Changes in the geographic scope of the supply chain function have been towards either a more pan-European or a global operation. The plastics division of Solvay, the Belgian chemicals company, now negotiates and administers contracts with a smaller number of ethylene suppliers responsible for supplying across Europe, having previously negotiated on a factory-by-factory basis with locally based suppliers. This has enabled the plastics division to negotiate better prices by buying significantly greater quantities of raw materials and also reduces the administrative cost of dealing with multiple suppliers.

The potential for sourcing on a pan-European basis may however be limited by the capabilities of the suppliers. Hewlett Packard found that several of its component suppliers were unable to supply in increased volumes, while Honeywell had to resort to local procurement in some instances because several of its suppliers did not have the necessary distribution structure in place to supply each of its twelve European plants on a timely basis.

(iii) Changes within the manufacturing, distribution and sales and service activities. No clear picture emerges in manufacturing. At one extreme there are companies that have restructured in order to gain the scale benefits that come from manufacturing a product designed, with only a few modifications, for the global market. Pharmacia was one firm that in the process of reducing the number of its factories worldwide from 45 in 1988 to 35 in 1993, shifted the focus of its remaining plants towards global product lines. At the other extreme, the need to respond quickly to customer demands, compounded by distinct national business practices, calls for more nationally focussed manufacturing sites.

Finally, in the distribution and sales and service functions there was a strong bias towards either a pan-European or a national focus. Only a handful of companies moved to organise these activities on a global basis.

Organisational locus of managerial responsibility
In all activities (except manufacturing) a majority of companies claimed that there had been a marked shift in the locus of decision making in the last few years. The general trend has been one of increased centralisation. This is particularly noticeable in procurement, where companies have moved to take advantage of emerging opportunities for greater cost savings, through such mechanisms as centrally negotiated procurement contracts. Likewise in R&D, where a company such as Pharmacia has adopted a more centralised approach in order to better control R&D spending (investing more money on fewer projects) and speed up the development process through its labs.

Again, within the IT infrastructure, distribution and manufacturing activities as well as the European management function, the pattern has been one of increased centralisation, although a few companies have demonstrated a counter trend by moving towards more decentralised control. Honeywell is one firm that has increased the degree of centralisation within its IT infrastructure through the creation of a pan-European department to take responsibility for IT staff and operations across Europe.

Only in the case of marketing and sales and service has there been a strong push to decentralise decision making. This is particularly noticeable in the management of the sales and service function where 17 companies (41% of the sample) reported a move towards a more decentralised approach, compared to only 8 companies that had centralised decision-making responsibility within sales and service.

The Swiss-based financial services group Credit Suisse was one firm that decentralised the management of its sales activity. In 1992, it revised its European reporting structures giving one Board member specific responsibility for European affairs and a further five executives reporting to him responsibility for a particular geographic territory within Europe. Subject to certain guidelines, each of these executives was directly responsible for the direction and content of the sales activity within their area. At the same time, the company established several centres of excellence to capture the expertise for developing, documenting and pricing financial products and services. This represented an increased centralisation of the group's operational capability.

What this last example highlights is that decision making within large organisations can be a complex mix of both styles of management control. This can be demonstrated further in the case of Petrofina, an oil and chemicals company, which centralised the management of all those activities that were not directly 'seen' by the customer (specifically R&D and logistics) and decentralised those that are (marketing, sales and service).

Industry Dynamics

This section examines the patterns of restructuring activity seen among the surveyed companies when grouped into the six broad industry sectors (see Table 9.3–9.5).[8] Overall the results suggest that firms within an industry pursue a similar pattern of restructuring yet the particular pattern varies industry by industry.

Firms representing the financial services (banking and insurance) and commercial services (contract services, management consulting, publishing, post and telecommunications services) sectors have generally expanded their sales, marketing and IT networks. The trend among financial service firms has also been to centralise control of IT and product development while decentralising decision making in the marketing and sales areas. Firms in the commercial services sector, and to a lesser extent, financial services have focussed on the creation of pan-European operations in their restructuring.

In the energy (oil, gas, chemicals and electricity generation) and construction materials (cement, steel and building materials) industries the dominant trend is for firms to rationalise their manufacturing base; there was also a cut back and a shift towards a more pan-European focus in the distribution activity among companies in the construction materials sector.

Firms in the computers and electronics sector have undertaken a significant rationalisation in the key areas of procurement, manufacturing, distribution and IT; in R&D and procurement there has been a move to operate on a global basis, while in other activities there is a strong pan-European bias. The growing internationalisation of its customer base (for example Original Equipment manufacturers (OEM) in the semiconductor business) was said by an executive of a major consumer electronics firm to be one of the factors behind his company's efforts to develop a more coordinated pan-European approach as part of an evolving global operational capability. These changes have been associated with a heightened degree of centralisation of the procurement, marketing and IT functions and an increased devolvement of responsibility to the local operations in the case of sales and service.

In consumer products, the results indicate a rationalisation of the procurement and manufacturing functions in the process of developing a more pan-European operation. There has also been a strong push towards increased centralisation of procurement, R&D, manufacturing and the European management function.

Table 9.3 Expansion and rationalisation, by industry sector

Sector (no of constituent companies) Activity	Financial services (7)		Commercial services (7)		Energy (7)		Construction materials (4)		Computers and electronics (9)		Consumer products (4)	
	E	R	E	R	E	R	E	R	E	R	E	R
Supply chain	1	2	4	2	0	3	1	1	2	5	1	3
R&D	5	1	2	1	0	4	0	1	2	4	0	2
Manufacturing	2	3	0	3	1	5	0	4	1	7	2	3
Distribution	2	4	1	3	2	3	0	4	2	6	1	2
Marketing	6	1	5	1	3	1	1	1	1	2	1	1
Sales and service	6	1	5	1	2	1	1	2	2	4	0	2
IT infrastructure	5	3	4	2	2	2	2	1	1	7	1	1

Key: E – expansion; R – rationalisation.
Note: Numbers in boxes refer to the number of companies indicating a change in this particular activity.

Table 9.4 Geographic scope of activities – by industry sector

Sector	Financial services			Commercial services			Energy			Construction materials			Computers and electronics			Consumer products		
Activity	G	P-E	N	G	P-E	N	G	P-E	N	G	P-E	N	G	P-E	N	G	P-E	N
Supply chain	1	0	1	2	2	1	2	2	1	0	0	2	4	4	0	2	3	1
R&D	1	4	2	1	4	0	0	1	3	0	1	0	5	1	0	2	2	0
Manufacturing	1	1	1	0	0	3	0	4	1	0	1	2	7	2	0	1	3	2
Distribution	1	1	4	2	2	3	0	3	2	0	3	1	0	7	0	0	1	2
Marketing	2	2	3	2	5	3	0	2	1	0	2	0	3	7	1	2	1	1
Sales and service	2	2	3	1	4	3	0	3	2	0	2	0	1	4	3	1	0	2
IT infrastructure	3	2	4	3	2	2	0	3	3	0	1	0	4	7	1	2	1	1
Euro management team	0	4	1	0	5	2	2	1	0	0	2	0	1	8	0	1	3	1

Key: G – global; P-E – pan-European; N – national.

Table 9.5 Organisational focus of managerial responsibility, by industry sector

Sector / Activity	Financial services		Commercial services		Energy		Construction materials		Computers and electronics		Consumer products	
	C	D	C	D	C	D	C	D	C	D	C	D
Supply chain	1	0	3	0	1	2	0	1	5	2	4	0
R&D	5	1	2	0	3	2	0	1	2	3	3	0
Manufacturing	2	2	0	2	1	0	0	1	4	1	3	0
Distribution	2	2	3	0	1	2	1	1	3	1	1	1
Marketing	2	4	2	3	2	1	0	2	5	1	2	1
Sales and service	1	4	1	3	2	2	0	1	1	5	2	1
IT infrastructure	4	2	1	3	3	3	1	1	5	2	1	0
Euro management team	1	1	5	2	2	1	0	1	4	1	3	1

Key: C – centralisation; D – decentralisation.

Stage of Organisational Development

We found that the company's stage of organisational development in Europe, its 'starting point' prior to the period of restructuring, was an important influence on the amount and type of restructuring it was likely to undertake (see Tables 9.6–9.8). Companies restructuring around an existing 'multi-domestic' configuration, comprising a number of vertically integrated national subsidiaries, were the most active restructurers. There were notable shifts to greater pan-European development of the marketing, R&D and IT functions and the integration of purchasing and manufacturing into a global network; in the cases of R&D and purchasing this was combined with a more centralised approach.

Table 9.6   Expansion and rationalisation, by stage of development

Stage of development (no. of constituent companies)	National champion (14)		Multi-domestic (13)		Pan-European (10)	
Activity	E	R	E	R	E	R
Supply chain	3	6	5	5	0	5
R&D	2	7	6	5	1	3
Manufacturing	2	9	4	7	1	10
Distribution	5	7	1	8	1	7
Marketing	7	2	7	4	2	1
Sales and service	6	2	7	5	1	4
IT infrastructure	6	7	6	5	2	4
Euro management team	2	3	7	2	2	3
Total	33	43	43	41	10	37

Table 9.7   Geographic scope of activities, by stage of development

Stage of development	National champion			Multi-domestic			Pan-European		
Activity	G	P-E	N	G	P-E	N	G	P-E	N
Supply chain	4	1	2	6	3	2	2	7	1
R&D	1	5	4	6	6	0	3	3	0
Manufacturing	1	2	5	6	3	2	3	6	1
Distribution	0	5	6	2	5	4	0	6	1
Marketing	2	6	3	5	7	3	1	5	2
Sales and service	1	6	6	1	3	6	2	4	3
IT infrastructure	2	6	7	6	6	1	3	5	2
Euro management team	3	6	1	1	10	2	1	6	1
Total	14	37	34	33	43	20	15	42	11

Table 9.8 Organisational focus of managerial responsibility, by stage of development

Stage of development	National champion		Multi-domestic		Pan-European	
Activity	C	D	C	D	C	D
Supply chain	2	3	7	1	6	0
R&D	5	4	6	2	3	2
Manufacturing	1	1	5	5	4	0
Distribution	3	2	4	3	3	1
Marketing	4	5	4	5	4	1
Sales and service	3	4	1	8	2	4
IT infrastructure	5	5	6	3	5	2
Euro management team	2	2	7	3	4	1
Total	25	26	40	30	31	11

At the same time, there was a move to rationalise manufacturing and distribution while expanding in the marketing area. The focus within sales and service was very much to expand the capability and devolve responsibility to an increasing number of local operations.

More generally, we observed that these companies were more likely to undertake expansion as part of their restructuring activities, than firms representing either of the other two categories. The likely explanation is that some nationally based operations become subscale once the opportunities to supply the pan-European market start to open up. As a result, existing facilities need to be expanded or larger greenfield operations established.

For those companies that had grown up as 'national champions', with historically little cross-border activity, restructuring has tended to focus on rationalising the upstream activities of procurement and R&D and expanding downstream in marketing and sales. It appears that existing manufacturing, R&D and to a lesser extent supply arrangements in the home market are considered adequate to supply the European marketplace, yet in order to sell to consumers in other European markets it requires a significant expansion of the marketing and sales functions into these new geographic territories.

While marketing has taken on a more pan-European dimension, manufacturing has become a more nationally focussed operation. In other activities, such as R&D, distribution, sales and IT, restructuring has taken on a national or pan-European dimension, depending on the company.

Those companies that had the basics of an integrated, pan-European network already in place have rationalised in almost all areas (with only a few instances of companies expanding activities). This is particularly noticeable in procurement, manufacturing and distribution. The degree of centralisation within the procurement and IT areas has also increased.

For this category of firms, restructuring has generally involved reinforcing the existing pan-European scope of operations, especially in the supply, manufacturing and distribution activities and the IT infrastructure and European management team support functions. Interestingly it is the pan-European firms that have exhibited the least inclination (amongst the three categories) to adopt a more decentralised approach.

THE CHANGING SHAPE OF EUROPEAN CORPORATE DEVELOPMENT

Overall, these results provide strong evidence to support the notion that European corporate development is undergoing a profound shift with a major realignment of activities taking place:

- There has been a distinct move to organise several activities on a pan-European basis. Research and development, manufacturing, distribution and the IT infrastructure increasingly are being undertaken on a greater scale and out of fewer sites.
- In contrast, there has been a marked expansion in marketing, again with a pan-European flavour. The development of European marketing programmes being led out of several locations, with each location being responsible for the marketing of a particular product category, is indicative of this trend.
- This pan-European focus is not evident through all activities. For instance, there has been a move for companies to source from a reduced number of suppliers but on an increasingly global basis.
- At the same time, a number of companies have expanded their sales and service function, continuing to operate on a national basis. In some instances companies have further devolved their sales activity to a more local level, to take advantage of culturally distinct customer groupings.

Taken together, these results are a strong indication that companies are adapting their existing operations, and relocating activities to sites that are better suited to their particular needs and on a scale that allows them to capture greater economies. These developments signal a significant change in the evolving pattern of corporate development for many European-based firms, particularly those indigenous to the European continent, with a major geographical reconfiguration and 'de-coupling' of activities taking place (see Box 9.1).

Box 9.1   Activity decoupling

Traditionally, the European corporate environment has been characterised by a physical separation of activities between countries and a clustering of activities within each of several countries, with the home country being the initial and primary location for most activities, as well as the site of the corporate headquarters. Effectively, each major country subsidiary would be a scaled-down version of the parent company's operations. It would generally serve the local market and operate with a high degree of autonomy within the overall group structure. This duplication of activities in several European countries combined with a close geographic proximity of one activity to another within a country, also contributed to a well-defined decision-making structure within companies.

Europe's national borders no longer have the same capacity to influence the configuration and scale of activities. Companies have closed some nationally focussed activities while expanded others. New investments are better placed to migrate cross-border to more suitable locations. As a result the remaining activities are becoming geographically 'decoupled' from their home base and from each other. While geographically disparate, these activities remain organisationally bound through an improved communications and information infrastructure. We can expect this decoupling process to continue, although this will present managers with new challenges of coordinating dispersed activities across Europe.

Such developments have been made possible by three recent trends. The first is a dramatic improvement in the quality and functionality of communications technology, allied to a reduction in cost. This has enabled disparate company offices and activities to be better coordinated without the need to physically co-locate them. The second trend is the increased availability of support services from third party specialist suppliers. By contracting out such non-core activities as IT, facilities management, assembly and transportation, firms are able to access certain services locally without necessarily owning them. The final trend is the gradual removal of national barriers to the flow of goods, services, finance and information. Such actions favour the relative economics of serving a broader European market rather than a number of individual national markets in Europe.

CONCLUSION

Despite some concerns about the pace of progress towards a more integrated Europe, this survey demonstrates that extensive restructuring has in fact taken place among European-based companies. Each of the companies in our sample of leading companies, regardless of their competitive situation, have restructured their activities in some way or another in the last few years. This flags a warning to those companies that have been unwilling to take the necessary steps to restructure their European activities: they risk falling behind in the quest to enhance their global competitiveness.

While the Single Market programme envisioned the creation of one integrated pan-European marketplace by the end of 1992, the reality is that companies have restructured their operations in a number of ways. There has undoubtedly been a shift towards a more pan-European dimension in the way key activities are organised, but this is by no means the universal direction of change. Some activities, such as sales and service are being carried out on a more localised basis, while others, such as procurement, are operating along more global lines.

The pattern of restructuring undertaken by each company is therefore much more complex than simple choices about the degree of rationalisation or centralisation. In designing a successful restructuring plan, two factors appear to be particularly important to take into account: the dynamics of competition in the specific industries in which a company operates and its stage of organisational development in Europe.

Notes

1. The study also looked at the ways in which companies have managed the restructuring process, in order to distil key elements of a best practice for effective implementation of a major restructuring programme. For further information on this aspect see Bleackley and Williamson (1995).
2. Consider two companies, each with assembly operations in only one European location. According to Porter, the configuration of this activity would be 'geographically concentrated' in each case. Yet, it is conceivable that the two companies could differ markedly in the scale of their assembly operations and the breadth of European markets that they choose to serve.
3. In total there are 56 possible combinations of restructuring (7 classifications under the 3 dimensions of restructuring, for each of 8 value-added activities).
4. 25 of the sample companies (or their parent company) were in *Business Week*'s top 1000 global companies (ranked by market capitalisation on 31 May 1995).

5. The year 1988 was chosen because it marked the date of publication of the Cecchini Report, a much publicised report that considered the costs and lost opportunities of not achieving a single, unified EC home market from 12 separate and distinct national markets (Cecchini, 1988).
6. Most of the respondents characterised their firm as having either a national champion, a multi-domestic or pan-European configuration. Only two companies considered themselves recent entrants into the European market, while the remaining two firms could not be classified according to the existing classification.
7. The data upon which the following comments are based have been omitted in the interests of brevity. They have been included in a statistical summary, copies of which can be obtained in writing from the authors.
8. These figures depict those activities within each industry sector, where more than half of the constituent companies have undertaken the particular type of restructuring shown. For supporting data see Bleackley and Williamson (1995).

References

Atamar, T. (1991) 'The single market: it's impact on six industries', *Long Range Planning*, 24(6): 40–52.

Bartlett, C. and Ghoshal, S. (1989) *Managing Across Borders: The Transnational Solution* (Boston, MA: HBS Press).

Bartmess, A. and Cerny, K. (1993) 'World class operations: seeding plants for a global harvest', *The McKinsey Quarterly*, 2: 107–132.

Bleackley, M.E. and Williamson, P. (1995) 'Restructuring corporate Europe: a survey of the restructuring patterns and processes of Europe's leading companies', Unpublished report commissioned by The Conference Board Europe, Brussels, Belgium.

Daniels, J.D. (1986) 'Approaches to European regional management by large US multinational firms', *Management International Review*, 26(2): 27–42.

Dekker, W. (1985) 'Europe 1990: an agenda for action', *European Management Journal*, 3(1): 5–10.

Doz, Y., Bartlett, C. and Prahalad, C. (1981) 'Global competitive pressures and host country demands: managing tensions in MNCs', *California Management Review*, 23: 63–74.

Financial Times (1994) *Can Europe Compete? A Financial Times Guide* (London: Financial Times).

Garnier, G. (1982) 'Context and decision-making autonomy in the foreign affiliates of US multinational corporations', *Academy of Management Journal*, 25: 893–908.

Geroski, P.A. (1989) 'The choice between diversity and scale', in *1992: Myths and Realities*, Centre for Business Strategy Report Series. London Business School.

Hill, J.S. and Still, R.R. (1990) 'Organising the overseas sales force: how multi-nationals do it', *Journal of Personal Selling and Sales Management*, 10(2): 57–66.

Kemezis, P. (1992) 'US firms voice optimism – look to lower costs in a single market', *Chemical Week*, 151(11): 41–44.

Morrison, A and Roth, K. (1993) 'Relating Porter's configuration/coordination framework to competitive strategy and structural mechanisms: analysis and impli-cations', *Journal of Management*, 19(4): 797–818.

Porter, M.E. (1986) 'Competition in global industries: a conceptual framework', in M.E. Porter (ed.) *Competition in Global Industries* (Boston, MA: HBS Press).

Pugh, D. *et al.* (1968) 'Dimensions of organization structure', *Administrative Science Quarterly*, 13: 65–105.

Shetty, Y.K. (1979) 'Managing the multinational corporation: European and American styles', *Management International Review*, 19(3): 39–48.

Tilles, D. (1992) 'Out of the fire, into the "pan"', *Brandweek*, November 9: 24–26.

Turner, I. and Henry, I. (1994) 'Managing international organisations: lessons from the field', *European Management Journal*, 12(4): 417–431.

Williamson, P. J. (1992) 'Sales and service strategy for the single European market', *Business Strategy Review*, Summer: 17–43.

10 Strategy Development in German Manufacturing Subsidiaries in the UK and Ireland

James H. Taggart and Neil Hood

INTRODUCTION

In recent years, international business research has thrown much light on the processes through which multinational corporations develop and implement strategy, and a number of useful paradigms have been developed to model aspects of such processes. Following the general methodology of Jarillo and Martinez (1990), this chapter evaluates and interprets the roles played by manufacturing subsidiaries of multinational firms in the UK and Ireland using a sample of German-owned firms to test the framework developed. An alternative taxonomy is evolved using decision-making autonomy, market technology scope, and integration as dimensions. This paradigm helps to explain strategy evolution within the subsidiaries and may guide policy makers responsible for encouraging cross-border investment within the European Union or, indeed, in other regions.

BACKGROUND

The topic of subsidiary strategy within multinational entrerprises (MNEs) has attracted growing attention in the recent past, as for example in the case of Canada (White and Poynter, 1984), Spain (Jarillo and Martinez, 1990), Northern Ireland (McNamee and Wang, 1994) and Scotland (Hood, Young and Lal, 1994; Taggart, 1996a, b). Jarillo and Martinez analysed the strategic role of multinational subsidiaries in Spain, developed a taxonomy to describe these roles, and suggested a methodology for examining the development of strategic roles over time (see also Taggart, 1998a). The intention of this chapter is both to extend the methodology of categorising subsidiary strategy and to probe more deeply into its nature using a sample of 102 German manufacturing affiliates in the UK and Ireland to test a proposed framework. The research issue here revolves around an attempt to characterise the strategy roles of these affiliates by reference to a number of endogenous variables. Thus, it is intended to supplement the rich stream of subsidiary research summarised above. The chapter is in three main sections, starting with an overview of recent relevant research on subsidiary and corporate strategies. The core section of the chapter concerns this particular research project, including related methodological questions and the statistical analysis applied to the data. The final section draws conclusions both about the model utilised and the findings on manufacturing affiliates; it also suggests some implications for managers and policy makers.

OVERVIEW OF RELEVANT RESEARCH

The purpose of this section is to focus on three key strategy dimensions at subsidiary level: the spread of and ability to supply the different markets available to the subsidiary, freedom to make decisions, and integration of activities with other subsidiaries within the parent's network.

Market Scope

White and Poynter (1984) propose three dimensions – product scope, market scope, value-added scope – from which they derive two 4-box models (market scope is common to both). The five classifications yielded by this approach – miniature replica, marketing satellite, rationalised manufacturer, product specialist, strategic independent – give useful perspectives on subsidiary strategy, but are essentially static in nature. Value-added scope is undoubtedly an important dimension, but one that is very difficult to operationalise. Technology, management skills and the use of information are contributors to value-added, though these broad variables will combine with different priorities and proportions in different circumstances. Product scope is also difficult to define, especially in the conglomerate MNE, where the subsidiary's comparison with 'the product range of parent company' may often be meaningless. Market scope is much easier to define and operationalise; it was first introduced as a key variable by Chandler (1962), and subsequently developed by others (e.g. Rumelt, 1974; Porter, 1980; Hedlund, 1981). However, its critical role was emphasised by White and Poynter (1984), who defined it as the range of geographic markets available to the subsidiary. This, however, is rather simplistic and unidimensional. If a subsidiary is required to service certain markets for or on behalf of its corporate parent it requires, above all, the necessary technological inputs to satisfy the demands of those markets.

Autonomy

Hedlund (1986) takes a different approach, suggesting the evolution of the 'heterarchical' multinational with many centres rather than a single corporate headquarters in the home country. This concept was further developed by Hedlund and Rolander (1990), and some empirical evidence from a study of Swedish multinationals is offered by Forsgren, Holm and Johanson (1992). While this view certainly introduces a dynamic element – albeit a one-way decentralisation – it focusses essentially on the nature of the subsidiary rather than on its strategy. The topic of centralisation and decentralisation in international firms has had very substantial exposure over the years. Much research interest has centred on decision making and the extent to which it is centralised or decentralised (Picard, 1977; Hedlund, 1981; Doz and Prahalad, 1981; van den Bulcke, 1984; Taggart, 1997a). In particular, a study of foreign-owned multinationals in the UK indicated that headquarters had a strong or decisive influence on the choice of non-UK markets served in about 45% of cases, but this figure fell to 25% in the case of product policy (Hood, Young and Hamill, 1985). Centralisation was also found to be significantly higher for financial decisions and significantly lower for personnel and human relations decisions. The determinants of greater centralisation were linked to the degree of multinationality, the degree of integration within the multinational's network, and subsidiary size. Finally, it was concluded that control was moving towards the centre for the most crucial strategic and long-term decisions. Gates and Egelhoff (1986) gathered data at headquarters level about headquarters–subsidiary relationships. This study suggested a negative correlation between size of foreign operations and centralisation, statistically significant in the case of marketing decisions. It also found statistically significant negative correlations between centralisation and decisions on foreign product diversity, extent of outside ownership in foreign subsidiaries, and the extent of foreign acquisitions. Finally, statistically significant positive correlations were found between centralisation and the overall size of the MNE, the relative size of the subsidiary, the absolute size of the subsidiary, and product change (the degree to which new products are being introduced by the subsidiary to its local markets).

Integration

Yet another view is developed by Bartlett and Ghoshal (1991) who base their view on two dimensions – the level of local resources and capabilities and the strategic importance of the local environment. They see the 'transnational' as a network of resources shared between corporate headquarters and subsidiaries, with an integrative overlay fostered by a distinct pattern of interdependencies. Conceptually similar is the perspective of Prahalad and Doz (1987) who view the problem as determined by two imperatives – the need for global coordination/integration and the need for national responsiveness/differentiation. As noted above, the Jarillo and Martinez (1990) model is essentially a refinement of this approach, applied specifically at subsidiary level. Integration of worldwide activities, as envisaged by

Prahalad and Doz, has been used extensively as a key strategy determinant for a long number of years; the concept was developed by Petroni (1983), Schofield (1987), Teece (1987), and Hitt and Ireland (1987); it was further operationalised by Young *et al.* (1988). In addition to the work of Jarillo and Martinez noted above, it has been subjected to intensive empirical investigation by Roth and Morrison (1990), Johnson (1995), and Taggart (1998b).

In identifying Market Scope, Autonomy and Integration as the broad strategy dimensions to be used in this study, it is not claimed that any one individual construct is better, more powerful, or offers more insights than local responsiveness, coordination, value-added scope, configuration or procedural justice. These three dimensions have been selected because they have been individually validated by extensive empirical work, and because a three-dimensional model with eight strategy variants (combinations of 'high' and 'low' on each dimension) is likely to prove a richer analytical and interpretative tool than the two dimensional paradigms discussed above. Thus, it may be that the proposed model will better explain the strategy roles of MNE manufacturing subsidiaries and the development of those roles over time. More specifically, the inclusion of the decision-making dimension may yield additional insights in terms of the way a subsidiary might use the bargaining power *vis-à-vis* headquarters that may develop as it expands its capabilities and activities.

THE RESEARCH PROBLEM

Choice of Variables

We now have to examine how MNE affiliates position themselves on the three dimensions by exploring the endogenous strategic variables deployed in this study as follows:

1. The current market area for products supplied by the subsidiary. This variable has been used by White and Poynter (1984) and by Young *et al.* (1988); it should be closely associated with the Market Scope dimension. The variable is measured on a six-point scale (1 = mainly the UK and Ireland, 6 = worldwide).
2. The percentage of export sales currently achieved by the subsidiary (Poynter and Rugman, 1982; Quelch and Hoff, 1986; Beamish *et al.*, 1993); this variable should also be closely associated with Market Scope.
3. Decision-making responsibility for markets served by the subsidiary (Hedlund, 1981; Young *et al.*, 1988); this variable should be closely associated with Autonomy. The variable is measured on a four-point scale (1 = decided by parent without consulting subsidiary, 2 = decided by parent after consulting subsidiary, 3 = decided by subsidiary after consulting parent, 4 = decided by subsidiary without consulting parent).

4. Decision-making responsibility for the product range supplied by the subsidiary (Garnier, 1982; Egelhoff, 1988); again, this variable should be closely associated with Autonomy. (Measured as variable 3.)

5. The nature of production operations, which is a measure of the level of production technology applied by the subsidiary (Prahalad and Doz, 1987; Axelsson *et al.*, 1991); this variable should be associated with Market Scope in terms of supporting the quality demands of markets. This variable is measured on a five-point scale (1 = assembly only, 5 = fully fledged manufacturing).

6. Percentage of outputs transferred to group plants abroad for further processing or final assembly (Jarillo and Martinez, 1990; Dicken, 1992); this variable should be associated with Integration, but may also be connected to aspects of Market Scope if the parent's manufacturing operations are widely dispersed.

7. The percentage of inputs to the subsidiary originating in group plants abroad (Jarillo and Martinez, 1990; Dicken, 1992); again, this variable should be closely associated with Integration, but may also be tied to aspects of Autonomy.

8. The nature of R&D activity carried out by the subsidiary (Young *et al.*, 1988; Roth and Morrison, 1990; Taggart, 1997b). This variable should be closely associated with Integration, but may also be linked with Market Scope in terms of product technology support for diverse markets, and with Autonomy in terms of the bargaining power of the subsidiary. This variable is measured on a six-point scale (1 = no R&D, 6 = generation of new technology for corporate parent).

9. Percentage of material inputs sourced locally (Buckley and Casson, 1979; Jarillo and Martinez, 1990; Porter, 1990); This variable should be associated with Autonomy and negatively associated with Integration.

Developing the Framework

White and Poynter's model is helpful in visualising current subsidiary strategy and how it may change over time, but it depends on a strategic dimension (value-added scope) that is difficult to operationalise. The paradigm of Jarillo and Martinez avoids this shortcoming, but is very tightly linked to the MNE strategy model of Prahalad and Doz, and may suffer from some of its weaknesses (Johnson, 1995). The framework proposed here is constructed along three independent dimensions – Autonomy, Market Scope and Integration; it is not tied to any particular corporate strategy model, and it offers the prospect of incremental richness via the third strategic dimension. As noted above, it has no claim to be better than existing models, but may yield additional insights into the development and evolution of subsidiary strategy through its underlying structure.

We may devise a basic typology by considering two states (high, low) of each strategic dimension, as follows.

A High Autonomy, high Market Scope, high Integration: this type is termed Strategic Independent and is characterised by extensive decision-making capability, strong ability to serve and develop a wide range of existing markets, while coordinating its activities closely with other parts of its parent's international network.

B High Autonomy, high Market Scope, low Integration: with much less inter-network coordination than the Strategic Independent, this type is described as Emergent Regional Supplier.

C High Autonomy, low Market Scope, high Integration: with tightly limited existing markets and less technological ability to sustain market development, the Constrained Subsidiary may well be a transitional phase for the emergent Strategic Independent; alternatively, it may be a sign of a centralising tendency on behalf of the parent corporation.

D High Autonomy, low Market Scope, low Integration: the mission of the Host Market Penetrator is largely to enter and serve the UK and Ireland market with current products and technologies; exports are likely to be particularly low.

E Low Autonomy, high Market Scope, high Integration: this subsidiary type, termed the Integrated Branch Plant, is very tightly linked with the parent's international network in terms of component and part-assembly inputs and/or outputs; strategy will probably be dictated by headquarters.

F Low Autonomy, high Market Scope, low Integration: this is a development stage beyond the Starter Plant (below) and, unlike the Slave Subsidiary (below), it represents a substantive subsidiary strategy rather than a transitional phase; it is termed Regional Exporter, as its main task is to serve the parent's regional (mainly European) market from a base in the UK and Ireland.

G Low Autonomy, low Market Scope, high Integration: this type is probably a transition phase between the Starter Plant (below) and the Integrated Branch Plant, and is described as Slave Subsidiary; there are likely to be few of these, and subsidiaries are unlikely to dwell long in this stage.

H Low Autonomy, low Market Scope, low Integration: this is the direct opposite of the Strategic Independent, and is termed the Starter Plant; it is likely to be fairly small, dependent on the parent for technology inputs, and carry out fairly basic manufacturing operations for the UK and Ireland market.

Sample Characteristics

The sample of German manufacturing affiliates was drawn from both UK and Irish sources. Thus, the German Chamber of Commerce and Industry

Directory (1993) yielded a total of 268 manufacturing subsidiaries in the UK; the Irish Development Authority provided a current listing of 141 German manufacturing subsidiaries in Ireland. The total initial sample therefore comprised of 409 firms throughout the UK and Ireland. A postal survey addressed to subsidiary managing directors was regarded as an appropriate method of obtaining relevant strategy data. The initial mailing was followed by two reminder stages, and the final response amounted to 25%.

In completing the research instrument, respondents were asked to make assessments for the strategy variables for 'five years ago' and 'five years' time', as well as for the current position. Jarillo and Martinez approached this problem by asking respondents to base answers on company plans rather than personal estimates, a solution not entirely feasible in this research due to the nature of some of the variables. So, especially for variables 3 and 4, the use of managerial judgment was essential and this individual aspect to response should be remembered when results are being interpreted. The variables selected have been used in the past by other researchers, but have also been checked through both postal questionnaire and personal interview by both of the present authors working individually in the past.

The average period of establishment for the 102 subsidiaries in the sample was 15.4 years, with sales revenue of £12.8m on average. Some 58% of the sample had sales under £10m and only 5% over £50m. As regards employment, the average figure was 178, with 35% employing fewer than 50 people. Finally, Table 10.1 shows the principal area of business followed by the subsidiaries. This broadly indicates the spread of classifications that would be expected for German investment in the region, except that the mechanical engineering sector is somewhat over represented. The large number of 'other' sectors applies more to the UK than to the Irish part of the sample and is perhaps merely a reflection of the different industrial structures of the two economies.

Table 10.1 Sample sectoral distribution

Sector	No. of firms
Food, drink, tobacco	1
Chemical	13
Mechanical engineering	29
Electrical engineering	9
Electronics	9
Vehicles & associated	11
Textiles	3
Paper, printing, publishing	3
Other	24
Total	102

It is evident from the foregoing data that the subsidiaries that are under scrutiny in this study are relatively small in terms of both revenues and employment. Although there are differences between the two elements of the sample that are considered elsewhere (Hood and Taggart, 1994), they are considered to be sufficiently homogeneous for the analysis of subsidiary strategies that now follows.

STATISTICAL EVALUATION

Factor Analysis

Principal components analysis was carried out on the nine strategy variables based on the survey data. A rank-order (Spearman) correlation matrix was derived for the variables and used as input for the factor analysis. Table 10.2 shows the factor loadings for a three factor solution after performing a varimax rotation.

Only factor loadings above 0.5 are included in this assessment; while this is arbitrary to some degree, it corresponds with the cut-off level of factor loadings used in other similar studies (Miller and Friesen, 1978; Dess and Davis, 1984; Robinson and Pearce, 1988; Morrison, 1990) and is well above the minimum level of 0.3 proposed by Morrison (1967).

The three factors in this solution explain nearly 70% of the variance, a satisfactory level in social sciences (Kaiser, 1960; Alt, 1990); and the matrix of residual correlations shows low off-diagonal values – all between -0.16 and $+0.15$ (Mulaik, 1972). An examination of the communalities indicated good homogeneity (all values between 0.50 and 0.79); none of the variables had a high multiple-R^2 together with a low communality, thus indicating

Table 10.2 Principal components analysis – varimax rotation: 9 variables

	Factor 1	*Factor 2*	*Factor 3*	
Variable 1	0.0206	−0.8345	−0.1805	Market areas supplied currently
Variable 2	−0.3411	−0.7954	−0.0835	Percent export sales
Variable 3	0.7959	0.3490	0.0445	Decisions about markets served
Variable 4	0.8691	0.0781	−0.0633	Decisions about product line supplied
Variable 5	0.2912	−0.5160	−0.5012	Nature of production technology
Variable 6	−0.0853	−0.6659	0.5798	Percent of output to other group plants
Variable 7	0.0409	0.1069	0.8364	Percent of inputs from other group plants
Variable 8	0.6047	−0.2915	−0.4273	Nature of R&D activity
Variable 9	0.4753	−0.0508	−0.5155	Percent of local material inputs

that the appropriate number of factors has been retained in the analysis (Stevens, 1986). While the solution has two variables that each load on two factors, it does nevertheless yield three easily interpreted dimensions.

(i) Autonomy dimension
Both variables 3 and 4 are direct measures of the subsidiary's decision-making autonomy in markets and products. Variable 8 is a measure of the subsidiary's R&D scope, and its heavy loading on this factor suggests that the complexity of R&D activity is also a measure of affiliate autonomy. Indeed, White and Poynter (1984) argued that the bargaining power of the subsidiary *vis-à-vis* headquarters is a substantial determinant of increased R&D activity. Note that, against expectation, variable 8 did not also load significantly on the Market Scope dimension, though it does have a loading of 0.43 on Integration.

(ii) Market Scope dimension
This relates to the markets served with the nature of manufacturing technology available to meet the needs of those markets. Variables 1 and 2 are direct measures of markets served, and variable 5 of the supporting level of manufacturing technology. It is less expected that variable 6 would load so heavily on this factor, but this is clearly related to export of components and part assemblies to other parts of the parent's international network for final assembly; consequently, the sister subsidiaries become part of 'markets served'.

(iii) Integration dimension
Both variables 6 and 7 measure linkages within the corporate network between its manufacturing operations, and variable 9 – the percentage of material inputs sourced locally – is, as expected, negatively correlated with variables 6 and 7. These three give a consolidated measure of the degree of integration within which the affiliate works. The heavy loading of variable 5 on this dimension is less expected, but is probably related to integration in that a certain level of manufacturing technology is necessary to accept components or part assemblies from other group plants for further processing or, alternatively, to produce these constituents to such a technological so as to make them acceptable as inputs for other group plants (Prahalad and Doz, 1987). It was expected that variable 7 might also load significantly on the Autonomy dimension, but the loading is very small indeed.

Cluster Analysis

The next step was to use the factor scores for the three derived dimensions to explore a taxonomy of subsidiary behaviour (Galbraith and Schendel, 1983; Dess and Davis, 1984; Robinson and Pearce, 1988; Jarillo and Martinez,

1990; Morrison, 1990). Both hierarchical and non-hierarchical clustering methods were used in combination to achieve a stable clustering solution. Due to the nature of the variables hierarchical methods may be more appropriate, but non-hierarchical clustering has the advantage of calculating derived statistics like analysis of variance, cluster centroids, distance between cluster centroids, and distance from each case to the corresponding cluster centroid. The hierarchical tree suggested that 7 or 8 clusters were present. The non-hierarchical approach was then used as a comparison, and to determine cluster centroids for further analysis. Solutions were developed for 2, 3, 4, 5, 6, 7, 8, 9 and 10 clusters and the analysis of variance for each examined. The proportion of 'between clusters' variance was plotted as a proportion of total variance. For 7 clusters the 'between clusters' variance was 75% of the total; for 8 clusters, 78%; and for 9 cluster, 80%. Thus, as a parallel to the 'scree test' (Cattell, 1966) for retaining factors in factor analysis, it was concluded that 8 clusters were appropriate for this study, and the basic statistics are shown in Table 10.3. Comparing the methods, 92 of the 97 cases were entered in the same cluster by each: 2 cases were differently classified in cluster 3, 2 in cluster 4, and 1 in cluster 7. This result suggests that the 8 cluster solution is fairly robust.

The results of the cluster analysis have confirmed the strategy prescriptions set out above (see 'Developing the Framework'), and moved us from typology to taxonomy. The data in Table 10.4 begins the process of interpreting the analysis in this context. The evidence from the sample points to relatively early-stage market entry strategies on the part of many of the German companies, even where the subsidiary has been in the host market for an extended period. There is strong evidence of host-country-centred strategies throughout the sample, but especially in groups 1, 2 and 5. Group 5 is styled Starter Plant as evidence of its being the earliest stage of manufacturing, perhaps having recently emerged from being a distribution and servicing unit; it operates, however, with fairly low levels of Integration, which differentiates it from group 1, the Slave Subsidiary, whose main role appears to be final assembly for the host market of components and sub-assemblies manufactured elsewhere in the international network. The Host Market Penetration (group 2) is the next stage from the Starter Plant, in that while the plant has high autonomy it has this along clearly defined product, market and technology lines, which allows it to focus strongly on the host market. It should be recalled that both the UK and Ireland have large numbers of major MNE subsidiaries manufacturing for European Union (EU) markets and hence this group of subsidiaries serve a large and demanding market. However, they do so in a particularly constrained manner in the terms of the factors considered in this analysis. Group 6 (Integrated Branch Plant) is distinguished from 2 and 5 by the high level of integration with other group plants and rather higher market-technology scope. They are less host country orientated and may suggest evidence of

Table 10.3   Cluster analysis results

A

Factor	Between-clusters variance	Within-clusters variance	F value	p level
Autonomy	75.64	21.36	45.01	0.000
Market Scope	77.99	19.01	52.16	0.000
Integration	73.66	23.34	40.11	0.000

B

Cluster	Number of firms	Dimension	Minimum value	Maximum value	Mean value	Standard deviation
1	6	Autonomy	−1.90	−0.37	−1.07	0.60
		Market Scope	−1.97	−1.09	−1.60	0.32
		Integration	1.52	2.36	1.86	0.29
2	24	Autonomy	−0.54	1.16	0.47	0.40
		Market Scope	−1.38	0.26	−0.57	0.46
		Integration	−1.73	−0.10	−0.89	0.47
3	16	Autonomy	−1.01	0.39	−0.33	0.38
		Market Scope	−0.11	1.39	0.63	0.45
		Integration	−1.47	0.28	−0.51	0.48
4	11	Autonomy	0.60	1.99	1.25	0.53
		Market Scope	0.39	1.06	0.72	0.20
		Integration	−1.19	0.86	−0.01	0.70
5	12	Autonomy	−2.04	−0.82	−1.49	0.42
		Market Scope	−1.63	0.64	−0.35	0.62
		Integration	−1.16	0.38	−0.57	0.53
6	5	Autonomy	−1.67	−1.03	−1.39	0.32
		Market Scope	1.23	1.91	1.64	0.27
		Integration	−0.27	1.05	0.36	0.58
7	11	Autonomy	−0.25	2.45	0.82	0.82
		Market Scope	−1.61	−0.01	−1.09	0.47
		Integration	0.20	1.87	0.89	0.54
8	12	Autonomy	−0.57	0.72	0.21	0.39
		Market Scope	0.22	1.74	1.11	0.56
		Integration	0.40	2.01	1.16	0.43

group networks effectively achieving some of the intra-EU integration gains across different manufacturing locations.

Groups 3 and 4 are in rather different categories. Group 3 (Regional Exporters) has high Market Scope, but is low on Autonomy and Integration. Group 4 (Emergent Regional Suppliers) is a development from the latter stage in that the firms here have substantially more Autonomy; both groups have a higher than expected incidence of export-dependent subsidiaries. Some of Regional Exporters may evolve as Integrated Branch

Table 10.4 Subsidiary groups

Cluster	No. of Firms	Title	Main characteristics
1	6	Slave Subsidiary	Low Autonomy, very low Market Scope, and a very high degree of Integration. Likely to be a transition phase between clusters 5 and 6
2	24	Host Market Penetrator	High Autonomy, low Market Scope and low levels of Integration. Mission largely to penetrate host markets with existing products/technologies. Very low dependence on exports.
3	16	Regional Exporter	Fairly low Autonomy, fairly high Market Scope, and low Integration. Mission largely to service existing customers of the parent in European countries.
4	11	Emergent Regional Supplier	High Market Scope, low Integration, above average Autonomy, but higher export dependency to EU markets.
5	12	Starter Plant	Almost direct opposite of Cluster 8. Relatively low level, small, initial manufacturing operations for host market.
6	5	Integrated Branch Plant	Very high Integration: low on decision making: above average in market-technology scope.
7	11	Constrained Subsidiary	High autonomy, very low Market Scope and high levels of Integration. This may be a transitional phase towards cluster 8, or it may merely indicate increasing centralisation by HQ.
8	12	Strategic Independent	Highly Autonomous, tightly Integrated into parent networks: serving many markets with high levels of product and process technology.

Plants (group 6), and some Emergent Regional Suppliers as Strategic Independents (group 8). It is probable, however, that many are in groups 3 and 4 because they have a small, but distinctive product or technology advantage that was acquired by the German company and hence their categorisation. In others, a probable explanation lies in the fact that they are parts of smaller German parent companies that no longer manufacture the particular product range in Germany and use the UK or Ireland as an export base.

Table 10.5 Strategy evolution within groups

		Autonomy	Market Scope	Integration
Group 1				
Mean:	1989	−1.17	−1.86	1.50
	1994	−1.08	−1.60	1.86
	1999	−0.45	−1.76	1.63
t-value:	1989–94	0.35	2.92	2.26
	1994–99	2.44	−1.68	−1.30
p-level:	1989–94	0.74	0.03	0.07
	1994–99	0.05	0.15	0.25
Group 2				
Mean:	1989	0.43	−0.29	−0.84
	1994	0.47	−0.57	−0.89
	1999	0.36	−0.55	−0.88
t-value:	1989–94	0.41	−3.27	−0.81
	1994–99	−1.12	0.43	0.42
p-level:	1989–94	0.68	0.00	0.43
	1994–99	0.27	0.67	0.68
Group 3				
Mean:	1989	−0.08	0.59	−0.44
	1994	−0.33	0.63	−0.51
	1999	−0.47	0.67	−0.43
t-value:	1989–94	−1.71	0.38	−0.56
	1994–99	−1.77	0.79	1.39
p-level:	1989–94	0.11	0.71	0.58
	1994–99	0.10	0.44	0.19
Group 4				
Mean:	1989	0.64	0.84	0.08
	1994	1.25	0.72	−0.01
	1999	1.14	0.66	−0.26
t-value:	1989–94	2.22	−1.94	−0.77
	1994–99	−0.80	−0.76	−2.42
p-level:	1989–94	0.05	0.08	0.46
	1994–99	0.44	0.47	0.04
Group 5				
Mean:	1989	−1.16	−0.35	−0.61
	1994	−1.49	−0.35	−0.57
	1999	−1.18	−0.26	−0.35
t-value:	1989–94	−1.14	−1.08	0.34
	1994–99	0.89	1.24	1.85
p-level:	1989–94	0.28	0.31	0.74
	1994–99	0.39	0.24	0.09

Table 10.5   (continued)

		Autonomy	Market Scope	Integration
Group 6				
Mean:	1989	−0.85	1.10	0.53
	1994	−1.39	1.64	0.36
	1999	−1.27	1.49	0.64
t-value:	1989–94	−5.31	3.51	−1.05
	1994–99	2.75	−0.79	0.92
p-level:	1989–94	0.01	0.02	0.35
	1994–99	0.05	0.48	0.41
Group 7				
Mean:	1989	0.84	−1.28	0.70
	1994	0.82	−1.09	0.89
	1999	0.37	−0.96	0.57
t-value:	1989–94	−0.10	2.62	1.16
	1994–99	−2.29	1.16	−2.68
p-level:	1989–94	0.92	0.03	0.27
	1994–99	0.05	0.27	0.02
Group 8				
Mean:	1989	−0.11	0.97	1.14
	1994	0.21	1.11	1.16
	1999	0.47	1.00	1.31
t-value:	1989–94	1.42	1.10	0.14
	1994–99	2.96	−1.90	1.98
p-level:	1989–94	0.18	0.29	0.89
	1994–99	0.01	0.08	0.07

(T-tests for correlated samples)

Group 8 (Strategic Independent) is a distinct category and accounts for a small proportion of the sample, though group 7 (Constrained Subsidiary) is probably an earlier developmental stage where substantial Market Scope has yet to be achieved. From this analysis, the Strategic Independent is close to that of White and Poynter (1984) and perhaps has some elements of Porter's (1986) global firm. At this stage of EU development (and its potential enlargement), together with the relatively recent growth of German FDI, a large representation in this category would not be expected. It will be noted that 65% of the sample are in the relatively less developed groups 1, 2, 3, 5 and 6.

It is tempting in this type of analysis to imply a deterministic evolution from one type of subsidiary to another over time. Clearly this is to be avoided, although in particular circumstances a progression might be expected as different roles are assigned by the corporate parent. The two polar positions are readily established as Starter Plant and Strategic Independent, with the latter normally being the product of development to maturity. More difficult is the sequence in between them. In some circumstances it might well be Host Market Penetrator, Integrated Branch Plant to Emergent Regional Supplier, but further investigation would be required to verify this and much would depend on the corporate positioning of the parent in the market concerned. Having said that, this project did examine the 10-year changes that were evident in the chosen dimensions and these are reported in the next section.

Strategic Change over Time

In completing the research instrument, respondents were asked to make assessments for the strategy variables for 'five years ago' and 'five years time', as well as for 'now'. This allowed an examination of strategy evolution. The factor solutions for 'five years ago' and 'five years time' were substantially similar to that for 'now', so the clustering procedure was carried out as described above (see Jarillo and Martinez, 1990). The resultant summary of variables is shown in Table 10.5.

The overall impression gained from Table 10.5 is of a remarkable stability of subsidiary strategy over time. From a very low base, Slave Subsidiaries increased Market Scope during the period 'five years ago to now' and expected to gain in Autonomy during 'now to five years' time'. Conversely, Host Market Penetrators became even more focussed on the UK and Ireland over the last five years. Emergent Regional Suppliers gained somewhat in Autonomy over the last five years, but expect to become even less integrated with the parent network during the next five years. This is broadly in line with the expected role of this group. As a wide market base is established together with the production technology to support it, there is likely to be a need to increase the scope of decision making to support increased market penetration efforts.

Integrated Branch Plants had a very substantial loss of Autonomy in the previous five years and, while this is expected to be reversed substantially over the next five years, it will not regain the position of 'five years ago'. In addition, these firms gained more latitude in terms of Market Scope in the last five years. It should be noted that these firms (together with Starter Plants) have very much less decision-making authority than the sample as a whole. It is consistent with their role that market-technology scope would grow in response to both customer and network demands. Equally, plant performance and management competence in a plant that has high levels of integration, could be expected to lead to more decision-making authority, as reflected in the 'now to five years' time' comparison.

Constrained Subsidiaries made the same type of gain during this period, albeit from a much lower base, but expect to lose in both Autonomy and Integration over the next five years. Strategic Independents remain unchanged over the whole period with the exception of an expected further gain in Autonomy over the next five years. Regional Exporters and Starter Plants show no change of any kind over the 10-year period. Thus it would seem that, having reached a strategic posture that is satisfactory to both parent and subsidiary, no change has occurred in these two groupings in the last five years, and none is envisaged for the next five. Overall, this analysis shows a number of changes in Autonomy (4 increases, 2 drops), fewer in Market Scope (3 increases, 1 drop), and only two changes in Integration (both drops).

Thus, Autonomy is the most volatile dimension and it tends to increase throughout the study period, as does Market Scope, though the movement here is weaker. Integration within the parent's own network is the most stable parameter and it could marginally drop in some cases during the next five years. All of this suggests a gradual increase in the overall autonomy of German subsidiaries in the UK and Ieland, though, as noted, there are substantial differences among the strategic groups identified. Specifically, the evolution of subsidiary strategy reported here is not so marked as that found in recent similar work (Prahalad and Doz, 1987; Jarillo and Martinez, 1990; Taggart, 1996b).

CONCLUSIONS

As indicated in the introduction, this chapter had three objectives. The first was to build on the well-tested and accepted strategy dimension of integration in the context of subsidiary management; and also to develop a three-dimensional model that identifies some of the main characteristics of strategic behaviour at subsidiary level – at least when viewed from the perspective of the senior management of the subsidiary. The second was to apply this model to a sample of German manufacturing affiliates in the UK and Ireland in order to attempt to add to the limited academic knowledge that exists about this particular aspect of FDI. The third objective was to use the derived framework to examine how the strategies of German subsidiaries changed over time. For the purposes of clarity, the conclusions distinguish between these three objectives.

Subsidiary Strategy Model

As a preliminary step, the approach taken here has had a measure of success, with acknowledged limitations. It has confirmed the importance of corporate–subsidiary integration, as well as highlighting the critical nature of the spread of market served and its link with the extent of process technology used to service different customer bases. This amplifies the White and Poynter (1984) concept of market scope, though it might also be conceived as the resolution of market scope and aspects of value-added scope on a single dimension. The model draws out the need for a decision-making dimension with reference to products, markets and the nature of R&D, showing this to be an important factor in understanding the strategic posture of the MNE subsidiary (see also Taggart, 1998c). It is, however, recognised that the underlying nature of this dimension requires confirmation from more fine-grained research with the individual companies and that only the broader perspective can be expected to emerge from data generated by postal questionnaire. For example, detailed company interviews may well reveal that the degree of decision-making autonomy as defined in this study is in itself an enabling factor in the operationalisation of the level of integration, the degree of localisation, the extent of market and product scope and so on.

The strategy prescriptions of the model derived in this chapter may be broadly compared to those of other researchers. The Strategic Independent is very similar to that of White and Poynter (1984) and to the Active Subsidiary of Jarillo and Martinez (1990); this also applies, though to a lesser extent, to the Constrained Subsidiary. In corporate terms, there are links with Porter's (1986) Purest Global strategy and with Bartlett's (1986) Transnational form of organisation. The Integrated Branch Plant, on the other hand, may be linked with Porter's High Foreign Investment strategy and with Bartlett's Global Organisational form. It has clear parallels with Jarillo and Martinez' Receptive Subsidiary and some similarities with White and Poynter's Rationalised Manufacturer. The Emergent Regional Supplier and, to a lesser extent, the Regional Exporter may be compared with Jarillo and Martinez' Autonomous Subsidiary, and possibly with White and Poynter's Product Specialist. It may operate within a Country-focussed strategy (Porter) and a Multinational Organisational form (Bartlett). Neither the Starter Plant, the Slave Subsidiary nor the Host Market Penetrator have any parallel within the Jarillo and Martinez paradigm or Bartlett's typology. However, the first two are close to the Miniature Replica (White and Poynter), operating within a parent with an Export-based strategy (Porter) in the early stages of internationalisation, while the latter represents some aspects of the Rationalised Manufacturer (White and Poynter) operating within a developing Country-focussed corporate strategy (Porter).

There are some caveats to be offered in the light of the evidence presented. For example, these findings may be largely due to the distinctive characteristics of German manufacturing in the UK and Ireland, an issue that is reviewed below. More related to the model itself, is the need to increase the number of variables used in the factor analysis to capture the three core dimensions of Autonomy, Market Scope and Integration. Perhaps there is less need for this in the case of the latter, since that aspect is well supported in the literature. However, the analysis may well be enriched in the Market Scope dimension, for example, by the inclusion of the specifics of product addition and deletion, market entry strategies, and the evaluation of competitive technologies.

Strategies in German Manufacturing Subsidiaries within the EU

In many ways these findings and the resultant eight-group taxonomy of German affiliates are rather revealing and develop considerably the knowledge base about this type of international investment. Corporate intentions are confirmed as largely directed to host country markets, but Integrated Branch Plants, Emergent Regional Suppliers, Constrained Subsidiaries and Strategic Independents all play rather different roles. The first of these largely in a production context, the second as perhaps the beginnings of source-points for wider markets. As emphasised, both the origins and the future of this group are particularly difficult to predict at this stage.

Taking a slightly wider perspective, it is clear that German parent companies are highly specific about the role/strategy taken up by the UK affiliate, and developed over time. The variety represented by the eight-group taxonomy (if it actually represents real life) gives both parent and affiliate wider choice of initial and subsequent strategic capacity, and a wider range of strategic trajectories. This research reveals little about the dynamics of choice and trajectory, but there is clearly scope for such enquiry in the future.

Strategy Evolution

Another important aspect of the findings lies in the relatively moderate changes over time both in a number of the subsidiary groupings as a whole and in the functional differences between them. In particular, the reported levels of integration (in terms of inputs and outputs) being static is somewhat of a puzzle. Differential cost and productivity levels, as well as customer requirements and related parameters, might have been expected to act on these variables. Equally, the refocussing of German investment interest towards Eastern and Central Europe, while likely to lead to further sourcing of components and sub-assemblies from these countries, does not apparently emerge at this level of analysis.

One final and important set of policy issues arise from those findings in terms of the attraction and development of FDI by the UK and Ireland, who are both very active in this field. From an economic impact perspective it is evident that the various strategic groupings make rather different contributions to the host economies (Young, Hood and Peters, 1994). The view that many of these affiliates have not moved along a development path towards higher value-added over a 10-year period will not be a welcome one; nor will the suggestion that a large number of them have relatively unpredictable futures in terms of their wider European roles. In that regard there is little evidence yet that German manufacturers replicate, or are likely to replicate, the patterns of US and Japanese investors who develop many of their UK and Ireland manufacturing subsidiaries into major export points for the EU as a whole.

References

Alt, M. (1990) *Exploring Hyperspace* (London: McGraw Hill).
Axelsson, R. *et al.* (1991) 'Decision style in British and Swedish organisations: a comparative examination of strategic decision making', *British Journal of Management*, 2(2): 67–80.
Bartlett, C.A. (1986) 'Building and managing the transnational: the new organisational challenge', in M.E. Porter (ed.) *Competition in Global Industries* (Boston, MA: Harvard Business School Press).
Bartlett, C.A. and Ghoshal, S. (1991) 'Global strategic management: impact on new frontiers of strategy research', *Strategic Management Journal*, 12: 5–16.
Buckley, P.J. and Casson, M. 'A theory of international operations', in P.J. Buckley and P. Ghauri (eds) *The Internationalisation of the Firm* (London: Academic Press).
Cattell, R. (1966) 'The scree test for the number of factors', *Multivariate Behavioural Research*, 1: 245–276.
Chandler, A. (1962) *Strategy and Structure* (Cambridge, MA: MIT Press).
Dess, G. and Davis, P. (1984) 'Porter's (1980) generic strategies as determinants of strategic group membership and organizational performance', *Academy of Management Journal*, 27: 467–488.
Dicken, P. (1992) *Global Shift* (London: Paul Chapman).
Doz, Y.L. and Prahalad, C.K. (1981) 'Headquarters influence and strategic control in MNEs', *Sloan Management Review*, Fall: 15–29.
Egelhoff, W.G. (1988) 'Strategy and structure in multinational corporations: a revision of the Stopford and Wells model', *Strategic Management Journal*, 12: 145–164.
Forsgren, M., Holm, U. and Johanson, J. (1992) 'Internationalisation of the second degree: the emergence of European-based centres in Swedish firms', in S. Young, S. Dunlop and J. Hamill (eds) *Europe and the Multinationals* (Aldershot: Edward Elgar).
Galbraith, C. and Schendel, D. (1983) 'An empirical analysis of strategy types', *Strategic Management Journal*, 4: 153–173.
Garnier, G.H. (1982) 'Context and decision making autonomy in the foreign affiliates of US multinational corporations', *Academy of Management Journal*, 25(4): 893–908.
Gates, S.R. and Egelhoff, W.G. (1986) 'Centralization in headquarters-subsidiary relationships', *Journal of International Business Studies*, Summer: 71–92.
Hedlund, G. and Rolander, D. (1990) 'Actions in heterarchies: new approaches to managing the MNE', in C.A. Bartlett, Y.L. Doz and G. Hedlund (eds) *Managing the Global Firm* (London: Routledge).
Hedlund, G. (1981) 'Autonomy of subsidiaries and formalization of headquarters-subsidiary relationships in Swedish MNEs', in L. Otterbeck (ed.) *The Management of Headquarters-Subsidiary Relationships in Multinational Corporations* (Aldershot: Gower).

Hedlund, G. (1986) 'The hypermodern MNE: a heterarchy?', *Human Resource Management*, 25: 9–36

Hitt, M.A. and Ireland, R.D. (1987) 'Building competitive strength in international markets', *Long Range Planning*, 20(1): 115–122.

Hood, N. and Taggart, J.H. (1994) 'German foreign direct investment in UK and Ireland: survey evidence', *Regional Studies*, 31(2): 137–148.

Hood, N., Young, S. and Hamill, J. (1985) 'Decision making in foreign-owned multinational subsidiaries in the United Kingdom', *Working Paper 35* (Geneva: International Labour Office).

Hood, N., Young, S. and Lal, D. (1994) 'Strategic evolution and Japanese manufacturing plants in Europe: UK evidence', *International Business Review*, 3(2): 97–122.

Jarillo, J.C. and Martinez, J.I. (1990) 'Different roles for subsidiaries: the case of multinational corporations in Spain', *Strategic Management Journal*, 11: 501–512.

Johnson, J.H. Jr (1995) 'An empirical analysis of the integration responsiveness framework: US construction equipment industry firms in global competition', *Journal of International Business Studies*, 26(3): 621–635.

Kaiser, H.F. (1960) 'The application of electronic computers to factor analysis', *Educational and Psychological Measurement*, 20: 141–151.

McNamee, P. and Wang, H. (1994) 'European integration and corporate strategy: an empirical study of multinational companies in a peripheral region', *Proceedings of the 21st Annual Conference of the UK Academy of International Business*, UMIST, 2–26 March, pp. 449–470.

Miller, D. and Friesen, P. (1978) 'Archetypes of strategy formulation', *Management Science*, 24: 921–933.

Morrison, A.J. (1990) *Strategies in Global Industries: How US Businesses Compete* (New York: Quorum Books).

Mulaik, S.A. (1972) *The Foundations of Factor Analysis* (New York: McGraw-Hill).

Petroni, G. (1983) 'The strategic management of R&D, Part II – organising for integration', *Long Range Planning*, 16(2): 51–64.

Picard, J. (1977) 'Factors of variance in multinational marketing control', in L.G. Mattson and F. Weidsheim-Paul (eds) *Recent Research on the Internationalization of Business* (Uppsala: Almqvist and Wiksel).

Porter, M.E. (1986) 'Changing patterns of international competition', *California Management Review*, 28: 9–40.

Porter, M.E. (1990) *The Competitive Advantage of Nations* (London: Macmillan).

Poynter, T.A. and Rugman, A.M. (1982) 'World product mandates: how will multinationals respond?', *Business Quarterly*, Autumn: 54–61.

Prahalad, C.K. and Doz, Y.L. (1987) *The Multinational Mission: Balancing Local Demands and Global Vision* (New York: Free Press).

Quelch, J.A. and Hoff, E.J. (1986) 'Customizing global marketing', *Harvard Business Review*, 64(3): 59–68.

Roth, K. and Morrison, A.J. 'An empirical analysis of the integration-responsiveness framework in global industries', *Journal of International Business Studies*, 21(4): 541–564

Rumelt, R. (1974) *Strategy, Structure and Economic Performance* (Cambridge, MA: Harvard Graduate School of Business Administration).

Schofield, N.A. (1987) 'Integration – the key to success with CAD/CAM', *Long Range Planning*, 20(3): 84–91.

Stevens, J. (1996) *Applied Multivariate Statistics for the Social Sciences*, (Hillsdale, NJ: Erlbaum).

Taggart, J.H. (1996a) 'Multinational manufacturing subsidiaries in Scotland: strategic role and economic impact', *International Business Review*, 5(5): 447–468.

Taggart, J.H. (1996b) 'Evolution of multinational strategy: evidence from Scottish manufacturing subsidiaries', *Journal of Marketing Management*, 12(6): 533–549.

Taggart, J.H. (1997a) 'Autonomy and procedural justice: a framework for evaluating subsidiary strategy', *Journal of International Business Studies*, 28(1): 51–76.

Taggart, J.H. (1997b) 'R&D intensity in UK subsidiaries of manufacturing multinational corporations', *Technovation*, 17(2): 73–82.

Taggart, J.H. (1998a) 'Strategy shifts in MNE subsidiaries', *Strategic Management Journal*, 19: 663–681.

Taggart, J.H. (1998b) 'Identification and development of strategy at subsidiary level', in J. Birkinshaw and N. Hood (eds.) *Multinational Corporate Evolution and Subsidiary Development* (London: Macmillan) pp. 23–49.

Taggart, J.H. (1998c) 'Configuration and coordination at subsidiary level: foreign manufacturing affiliates in the UK', *British Journal of Management*, 9: 327–339.

Teece, D. (1987) 'Profiting from technological innovation: implications for integration, elaboration, licensing and public policy', *Research Policy*, 15: 285–305.

Van den Bulcke, D. (1984) 'Decision making in multinational enterprises and the information and consultation of employees: the proposed Vredling Directive of the EC Commission', *International Studies of Management and Organization*, 14(1): 36–60.

White, R.E. and Poynter, T.A. (1984) 'Strategies for foreign-owned subsidiaries in Canada', *Business Quarterly*, Summer: 59–69.

Young, S. Hood, N. and Dunlop, S. 'Global strategies, multinational subsidiary roles and economic impact in Scotland', *Regional Studies*, 22(6): 487–497.

Young, S., Hood, N. and Peters, E. 'Multinationals and regional economic development', *Regional Studies*, 28(7): 657–677.

11 Foreign Direct Investment, Economic Transition and the Impact on Marketing Practice in Slovenia

John Fahy, Graham Hooley, Tony Cox and Boris Snoj

M31 F23
P31 P33

INTRODUCTION

Central Europe (CE) has been an important locus for research in the area of marketing since the fall of Communism. Researchers have adopted both the perspective of a potential investor in the region (Quelch, Joachimsthaler and Nueno, 1991) and well as that of indigenous firms (Hooley, 1993; Noar, 1989). This study builds on an emerging line of research that examines the impact of foreign direct investment (FDI) on marketing practice in countries in CE. The extant research has highlighted, for example, that Hungarian firms tend to be more market orientated than their Polish counterparts (Shipley *et al.*, 1994) and that firms with foreign participation in Hungary are more likely to have long-term, growth-orientated marketing objectives than state-owned enterprises (Hooley *et al.*, 1996). To date, however, most research has focussed on the larger countries in CE, such as Bulgaria, the Czech Republic, Hungary and Poland. In particular, there is a dearth of knowledge on the status of marketing in several of the smaller economies, such as the Baltic states, Slovakia and the states of the former Yugoslavia. The research outlined in this chapter is the beginning of the process of filling this void, presenting an assessment of the impact of foreign direct investment on the marketing practice of a sample of Slovene firms.

The purpose of this chapter is to examine the nature of marketing strategy and performance of Slovene firms. Organisation theorists have noted the existence of equifinality in organisational interactions with the environment (Hrebiniak and Joyce, 1985). In other words, in any given set of competitive conditions, organisations will exhibit a number of different approaches in key areas of decision making, such as structure and strategy. A cross-sectional study of a transition economy such as Slovenia provides a vivid illustration of the presence of equifinality resulting from a range of influences, such as the tenacity of old, established practices and structures as well as the innovation of new firms seeking to exploit emerging opportunities. In general, four broad sets of firms currently operate in Slovenia. These include enterprises that are still state owned (SOEs), former state-owned enterprises that have been privatised through domestic investment (domestically privatised firms), firms with some or full foreign ownership (firms with FDI) and private domestic firms including both those that existed before Slovene independence and those founded subsequently (organic firms). Given the presence of this variety of organisational types, important differences in marketing strategy and performance might be expected, with implications for research, practice and policy making in the region.

BACKGROUND TO THE STUDY

Slovenia is one of the more progressive and better developed economies in the CE region. When it was still a part of Yugoslavia, Slovenia covered less than 8% of the land area and had 8% of the population, yet it accounted for almost 17% of the total GNP, 27% of exports and more than 30% of exports in convertible currency. Its population is just under two million people, but its GDP per head as a percentage of the European average is 34.6%, which is superior to all other CE countries with the exceptions of the Czech Republic and Slovakia (Economist, 1997a). All of Slovene exports went to the European Union (EU) in 1995, which was higher than any of its CE neighbours (Economist, 1997a). No longer required to finance the Yugoslavian federation and its army, Slovenia has been investing in building its infrastructure and marketing itself as being central European, or 'between Venice and Vienna' (Financial Times, 1997). Its economy is orientated towards services and manufacturing and the services sector accounts for approximately 57% of its output. Despite Slovenia's small population, its economy is well developed economically and in terms of international trade.

Slovenia enjoyed the highest standard of living among the former Yugoslav republics, but the disintegration of that federation led to disruption in trade, production and tourism in the early 1990s. Fixed investment declined and the unemployment rate rose from 5% in 1990 to more than 14% in 1993 (World Bank, 1996). However, since its independence in October 1991, Slovenia has made substantial progress from these disruptions. A new currency, the Slovene tolar was introduced and yearly inflation fell from 247% in 1991 to 23% in 1993 (World Bank, 1996). In early 1993, a comprehensive structural reform programme was launched, including the privatisation of socially owned enterprises, the development of the private sector and restructuring of the banking sector. Progress in privatisation efforts was initially slow due to the negative legacy of the Yugoslav experiment with self-management, which gave rise to the belief that socially owned companies were the property of managers and workers and not something that can be bought and sold. Less than one-third of Slovenia's 1400 eligible companies had been privatised by early 1996 (Business Central Europe, 1996) in a complicated system involving the transfer of equity stakes to managers and employees as well as placing up to 40% of the value of companies in a variety of investments, such as pension funds and voucher privatisation funds. By mid-1996, insiders owned more than half of the equity in almost 80% of privatised companies (EIU, 1997a and b). However, the privatisation process has also effectively excluded foreign participation with the result that Slovenia has among the lowest levels of inward FDI in the region, ranking with Romania and Slovakia (Business Central Europe, 1996). This contrasts sharply with the relatively higher levels of inward investment, measured on a per-person basis, in countries like Hungary and the Czech Republic. Against this, the growth in new private enterprises has been robust, partly due to progress in adopting important elements of reform in the legal framework for private-sector development (World Bank, 1996).

In short, Slovenia is an important country for a number of reasons. First, it is one of the more stable and better-developed economies in CE. Understanding the impact of the transition in Slovenia on the firms there provides an indicator of the likely future impact of changes in neighbouring countries. Second, as part of the former Yugoslavian federation and one that escaped the ravages of war, it represents an important gateway into other markets in the Balkans region making a knowledge of the status of marketing practice in the country important. Third, it is a prospective member of an enlarged European Union, having applied for membership in 1996. The success of its application would increase its potential opportunity as a new market as well as offering competitive Slovene firms the chance to threaten their more established European rivals. For these reasons, an understanding of the status of transition and the nature of marketing strategy and performance in Slovenia is desirable.

RESEARCH PROPOSITIONS

Since the work of Porter (1980), the impact of industry conditions on organisational performance has been the focus of much interest. Porter's initial work, and ongoing empirical research (McGahan and Porter, 1997), attests to the important role played by competitive conditions in determining performance. Several dissenting voices have emerged over the past decade, with conceptual work, such as that falling within the realm of the resource-based view of the firm (Barney, 1991; Grant, 1991) and empirical research (Hansen and Wernerfelt, 1989; Rumelt, 1991), highlighting the importance of firm-level factors. Whatever the respective importance of firm versus industry factors, the Porter five forces model (Porter, 1980) has become the established framework for assessing industry competitiveness. Heightened competition arises in situations of low barriers to entry, intense rivalry among numerous competitors of similar size, the presence of demanding buyers and suppliers, and the threat of substitutes. The transition to a market-led economy is characterised by an increase in the intensity of competition as industries are deregulated and protective measures that had been put in place by governments are swept away. However, while many state-owned companies and domestically privatised firms retain their monopoly status, the entrance of foreign-owned and organic firms potentially increases the level of rivalry and may alter levels of bargaining power at different stages of the industry chain. Therefore:

P1:   *Firms that are fully or partly foreign-owned and those which have never been state-owned will be operating in more competitive environments than those that have been or are still state-owned.*

The extant marketing literature has long stressed the importance of adopting a market orientation whereby firms understand and respond to the needs of their customers. The question of market orientation is of particular relevance in the context of the former centrally planned economies, where it would be expected that the absence of a market imperative would have hindered its development. Previous research in Central Europe has demonstrated that this is indeed the case. For example, research in Poland has found that firms there exhibit a predominantly sales/advertising orientation (Shipley and Fonfara, 1993) while in Bulgaria the presence of a predominantly production orientation has been observed (Marinov *et al.*, 1993). Further work by Hooley *et al.* (1996), in Hungary, found that the business orientation observed varied with organisational type. For example, their study found that state-owned enterprises were most likely to be production orientated, while the most market-orientated firms were those with private Hungarian participation. As Slovenia is one of the better-developed CE economies and one that has had relatively well developed relations with Western firms for some time, it is to be expected that the majority of Slovene firms will exhibit a market orientation. However, the problems that can be created by a firm's administrative heritage (Bartlett and Ghoshal, 1989), whereby it has difficulty breaking with its past traditions, are well recognised in international business research. In this context, it is expected that firms with some level of FDI will be more market orientated than their domestic counterparts, therefore:

P2: *Firms that are fully or partly foreign-owned will be more market orientated than their domestic counterparts.*

Industrial organisation theorists, such as Hymer (1960), have proposed that FDI is driven by a desire to counter competition in foreign markets and to appropriate fully the returns deriving from advantages developed domestically. Firms operating in foreign markets face disadvantages compared with local competitors, including the latter's greater familiarity with local conditions, political and exchange risks, and the travel and communication costs incurred in conducting foreign business (Caves, 1971; Hymer, 1960). To overcome these disadvantages, it was argued that firms must possess idiosyncratic advantages that, when used in foreign markets, generate economic returns over and above their opportunity costs (Graham, 1978). These advantages may derive from imperfections in goods markets (e.g. product differentiation, seller concentration), factor markets (proprietary technology, managerial skills) and government-imposed restrictions (tariffs) (Kindleberger, 1969). Caves (1971), for example, outlined how imperfections in the market for goods, such as product differentiation, helps to explain horizontal foreign direct investment. Firms that successfully develop differentiated products possess specific marketing capabilities that can be transferred to foreign markets at little or no cost and thus enable the effective appropriation of returns. Consequently, it is to be expected that firms with FDI will exhibit different business objectives and strategies than will domestic firms. In particular, it is expected that firms with FDI will have more long-term, growth-orientated marketing objectives, which build on their domestically derived strengths, and that their competitive strategies will be characterised by a focus on differentiation due to the inherent cost disadvantages noted above. Therefore:

P3a: *Firms that are fully or partly foreign-owned will have more long-term, growth-orientated marketing objectives than their domestic counterparts.*

P3b: *Firms that are fully or partly foreign-owned will be more likely to be characterised by differentiation strategies than their domestic counterparts.*

Finally, the question of performance is one that is of interest to managers, investors and policy makers alike. One of the objectives of the transition to a market-led economy is to stimulate the kinds of strategic and structural changes that enable the development of a pool of internationally competitive firms. However, the problems of structural inertia (Hannan and Freeman, 1984) and administrative heritage (Bartlett and Ghoshal, 1989) hinder the ease with which firms can make the kinds of strategic changes necessary to positively influence their performance. As noted above, the legacy of Slovenia's participation in the Yugoslav self-management experiment has been such that it has hindered the pace of the privatisation process. It is to be expected that old patterns of behaviour will prevail to some extent in domestic firms, with the effect that the strategic changes necessary to respond to recent developments in the environment will be more difficult to introduce in these firms. Therefore:

P4:   *Firms that are fully or partly foreign-owned will outperform their domestic counterparts.*

METHODOLOGY

Data were collected in two phases. First, a series of in-depth case studies was conducted covering issues such as the privatisation process and foreign direct investment, market orientation, marketing strategy and performance. A total of eleven interviews, conducted in Slovene, were held with senior managers in the retailing and electronics sectors. These interviews enabled an assessment of the ability of local Slovenian managers to understand marketing terminology and concepts. This preliminary phase was followed by a quantitative study, the results of which are reported here. The questionnaire was first developed in English and then translated into Slovene. It was pre-tested on a number of executive directors of local firms and subsequently some minor modifications were made to correct misinterpretation. This was followed by a mail survey of all firms in Slovenia employing more than 20 people ($n = 1581$). The fieldwork was conducted in three stages. One week after the initial round of questionnaires, a remainder letter was sent to all non-respondents. A second wave of reminder letters followed one week later. A total of 629 usable responses had been received by the cut-off date, giving a response rate of 40%, which compares very favourably with the norm for mail surveys not offering anonymity (Hart, 1987). A follow-up telephone survey of non-respondents yielded 72 firms that provided basic classificatory information. This was used in conducting tests of non-response bias and no significant differences were observed between the responding and non-responding groups.

RESULTS

The findings of the study are summarised in Tables 11.1–11.5. The first proposition concerned the nature of the competitive environment. This construct was operationalised using the Porter five forces framework (Porter, 1980) and the findings of an examination of the competitive environment in Slovenia are presented in Table 11.1. Almost two-thirds of the sample operated in industrial markets, with their main customers being other businesses, and almost 80% of these firms described customer bargaining power as being strong. A similar proportion considered competition in their industries to be intense. Two-thirds of the suppliers of the responding group

Table 11.1   Competitive conditions in Slovenia (percent of each group)

Industry dimension	State-owned firms (n = 163)	Domestic private firms (n = 287)	Firms with FDI (n = 48)	Organic firms (n = 122)
Bargaining power of buyers				
Strong	77.3	81.1	83.0	80.0
Moderate/weak	22.7	18.8	17.0	20.0
Total	100.0	99.9	100.0	100.0
Chi-Square = 0.62 (not significant)				
Rivalry among competing firms				
Intense	69.8	75.9	72.3	73.9
Moderate/non-existent	30.3	24.2	27.6	26.0
Total	100.1	100.1	100.0	99.9
Chi-Square = 0.70 (not significant)				
Bargaining power of suppliers				
Strong	36.3	24.9	30.4	46.0
Moderate	56.3	64.8	60.9	48.7
Weak	7.5	10.3	8.7	5.3
Total	100.1	100.0	100.0	100.0
Chi-Square = 0.01 (Significant at $p = 0.05$)				
The threat of substitutes				
Substantial	30.4	33.9	47.8	35.7
Some threat of substitutes	46.0	49.1	34.8	47.8
Little possibility	23.6	17.0	17.4	16.5
Total	100.0	100.0	100.0	100.0
Chi-Square = 0.25 (not significant)				
The threat of new entrants				
Substantial	37.0	38.8	39.1	36.5
Some threat of new entrants	40.1	47.0	41.3	50.4
Little possibility	22.8	14.2	19.6	13.0
Total	99.9	100.0	100.0	99.9
Chi-Square = 0.24 (not significant)				

Percentage totals may not equal 100 due to rounding and/or missing data.

are other Slovene firms who, in the main (almost 60%) exert moderate levels of supplier power. The perceived threat of new entrants and substitutes are both very high, with over 80% of respondents in both cases commenting that these represented at least some threat. Consequently, across a range of industries in Slovenia, competition is perceived to be intense. It is also important that this is perceived to be the case irrespective of the type of firm

Table 11.2 An analysis of market orientation by firm type

Statements on market orientation – selected items (Narver and Slater, 1990)	State-owned firms (A) (mean)[1]	Domestic private firms (B) (mean)	Firms with FDI (C) (mean)	Organic firms (D) (mean)	Significance
1. Our commitment to serving customer needs is closely monitored	2.56 < C, D	2.33	2.04	2.06	0.006[2]
2. We achieve rapid response to competitive actions	3.18	3.04	2.87	2.54 > A,B	0.005[2]
3. Information about customers is freely communicated throughout the firm	4.04	3.96	4.13	3.41 > A	0.025[3]
4. Competitive strategies are based on understanding customer needs	2.79	2.56	2.29	2.25 > A	0.006[2]
5. Business functions are integrated to serve customer needs	2.48	2.60	2.29	2.16 > B	0.041[3]
6. Close attention is given to after sales service	3.54	3.41	3.22	2.88 > A,B	0.008[2]
7. Customers are targeted when we have an opportunity for competitive advantage	3.47	3.44	3.38	2.95	0.043[3]

[1] Means are calculated on a seven-point scale with a score of one indicating the strongest level of agreement with the statement.
[2] Significant at $p = 0.01$.
[3] Significant at $p = 0.05$.

Table 11.3   An analysis of strategic and marketing objectives by firm type

Strategic and marketing objectives	State-owned firms (n = 163)	Domestic private firms (n = 287)	Firms with FDI (n = 48)	Organic firms (n = 122)
Strategic priorities for the last two years				
Survival	65.4	45.9	34.8	28.6
Good short-term financial returns or profits	16.7	23.1	28.3	23.2
Long-term building of market position	17.9	31.0	37.0	48.2
Total	100.0	100.0	100.1	100.0
Chi-Square = 0.000 (Significant at $p = 0.001$)				
Strategic priorities for the next two years				
Survival	18.9	10.8	6.5	8.8
Good short-term financial returns or profits	17.0	13.7	13.0	16.8
Long-term building of market position	64.2	75.5	80.4	74.3
Total	100.1	100.0	99.9	99.9
Chi-Square = 0.064 (Not significant)				
Marketing objectives				
To maintain/defend current position	21.5	31.2	25.5	13.9
To achieve steady sales growth	71.2	60.0	63.8	72.2
Achieve aggressive growth/ dominate market	7.4	8.8	10.6	13.9
Total	100.1	100.0	99.9	100.0
Chi-Square = 0.008 (Significant at p = 0.01)				

Percentage totals may not equal 100 due to rounding and/or missing data.

responding. Competitive intensity is being felt just as much by state-owned enterprises as it is by new organic firms, for example. The only dimension of the five forces model in which differences in perception between the groups are observed is in the case of the bargaining power of suppliers. This is perceived to be strongest in organic firms and weakest in the domestically privatised group. Overall, it can be concluded that the proposition P1 is not supported by the research.

Previous research in Central Europe found that a market orientation is not well developed in the region (Marinov *et al.*, 1993; Shipley and Fonfara, 1993). It was expected that given the level of development of the Slovene economy and its length of exposure to international trade, particularly with

Table 11.4 An analysis of product and pricing strategy by firm type

Statements on product and pricing strategy	State-owned firms (A) (mean)[1]	Domestic Private Firms (B) (mean)	Firms with FDI (C) (means)	Organic firms (D) (mean)	Significance
1. We place an emphasis on enhancing the total product offering to our customers	1.56	1.57	1.70	1.59	0.694
2. We use superior service as a way to build closer relationships with customers	2.18	2.02	2.02	1.92 > A	0.037[2]
3. We are investing in creating strong, well-known brands	2.16	2.18	1.89	1.96	0.029[2]
4. Company and brand reputation are less important than keeping prices down	2.09	1.99	2.02	2.14	0.274
5. We can charge more for our products because we offer superior value	2.57	2.60	2.54	2.39 > B	0.046[2]
6. We set prices on the basis of the cost of production plus a fixed margin	2.11	2.08	2.06	1.87	0.149
7. We set prices based on what the market is prepared to pay	1.61	1.52	1.79	1.73	0.059
8. Prices are set by our competitors and we have to follow	2.29	2.32	2.23	2.47	0.251

[1] Means are calculated on a three-point scale with a score of one indicating the strongest level of agreement with the statement.
[2] Significant at $p = 0.05$

Table 11.5 An analysis of performance by firm type

Dimensions of performance	State-owned firms (%)[1]	Domestic private firms (%)	Firms with FDI (%)	Organic firms (%)	Chi-Square
1. Overall profit is better than competitors	12.9	19.9	18.8	26.2	0.009[2]
2. Sales volume is better than competitors	19.0	25.1	35.4	32.0	0.002[2]
3. Market share is better than competitors	12.9	18.8	27.1	30.3	0.015[3]
4. ROI is better than competitors	6.7	8.0	12.5	17.2	0.010[3]
5. Cash flow is better than competitors	14.1	16.0	16.7	13.9	0.196
6. Unit costs are better than competitors	19.6	16.4	22.9	15.6	0.037[3]
7. Employment is better than competitors	10.4	17.4	25.0	23.8	0.010[3]

[1] Percentages represent the proportion of each group who responded that the were performing better than their competitors on a given performance dimension.
[2] Significant at $p = 0.01$
[3] Significant at $p = 0.05$

EU countries, that a market orientation would be well developed in Slovene companies, but also that it is likely to vary by firm type due the persistence of past practices. The measurement of market orientation has become the focus of much interest in recent years (Kohli and Jaworski, 1990; Narver and Slater, 1990). Narver and Slater (1990) propose advancing beyond the basic idea of meeting customer needs to also taking account of the extent of competitor focus as well as levels of inter-functional coordination. Respondents were presented with the 14-item scale developed by Narver and Slater (1990) and asked to indicate their level of agreement with each statement on a seven-point Likert scale ranging from one (strongly agree) to seven (strongly disagree). Findings relating to this question are summarised in Table 11.2. A one-way analysis of variance was conducted to examine the extent of differences between each of the four groups of firms in their level of market orientation. Significant differences at the $p \leq 0.05$ level between the groups were observed on seven of the 14 dimensions (see Table 11.2). In the main, mean values of agreement with the listed statements were higher for organic firms and for firms with foreign direct investment than either state-owned enterprises or domestically privatised enterprises. A Bonferroni test was conducted to establish more precisely the extent of the differences between the groups. The Bonferroni test is a popular post hoc test that adjusts the observed significance level based on the number of comparisons being made. In this case where three comparisons are being made, the observed significance level must be less than 0.05/3 or 0.016 for the difference to be significant at the 0.05 level. Significant between-group differences were observed in six cases with the most evident pattern being that organic firms were more market oriented that their state-owned or former state-owned counterparts. Based on these findings, it emerges that the level of market orientation exhibited by organic firms is comparable to that of firms with FDI and therefore that proposition two (P2) is not supported.

Differences between the groups were also expected in relation to their marketing objectives and the types of strategies that they employ. The findings of the research on these questions is presented in Tables 11.3 and 11.4. A quasi-longitudinal approach was taken to the measurement of objectives. Respondents were asked to indicate what had been their main strategic objectives over the last two years and also what they expected their main focus to be over the next two years. Some interesting patterns emerged, reflecting the nature of the transition to a market-led economy. Over the past two years, almost two-thirds of state-owned enterprises and almost half of the domestically privatised firms have been concerned with simply surviving, while this has been the case in one-third of firms with FDI and less than 30% of organic firms (significant at $p = 0.001$). This supports the findings of previous research conducted in Hungary, which has shown that a lower proportion of firms with foreign participation have been pre-occupied with survival than wholly domestically owned firms (Hooley *et al.*, 1995). No significant differences between the groups were observed in the case of intended priorities for the next two years, with the majority of firms reporting that they would be concerned with building their long position in the market (see Table 11.3). However, some differences did emerge when the specific marketing objectives of each of the four groups were examined. Organic firms were least concerned with defending their current position, while this was a concern for an average of one-quarter of the other three groups (significant at $p = 0.01$). Achieving a steady sales growth was of highest and of relatively equal importance to state-owned enterprises and organic firms while an average of less than 10% of all firms intended to use aggressive sales growth to achieve market domination, though organic firms were twice as likely to adopt this approach as state-owned enterprises. In summary, the strategic priorities of all four groups are relatively similar in that they are concerned with building market potential, while organic firms appear to be most likely to be aggressive in their approach to doing so. Therefore, the proposition P3a is not supported by the research.

The relative similarity of future objectives among the four groups focusses attention on the nature of marketing strategies being adopted. Respondents were presented with a series of statements describing product and pricing strategies in their firm and asked to indicate their level of agreement on a three-point scale from 'agree' to 'no opinion' to 'disagree'. Significant differences were observed between the groups relating to dimensions such as service quality, branding and pricing (See Table 11.4). The findings reveal that firms with FDI and organic firms are characterised by a greater propensity to use differentiated strategies. In particular, organic firms emphasise superior service as a way of building closer relationships with customers (significant at $p = 0.05$), firms with FDI invest in creating strong, well-known brands (significant at $p = 0.05$) and organic firms can charge higher prices for their products because they offer superior value to customers (significant at $p = 0.05$). That firms with FDI seek to invest in brands supports the views of industrial organisation theorists who propose that multinational firms rely on domestically derived advantages, such as brands and marketing expertise, in competitive battles against local firms and provides some limited support for proposition P3b.

Finally, it was predicted that firms with foreign direct investment would outperform their domestic counterparts given the difficulties encountered by the latter in attempting to overcome past practices. The operationalisation of the performance construct has received a great deal of attention in the literature and a consensus appears to be emerging advocating a move away from a sole reliance on financially-based measures to include others such as market share and employment (Eccles, 1991; Kaplan and Norton, 1992). Similarly, relative performance can be compared against a variety of bases, including original objectives set, the previous financial year and the firm's major competitors. Seven measures of performance were assessed, including profitability, sales, market share and employment levels. As this study is concerned with the ability of different types of firms to compete in the changing business environment in Slovenia, respondents were asked to compare performance levels against their major competitors. The findings of this part of the research are summarised in Table 11.5. It shows that organic firms and firms with FDI generally outperformed the other two groups with the exception of cash flow. The findings are similar to those of previous research conducted by Hooley *et al.* (1996) in Hungary, which found that firms with FDI outperformed both state-owned firms and state–private joint ventures on the bases of profit as a percentage of turnover and return on investment. However, a surprising finding is that organic firms outperformed firms with FDI on the basis of both overall profit achieved and return on investment. The strong performance of organic firms bears out the sophistication of their marketing orientation, objectives and strategies described in the foregoing paragraphs.

DISCUSSION

In the transition to a market-led economy, Slovenia has had a significant head start over other countries in the CE region. It had well established trade links with the West and despite its small size, it accounted for almost one-third of the exports of the former Yugoslavia. Therefore, after transition it had only to develop and upgrade existing links rather than establish trading operations from scratch (Business Central Europe, 1996). Trade links also gave Slovenia product development advantages. Licensing and cooperative agreements kept Slovene companies up to date on technological developments and gave them experience in brand building. Its experience with self-management created a generation of managers experienced in running their own relatively autonomous profit centres (Business Central Europe, 1996). These initial advantages eased the transition process in Slovenia and made it one of the region's big success stories. However, the country has no cause for complacency. The difficulties encountered in forming a coalition after elections in November 1996 has highlighted the fragility of the government. Economic indicators are not good either, with growth slowing, inflation rising, the tolar continuing to depreciate and its proportion of exports to the EU falling back from the high levels achieved in 1995. An analysis of the Slovene economy by the EIU suggests that an underdeveloped marketing expertise in many companies may be contributing to the lack of buoyancy in export orders (EIU, 1997b).

This study found a marked variation in the quality of marketing practice among different groups of companies operating in Slovenia. It showed that state-owned companies and companies that had been privatised through domestic investment have had the most difficulty in making the transition. In contrast, firms with foreign participation and organic firms are adopting more sophisticated marketing practices. These groups are characterised by a greater adoption of a market orientation, superior differentiation strategies and by superior performance on a variety of dimensions. The performance of the organic sector will be a source of some satisfaction to policy makers in Slovenia. Most of these firms are small, employing less than 100 people and, consequently, are experiencing particular pressures such as a high level of bargaining power from suppliers. Yet they demonstrate professional marketing competencies and an ability to generate comparatively strong profit levels and market shares in a competitive business environment. Policy efforts should concentrate on supporting the development of these firms and in finding ways of assisting them to regain Slovenia's strong export performance in EU markets.

However, the most surprising element of the study is the issue of FDI in Slovenia. To date, it has lacked support at both a policy and business level though the most recent figures shows that it is holding its level of inward FDI while many other CE countries are experiencing sharp declines (Economist 1997b). However, in this study, only 48 companies, or less than 8% of the responding group, has some level of foreign investment, indicating the paucity of inward FDI in the country to date. Yet these firms were consistently superior to state-owned and domestically privatised firms on marketing practice and performance dimensions, though surprisingly they were only comparable to and in some cases behind, organic firms on these dimensions. Slovenia's relatively high wage levels and the impact of the Balkans war have often been used to explain the country's relatively low levels of FDI (Economist, 1995). However, inward investment has also lacked government support and its official strategy for economic development argues that economic activities that are highly profitable must be protected from acquisition by foreigners (Business Central Europe, 1996), which may help to explain why firms with FDI matched but did not outperform domestic organic firms. From a policy perspective, it should be noted that not all foreign investment is directed at the purchase of local firms and the Slovene government should market the country's advantages, such as its level of development and its strategic location, as reasons why multinational firms might want to set up manufacturing or distribution and service operations there. Other small countries in Europe, such as Ireland, have benefited from an openness to foreign investment and a willingness to market their other advantages in the absence of low labour costs (Economist, 1997c).

The findings of the study also provide issues of interest to researchers. First, the research demonstrated that though most respondents perceived their firms to be facing a similar set of industry conditions, significant variations in performance were observed. This suggests further support for the view that firm-level factors are important in explaining performance heterogeneity. Second, this study marks a step in advancing our understanding of the status of transition to a market-led economy and the nature of marketing practice in a smaller CE country. It provides additional evidence of differences in the pace of development of marketing practice in the region related to the heritage of organisations and the impact of privatisation and foreign direct investment processes. In particular, it has shown that a small country like Slovenia has been able to develop a buoyant and competitive indigenous sector comprising of small, organic firms. Foreign direct investment has not been greatly encouraged and has not had the major impact on marketing practice and firm level performance in Slovenia that it has had in other countries such as Hungary (Hooley *et al.*, 1996). It indicates the importance of extending research in the CE region beyond the traditional countries of interest, such as the Czech Republic and Bulgaria, and of further understanding the determinants of successful marketing practice in the region generally.

References

Barney, J.B. (1991) 'Firm resources and sustained competitive advantage', *Journal of Management*, 17(1): 99–120.
Bartlett, C.A. and Ghoshal, S. (1989) *Managing Across Borders: The Transnational Solution* (Cambridge, MA: Harvard Business School Press).
Business Central Europe, (1996) 'Slovenia survey', *Business Central Europe*, February: 35–46.
Caves, R.E. (1971) 'International corporations: the industrial economics of foreign investment', *Economica*, 38: 1–27.
Eccles, R.G. (1991) 'The performance measurement manifesto', *Harvard Business Review*, 69(1): 131–137.
Economist (1995) 'Survey: Central Europe', *Economist*, November 18: S1–S28.
Economist (1997a) 'Survey: European Union', *Economist*, 343, 8019: S1–S22.
Economist (1997b) 'Survey: Business in Eastern Europe', *Economist*, 345, 8044: S1–S30.
Economist (1997c) 'Europe's tiger economy', *Economist*, 343, 8017: 23–26.
EIU (1997a) 'Country report: Slovenia' (London: Economist Intelligence Unit) 1st quarter, pp. 20.
EIU (1997b) 'Country report: Slovenia' (London: Economist Intelligence Unit) 2nd quarter, pp. 17.
Financial Times (1997) 'Survey: Investing in Central and Eastern Europe', *Financial Times*, April 11: S5.
Graham, E.M. (1978) 'Transatlantic investment by multinational firms: a rivalistic phenomenon?', *Journal of Post Keynesian Economics*, 1: 82–99.
Grant, R.M. (1991) 'The resource-based theory of competitive advantage: implications for strategy formulation', *California Management Review*, 33(3): 114–135.
Hannan, M.T. and Freeman, J. (1984) 'Structural change and organisational inertia', *American Sociological Review*, 49: 149–164.
Hansen, G.S. and Wernerfelt, B. (1989) 'Determinants of firm performance: the relative importance of economic and organisational factors', *Strategic Management Journal*, 10(5): 399–411.

Hart, S. (1987) 'The use of mail surveys in industrial market research', *Journal of Marketing Management*, 3: 25–38.

Hrebiniak, L.G. and Joyce, W. F. (1985) 'Organisational adaptation: strategic choice and environmental determinism', *Administrative Science Quarterly*, 30(3): 336–349.

Hooley, G.J. (1993) 'Raising the iron curtain: marketing in a period of transition', *European Journal of Marketing*, 27(11/12): 6–20.

Hooley, G.J. *et al.* (1995) 'The marketing implications of foreign direct investment in private Hungarian firms', *International Marketing Review*, 12(5): 7–17.

Hooley, G.J. *et al.* (1996) 'Foreign direct investment in Hungary: resource acquisition and competitive advantage', *Journal of International Business Studies*, 27(4): 683–709.

Hymer, S.H. (1960) *The International Operations of National Firms: A Study of Direct Foreign Investment* (Cambridge MA: The MIT Press).

Kohli, A.K. and Jaworski, B.J. (1990) 'Market orientation: the construct, research propositions and managerial implications', *Journal of Marketing*, 54(3): 1–18.

Kaplan, R.S. and Norton, D.P. (1992) 'The balanced scorecard: measures that drive performance', *Harvard Business Review*, 70(1): 71–79.

Kindleberger, C.P. (1969) *American Business Abroad: Six Lectures on Direct Investment* (New Haven and London: Yale University Press).

McGahan, A.M. and Porter, M.E. (1997) 'How much does industry matter, really?', *Strategic Management Journal*, 18: 15–30.

Marinov, M. *et al.* (1993) 'Marketing approaches in Bulgaria', *European Journal of Marketing*, 27(11/12): 35–46.

Narver, J.C. and Slater, S.F. (1990) 'The effect of marketing orientation on business profitability', *Journal of Marketing*, 58(5): 20–35.

Noar, J. (1989) 'Research on Eastern Europe and Soviet marketing: constraints, challenges and opportunities', *International Marketing Review*, 7(1): 7–14.

Porter, M. E. (1980) *Competitive Strategy* (New York: The Free Press) pp. 3–33.

Quelch, J.A., Joachimsthaler, E. and Nueno, J.L. (1991) 'After the wall: marketing guidelines for Eastern Europe', *Sloan Management Review*, 32(2): 82–93.

Rumelt, R.P. (1991) 'How much does industry matter?', *Strategic Management Journal*, 12(3): 167–185.

Shipley, D. and Fonfara, K. (1993) 'Organisation for marketing among Polish companies', *European Journal of Marketing*, 27(11/12): 60–79.

Shipley, D. *et al.* (1994) 'The internal status and organisation of marketing in Hungary and Poland', *Developments in Marketing Science*, 24: 320–327.

World Bank, (1996) 'Slovenia: Country overview' (New York: World Bank) pp. 1–3.

12 The Patterns and Management of Foreign Direct Investment in Central and Eastern Europe: Poland, Hungary and Romania Compared

Robert Carty and Carla C.J.M. Millar

INTRODUCTION

The flow of FDI into Eastern Europe has been directed largely at the 'front-line' states (Millar, 1993) of Poland, Hungary and the Czech Republic (Ivanov, 1995). This FDI can take the form of building on greenfield sites, acquisitions, joint ventures or other types of non-equity alliances. These are the typical mode of entry options open to the foreign investor (Albaum *et al.*, 1994).

This chapter concentrates on how this FDI is used at the level of the firm, using the example of one large multinational that has invested in several Eastern European countries. The chapter further discusses the differences in patterns of use of FDI between Eastern and Western Europe and investigates whether the flow of FDI is managed differently in the case of a non front-line state compared to front-line states.

PATTERNS OF FDI

El-Hajjar (1991) studied the demographics and motivations of British alliances (joint ventures, mergers and acquisitions) between 1980 and 1989. In a survey covering various types of alliances, she found that 78% of alliances were accounted for by four industries: electronics, aerospace, telecommunications and automobiles.

Only two partners were involved in 77% of all alliances, and 70 British companies accounted for 337 alliances, indicating that the same companies

238

can, over time, be involved in several alliances, and pointing towards an experience curve for the companies involved.

Hibbert (1992) found that 87% of activity in 'cooperative ventures' was within the Triad (North America, Europe, and Japan), and that 81% of alliances involved one partner. The sectors of aerospace, telecommunications, computers, motor vehicles, and other electricals accounted for 87% of agreements.

In a similar but more comprehensive study over the same period, Glaister and Buckley (1994) surveyed the formation of joint ventures between UK firms and Western Europe, the US and Japan. These regions accounted for 94% of activity. The researchers found that there had been an uneven pattern of joint venture formation, with a distinct increase in the final two years of the decade caused by joint ventures in Western Europe. The majority of the joint ventures were formed within Western Europe, the US being the second most common source of partners. The authors found that 50% of all joint ventures fell into 4 groups of industry: financial services, telecommunications, aerospace and manufacturing.

No pattern of success by industry could be determined. The vast majority of ventures (85%) were formed with just one partner, though the UK organisations tended to be more promiscuous. In method of formation, equity-based were more common than non-equity-based, although no clear preference was determined from the sample.

Within these three publications, there is broad agreement on the pattern of alliance formation, irrespective of the form of alliance, with the exception of Glaister and Buckley's findings of alliances in financial services (14%), which are not mentioned by the other researchers.

The growth in alliance activity during and after this period reflects the growth of FDI and is well chronicled by many authors. Whitelock and Rees (1993) suggest that the formation of the Single European Market encouraged the growth in joint ventures and merger and acquisition activity, Schoenberg *et al.* (1994) reported a quadrupling of joint ventures and merger and acquisition activity, and Cartwright and Cooper (1996) noted a large increase in mergers and acquisitions.

More recently the growth has continued. Merger and acquisition deals in 1996 reached a record high of $262 billion and the drivers to sustain this growth are still in place (Finkelstein, 1998): 'Whilst cross-border direct investment is expanding rapidly, acquisitions and especially alliances are increasing even faster' reports the Financial Times (Wagstyl, 1997), and David Ernst of McKinsey's is quoted as predicting a 20% annual growth rate in the future; 'A mergers runaway', exclaims Shearlock (1997). A further record $2100 billion was achieved in 1998 (Harris, 1999).

The conclusion to be drawn from the research in this area is that there is little doubt that activity has increased considerably in the past decade and will continue in the future. The drivers appear to be FDI in cross-border deals and international restructuring of industry. There is little difference in the patterns of development for different forms of alliance – all forms have shown tremendous growth during the 1990s.

MOTIVATIONS

The historic view of the use of FDI in international alliances has been to create a mode of entry, and this use of alliances is most often described in typical textbooks (Keegan, 1994; Norgan, 1994; Rugman and Hoggets, 1995) to the exclusion of all other considerations. Other authors take a broader perspective, suggesting the growth of FDI is part of organisational strategic development necessary to face the challenges of global competition. For example, Bleeke and Ernst (1992) query whether a joint venture is part of a continuum of strategic development, which most often results in an acquisition. Corrigan *et al.* (1993) consider that a new style of joint venture is taking place across Europe, in which the development of international relationships and rationalisation act as drivers. Development of the core business is the new strategic logic, and joint ventures are seen as a way of reducing risk. Banks and Baranson (1993) support the view that a new type of strategic alliance is emerging, which allows for the sharing of complementary resources and capabilities across borders to develop global business strategies. Porter and Fuller's (1986) view is simply that global companies must compete on a global basis, and alliances are a mechanism that enables them to do so. Perlmutter and Heenan (1986) were among the first to note that the use of alliances could facilitate the evolution of an international organisation's strategy from competitive to cooperative, and Moss-Kanter (1994) foresees as inevitable a move from a competitive to a collaborative strategy. Moss-Kanter and Stonham (1994) regard alliances as part of the inevitable route to globalisation. Alliance relationships are a key asset and a requirement for successful globalisation. Opportunities have developed from the opening up of Eastern Europe. Much the same viewpoint was adopted earlier by Ohmae (1989), who states that alliances are a necessary part of the path to globalisation, because of the impossibility of one organisation being able to totally service global markets. The advantages of alliances lie not only in cost savings but also in greater market spread.

Other researchers take the development of alliances a step further. Gomes-Casseres (1994) suggests that future competition will take place between competing networks rather than between individual companies. The drivers that will enable this to happen are new technology, globalisation, increasing complexity of products and shared technology. A network will compete to ensure acceptance of its technical standards and gain critical mass to aid acceptance of its designs. Technologies are creating links between businesses that were formerly separate and allowing specialists in each field to cooperate. Gomes-Casseres points out that networks are not new and gives the Japanese *keiretsu* as an example. He sees network growth as incremental and observes that to be successful the network must be greater than the sum of its parts. Barnatt and Wong (1992) note that networks, 'allow firms to exist without the encumbered inefficiencies of overburdened line structures' and have become feasible because of the development of information technology (IT). The network model and the more traditional multinational configuration are compared and contrasted by D'Cruz and Rugman (1994). While no conclusions concerning performance are drawn, clear differences between the cooperative and competitive modes of international competition are made. Lorenzoni and Baden-Fuller (1995) essentially agree with Ohmae and Gomes-Casseres' vision. They envisage the international organisation as being at the centre of a web of alliance partners, in which it must fulfil the role of leading the web, creating value for its partners and directing the structure and strategy.

Whether the growth in FDI will result in global organisations of competing networks or not, it is clear that the above authors view FDI via alliances as far more than only an alternative mode of entry. There is, however, broad agreement on the use of alliances as part of the organisational development process, particularly to channel FDI to aid internationalisation. It is interesting to see whether the flow of FDI into Eastern Europe though alliances follows the same patterns of development.

FDI IN EASTERN EUROPE

According to Ivanov (1995), by the mid-1990s the Czech Republic, Hungary, and Poland accounted for two-thirds of the total of FDI in Eastern Europe, though the region as a whole attracted less inward investment than China and captured only 3% of global FDI in 1993. The main risk factors identified by the European Bank for Reconstruction and Development (EBRD) were the lack of a clearly defined legislative framework, confusion over property rights, lack of a developed market economy, lack of a capital market and uncertainty with respect to price trends.

Motivations

Corrigan *et al.* (1993) found that the most important motivation for FDI via alliances by Western investors was market growth, because the underdeveloped markets of Eastern Europe present opportunities to companies competing in the mature markets of Western Europe. Secondly, FDI was invested to take advantage of the low-cost production opportunities in the region. Motivations for Eastern European partners include access to Western technology and expertise, access to Western markets, and the prestige involved in having links with an international name. Lane (1995), in an empirical study of joint ventures, comes to similar conclusions about motivations, but notes that the sectoral distribution differs in that most are involved in service industries including the media, and hotels. Other alliances involve consumer goods – foodstuffs, tobacco, cosmetics and pharmaceuticals – construction materials and automobiles. One of Lane's major findings was that foreign firms were no more likely to take advantage of lower labour costs than domestic investors and are not entering sectors that require higher capital. This contradicts some of the findings of Corrigan *et al.* and points to the need for further research in this area, as relatively few studies have yet been performed.

The direction of the restructuring of the economies of Eastern Europe is reviewed by Amsden *et al.* (1996). The embeddedness of communism across the region is questioned because controls and implementation of Soviet policy differed country by country, and each country had its own culture and social norms. They also take the view that free market forces should be left to evolve, and market-led capitalism grow naturally 'from pseudo- socialism to pseudo-capitalism'. Western capitalism did not evolve spontaneously; they argue that without government planning backed by the injection of capital into state-controlled financial institutions to support and control development, desired outcomes will be hard to achieve. FDI investment directly in enterprises without regard to the economic infrastructure is likely to be unsuccessful. They suggest that a model of development based on East Asia may be most appropriate for the region.

RESEARCH OBJECTIVES

There are obviously differing perspectives and views expressed in the literature concerning the motivations for, channelling of, and use of FDI in the region. The study below adds to the body of knowledge by examining how and why one Western European multinational managed its FDI in markets of Eastern Europe.

Research Sponsor

A search through *Acquisitions Monthly* and inquiries of organisations concerned with investment in Eastern Europe (DTI, embassies, EBRD) revealed that there was remarkably little UK investment in the region, let alone organisations involved in FDI investment in several countries. This circumstantial research confirms Corrigan *et al.*'s (1993) findings concerning the low proportion of global FDI entering the region. In fact only two UK organisations, one a multinational involved in the manufacture and distribution of fast-moving consumer goods, and the other a well-known retailer, had entered several of the markets. The former allowed access for the research.

The multinational was involved in four industry sectors – detergents, margarine, personal products and frozen food – worldwide. In CEE (Central and Eastern Europe) these industries were managed by one subsidiary organisation in each country which reported to the headquarters in Western Europe.

The organisation provided the opportunity to investigate the management of its FDI in Poland, Hungary and Romania, the latter being chosen to provide a contrast with the 'front-line' states.

Sample Design

It made sense to reduce the number of organisations involved as far as possible, in order to reduce the organisational variables. Following the methodology of Hamill and Hunt (1993) and guidance by Yin (1994), the number of alliances chosen was 3, resulting in a minimum number of 4 organisations, the parent and three Eastern CEE subsidiaries.

A UK-based Western organisation, operating in discrete industries, was desirable for matters of convenience, and also to reduce the industry variables. It was also preferable that the CEE subsidiaries were at the same stage of economic development and that this stage was economic expansion rather than survival. This was to ensure that the CEE organisations were not seeking FDI out of desperation. It was also important that the investments were strategic, or long term. Investigating subsidiaries at the same stage of development also reduced time-related organisational development variables. The mode of entry (acquisition) was also held constant to ensure comparability of process and control. Comparing joint ventures with acquisitions at this stage, for example, would have proved problematical in this respect. To further focus the research the study concentrated on the detergents industry in each subsidiary.

Research Process

The methodology chosen was essentially the inductive method following Glaser and Strauss (1967). The methods used were interview and observation. Interviews were conducted at comparable senior management level at headquarters and in each subsidiary. In the subsidiaries, the expatriate chairmen and senior local managers who had lived through the acquisition were interviewed.

RESEARCH RESULTS

Motivation for FDI

The main, if not only, motivation for FDI was market access. The reason for this was that markets in Western Europe were saturated and there were greater opportunities for growth in Central and Eastern Europe, which had as big a population as Western Europe. It was also felt that there would be similarities in consumer needs, though it was recognised that adjustments would have to be made.

It was not felt that the development of networks or organisational redesign would be important, but an (unlikely) scenario where the organisation might combine with another to compete against a mutual enemy had been considered.

These motivations are in agreement with authors (Keegan, 1984; Norgan, 1994; Rugman and Hoggets, 1995, who regard overseas acquisitions primarily as a mode of entry, and with the researchers (El-Hajjar, 1991; Hibbert, 1992; the Economist, 1993; Glaister and Buckley, 1996), who found growth and market development to be the most common motivations in practice.

Mode of Alliance

The choice of FDI via acquisition was born out of experience. An acquisition gave the parent organisation the freedom to run its subsidiaries in the way in which it wanted, and enabled the subsidiaries to become and feel part of the 'family'. A second advantage was speed, an acquisition being the quickest way to market. The organisation was flexible enough to incorporate 'gut feeling' in its acquisition process and had existing links with organisations in Central and Eastern Europe. For example, the organisation had had an association with the Hungarian subsidiary for decades, and there had been an existing licensing agreement before the acquisition.

The acquisition price was almost irrelevant, but growth potential was supremely important. However, in Eastern Europe the cost of an acquisition was less than that of a greenfield site after taking into account time and the cost of assets. In some ways, the less developed the target organisation the better, because it would be easier to acquire and would have greater growth potential. The parent organisation looked for potential market leadership; hence the acquisition target would normally be the market leader in the country or an organisation with the potential to become the market leader. The growth potential would be realised by the application of the expertise and experience of the parent organisation to the acquired subsidiary.

The parent organisation would not normally consider a hostile acquisition because of the importance of the goodwill of the subsidiary workforce. In terms of strategic fit, while there were no hard rules, in general subsidiaries would be acquired in one of the four sectors in which the organisation operated, thus 'sticking to the knitting'. The intention was to use the acquisitions as building blocks within these core industries to achieve market leadership. There was no formulaic way in which integration was to be achieved; each subsidiary could be managed differently. The whole parent organisation's management structure worked according to the same principles and so there was little headquarters–subsidiary conflict. Obviously it was the subsidiary chairmens' responsibility to impart the parent organisation's way of doing things and its values, but there was no totalitarianism. The parent organisation was guided by experience and practice rather than theory. In the words of its President, 'flexible pragmatism' was its guiding principle.

Legal Framework

The organisation did have a common policy on legal matters, and would not acquire if the legal position was uncertain. It was necessary to have title to the assets purchased and to have trademark and patent protection. Romania had always had a minimum acceptable standard, despite being less developed than elsewhere in the region. In Eastern Europe, commercial law was often underdeveloped and unpredictable, having not kept pace with recent developments in commerce, and subsidiary chairmen spent a considerable time with the government suggesting improvements and establishing a good relationship.

By establishing as criteria for FDI the need for a legal framework and property rights, the parent organisation circumvented two of the difficulties reported by the EBRD (Ivanov, 1995). The other obstacles – lack of a market economy and capital markets, and uncertainty of price trends – were of little consequence.

The Management of FDI

The FDI was channelled into three areas – asset development, organisational development and human resource development.

Asset development
In each country, the manufacturing plant and processes were upgraded to world-class standards. In Romania, this entailed building from scratch because of the state of the plant and equipment.

Basic administration systems had been based on the status quo, recording data rather than providing management information. The former communist governments had had peculiar reporting requirements for which the administration system provided figures, none of which were of any use in running a modern organisation. Big accounts departments had produced these figures, but, for example, there had been no systems for measuring cost control at factory level. Hence, computerised management information and control systems from Western Europe were installed.

A major difficulty had been rationalising logistics, and FDI was spent to develop the distribution function. Previously, the product had been merely produced and collected by wholesalers if and when available. Production would be closed for three weeks for maintenance, for example, regardless of stock shortages. No product – no problem, provided output targets had been met. Now, each subsidiary had to produce, market, sell and distribute to fragmented outlets. This involved making employees appreciate that non-manufacturing was part of the supply chain; previously, the supplier or wholesaler as a partner was not part of the mind set.

Organisational development
Organisational development was focussed on two objectives. The primary objective was to turn each subsidiary from a factory producing products into a modern marketing-led organisation. This involved investment to initiate the marketing function, the development being led by expatriates because of the lack of local expertise. Consequently, the factories were now at a lower level in the subsidiary organisations' hierarchies compared to the marketing functions, and the management of added value was now the most important task. Human Resource Management had also to be developed.

The second objective was internal restructuring. Within each part of each organisation, rigid barriers and hierarchies were broken down to build a flatter, leaner organisation, populated by flexible teams of workers. Previously, there had been political officers and trade-union-led councils of workers, which had resulted in parallel political hierarchies. Senior appointments had to be approved by the government. This structure had now gone, though the unions remained but were not involved in day-to-day decisions.

Change agents in these processes were often the former local directors, whom the parent organisation encouraged to remain if they wished. They also provided links with the past and possessed invaluable country specific knowledge. In terms of the new organisational management teams, the parent organisation intended that eventually 80% of the subsidiary boards of directors would be composed of locals.

It was the chairmen's responsibility to mould the organisational cultures and their personal management style was very important. They saw it as their role to change the organisational culture from quantity- to quality-orientated, from individualism to team-orientated working, from a focus on job descriptions to a focus on responsibilities, involving crossing organisational boundaries to get things done. They also nurtured the latent entrepreneurship within the workforces, and built trust where none had previously existed. The chairmen maintained the interface with headquarters, being anxious to avoid headquarters being perceived as 'Moscow' from the employees' perspective and to avoid 'the arrogance of the multinational'.

Human resource development

This was the area that commanded most attention and that consumed most effort and a large proportion of the FDI. The work forces were first rational-ised, using generous voluntary redundancy schemes (up to two years' pay) where possible. Most workers had a good technical background, but there was a skills shortage in wider business skills, depending on the function. The skills shortage was especially pronounced in finance and accounting and marketing, and few employees had the necessary experience to operate at senior and board levels. Workers were retained if they had the right skills or potential. To develop the workforce, younger employees, generally educated to degree standard and under the age of 35, were recruited, because the experience of the parent organisation suggested that they were more flexible and responsive to change.

Instead of one job for life, multiskilling and teamworking were developed, with the devolvement of responsibility to team level. For example, the quality control department in Poland had been abolished and the teams given their own equipment to check the quality of their output. There were constant programmes of secondment of employees, not only to headquarters, but also to other worldwide subsidiaries. Workers were encouraged to make improvements and appraisal systems, with links to pay flexibility, were being introduced. Specific employee benefits were the encouragement to learn English at the subsidiaries' expense, health checks and above average pay.

The Future

It is worth mentioning that the result of the FDI into the Eastern European subsidiaries was considered successful from three points of view – head-quarters, the subsidiary chairmen and the local senior managers. The easiest task was the introduction of new technology, reflecting the quantitative and technical skills of the workforces in each country. More difficult was the introduction of teamworking.

There was an awareness that there was likely to be a pan-European rationalisation, particularly of production, at some time in the future. The subsidiaries were considered well placed to play a leading part in this process.

CONCLUSIONS

The parent organisation followed a classic policy of integration described as *symbiosis* (Haspeslagh and Jemison, 1991), by which there was mutual learning between parent organisation and each subsidiary.

Table 12.1   Organisational outcomes of the integration process

	Before acquisition	*After acquisition*
Management structure	Vertical Rigid	Flat Flexible
Management style	Top down Closed systems Political	Participative Open systems Professional
Jobs	Job for life Single skilled Individual tasks	Job rotation Multiskilled Teamwork
Market orientation	Monopoly Product led Quantity orientated	Competition Market led Quality orientated
Pay	Fixed wage	Performance related

Table 12.1 summarises the internal changes within the integration process.

Motivation

The interviews show that the motivation for the acquisitions in Eastern Europe was, straightforwardly, market development because of the saturation of Western European markets and the opportunities presented by a new market of larger size. It is worth reiterating, however, that headquarters was aware of the use of alliances for collaborative rather than competitive strategy and the development of competing networks (Lorenzoni and Baden-Fuller, 1995).

A conclusion to be drawn from this is that there is a time lag in the region between the present use of FDI to facilitate market entry and the future creation of new organisational forms.

Management of FDI

There is no evidence that the management of FDI in the 'third-line' country, Romania, proved any more difficult than in the 'front-line' states. Within each classification there were, as might be expected, differences in the management of FDI between countries. Hence, the management of FDI differed between Poland and Hungary. The FDI in Romania benefited from the parent organisation's previous experience in Eastern Europe, but this research suggests that the classification of Eastern European countries is not particularly useful in management terms, other than as an economic descriptor. The 'front-line' are preparing for accession to the EC, but there was no evidence to suggest that Poland and Hungary were treated differently from Romania. The differences between countries are as predicted by Amsden *et al.* (1996); however the parent organisation did not concern itself with state-controlled financial institutions or the economic infrastructure.

The overriding management principle was 'pragmatic flexibility'. FDI via acquisitions was made according to experience rather than management theory, and best practice had evolved from experience. General guidelines for making the FDI successful within Eastern Europe were:

1. The parent organisation had discussions with the owners of local companies prior to the FDI – sometimes continuing for several years.
2. The mode of FDI was acquisition, for speed and to ensure parent organisation control.
3. Hostile takeovers were avoided, to help the establishment of a good relationship with the subsidiary.
4. The parent organisation retained existing management, to gain local knowledge, build trust and help the integration process.
5. The parent organisation invested in local plant to bring it up to world-class standards.
6. The parent organisation invested in local manpower development, with the intention of having a large component of the local subsidiary board of directors consisting of local directors.
7. The parent organisation developed good relationships with the local authorities.
8. The overall integration process was that of symbiosis, or mutual learning.

The first point would help to establish trust and commonality of purpose, and is in agreement with the advice of Haanes *et al.* (1995).

The policy of FDI via acquisition (point 2) was developed from experience. However, total ownership of the shares, though desired, was not a necessity. A few minority shareholders in Poland, for example, still existed, but they played no part in the running of the subsidiary.

Points 3 to 8 helped foster goodwill and reflected the parent organisation's beliefs and value systems. Point 5 was a very tangible sign of FDI in the subsidiaries. This is also in agreement with Haanes *et al.* (1995), who also recommend technology transfer and the production of goods for export, which the subsidiaries had started to achieve.

Hamill and Hunt (1993) recommend investment in manpower development and establishing good relationships with the authorities (points 6 and 7), which the parent organisation undertook. In human resource development the emphasis was on the recruitment of young potential managers under 35 years of age, because the parent organisation's experience was that these employees were more adaptable than older workers. This view is supported by the analysis of the interviews, which suggests that the older workers had found the organisational changes more difficult.

The integration process of symbiosis (point 8) follows the advice of Haspeslagh and Jemison (1991).

There are two further factors in the parent organisation's FDI management process which contributed to its success, but which have hitherto not been prominent in the literature: experience and reputation.

Experience

The effect of experience on alliance longevity was tested empirically by Barkema *et al.* (1996), who found that firms benefited significantly from previous experience, particularly in the same locality. One could therefore expect the experience effect to be important in Eastern Europe, and it has already been mentioned several times in this chapter. The importance of experience is supported by Gomes-Mejia and Palich (1997), but is not evidenced by the body of literature in general, which leads to the conclusion that the experience effect is perhaps under researched.

Reputation

The Hungarian subsidiary had known the parent organisation for many years, and in Poland the parent organisation had won the 'beauty' contest. In Romania, the parent organisation was known and respected. A conclusion is that the parent organisation's reputation was important in enabling it to make the FDI. The effect of reputation is almost completely missing from the literature. It is hinted at by Corrigan *et al.* (1993), but save for a recent paper by Dollinger *et al.* (1997), in which the authors find that reputation plays a significant role in partner choice, studies are absent.

FUTURE USES OF FDI

As the markets of Eastern Europe evolve it can be expected that the uses of FDI will start to change:

- *Asset development.* The cost of acquiring assets is likely to increase as economies advance, and FDI is likely to be more directed to purchase and restructuring, rather than upgrading. Greenfield operations may become less costly than acquisitions.
- *Organisational development.* The organisational structures and behaviours are likely to evolve naturally rather than having to be built or guided. A decrease in FDI in this area can be expected.
- *Human resource development.* While training and development will be ongoing, there is likely to be less investment in the development of basic skills. Secondments, and the inculcation of world best practice will remain, however.

To summarise, there may be a shift in the use of FDI from the 'soft areas' of organisational and human resource development to the 'hard' areas of the purchase of assets. In the long term, use of FDI is likely to follow the patterns of the US and Western Europe.

REVIEW OF METHODOLOGY AND FUTURE RESEARCH

The researchers chose to control variables (one MNC, one industry) and this, to some extent, affects generalisability. Any research in any one group of organisations is bound to be affected by this concern. Hence, replication studies involving other organisation in other countries within the region are awaited. Further research directions indicated by this study are:

- Is the channeling of FDI into 'soft areas' a typical use of FDI throughout Eastern Europe?
- Would the factors for success in the management of FDI developed by the parent organisation be appropriate in different industries or in different markets?
- This study has identified two factors that were important to the success of FDI via alliances that are not prominent in the literature. Further research needs to be done on the effects of *experience* and *reputation* on the alliance process.

References

Albaum, G. *et al.* (1994) *Export Marketing Management*, 2nd edn (Wokingham, UK: Addison-Wesley): Chapter 8.

Amsden, A. *et al.* (1996) 'The market meets its match: restructuring the economies of Eastern Europe', *Journal of Economic Issues*, 30: 332–335.

Banks, P. and Baranson, J. (1993) 'New concepts drive transnational strategic alliances', *Planning Review*, 21(6): 28–32.

Barkema, H. *et al.* (1996) 'Foreign entry, cultural barriers, and learning', *Strategic Management Journal*, 17: 151–166.

Barnatt, C. and Wong, P. (1992) 'Acquisition activity and organization structure', *Journal of General Management*, 17(3): 1–14.

Bleeke, J. and Ernst, D. (1992) 'Is your strategic alliance really a sale?', *Harvard Business Review*, Jan/Feb: 97–105.

Cartwright, S. and Cooper, C. (1996) *Managing Mergers, Acquisitions and Strategic Alliances: Integrating People and Cultures*, 2nd edn (Oxford: Butterworth-Heinemann).

Corrigan, T. *et al.* (1993) 'International mergers and acquisitions', *Financial Times*, 17 Sept.

D'Cruz, J. and Rugman, A. (1994) 'The five partners model: France Telecom, Alcatel, and the global telecommunications industry', *European Management Journal*, 12(1): 59–66.

Dollinger, M. *et al.* (1997) 'The effect of reputation on the decision to joint venture', *Strategic Management Journal*, 18(2): 127–140.

The Economist (1993) 'Holding hands', *The Economist*, 27 (March): 14–16.

El-Hajjar, S. (1991) *Strategic alliances: motivations, management, and international competitiveness. The British experience*, Ph.D. thesis, University of Strathclyde.

Finkelstein, S. (1998) 'Safe ways to cross the merger minefield', in Mastering Global Business, *Financial Times*, 20 (February): 8–10.

Glaister, K. and Buckley, P. (1994) 'UK joint ventures: an analysis of patterns of activity and distribution', *Journal of Management*, 5(1): 33–51.

Glaser, D. and Straus, A. (1967) *The Discovery of Grounded Theory* (Chicago: Aldine).

Gomes-Casseres, R. (1994) 'Group versus group: how alliance networks compete', *Harvard Business Review*, Jul/Aug: 62–70.

Gomes-Mejia, L. and Palich, L. (1977) 'Cultural diversity and the performance of multinational firms', *Journal of International Business Studies*, 28(2): 309–335.

Haanes, K. *et al.* (1995) 'Critical success factors of the "co-operative entry mode": the cases of ABB and Fiat Auto in Poland', in *Global Perspectives on Co-operative Strategies*, conference proceedings IMD, Lausanne.

Hamill, J. and Hunt, G. (1993) 'Joint ventures in Hungary: key success factors', *European Management Journal*, 11(2): 238–247.

Harris, C. (1999) 'Dizzy ride promises fresh test of nerves', in Global Investment Banking, *Financial Times*, 29 (January): 1.

Haspeslagh, P. and Jemison, D. (1991) *Managing Acquisitions* (New York: Free Press).

Hibbert, E. (1992) 'The growth of international coalitions in global product and market strategy', *Journal of European Business Education*, 1(2): 63–95.

Ivanov, D. (1995) 'Doing business in Eastern and Central Europe', in B. Dawes (ed.) *International Business: a European Perspective* (Cheltenham, UK: Stanley Thornes): Chapter 8.

Keegan, W. (1994) *Multinational Marketing Management*, 3rd edn (Englewood Cliffs, NJ: Prentice-Hall): Chapter 10.

Lane, S. (1995) 'The sectoral distribution of joint ventures in Eastern Europe', paper published by Boston University, USA.

Lorenzoni, G. and Baden-Fuller, C. (1995) 'Creating a strategic center to manage a web of partners', *California Management Review*, 37(3) C: 46–163.

Millar, C. (1993) 'The question of marketing in Central and Eastern Europe', in *Developments in Marketing Science* (Miami: Academy of Marketing Science) 586–592.

Moss-Kanter, R. (1994) 'Collaborative advantage: the art of alliances', *Harvard Business Review*, Jul/Aug: 96–108.

Moss-Kanter, R. and Stonham, P. (1994) 'Change in the global economy', *European Management Journal*, 12(1): 1–9.

Norgan, S. (1994) *Marketing Management: A European Perspective* (Wokingham, UK: Addison-Wesley): Chapter 3.

Ohmae, K. (1989) 'The global logic of strategic alliances', *Harvard Business Review*, Mar/Apr: 143–154.

Perlmutter, H. and Heenan, D. (1986) 'Co-operate to compete globally', *Harvard Business Review*, Mar/Apr: 136–155.

Porter, M. and Fuller, M. (1986) 'Coalitions and global strategy', in M. Porter (ed.) *Competition in Global Industries* (Boston USA: Harvard Business School Press).

Rugman, A. and Hogetts, R. (1995) *International Business* (London: McGraw-Hill): Chapter 17.

Schoenberg, R. (1994) 'European cross-border acquisitions: the impact of management style differences on performance', in *21st Annual Conference of the UK Academy of International Business Proceedings*, pp. 950–977.

Shearlock, P. (1997) 'A mergers runaway', *The Banker*, February: 17–20.

Wagstyl, S. (1997) 'When even a rival can be a best friend', *Financial Times*, 22 (October): 17.

Whitelock, J. and Rees, M. (1993) 'Trends in mergers, acquisitions, and joint ventures in the Single European Market', *European Business Review*, 4: 26–32.

Yin, R. (1994) *Case Study Research Design and Methods* (London: Sage Publications).

13 Local Sourcing Practices of Foreign Owned Multinational Subsidiaries Operating in Poland

David Floyd

F21 F23 L24
P31 P33

INTRODUCTION

Much of the current literature on Central and Eastern Europe (CEE) focuses on macroeconomic issues, including macroeconomic reforms and the development of the transition process. However, one needs also to question the 'micro' side and see, for example, the contribution foreign direct investment made to the transition process and the activity of foreign multinational enterprises. This chapter will first define what is meant by the transition process and outline current trends in FDI activity in Poland. It will then set out to analyse the impact of local sourcing activities on the transitional economy of Poland. Based on the theoretical literature of Dunning (1993) and others, a set of criteria have been developed for evaluating the effects of multinational enterprise supplier linkages to national economic competitiveness. These include linkages introducing complementary assets – for example, technology – raising standards of product quality and stimulating local entrepreneurship. These effects are analysed by drawing on empirical evidence from foreign-owned manufacturing multinational firms operating in Poland. The findings define the impact of these firms by comparing their sources of supply when entering the Polish market with the present-day situation. The findings indicate that foreign multinationals are starting to make a more favourable impact on the Polish economy through the use of increased supplier linkages, though at a very slow pace. Other interesting observations include the fact that foreign-owned multinationals operating in this Central European economy are starting to make less use of suppliers from other countries within the company group in favour of using more European suppliers, both West and East. In addition, the study examines supplier linkages in terms of both major and minor sources of supply.

The chapter then highlights the less desirable consequences of globalisation and increased FDI activity on a transitional economy by discussing the main winners and losers with reference to the Polish case. A more critical focus is then developed, which addresses efficiency, distribution and

254

sovereignty issues. The chapter concludes with a less biased approach and suggests reasons for the future development of such activity that are both optimistic and pessimistic.

BACKGROUND

Until very recently, the information available on transition economies was very limited. Today, it has become clear that the economies of CEE experienced a fall in output just after the collapse of communism in 1989. It is also worthy of note that Poland experienced a 'Big Bang' in 1990, with deregulation taking place at far too great a pace. This consequently lead to high inflation (over 30%) and a fall in real earnings. This leads to the hypothesis that, in the long term, more substantial reform can lead to higher growth though there may be much pain in the short term.

The new literature on transition further indicates that there are substantial differences in the progress being made across the different former Eastern Bloc countries. For example Allsopp (1997) shows that the perceived most-advanced CEE country, Hungary, has a GDP per capital equal to half that of the lowest-ranked EU member (Greece), whereas the figure for Bulgaria is just one-eighth. (Table 13.1). Inflation rates and growth rates have also varied considerably, for example, the Czech Republic opted for lower growth and lower inflation, whereas Poland started with higher inflation and high growth (Table 13.2). These differences were further highlighted by Buckley and Ghauri (1994) who classified CEE countries into various groupings.

Transition

The term 'transition' implies one particular economic and political system being replaced by another. Allsopp (1997) suggests this is a process that goes

Table 13.1   GDP levels in selected transmission economies (1989 = 100)

	Eastern Europe			Former Soviet Union	
	1991	*1996*		*1991*	*1996*
Czech Republic	80	89	Russia	71	51
Hungary	82	86	Balarus	87	63
Poland	84	104	Ukraine	79	42
Slovakia	79	90	Estonia	73	69
Bulgaria	74	68	Latvia	61	52
Romania	75	88	Lithuania	51	42

Source: *EBRD* (1997).

Table 13.2 Inflation 1991–96. End year (% per annum)

	1991	1992	1993	1994	1995	1996
Central Europe						
Czech Republic	52	13	18	10	8	9
Hungary	32	22	21	21	28	22
Poland	60	44	38	29	22	19
Slovakia	58	9	25	12	7	6
South East Europe						
Albania	104	237	31	16	6	20
Bulgaria	339	79	64	122	33	165
Croatia	429	937	1.150	−3	4	5
FYR Macedonia	115	1.935	230	55	9	2
Romania	223	199	296	62	28	60
Slovania	247	93	23	18	9	10
Baltics						
Estonia	304	954	36	42	29	24
Latvia	262	958	35	26	23	19
Lithuania	345	1.161	189	45	36	26

Source: *EBRD* (1997).

through several stages. Firstly, stabilisation needs to occur and this includes a gradual lifting of price fixing. If this is done too quickly there is a risk of inflation and political backlash hence the need for more gradual reform. Only once stabilisation has occurred can the necessary legal reforms to ensure effective operation of a market system be made; Allsop refers to this as stage 2 of the process.

The word 'transition' has also been defined as the dismantling of one system that is then replaced by another. However, this definition does not stress enough the importance of allocation and efficiency, which are inherent in the transition process (Allsopp, 1997). In a definition of transition it is also important to emphasise the role of external influences in the process, such as allowing free trade and the use of an effective exchange rate. Equally important, there is inherent in a market economy a need for an efficient banking system to support entrepreneurship as well as encouraging the necessary management skills. We postulate that there is a specific role for multinationals to play in contributing to these various characteristics of the transition process. Transition is also sometimes misunderstood, in that transition is not necessarily the movement from a centrally planned system to a free market system.

In addition to the complex problem of defining transition, one might also question how long the process may take to complete. Some of the recent literature (Allsopp, 1997) suggests fulfilling certain criteria prior to actually being able to say the transition process is complete. One example could include the time it takes to move from one point towards optimal production efficiency to a more efficient point closer to that goal. A second approach could be to suggest the transition process is over once the country has become a successful market economy. This would include adoption of various institutions, for example, banks, regulatory procedures, corporate law, property rights and markets. This could imply that countries would have to follow a similar route to meeting the criteria required for becoming a member of the EU. As mentioned earlier, there are huge differences in what needs to be done to meet the criteria across the various Eastern European countries.

With these definition of transition in place it is now possible to determine how far the Polish economy has progressed.

Changes in the Polish Market

Poland is the largest in physical size and population of the ex-Communist countries wishing to join the EU. Poland has a population of around 40 million, similar to that of Spain. The Polish situation may prove to be more viable in the future due to a number of reforms that have taken place. Firstly, the abolition of price controls; only 6 years ago prices were controlled and divorced completely from production and costs. Wide-ranging privatisation has occurred, improving efficiency of production and the ownership structure of enterprises. Around 70% of the labour force work outside the public sector and contribute around 53% of the GDP. Poland now has a convertible currency, inflation has stabilised from 50% in 1991 to 19% in 1999 and, more positively, GDP growth has been averaging 5%. There have been reforms in the banking system, including the National Bank of Poland becoming the central bank for regulating money supply and exchange rates.

Between 1990 and 1993, changes in the legal system have been substantial; 50% of the legal regulations valid in Poland underwent change. According to Blazyca (1995), 200 legal acts have been assessed, almost 100 of them in the last few months of 1994. Furthermore a government programme for enhancing competition has been approved by the Council of Ministers specifying the creation of SME-sized businesses, the creation of anti-trust regulations, the reduction in the scope of price interventionism, the improvements in enterprise access to credit and the reduction of import restrictions.

In addition, measures have been taken to bring the country into line with the EU, for example, norms and technical regulations have started to be harmonised. The European agreement of March 1992 provides for the creation of a free trade zone for industrial goods within a period of 10 years. In 1993, the EU removed import duties on 55% of Polish products, while

Poland lowered import duties for 27% of non-agricultural products, and Poland enjoys privileges on this agreement. In 1993, 63% of Polish exports were directed to the EU market. Poland has also agreed to reduce state aid and become compliant with Article 92 of the Treaty of Rome. However, the greatest obstacle to Poland's membership of the EU is the impact of its agriculture on the EU common agricultural policy budget. It is estimated that absorbing Visegrad countries would cost $47 billion annually.

In July 1997, a historic announcement by the European Commission stated that the six early accession countries – Poland, Hungary, the Czech Republic, Slovenia, Estonia and Cyprus – had achieved the necessary economic and political reforms to allow accession negotiations to open in January 1998, and this raises the prospects of these countries joining the EU by 2004. £54 million is to be spent between 2000 and 2006 to help applicants develop their economies before and after accession. This news can be seen as positive for potential foreign investors hoping to gain from market access to an enlarged EU.

In relation to the other definitions of transition, progress has been made with regards to efficiency, for example. The removal of price controls and the opening up of trade has led to a wider variety of competition.

Evidence suggests that foreign firms are not rushing in to take advantage of the abundant supply of low cost labour, however. In a survey of the top 300 multinational firms investing in Poland, Floyd (1997) found low-cost labour to be one of the least important factors in attracting further FDI. Market access and access to raw materials proved to be much more important. Husan's study of the automobile industry in Poland further indicates the drawbacks of operating in Poland (Husan, 1996). He suggests that the advantage Poland has in terms of low labour costs is more than counter-balanced by the fact that the Polish car industry is much less productive than its Western counterparts. Furthermore plants in Poland are producing on such a small scale that it is not possible to achieve the scale economies that are possible in a Western plant. There is a need for further investment in skills and new machinery in the car industry in order to improve productivity and, therefore, move towards the optimal production efficiency frontier. This will take a great deal of time and effort.

Other recent studies have also suggested there are further problems to be overcome before Poland completes the process of transition. Floyd (1997), cited lack of infrastructure as being the greatest problem to be overcome.

Other problems of a more minor nature included government bureaucracy and political instability. In order to move closer to the optimal production efficiency point, there is a need for an effective and efficient government that will encourage enterprise. Indeed, part of the growth increases in South East Asia have been due to effective government intervention and not just the establishment of free trade and the market mechanism. Recent developments have indicated a changing role for governments. Government now needs to be more efficient and more accountable for expenditure at a time when more money is being spent on public goods, such as health and education. CEE governments need to take these developments on board in establishing a specific role to encourage enterprise.

Trends in Foreign Direct Investment Flows

Recently, FDI flows into CEE have soared. This has been attributed to waves of privatisation as well as to economic recovery, particularly in Poland and the Czech Republic. After the initial flows into Eastern Europe in the early 1990s, FDI remained stagnant until 1994. However, flows doubled in 1995 for the region to reach an estimated $12 billion. The region accounted for 5% of world flows in 1995, compared with only 1% in 1991. Hungary and the Czech Republic accounted for about two-thirds of the 1995 increase. By 1995, foreign investment into CEE had reached US$ 4.3bn for Poland and US$ 7.1bn for Hungary. The 1995 FDI flows into the Russian Federation are estimated at US$ 2bn, twice the 1994 level.

A large percentage of the FDI received in CEE (18%) is attributable to the privatisation of state enterprise, however this share has declined considerably compared with the 1989–1993 period. The more significant reason for the recent growth in FDI has been the growth in GDP in Central Europe after the recession of the early 1990s; hence, there is a strong correlation of FDI growth and domestic output. Interestingly, the largest increases in FDI have been seen in countries reflecting higher levels of GDP; this further reflects the recognition by MNEs that some Central and Eastern European countries, including Poland, Hungary and the Czech Republic, are well on the way to becoming market economies.

The largest proportion of investment into Eastern Europe is from the US (21%) (Table 13.3) though investment from Germany (18%) and Austria (14%) has also been strong, due to the proximity of the countries. France and the UK account for 7% and 6%, respectively; there is an absence of major Japanese investment. Activity has focussed both on the manufacturing and service sectors, with manufacturing accounting for 45% of investment in Poland. The most important industries for FDI focus in CEE have been food (18.5%), electronics (11%), transportation (10%), glass concrete (9%), publishing (9.6%) and computer equipment (8.6%). The mode of entry has changed considerably. In the early transition period of the late 1980s, most were joint ventures but now joint ventures account for 38%, acquisitions for 25% (though 43% for manufacturing in the CEE as a

Table 13.3 Foreign investment by top ten investor countries and investee country

			Investee country					
Investor country	*Hungary*	*Czech Rep*	*Poland*	*Bulgaria*	*Slovakia*	*Romania*	*Total*	*%*
USA	164	94	121*	24	27	18	448	21.1
Germany	163	101	67	23	25	11	390	18.4
Austria	139*	79	27**	11**	36*	5**	297	14
France	47**	46	36	8	7	10	154	7.3
UK	44	30	26	10	3	4	117	5.5
Italy	39	16	13	6	3	8*	85	5
Switzerland	23	23*	8	4	5	2	65	3.1
Sweden	18	13	18*	5	5	0	59	2.8
Japan	27	11	9	4	2	2	55	2.6
Netherlands	20	12	8	2	3	0	45	2.1
Other	160	76	87	41	19	24	407	19.2
Total	844	501	420	138	135	84	2122	

*The actual number of investments is significantly greater than the number of expeced investments.
**The actual number of investments if significantly less than the number of expected investments.
Source: Multinational Business Review (Fall 1996).

whole, and 50% for manufacturing in Poland) and 36% for greenfield investments, though only 12% in the manufacturing sector.

German companies have invested most heavily in manufacturing, accounting for 25% of the total manufacturing investment; the US managed only 17% investment in manufacturing despite being the largest overall investor. Austrian companies have invested more significantly in food, clay, stone and glass products; French firms have invested mostly in printing, UK firms have shown a preference for glass, stone and clay; and the US has had a mixed portfolio. Asian companies have invested in television and car production, though their total investment is still very small compared with that of the US.

RESEARCH FRAMEWORK

According to Dunning (1993), market-orientated FDI has several effects in terms of impact of supplier linkages. Firstly, backward and forward linkages may be achieved. Backward linkages include purchasing goods from local suppliers, forward linkages arise through the firm's marketing channel creating an economic multiplier effect. More highly developed linkages lead to greater economic benefit. McAleese and McDonald (1978), in a study in Ireland, found that domestic firms use more local sourcing than foreign firms but local content improves over time. Over half of the firms surveyed in this study stated that quality was the most important factor when deciding whether to use more local firms, infrastructure was more of a secondary consideration. Local sourcing may help get over the obstacles of poor infrastructure often found to be a key drawback to operating in a Central European country such as Poland, though a MNE will only use local suppliers if quality can be maintained. Linkages can also include second round effects, for example, the establishment of an overseas operation can help the transport industry as well as providing wages that can be spent in the local economy thus providing further multiplier effects.

The second effect that FDI has on a host economy is that of introducing complementary assets. This includes the fact that FDI can be used as a vehicle for introducing new technology into the country as well as management skills. The introduction of 'Just in Time' from the Japanese MNE to Europe is a prime example. In the case of CEE, large MNEs have often played a role in providing short management courses, for example, for General Bottlers (Estrin, 1996). This could involve the production process or be associated with forward linkages, merchandising and sales techniques, and we postulate that there is a role for the foreign MNE in providing education. The benefits from training can also be passed on from job to job and can increase potential earnings.

Dunning also states that MNEs can help raise the standard of product quality. For example, in the food producing industry, which accounts for a substantial amount of FDI in Poland, firms have to adhere to international standards of quality. Quality improvement could also be linked to reliability of product delivery. As well as these benefits, FDI may also have a role to play in increasing competition or domestic rivalry, as often referred to by Porter (1990). In addition, Vernon (1966) has shown that once an MNE enters a market this may stimulate a 'follow-the-leader' approach. Applied to the Polish car industry, Fiat entered earlier followed more recently by Peugeot, General Motors and Daewoo.

The presence of an MNE not only influences rivals but also stimulates competitiveness through backward linkages. For example, firms that have worked with the MNE may gain additional clients and contacts while working with the MNE and entrepreneurship may be stimulated in this way. In another sense, entrepreneurship could be stimulated as the presence of the MNE in the local marketplace may encourage local firms to find ways of servicing the MNE, as well as gaining understanding of what is required in the marketplace and the necessary skills to address these needs.

Limitations to the Benefits of Supplier Linkages

Despite some of the positive benefits suggested there is also evidence that there maybe limitations. Hardy (1998), for example, in a study considering the possible benefits of FDI in Poland through suppliers linkages, suggested benefits to be patchy. In Wroclaw, for example, much development has taken place arising from FDI activity but this has not filtered through to the regions where infrastructure is particularly poor. Hardy refers to such developments as 'cathedrals in the desert'. Secondly, counter-balancing possible benefits arising from competitiveness through backward linkages and the stimulation of entrepreneurship there may again be some limitations. Due to the limitations of the Polish banking system, for example, prospective entrepreneurs may find that bank loans are subject to higher interest rates that may hamper development. In addition, Poland still has cultural vestiges of its Communist past associated with state-run enterprises, including the expectation of job security. Other factors include weakness in innovation, in personnel skills and in stakeholder interests. While Poland is generally felt to be stable politically, the coalition government's cautious macroeconomic policies are not universally popular and economic slowdown could lead to declining support for these measures, both within the coalition and in the population generally. With its eyes firmly focussed on EU membership between 2002 and 2004, the government is pursuing reform and restructuring programmes, not only in terms of economic restructuring, but also in the areas of local government, public administration and the tax system. While viewed with suspicion by many

Poles, these reforms will be welcome to foreign investors who view bureaucratic procedural hurdles and lack of transparency as obstacles to developing linkages. Further integration with Western economies is a priority of the government, mindful of the perception that the Polish economy is heavily dependent on Russia. In fact, only 8% of Poland's exports go to Russia, while 60% are westward bound. Still, the Warsaw stock market has dropped 30% since the most recent Russian crisis, largely due to the exposure of Polish banks in Russia. (*Financial Times*, October 27, 1998). The Polish government's GDP growth forecast for 1999 is down from 6.1% to 5.1%, mainly due to global economic factors. However, the government's plans for restructuring and further privatisation, although halting in progress and facing political obstacles, should help to win the confidence of foreign investors, especially given the country's large domestic market and proximity to EU markets.

DATA COLLECTION

The data for this study were collected through a mail survey of 145 manufacturing firms that were in the top 300 foreign investment firms in Poland. The sample was drawn from lists prepared by the Polish agency for foreign investment and information obtained from the Polish embassy. The questionnaire, accompanied by a standard cover and directions for completion, was mailed to the Managing Director of each of the foreign-owned manufacturing MNEs. Many of the largest foreign-owned MNEs investing in Poland questioned were focussing on resource-based industries, including aluminium, copper, paper and gas; around 50% of respondents were involved in resource-based industries; another third were focussing on the food industry and most of the rest were from the car and electronics industries. Given the purchasing power of Polish consumers at this stage of economic development, many of the firms focus on products that are necessities rather than expensive luxuries.

Firms Chosen for the Sample

Firms identified for the sample fulfil the following criteria: they have committed over US$ 1 million equity and loans to the Polish market (see Table 13.4).

In addition the share of foreign investment in these companies is at least 10%. The companies surveyed consist of foreign investors who have shares in Polish companies. By this strict definition, the World Bank, which granted Poland many credits, is not a foreign investor. The EBRD, the sixth largest foreign investor is by definition a foreign investor since it takes over

Table 13.4 Largest foreign investors in Poland

Number	Investor	Equity and loans granted by Investor (US$m)	Commitment (US$)	Country of origin	Branch
1	Fiat	260	1,750	Italy	Manufacturer of passenger cars
2	Coca-Cola	180	50	USA	Soft drinks
3	Polish American Ent. Fund	164	63	USA	Capital participation in private service
4	Thomson Consumer Electronics	147	37	France	TV tubes and sets
5	IPC	140	175	USA	Paper products
6	EBRD	138	0	International	Banking, capital participation in enterprise
7	International Finance Corporation	123	0	International	Investment in private sector projects across all sectors of industry
8	ABB	100	20	International	Power supply systems, turbines, electric engines
9	Curtis	100	0	USA	Electronics construction
10	Unilever	96	0	International	Washing powder, food processing
11	Epstein	90	110	USA	Construction development, meat processing
12	Procter & Gamble	60	1,130	USA	Personal hygiene products
13	Philips	660	26.5	Netherlands	Electric appliances
14	ING Bank	56	0	Netherlands	Banking
15	Pepsico	55	50	USA	Sweets, soft drinks, potato snacks

Source: State Agency for Foreign Investment (PAIZ) (February 1998).

Table 13.5 Sources of supply of inputs of MNEs operating in Poland

	Poland on entry	Poland currently	Other companies within group on entry	Other companies within group currently
Major source	65%	75%	42.86%	35.71%
Minor source	25	25	14.28	50
Not a source	10	0	42.86	14.28

	Western European countries on entry	Western European countries currently	Parent company on entry	Parent company currently
Major source	41.25%	43.75%	20.00%	14.28%
Minor source	56.25	56.25	26.67	50
Not a source	2.5	0	53.33	35.71

	Elsewhere on entry	Elsewhere currently	Other Eastern European companies on entry	Other Eastern European companies currently
Major source	16.67%	15.38%	0%	6.67%
Minor source	33.33	53.85	21.43	33.33
Not a source	50	30.77	78.57	60

Source: David Floyd Database (1997).

the shares of Polish companies as well as granting loans. However, EBRD was not included in the sample, nor were firms engaging in service industries, including banking, since the survey is aimed solely at manufacturing firms that engage in production and are likely to be involved in a great deal of outsourcing. The location of the foreign investment, as well as the percentage purchase of shares and the major activities of the plant were obtained from the Polish agency for foreign investment (PAIZ). Table 13.4 shows the main list of the 15 largest investors. Most of these firms were included in the survey, except the three engaged in financial activities rather than manufacturing. The major categories of activity of the 145 manufacturing firms were food, chemicals and pharmaceuticals.

METHODOLOGY AND HYPOTHESIS

The study examines the activities of 45% of the top 300 foreign-owned multinational firms operating in Poland, which are manufacturing firms.

Table 13.6 Sources of inputs – the food industry (% source of supply)

Sources of purchase on entry	Poland	Other companies within group	Other European countries	Country of the parent company	Elsewhere	Other Eastern European countries
Major source	71.43	28.57	14.29	0	14.29	0
Minor source	14.29	14.29	57.14	28.57	14.29	0
Not a source	14.29	57.14	28.57	71.43	71.43	100

Sources of purchase currently	Poland	Other companies within group	Other European countries	Country of the parent company	Elsewhere	Other Eastern European countries
Major source	100	28.57	42.86	0	14.29	0
Minor source	0	42.86	42.86	57.14	28.57	14.29
Not a source	0	28.57	14.29	42.86	57.15	85.71

Source: David Floyd Database.

The study focusses on the activities of these manufacturing firms and sets out to identify the sources of supply for the Polish subsidiary. In addition, the study shows the sources of supply on entry to Poland and compares this with the present situation. Sources of supply from various countries are compared and the nature of sources of supply are questioned. If there is shown to be more use of local suppliers one could conclude that the various linkages outlined in the earlier framework are actually being achieved.

RESULTS

As shown in Table 13.5, on entry approximately 65% of supplies were purchased locally for the firms questioned; these were of a major source. This figure has now risen to 75% in terms of current purchases. Table 13.5 also shows that the percentage of supplies sourced from other group companies of the multinational as a major source has decreased, a fall of almost 7% from 42% on entry to 35% currently. There has been a further fall in supplies coming from the parent company base, from 20% to around 14% in terms of major sources. In both of these categories there has been a shift from major to minor sources. To compensate for these falls, the Polish subsidiary is making more use of sources from other European countries, an increase of around 12% comparing the current figure with the one on entry.

Table 13.7   Sources of inputs – the tobacco industry (% source of supply)

Sources of purchase on entry	Poland	Other companies within group	Other European countries	Country of the parent company	Elsewhere	Other Eastern European countries
Major source	50	50	50	50		
Minor source					50	50
Not a source	50	50	50	50	50	50

Sources of purchase currently	Poland	Other companies within group	Other European countries	Country of the parent company	Elsewhere	Other Eastern European countries
Major source	50	50	50	50		
Minor source	50	50	50	50	100	20
Not a source						50

Source: David Floyd Database.

Table 13.8   Sources of inputs – the chemical and pharmaceutical industries (% source of supply)

Sources of purchase on entry	Poland	Other companies within group	Other European countries	Country of the parent company	Elsewhere	Other Eastern European countries
Major source	75	12.5	12.5	0	0	0
Minor source	12.5	12.5	62.5	12.5	25	25
Not a source	12.5	75	25	87.5	75	75

Sources of purchase currently	Poland	Other companies within group	Other European countries	Country of the parent company	Elsewhere	Other Eastern European countries
Major source	75	12.5	25	12.5	12.5	12.5
Minor source	25.5	37.5	50	12.5	25	37.5
Not a source	2.5	50	25	75	62.5	50

Source: David Floyd Database.

There has also been a small increase (around 7%) in major sources of supplies from other Eastern European countries, again comparing to figures on entry with the current ones, though, as noted, the largest increase has been due to greater use of local Polish suppliers: an increase of 10% comparing the situation on entry and at present.

Table 13.9   Sources of inputs – the car industries (% source of supply)

Sources of purchase on entry	Poland	Other companies within group	Other European countries	Country of the parent company	Elsewhere	Other Eastern European countries
Major source		50	50	50		
Minor source	50					
Not a source	50	50	50	50	100	100

Sources of purchase currently	Poland	Other companies within group	Other European countries	Country of the parent company	Elsewhere	Other Eastern European countries
Major source		50	50			
Minor source	50					
Not a source	50	50	50	50	100	100

Source: David Floyd Database.

Table 13.10   The main motivation factors of FDI in Poland

	Polish market	Eastern markets	Resources	Low wage costs	Global strategy
1 Most important	76.92%	16.67%	16.67%	4.76%	15.97%
2	7.69	50.00	5.56	16.67	26.31
3	7.69	5.56	11.11	33.33	10.53
4	3.85	5.56	27.78	19.05	6.00
5 Least important	3.85	16.67	38.89	23.81	31.58

Source: David Floyd Database (1997).

Industry Analysis

When examined separately for industry comparison, local sourcing for the food industry is almost 100% in Poland now compared with 70% on entry (see Table 13.6). This could be due to the necessity of having local suppliers for perishable goods. In the tobacco industry, around 50% of inputs are purchased in Poland now, which is similar to the level of purchase on entry, hence little change (see Table 13.7). Also, in the chemical and pharmaceutical industry there has been little change in major sourcing, when comparing the current situation with that on entry. It is still around 75% though there has been an increase in minor sourcing from 12.5% to 26% (see Table 13.8). In the car industry, sourcing has remained almost the same.

There is, for example, 50% minor sourcing, similar to the figure on entry (see Table 13.4).

As a general observation it can therefore be said that the largest percentage of local sourcing is taking place in the chemical and food industries. This can be explained by the fact that it maybe more favourable for firms to source locally for products for which a larger supply of raw materials is present in the country concerned. Although the percentage of local sourcing for foods and chemicals has barely changed, firms in the food and chemical industries were the first industries to enter Poland, have consolidated their sourcing and are now more established. Indeed some of the investments in the car industry were made later on: for example, Daiwoo and General Motors did not arrive in Poland until 1995.

DISCUSSION

The data of this study have shown that Polish subsidiaries of foreign MNEs are largely sourcing locally, and in some instances increasing the use of local suppliers. There has been an increase of around 10% comparing their entry in late 1980s and early 1990s and the current day situation. This should lead to a more favourable impact on the local economy given the possible linkages that this could produce, as explained in the framework outlined earlier.

From these trends one might imply that the pace of change is not as rapid as one could have hoped. We would like to put forward several reasons for this. Firstly, the parent company may have reservations about using more local suppliers. As the framework outlined earlier suggested, some of the spin-offs from FDI impact could include management skill and quality improvement. However, the lack of some of these skills in current suppliers may be causing concern for the parent MNE and, consequently, the parent is reducing the risk by only increasing the source of supply when it can be sure of adequate quality. The framework also suggested that there can be spin-offs from forward linkages in the form of improved infrastructure and distribution channels. Again, however, the foreign MNE parent companies may be more sceptical about increasing the number of locally sourced supplies due to the lack of infrastructure and established distribution channels. Indeed, the firms questioned in this study ranked lack of infrastructure as one of the most important drawbacks to expanding their operations further.

Additional reasons explaining why MNEs have not increased the number of local suppliers at a more rapid pace relate to location factors in accordance with Dunning OLI framework of international production (Dunning, 1993). Access to resources was chosen as the most important factor why foreign MNE's were investing in Poland by the second largest number of firms.

Therefore, if asset seeking is a major objective of foreign firms rather than solely production, this consequently leads to less of a need for firms to use local suppliers. Indeed this would confirm a changing role for MNE subsidiaries, as it is evident that firms are locating in Poland not just in pursuit of low-cost labour as previously thought, but also to play a role in the overall global strategy of the firm. This changing strategic role would also need to be taken into account when measuring the impact of such linkages. The Meyer (1995) study found low-cost labour to be the third most important factor, with market access being the most important. Further evidence on the importance of low-cost labour is shown by Lankes and Venables (1996), who states that production costs are more important when a firm is involved in exporting and if the project is wholly owned rather than a joint venture.

In terms of internalisation factors, our study showed that around 50% of firms questioned had opted for a greenfield site, with the other 50% deciding on a merger or joint venture. The fact that half of the firms chose in some respects less advanced forms of contractual arrangements rather than greenfield indicates that linkages would not be so great as when all were greenfield. A joint venture, for example, may involve the Western firm bringing in more of its own suppliers. However, on a more positive note, 15% of the firms questioned stated that they would move to a greenfield mode of entry within the next 5 years.

The results of the study also showed that foreign-owned MNEs in Poland are starting to make less use of traditional suppliers from the (say US) parent company or within the group in favour of more use from Western European suppliers and Eastern Europe suppliers. This could be due to the fact that over time the parent company begins to trust the local suppliers more. Also more locally based European suppliers have a cost advantage over more distant suppliers within the group due to the location advantage of distance leading to reduced transport costs.

Overall then, the impact of foreign MNEs on the Polish economy is becoming more favourable. There has been a gradual shift towards more use of local suppliers. However, it is evident that much more progress has to be made in terms of improved infrastructure, quality and management skills before foreign MNEs are confident enough to rapidly increase the use of local suppliers. Indeed, the pursuit of quality assurance and help in this field from the MNE may further enhance benefits for the Polish economy. This is likely to take place as foreign MNEs move, in time, towards a more advanced form of entry mode. More positively, it has also been shown that less supplies are being provided by the parent company and company group in favour of more suppliers from European firms. These positive results in terms of impact are further supported by the fact that 95% of the firms stated that the Polish subsidiary was supplying the local Polish market. This would support the view that impact and multiplier effects are much greater if the firm supports the local market rather than becoming a branch plant for export. In addition, 40% of the firms questioned supplied the Western European market and 50% supplied other CEE markets. Only around 15% of firms questioned were supplying the rest of the world. This would further suggest a specific strategy role for the Polish MNE of supplying the CEE and EU markets, for the most part, therefore, emphasising the export-orientated focus of modern subsidiaries. This new development further supports the recent study by Pearce (1997) on the role of MNE subsidiaries towards a larger focus of supplying regions as a whole rather than the traditional focus on supplying specific individual countries only. In this way subsidiaries can focus on supplying a narrower range of products for a larger regional market, the MNE can gain from economies of scale and scope and reduce costs further by using the company group-level distribution channels.

This more creative role for the subsidiary could also lead to gains in good will of the host country for the foreign multinational. On the one hand, the subsidiary is playing a greater part in world production and, on the other hand, greater exports could lead to a more favourable impact of the foreign MNE subsidiary on the Polish economy.

Some Positive Recent Evidence

A recent survey by the Polish agency for foreign investment (1998) has indicated that firms investing in Poland seem optimistic. Firstly, firms have suggested there is a high labour supply in the region which fits in well with their requirements. Secondly, the OECD acceptance of Poland as a nation striving to achieve European and international economic and political structures has enhanced the international communities' image of Poland as an acceptable investment destination. Poland is also close in proximity to the largest economy in Europe, Germany. Furthermore, the survey indicated that the vast majority of Poles are in favour of foreign investment and that a good portion feel there should be more. There is also a broad consensus in the country concerning the advantages that foreign investment brings to Poland.

The Downside to Globalisation and Foreign Direct Investment

Much of this chapter has focussed on the positive aspects of FDI in Poland and has suggested how benefits may be achieved in terms of low prices and better quality from exposure to competition, as well as increased use of local suppliers. It has also been suggested that FDI may be used as a vehicle for bringing in management skills and encouraging entrepreneurship, as well as creating employment.

It is also necessary, however, to take a more critical view of the FDI process. The advanced multinational of today has shown an ability to adapt to changes in the business environment, for example, most recently, currency fluctuations. There have been numerous cases of shifts in production from one country to another, including the well-documented case of Hoover and the more recent cases of Ford shifting from the UK to Germany. There was much movement by multinationals from France and Germany to the UK and Italy a few years ago when currencies were strongly devalued in the European exchange rate mechanism. Advanced communications make this an easier option for today's MNE. It therefore has to be pointed out that earlier positive benefits from multinational activity in Poland may be short term, and that, in addition to gaining benefits, problems need to be overcome, including lack of capital, infrastructure and quality. Indeed, some of the benefits may later disappear if multinationals pull out as wage costs rise.

Modern multinationals have also become involved in new activities that may be detrimental to host nations in other ways. There is evidence from the data in our study that MNEs in Poland may get more involved in the intra-group trade (trading inputs from one country to another, for example, the data showed an increased reliance on East European parts rather than on parts from the group). It has been shown earlier how CEE countries were at different stages of economic development. Firms may be able to buy parts more cheaply from countries that have not yet achieved abolition of price controls. This may provide opportunities for arbitrage, smuggling and corruption and this can be seen as a downside to the globalisation and FDI process in Poland. The involvement of transfer pricing in the activities of the modern multinational is also well documented.

Many writers, like Dunning and Pearce (1991), have also focused on the distribution of benefits arising from multinational activities and globalisation. As the benefits often go directly to the multinational and the most efficient firms, globalisation generates both winners and losers. Indeed, it has been suggested by Handy (1997) that while profits have risen due to globalisation, the gap between the poorest and richest people in society has widened. More jobs have been created as a result of globalisation, particularly in the US, but the quality of jobs has often been questioned. Other undesirable effects of globalisation include higher suicide rates, road rage and increased crime. Those in work are working longer hours and spend less time with their children. With reference to Eastern European economies, the former system left a large gap between rich and poor. It resulted in a large amount of less well-off people and the creation of a richer elite of people who benefit from the system or the black market; there is a risk, therefore, of exacerbating this particular problem. It is worthy of note that many workers in CEE are working for several companies through their main and second jobs.

Writers on globalisation have also focused on sovereignty issues in assessing the impact of MNEs. Governments are committed to offering favourable conditions to attract multinationals. As these have included limitation of trade union power and labour laws, low inflation, open access to trade, as well as government incentives, governments may be losing sovereignty in economic policy making.

CONCLUSION

To summarise, there are both positive and negative aspects to the MNEs that are playing a substantial part in developing the Polish economy through the transition process. These are taking the form of employment, management skill and various other forms of supplier linkages. More competition is helping to create efficiency and increased quality. However, it has been shown that some of the benefits may be short-term due to the flexibility of the multinational in today's world. Other limitations were also discovered. It is also necessary to draw attention to the downside of globalisation, as addressed in the later section of this chapter and to remember that increases in such activity will generate both winners and losers in society.

References

Allsopp, C. (1997) 'The assessment of economic transition in Eastern and Central Europe', *Oxford Review of Economic Policy*, 13(2) 7–32.
Blazyca, G. (1995) *Monitoring Economic Transition* (Avebury).
Buckley, P. and Ghauri, N. (1994) *The Economics of Change in Eastern and Central Europe* (London: Academic Press).
Dunning, J.H. (1993) *Multinational Enterprises and The Global Economy* (New York: Addison-Wesley).
Dunning, J.H. and Pearce, R. (1991) *The Nature and Growth of MNEs* (Prentice-Hall).
Estrin. S. (1966) 'Investing in Eastern Europe, two case histories', *Business Strategy Review*, 17(1): 24–36.
Floyd, D (1997) 'The determinants of FDI in Poland: further empirical results, Conference proceedings selected papers', *Business and Economics Society International*, Worcester MA: 152–157.
Handy. C. (1997) *The Hungry Spirit* (Hutchinson).
Hardy. J. (1998) 'Cathedrals in the desert. Corporate strategy and local sourcing in Wroclaw', *Regional Studies*, 32(7): 264–279.
Husan, R, (1996) 'The limitations of low cost labour as an inducement to foreign direct investments: an example from the motor industry in Poland', *European Business Review*, 96(4): 26–29.
Lankes, H. and Venables, A.J. (1996) 'Foreign direct investment in economic transition', *Economics of Transition*, 4: 331–347.

McAleese, D. and McDonald, D. (1978) 'Employment growth and the development of linkages in foreign-owned and domestic manufacturing enterprise', *Oxford Bulletin of Economics and Statistics*, 40(4): 321–339.

Meyer, K. (1995) 'FDI in the early years of economic transition: a survey', *Economics of Transition*, 3(3): 301–321.

Pearce, R., and Papanastassiou, M. (1997) 'European markets and the strategic role of multinationals', *Journal of Common Market Studies*, 35(2): 243–267.

Pearce, R. (1987) 'Host countries and the R&D of multinational issues and evidence', University of Reading Discussion Papers in International Investment and Business studies, No. 101.

Porter, M. (1990) *The Competitive Advantage of Nations* (New York: The Free Press).

Vernon, R. (1966) 'International investment and international trade in the product cycle', *Quarterly Journal of Economics*, 80: 190–207.

14 Japanese Ownership Strategies in Singapore, Malaysia and the Philippines: Japanese and US Foreign Direct Investment Preferences Compared

Yukio Takagaki

F23 G32
016
019

INTRODUCTION

This chapter examines the Japanese manufacturing industry's ownership strategy in three South East Asian countries (Singapore, Malaysia, and the Philippines) to determine whether the same variables that have explained US overseas firms' FDI preferences can also account for those of the Japanese. Vernon (1977), whose analysis was based on data from the Harvard Multinational Project, found that US firms preferred wholly owned subsidiaries (WOS), while Japanese firms preferred joint ventures (JV) over WOS (US firms, 66% WOS; Japanese firms, 6% WOS). Differences in ownership policies of US and Japanese parent companies and in the activities of the companies have been offered as explanation of the disparity in ownership preferences. The research reported here utilises hypothesis tests and regression analysis to determine the merit of a number of explanatory variables, key factors that may reflect the parent company's decision-making policies regarding ownership.

PREVIOUS WORK

The earliest well-known research of ownership strategy found that MNEs with product quality, design, and image standardised across countries had little tolerance for joint ventures (Franko, 1971). Subsequently, two studies that did not employ hypothesis-test analysis indicated that an important characteristic of Japanese FDI was the Japanese firms' high propensity for

JV (Yoshino, 1976; Tsurumi, 1976). Japanese FDIs in the mid-1970s were found to be similar in having a heavy concentration on the mature industries and in having fewer intangible assets, such as international goodwill (Hennart, 1982). Ownership preferences of US parent companies were categorised according to parent-firm characteristics, with empirical analysis revealing that WOS is preferred by firms having a greater intensity of research and development (R&D) and/or advertising (Stopford and Wells, 1972). Similarly, parent-firm preferences for UK firms were categorised according to firm-level characteristics such as R&D, advertising and international experience (Stopford and Haberich, 1978). Investigation of US MNEs in Latin America showed that WOS were preferred by firms who were active in R&D and/or advertising and who could employ their own intrasystem transfer (Fagre and Wells, 1982). Regression analysis using explanatory variables such as R&D intensity, advertising intensity and others, was employed to examine the ownership strategy of Japanese as well as US and European firms (Lecraw, 1984). The probability of ownership strategy choice of US MNEs was found to be attributable to the parent's level of R&D, advertising and international experience (Gatignon and Anderson, 1988), and the same data were again used, along with additional variables to identify the conditions of the local market, in a subsequent effort to analyse US MNEs in Less Developed Countries (LDCs) (Gomes-Casseres, 1989). These studies of ownership strategy are highlighted in Table 14.1.

Research into ownership strategy has shown the following factors to be of importance for providing significant explanatory power:

1. R&D
2. advertising
3. marketing (except advertising)
4. capital/labour (K/L)
5. early entry.

The order here does not indicate any degree of significance but rather commonalty of identification or usage in previous research.

Another characteristic of Japanese firms is the tendency to be located in less-developed countries where alien ownership is often restricted, and in 'matured' labour-intensive manufacturing, where the pressure for local ownership is particularly strong. This tendency can be captured somewhat by the factors 'Early entry', 'K/L' (capital/labour) and, to some degree, 'R&D'. Also important to an understanding of Japanese FDIs is the role of trading companies: (a) a trading company may function as a parent company, initiating FDI; and (b) a small- or medium-sized manufacturing company may act as a parent company in partnership with the trading company. Trading companies are specialised in the distribution of commodities and are consequently less advertising-intensive and less R&D-intensive, and are

Table 14.1 Empirical evidence from the analysis of ownership strategy

	Researchers						
Factor	S&W	S&H	P&W	LC	A&G	G&C	HN
R&D	WOS	WOS	WOS	WOS[1]	WOS	–	IS
Advertising	WOS	WOS	WOS	WOS	WOS	–	WOS
Marketing	–	–	–	–	–	WOS	–
Capital	–	–	–	IS[2]	–	–	–
International Experience	–	WOS	WOS	–	WOS	WOS	–
Time (Age)	–	–	–	JV	–	–	JV

WOS – wholly-owned subsidiary
JV – joint venture
– – not analysed
IS – not analysed
S&W: Stopford and Wells (1972): US MNE
S&H: Stopford and Haberich (1978): British MNE
F&W: Fagre and Wells (1982): US MNE in Latin America
LC: Lecraw (1984): Europe, US, Japan and LDCs
A&G: Anderson and Gatignon (1986): US MNE
G-C: Gomes-Casseres (1989): US MNE
HN: Hennart (1988): Japanese JV in US
[1] Technological leadership.
[2] Capital/output.

generally external to their main field of business. Therefore, a subsidiary company may well be a joint venture when the parent company is a trading company. The characteristics associated with trading companies may be covered by factors such as 'R&D' and 'advertising-intensity'.

HYPOTHESES

As indicated in the preceding paragraph, five factors have been identified in the literature as being significant for explaining the ownership strategy of MNEs. Considering these factors enables us to construct the following five hypotheses to be tested. For all except the last, it is expected that higher values are to be associated with a greater probability of wholly owned subsidiaries and a lesser probability of a joint venture. By contrast, the last factor is predicted to be inversely correlated with the occurrence of wholly owned subsidiaries. The expression of 'wholly owned subsidiaries' is meant to include a condition of a high equity share in the subsidiary (95% or higher).

- *Hypothesis 1: R&D.* The higher the level of research and development intensity, the greater the tendency for the parent company to keep its

R&D related ownership advantage (firm-specific advantage) by having wholly owned subsidiaries.

- *Hypothesis 2: Advertising.* The greater the level of advertising, the greater the likelihood that the parent company has wholly owned subsidiaries.
- *Hypothesis 3: Marketing (except advertising).* The greater the subsidiary's dependency on the parent's marketing skill (except advertising), the greater the likelihood for the parent company to have wholly owned subsidiaries.
- *Hypothesis 4: Capital/labour (K/L).* The greater the level of capital/labour (K/L), the greater the likelihood that the parent company has wholly owned subsidiaries.
- *Hypothesis 5: Early-entry.* The earlier the entry into local production, the greater the likelihood for the parent company to have a joint venture subsidiary (or smaller portion of equity share in the subsidiary).

Therefore, early entry values are predicted to be negative, indicating decreased likelihood of wholly owned subsidiaries (WOS).

METHODOLOGY AND MODEL

Analysis of the factors selected and testing of the above-identified hypotheses, as indicated above, entailed first collecting relevant data on subsidiary companies and their parent companies. A number of restrictions were introduced in the data collection as explained below. Those restrictions contributed to the effectiveness of the observations and the reliability of the statistical results.

Data on subsidiary companies were obtained from 'Kaigai Shinshutsu Kigyo Soran', (Toyo Keizai Shinpo, 1988), from which it was possible to assemble a list of subsidiaries having a Japanese company as parent in the three host countries selected. The total number of Japanese subsidiaries was 535 in Singapore, 325 in Malaysia, and 138 in the Philippines. The subsidiary companies considered here were then limited to manufacturing industries by ignoring representative offices and sales subsidiaries. Additionally, extremely small subsidiaries (total number of employees less than 50) were omitted. The resultant list classifying the relationship as wholly owned subsidiary (WOS) or joint venture (JV), provides a sample of 190 subsidiaries owned by 132 Japanese parents, among which the Japanese parent companies control 36 WOS and 29 JV in Singapore, 15 WOS and 78 JV in Malaysia, and 2 WOS and 30 JV in the Philippines.

This notable difference in the distribution of WOS and JV among these three host countries suggests that host-country conditions or regulations affect the differences in ownership strategy of the Japanese parent. The sample of 190 subsidiaries in the three South East Asian countries was then further reduced to a sample of 68 business units operated by 53 parent firms, a reduction necessitated by an absence of sufficient data on the parent companies. In order to arrive at reasonably comparable figures for three countries with very different historical conditions of receptivity to investment, it was necessary to adjust the numerical values with an adjustment that would appropriately reflect the diverse conditions of the local host countries.

In comparison with 1988, we observe from the same database series (Toyo Keizai Shinpo, 1993) that between 1988 and 1992 the number of Japanese subsidiaries in the three countries increased to 205. Japanese parent companies control 13 WOS and 18 JV in Singapore, 72 WOS and 81 JV in Malaysia, and 10 WOS and 11 JV in the Philippines. However, as the purpose of our analysis in this chapter is to analyse a comparison between US and Japanese FDI, the analysis concentrates on the data up to 1998.

Data on the parent companies were taken mainly from 'Yukashoken Hokokusho (company's financial report)' obtained from the magnetic tape of 'Needs-Zaimu Data Base (Nikkei Financials)' (Nihon Keiza Shinbun, (1988).

TOBIT and LOGIT models were used to analyse what influenced the decision making of Japanese parent firms when arriving at their specific ownership strategy. Both models are shown below.

1. TOBIT Analysis (Equation 1):

$$\text{SHARE} = f(\text{IRNDINT, ADINT, MKTINT, K/L, YR})$$

2. LOGIT Analysis (Equation 2):

$$\text{LOGIT} = f(\text{IRNDINT, ADINT, MKTINT, K/L, YR})$$

The two dependent variables are defined as follows.

SHARE: Japanese parent's percentage share of ownership in the subsidiary
LOGIT: a dummy value defined as
LOGIT = 1 if the subsidiary is wholly owned (WOS) (when the value of 'SHARE' equals or exceeds 95%)
LOGIT = 0 if the subsidiary is a joint venture (JV) (when the value of 'SHARE' is less than 95%)

The five independent variables are as follows; the first four concern only the Japanese parent, and the last concerns only the subsidiary, but with particular reference to the country:

IRNDINT: Research and Development intensity of the industry within which the principal business of the Japanese parent is located.
ADINT: Advertising intensity of the Japanese parent.
MKTINT: Marketing intensity (except advertising) of the Japanese parent.

K/L: Capital/labour ratio of the Japanese parent (that is, fixed-cost/labour-cost).

YR: Adjusted age of the subsidiary.

In the case of the TOBIT analysis (Equation 1), the dependent variable (SHARE) is limited in its range, in that the Japanese parent's equity share has no negative value and has an upper limit of 100. Therefore, a Limited Dependent Variable Model, of which TOBIT is one, is best applied because OLS (ordinary least squares) estimates are biased when the dependent variable is truncated. The TOBIT model can therefore correct for this deficiency.

In the LOGIT analysis (Equation 2), because the dependent variable is set up as a zero-or-one dummy variable and regressed for the independent variables the predicted value of the dependent variable can be expected to fall mainly within the interval between 0 and 1 and can be interpreted as indicating the probability of the parent firm's choosing WOS (wholly owned-subsidiary).

INDEPENDENT VARIABLES AND HYPOTHESES

In the section on hypotheses, five hypotheses were provided, each associated with one of the five factors that have been previously identified as significant to the operation of MNEs. In the section on methodology and model, five associated variables were introduced and given the labels used in the relevant equations. Here we repeat the five variables to be used in the statistical models, along with a brief explanation of expected numerical values, and for two of the variables a somewhat more detailed discussion of the associated hypotheses or of the numerical adjustments made for purposes of calculation.

The first three variables are determinants of intensity of research and development (R&D), advertising, and marketing. The fourth variable is related to the capital/labour ratio (K/L), which is associated with the firm's characteristics of operation. The fifth variable, early entry, takes into account the duration of the parent's foreign experience as well as the host country's attractiveness.

R&D Intensity (IRNDINT)

In this model, R&D intensity is expected to have the value 'IRNDINT'. Research and development intensity is calculated by dividing R&D expenditure of the industry by the total sales of the industry. The coefficient of R&D intensity is predicted to be positive.

- *Hypothesis 1: R&D.* The higher the level of research-and-development intensity, the greater the tendency for the parent company to keep its R&D related ownership advantage (firm-specific advantage) by having wholly owned subsidiaries.

Internalisation of the parent's knowledge and know-how (such as R&D, advertising, and marketing) may be greater if the market for such knowledge and know-how is imperfect due to asymmetric information. R&D intensive firms, therefore, often prefer to exploit their ownership advantage (firm-specific advantage) by internalising the transaction through FDIs in wholly owned subsidiaries rather than in joint ventures. Possession of a proprietary product or technology may also increase the bargaining position of the parent firm over the host partner, particularly if other rivals or local investors cannot supply technology of the same type or level of advancement. Advertising-intensive firms, and/or marketing-intensive firms, therefore also prefer wholly owned subsidiaries.

Advertising Intensity (ADINT)

For this model, advertising intensity (ADINT) is calculated by dividing the advertising expenditure of the Japanese parent company by the total sales in the parent company, both figures being values from the year of the subsidiary's establishment. The coefficient of advertising intensity is, like R&D intensity, predicted to be positive.

- *Hypothesis 2: Advertising.* The greater the level of advertising, the greater the likelihood that the parent company has wholly owned subsidiaries.

Marketing Intensity (MKTINT)

In this model, marketing intensity (MKTINT) is determined by dividing the sales expenditures of the parent by the total sales of the parent company, again with both figures having values from the year of the subsidiary's establishment. Again, the coefficient of marketing intensity is expected to be positive.

- *Hypothesis 3: Marketing.* The greater the subsidiary's dependency on the parent's marketing skill (except advertising), the greater the likelihood of the parent company having a wholly owned subsidiary.

Capital/labour (K/L) Ratio

In this model, the capital/labour ratio (K/L) is determined by dividing the Japanese parent's fixed cost as of the year of the subsidiary's establishment by the labour cost for the same year. The value of the coefficient of capital/labour (K/L) ratio is expected to be positive.

- *Hypothesis 4: Capital/labour.* The greater the level of capital/labour (K/L), the greater the likelihood that the parent company has a wholly owned subsidiary.

The capital/labour ratio (K/L) should be able to explain a number of the firms' characteristics. Capital intensive firms need a greater amount of capital in the foreign production site. Firms that are good at obtaining capital resources may have greater bargaining power towards the local partner; they may prefer, therefore, to exploit their ownership advantage (firm-specific advantage) by internalising transactions through FDIs in wholly owned subsidiaries rather than in joint ventures. On the other hand, a labour-intensive firm needs management skills for its operation; therefore, it may need a local partner who has greater experience in managing local workers.

Early Entry (YR)

In this model, calculations are based on the reference year 1988 (the year of the original database). However, in order to represent the value of the length of time of international experience, it was necessary to calculate a 'relative year figure', the relative year figure being the difference between the base year, when the parent firm established its subsidiary, and our reference year, 1988. The relative year figure is therefore a one- or two-digit number.

Furthermore, as indicated under 'Methodology' above, it was necessary to adjust the numerical values by a numeral adjustment that would appropriately reflect the diverse conditions of the three local host countries.

In this model, therefore, 'early-entry' is calculated from the *relative year figure* minus an *adjustment* of 5 years for the Philippines, 10 years for Malaysia, and 15 years for Singapore. That is, a subsidiary established in 1977 would have a relative year of 11 (1988 *minus* 1977). The corresponding early entry value would be 6 if established in the Philippines (11 *minus* 5), or −4 if in Singapore (11 *minus* 15). The values of early entry are predicted to be negative, indicating decreased likelihood of WOS.

- *Hypothesis 5: Early Entry.* The earlier the entry into local production, the greater the likelihood for the parent company to have a joint venture subsidiary (or smaller portion of equity share in the subsidiary.

An adjustment was necessary in calculating the 'early-entry' parameter in order to accommodate the effect of the attractiveness of conditions in the host country (e.g. the level of per capita income, market size, availability of skilled labour, government regulations, country risk, etc.). As mentioned before, the pattern of ownership is different for each of the three countries in the sample. The adjustment figure enables the model to capture the fact that Singapore appears to be very attractive for WOS-type investors, Malaysia intermediately attractive, and the Philippines less attractive. Although the adjustment figures were at first arbitrarily set for each country, and confirmed for suitability by trial and error, an economic and political environment analysis carried out historically formed the non-arbitrary basis for the choice of these figures. For example, Singapore started its open door policy for FDI in the late 1960s, and since that time many foreign firms have invested in that country. This took place especially after 1973, and hence that date, exactly 15 years before 1988, was taken as a suitable turning point for country-attractiveness, and the adjustment value needed was tentatively set at 15. Adjustment values for Malaysia and the Philippines were similarly set, but at lower values to reflect their apparently less attractive conditions, or later 'turning points'.

RESULTS AND DISCUSSION

The results clearly support the hypotheses concerning R&D intensity (IRNDINT), marketing intensity (MKTINT) and also the hypothesis for early entry (YR). That is, higher values of R&D intensity and marketing intensity suggest greater likelihood of WOS, while an earlier entry suggests decreased likelihood of WOS. However, the hypotheses for advertising intensity (ADINT) and capital/labour ratio (K/L) are not supported. An explanation of the results and of each of the variables now follows. In the cases of R&D intensity and marketing intensity, the discussion includes suggestions for future research.

The results are shown in Table 14.2. Column 1 shows the expected sign of each coefficient. Column 2 displays the results of the TOBIT model for the percentage equity share on the independent variables, which were described earlier. Column 3 shows the results of the binary LOGIT model according to the subsidiary's ownership pattern, joint venture (JV) or wholly owned subsidiary (WOS); the same independent variables were also used for the TOBIT model.

The correlation matrix for independent variables is shown in Table 14.3. Some degree of collinearity may be observed between marketing intensity (MKTINT) and advertising intensity (ADINT). In this case, however, this apparent collinearity does not affect the results of the analysis because both sets of data are taken independently from the same database. The collinearity simply means that there are several firms that emphasise both media advertising and sales promotion (marketing). Among the samples, there are many consumer product industries, such as cosmetics and home

Table 14.2 Parameter estimates from regression analysis

	Expected sign		TOBIT	LOGIT
Number of observations			68	68
Long-likelihood			230.07	30.506
INTERCEPT		coefficient	20.431	2.98833
		t-statistics	1.7	3.148
		significance level	0.08914	0.00165
IRNDINT	+	coefficient	7.81819	0.360537
		t-statistics	3.84	2.634
		significance level	0.00012	0.00845
ADINT	+	coefficient	−51.7882	−21.058
		t-statistics	−0.179	−0.844
		significance level	0.85761	0.3985
MKTINT	+	coefficient	150.266	8.2067
		t-statistics	1.585	1.429
		significance level	0.11286	0.15299
K/L	+	coefficient	0.524285	0.233793
		t-statistics	0.787	0.564
		significance level	0.431	0.57249
YR	−	coefficient	2.85441	0.146445
		t-statistics	−3.368	−2.445
		significance level	0.00076	0.01449

Table 14.3 Correlation matrix

	IRNDINT	ADINT	MKTINT	K/L	YR
IRIDINT	1				
ADINT	−0.178	1			
MKTINT	−0.145	0.607	1		
K/L	−0.211	0.448	0.453	1	
YR	−0.013	0.181	0.001	0.158	1

appliances, that are targeting the local market. Such industries need to display a marketing orientation in which both advertising and marketing play a role.

Analysis of Results per Hypothesis

R&D intensity (IRNDINT) – hypothesis supported
The coefficient of industry-level R&D intensity is positive (7.82 for TOBIT; 0.36 for LOGIT) and the value is significant (less than 0.01 for both models). This result is consistent with the results of Stopford and Wells (1972),

Stopford and Haberich (1978), Fagre and Wells (1982) and Gatignon and Anderson (1988). Japanese ownership is influenced by R&D like US and British MNEs. In the early stage of the analysis, another figure, calculated from corporate-level parent-firm's R&D divided by sales was also used, based on data from Yukashoken Hokokusho, and that figure served as a proxy for R&D intensity; however, that variable proved to be insignificant. Although further research for a better proxy is desirable, the results obtained here support the use of industry-level R&D intensity rather than individual corporate-level R&D intensity as a proxy for technological level.

Advertising intensity (ADINT) – hypothesis not supported
For media advertising intensity, the value is not significant (at 0.86 level for TOBIT and 0.4 level for LOGIT). Although Stopford and Wells (1972), Gatignon and Anderson (1988) and some others found that advertising intensity significantly influenced the choice of ownership, the results here suggest that Japanese parent's advertising practice or skill may have little influence on ownership strategy. We may tentatively explain the results as follows. (a) Advertising or product differentiation may not be an effective ownership advantage (firm-specific advantage), at least not in industries invested in those three South East Asian countries. (b) The purpose of some Japanese firms' FDI is not orientated to the local market but rather to exporting to Japan or to third countries; therefore, advertising is not particularly necessary or valuable. Alternatively, (c) difficulties may be involved in transferring advertising know-how and therefore a local partner is necessary.

Marketing intensity (MKTINT) – hypothesis supported
The coefficient for marketing intensity of Japanese firms is positive (150.3 for TOBIT and 8.2 for LOGIT) and the value is near the 0.10 cut off point (0.11 level for TOBIT and 0.15 level for LOGIT). The results are consistent with those of Gomes-Casseres (1989). In consumer product industries, such as home appliances, there may be emphasis on both advertising and marketing. In high technology industrial product industries – such as Numerically Controlled (NC) machinery, measuring instruments, fine chemicals, and such – emphasis will not be on advertising but as on customer focus and marketing instruments in general, including sales promotion. Although many researchers focus only on advertising intensity, it may be that in doing so they miss this important aspect of marketing.

Capital/labour ratio (K/L) – hypothesis not supported
Although, as predicted, the coefficient of the Japanese firms' capital/labour ratio (K/L) is positive, the value is not significant (neither at the level of 0.43 for TOBIT, nor at 0.57 for LOGIT). This suggests that the parent's capital/labour ratio does not clearly affect the ownership strategy. Part of the

reason for this is that in the sample there were many low K/L ratio companies, such as textile industries and home appliances, as contrasted with higher K/L ratio companies, such as petrochemicals or heavy industries.

Early entry (YR) – hypothesis supported

As predicted, the coefficient of 'early-entry' is negative (−2.85 for TOBIT and −0.146 for LOGIT) and the value is significant at less than 1 level for TOBIT and at 0.01 level for LOGIT. This strongly supports the hypothesis of early entry (YR). As many researchers have already mentioned, the earlier a subsidiary is founded the more likely that it is a joint venture (JV) because the parent company is wary of and does not know enough about the local environment. The value of the coefficient can be explained by the fact that as time passes the parent accumulates knowledge of the local business activity while at the same time the government in the country concerned loosens its regulations regarding FDI – hence, the parent firm feels there is less of a need to work with a local partner. As discussed above, the attractiveness of conditions for entry should be taken into consideration for each country. In our analysis the relative year figure of the subsidiary was adjusted for each country; the adjustment figure was arrived at by a best guess method, combining a reasoned approach, historical environmental analysis, and trial and error to obtain statistically workable results. In this way the 'turning point' year, marking the beginning of more favourable FDI conditions was established as 1973 for Singapore, 1978 for Malaysia and 1983 for the Philippines.

The year 1973 represents a turning point for Japanese FDI. Because of the Nixon shock (16 August 1971), floating rate system (14 February 1973) and the oil crisis (October 1973), the foreign exchange rate was drastically changed. Accordingly, as the Japanese wage level shot up, many Japanese firms tried to shift their production sites to cheaper South East Asian countries in order to be able to maintain their competitive advantage towards advanced countries. Hence the adjustment figures used in our analysis enabled the model to capture the fact that Singapore appeared to be very attractive for WOS-type investors. While our adjustment figures of 15, 10 and 5 were 'arbitrarily' set, their respective values reflect the apparent attractiveness of the three countries concerned, indicating an earlier or later 'turning point' and portraying Malaysia as intermediately attractive, and the Philippines as less attractive. This is consistent with the fact that, at that time, there were more than 2 WOS, and the accumulated paid-in capital for Japanese subsidiaries was more than 350 billion yen in each country. Therefore, this adjustment represents a good proxy for country attractiveness.

Thus, everything else constant, the younger a subsidiary – or the later the local market entry of the firm – the more likely that is will be wholly owned. This finding is in line with that of Gatignon and Anderson (1988) and

Gomes-Casseres (1989), both of whom found that the number of previous foreign investments appears to support an increased probability that the parent would opt for a wholly owned subsidiary.

CONCLUSIONS

This chapter set out to establish whether the variables which were successful in explaining ownership preferences of US firms could also account for the preferences of Japanese firms. One contribution of our research has been to throw some light on the possible differences between US and Japanese firms.

After reviewing previous studies, we concentrated on five key factors: R&D, advertising, marketing, capital/labour (K/L) and early entry. These five key factors were used to examine possible influences on a parent firm's decision making regarding ownership strategy, specifically focussing on preferences for wholly owned subsidiaries over joint ventures. Analysis involved using both TOBIT and LOGIT models.

The results show that most of these previously identified independent variables are significant in explaining the ownership type preferred by Japanese firms. In particular, among firm-specific advantages for Japanese firms, R&D was found to be the most important ownership advantage, just as it is for US and British firms. In highly R&D competitive industries the Japanese firm tends to prefer wholly owned subsidiaries. Since the competition in R&D is increasing this suggests that the number of Japanese wholly owned subsidiaries in South East Asian countries may increase. This analysis also indicated that industry-level R&D intensity provides a better proxy for R&D intensity than firm-level R&D.

As was the case for US and British firms, for Japanese firms marketing intensity proved to be one of the key ownership advantages (firm-specific advantages). Marketing intensive firms prefer a wholly owned subsidiary since they need to manage their brand image and maintain customer focus and the quality of their product. Although few researchers have specifically analysed marketing intensity, our research indicates that there would be good reason to include this category in subsequent research and analysis.

Our research provided unclear results on two of the factors: the effect of advertising intensity and the capital/labour ratio. This would suggest that further research in this area is necessary to clarify the factors of influence, even though at present there appears to be some possible explanations for our results, as indicated above.

The results of our 'early-entry' analysis suggest that joint venture is a good vehicle for acquiring local knowledge in the early stages. JVs tend to be used by Japanese firms with little experience of the local market or management, or for skirting local government regulations. However, as time passes, Japanese firms prefer a wholly owned subsidiary because they gain local knowledge through other channels and also because as the host economy grows, government regulations loosen. Hence, the external environment improves for the establishment of wholly owned subsidiaries, which in turn are good for maintaining ownership advantages. The factor 'country attractiveness' was treated as an adjustment for the calculation of early entry for each country. Although previous researchers have used a variety of variables, often involving complex computations, to treat this factor, the results obtained here suggest that this simple adjustment provides an easily used proxy for this purpose.

Because of the absence of associated firm-level data, the sample size was smaller than had been planned. Although this reduced sample size may have introduced some bias, the results indicate that overall the models successfully explained the Japanese firms' preference for ownership structures. Thus, it was established that the variables that were found to be successful in explaining ownership preference patterns of US firms can equally be used to explain Japanese ownership patterns, though, of course, there are some differences in data analysis compared with what has been reported for previous studies.

In brief, the analysis undertaken here suggests that, like US or British firms, Japanese firms currently tend to show a preference for wholly owned subsidiaries (WOS-type ownership) although some decades ago joint venture (JV-type ownership) was more common.

Our research has indicated two reasons why in the future some Japanese manufacturing firms may tend to prefer wholly owned subsidiaries rather than joint ventures: R&D intensity in certain industries, and the increase in global marketing: We postulate that firms with ownership advantages (firm-specific advantages) such as R&D and marketing will prefer wholly owned subsidiaries in international business activities, that the currently strong competition in R&D may increase the proportion of wholly owned subsidiaries among Japanese FDIs in South East Asia and that the current trend of global marketing may also push Japanese FDIs towards wholly-owned-subsidiary-type ownership. However, our research also suggests that JVs tend to be preferred by Japanese firms in labour-intensive industries, by those with little experience of local market or management, and by those who wish to skirt local government regulations. Even so, as time passes, Japanese firms will prefer and transfer to a wholly owned subsidiary.

References

Fagre, N. and Wells, L.T. (1982) 'Bargaining power of multinationals and host governments', *Journal of International Business Studies*, 13 (Fall): 9–23.
Franko, L.G. (1971) *Joint Venture Survival in Multinational Corporations* (New York: Praeger).

Gatigon, H. and Anderson, E. (1988) 'The multinational corporation degree of control over subsidiaries: an empirical test of a transaction cost explanation', *Journal of Law, Aconomics and Organizations*, 4 (Fall): 305–336.

Gomes-Casseres, B. (1989) 'Ownership structures of foreign subsidiaries: theory and evidence', *Journal of Economic Behaviour and Organization*, 11 (January): 1–25.

Hennart, J.-F. (1982) *A Theory of Multinational Enerprise* (Ann Arbor: University of Michigan Press).

Lecraw, D.J. (1984) 'Bargaining power, ownership, and profitability of transactional corporations in developing countries', *Journal of International Business Studies*, 5 (Spring/Summer): 27–43.

Stopford, J. and Haberich, K.O. (1978) 'Ownership and control of foreign operations', in Ghertman and Leontiades (eds) *European Research in International Business* (New York: North Holland) pp. 141–176.

Stopford, J.M. and Wells, L.T. (1972) *Managing the Multinational Enerprise: Organization of the Firm and Ownership of the Subsidiaries* (New York: Basic Books).

Tsurumi, Y. (1976) *The Japanese Are Coming: A Multinational Spread of Japanese Firms* (Massachusetts: Ballinger).

Vernon, R. (1977) *Storm Over the Multinationals: The Real Issues* (Cambridge, MA: Harvard University Press).

Yoshino, M. (1976) *Japan's Multinational Enterprises* (Cambridge, MA: Harvard University Press).

15 The Restructuring of the Chinese Automotive Industry: the Role of Foreign Direct Investment and the Impact of European Multinational Enterprises

Zhang Hai-Yan and Daniel van den Bulcke

INTRODUCTION

This chapter studies the restructuring of the Chinese automotive industry since the 1980s and the impact of FDI on this ongoing process. The main focus is the evaluation of the role of European MNEs in the development of Chinese automotive assembly and parts manufacturing,[1] especially in the passenger car industry. The first section provides an analytical framework for assessing the dynamic interactions between the government's sectoral policy and the strategic setting of automotive MNEs in different stages of the industrial restructuring, in particular with regard to the creation of local added value and the development of global competitiveness. In the second section, the restructuring process of the Chinese automotive industry is analysed. This chronological overview is designed to highlight the evolution of the Chinese government's sectoral policy and its impact on the structure and development pattern of the industry. In the third section, the entry and expansion path of foreign automotive manufacturers and automotive part and component producers in the Chinese automotive industry, especially those from the EU, is discussed against the background of the industrial restructuring process.

ANALYTICAL FRAMEWORK

The successful development of any industry in today's global economic system depends on two basic objectives; the creation of high local added value and the achievement of strong worldwide competitiveness. In order to sustain the profitability of indigenous industries and to strengthen international competitiveness, emerging countries have developed different policies during their various stages of development. As the evolution of the indigenous industries in emerging countries is becoming more determined by the infusion of foreign technology, MNEs are increasingly regarded as cross-border 'allocaters' and 'upgraders' of resources and capabilities in this process (Lall, 1985; Cantwell, 1991; Tolentino, 1993; Dunning, 1997). In order to monitor the technology transfer process and its spill-over effects on indigenous industries, a large number of developing host governments try to influence the investment patterns and strategic setting of MNEs through regulations, such as entry conditions for a particular industry, competitive practice, profitability and exit barriers (Aggarwal and Agmon, 1990). The dynamic interaction between government policy and corporate strategy in the development and restructuring of the automotive industry in emerging markets can be examined in different stages (World Bank, 1993) (Figure 15.1).

Stage 1. During a first stage, many developing countries are characterised by their limited market size and minimal levels of demand as a result of the low income per capita. Assuming that an indigenous automotive industry has been set up in the context of a country's import substitution policy, it will supposedly have relatively few technological capabilities and, therefore, have low competitiveness. Although local added value in the industry may be high, the national competitiveness of the industry may depend totally on

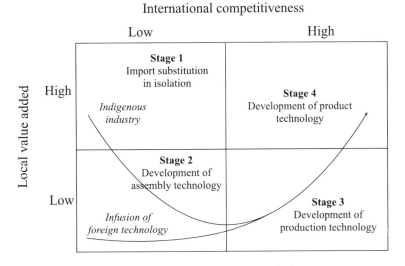

Figure 15.1   The development path of the automotive industry

the protection provided by the government through tariff and non-tariff barriers. The industrial structure is likely to be fragmented and dispersed because of inappropriate government policies and an inefficient economic system, as has often been the case in centrally planned economies. MNEs will not be encouraged to establish plants within the country, because the host government increases entry barriers to protect its 'infant industry'. During this stage, foreign automotive companies have few opportunities even to export to these markets, except when their parts or products are rather exclusive and are so specific that they are not readily available locally and have to be bought from them in the international markets.

Stage 2. In the second stage, governments change their sectoral policy in order to restructure and strengthen their indigenous automotive industry. New products and process technologies are introduced into existing enterprises by using foreign production licences, while greenfield plants are put up by, or together with, foreign companies. The limited import of finished vehicles will be replaced by the domestic assembly of CKD and SKD kits (i.e. completely and semi-knocked-down vehicles), which are imported either from the foreign partners of the joint ventures or from foreign licensors of the production technology. By using imported foreign assembly technology, however, the domestic industry gets an opportunity to catch up with the technological advances. At this stage there is still a huge technology gap between indigenous firms and foreign-invested enterprises. The local added value in assembling CKD kits is rather low and the infusion of modern assembling technology often results in increased imports of components and parts, because local suppliers are inefficient and not sufficiently competitive by world standards. The local sourcing capability is in fact quite limited. Host governments may react to this situation by imposing local content regulations for assembly plants – which are often related to tax and tariff incentives – in order to benefit more fully from the positive effects of foreign investment in the local industry by changing the relationship between the car manufacturers and the suppliers of parts. However, as long as the local market is too small the suppliers of parts and components are unlikely to invest into local production. Foreign car producers react to these measures by introducing less sophisticated finished products to the local market that are less demanding of local inputs in terms of quality. If this scenario does indeed unfold, the result will be that production in the host country will almost entirely be orientated towards, the small, but growing domestic market, as it will not be up to international standards.

Stage 3. The third stage will be reached when the national automobile industry develops mass-production capabilities by mastering the imported production technology or by introducing innovative new production systems. In this stage, the entry barriers for newcomers may become quite high, because on the one hand the government limits the establishment of complete vehicle manufacturing plants and on the other hand the early foreign entrants have acquired dominant positions in the domestic market. Facing this situation, early foreign licensors tend to switch from production licensing contracts to joint ventures agreements with their local contractors, while newcomers will try to take over existing local companies or will invest in the production of components in order to catch up. Although product design remains rather simple, production becomes more efficient, reaches a higher quality level and achieves lower costs, mainly as a result of technological upgrading and the improvements that occur in the sector of automotive parts and components. The traditional in-plant or vertically integrated supply system is changed into horizontal assembler–supplier linkages. The realisation of economies of scale leads to 'follow-up' investment by foreign component producers in the local industry. Production costs are reduced by localisation and management gains. Economies of scale also allow for lower costs and prices and lead to an expansion of the size of the domestic market. Trade barriers tend to be lowered in order to introduce competition in the local industry so as to strengthen the companies' competitive position in the global industry. At this stage, the industry in the emerging economy moves closer to the world production system that relies on subcontractors and related industries to achieve efficiency and reliability.

Stage 4. In Stage 4, the industry reaches a mature phase of development, characterised by its capability to design and market its own products through strong brand names, well-managed distribution channels and efficient logistic systems. Product innovation becomes the key success factor. The industry has become competitive in the global market and no longer requires protection. Product quality reaches world standards and frequent model changes become both necessary and possible as the automobile industry has to deal with increasingly sophisticated buyers. Marketing strategy becomes an essential competitive tool therefore. Only a few economies, such as the US, Japan, Germany and France, have actually reached this stage in the automobile sector because this phase requires substantial creative capabilities in technology and product development.

DEVELOPMENT OF THE CHINESE AUTOMOTIVE INDUSTRY

The development of the Chinese automotive industry since the 1950s fits into the first two stages and the early period of the third stage outlined above. The sector targets, technological development, product segmentation, growth tendency, level of trade barriers and foreign participation are quite different during this phased development process.

Establishment (1953–1982)

The Chinese automotive industry was launched in 1953 when construction was started for the First Auto Works (FAW), now renamed the China First Automobile Group Corp., in Changchun, Jilin Province. The start up of the indigenous automotive industry relied exclusively on Soviet assistance for product and production technology,[2] equipment and training. This pioneer enterprise initially consisted of several plants for the production of parts and the assembly of five-ton trucks (Jiefang Truck). Actual production only started in 1956, with an annual target of 30 000 units. However, during the time of the 'Great Leap Forward' in 1958 and again in 1969–1970, when the industrial decentralisation took place, many local governments set up their own truck factories. This resulted in a geographically dispersed automotive industry with the production of light trucks being located in Nanjing, heavy trucks in Jinan and passenger cars in Changchun (Dongfeng, 1958 and Red Flag, late 1950s) and Shanghai (Shanghai, early 1960s), and jeeps in Beijing (Beijing Jeep, 1966). The annual production of all types of vehicles in China went up from about 2000 units between 1953–1957 to 30 000 between 1963–1965. Yet, before 1964 the production of passenger cars was still less than 100 units (Table 15.1).

In 1965, another large complex – the Second Auto Works (SAW), known today as the Dongfeng Automotive Group – initiated the production of medium-size trucks (Dongfeng Truck). The construction of the plant was largely based on China's indigenous technical capabilities. However, as a result of the limited availability of domestic resources in capital and technology, SAW only started production in 1978 and reached its full production capacity as late as 1980. The enterprise was set up in a remote location, in Shiyan, Hubei Province, because of political and military considerations.[3] The unfavourable location and the poor industrial infrastructure in the region obliged SAW to enter into cooperation agreements with firms in other regions from the very beginning of its operations (see below).

By the end of the 1970s, the Chinese automotive industry counted almost 2400 enterprises, of which 2070 were producing automotive components and parts. The annual output of finished vehicles in the Chinese automotive industry reached about 220 000 units in 1980, i.e. 0.58% of the world production. Until the end of 1970s, the Chinese automotive industry predominantly produced trucks. At that time, passenger cars produced with domestic technology, i.e. the models Shanghai, Beijing Jeep and Red Flag, accounted for less than 1% of the total vehicle production in the country. Although this ratio reached 22% in 1995, it is still very low compared to proportions such as 53% in the US, 75% in Japan, 93% in Germany, 87% in the UK and 88% in France (AIB, 1996). Imports of foreign passenger cars largely surpassed domestic production: between 1953–1980, about 35 000 passenger cars were imported, while local companies produced less

Table 15.1 Number of enterprises and volume of production in the Chinese automotive industry (1953–95)

Period	All types of motor vehicles					Passenger cars			
	Number of plants*	Vehicle plants	Total output	Average annual output	Annual growth rate (%)	Total output	Average annual output	Annual growth rate (%)	As % of all vehicles
1953–57	115	1	9 619	1 924	–	–	–	–	–
1958–62	327	17	71 504	14 301	4.27	272	54	–	0.38
1963–65	522	21	89 183	29 728	60.86	244	81	129.52	0.27
1966–70	1228	45	241 608	48 322	16.54	1 084	217	8.06	0.45
1971–75	1852	52	580 013	116 003	9.91	5 680	1 136	56.14	0.98
1976–80	2379	56	817 650	163 530	9.72	17 151	3 430	24.39	2.10
1981–85	2904	114	1 371 588	274 318	14.81	24 721	4 944	–0.79	1.80
1986–90	2596	117	2 588 420	517 684	2.81	147 819	29 564	52.12	5.71
1991–95	2479	122	5 873 384	1 174 677	23.32	1 049 271	209 854	50.32	17.86

Note: * At the end of the period.
Source: AIB (1996).

Table 15.2 Local production and imports of passenger cars in China
(1953–95, units)

Year	Local production	Imports of finished cars	Imports as % of local production	Imported CKD	CKD as % of local production
	(1)	*(2)*	*(1)/(3)*	*(4)*	*(4)/(1)*
1953–57	0	4 067	–	–	–
1958–62	272	3 048	1 120.59	–	–
1963–65	244	4 266	1 748.36	–	–
1966–70	1 084	949	87.55	–	–
1971–75	5 680	2 317	40.79	–	–
1979–80	17 151	20 292	118.31	–	–
1981–85	24 739	135 734	548.66	–	–
1986–90	147 810	152 205	102.97	63 103	42.69
1991–95	1 049 271	169 969	16.20	352 132	33.56

Source: AIB (1996).

than 25 000 units (Table 15.2). This was in line with the development
objectives of the Chinese authorities who gave priority to the support of the
road transport system by establishing a truck fleet (World Bank, 1993). The
production of passenger cars was mostly reserved for official government
and military purposes and the private use of cars was strictly limited until
the early 1990s.

Restructuring (1983–1994)

Until the early 1980s, the Chinese automotive industry expanded very slowly
because of several structural problems (Marukawa, 1995). First, as already
mentioned, the Chinese automotive industry was extremely fragmented,
with small-scale and geographically dispersed production capacity.[4] In 1980,
for instance, only 2 (2.6%) of the 75 enterprises active in finished vehicle
assembly reached an annual production level of 10 000 units, while for 32
(44%) of them, the output was less than 500 units (National Information
Centre, 1994). The productivity of the automotive industry was extremely
low. In 1981, the industry employed 904 000 people for the production of
176 000 four-wheeled vehicles. This amounted to only 0.2 vehicle per
employee per year, as compared with 16.2 in Japan in 1980. China's labour
productivity was a mere 1/83 of Japan's in terms of number of vehicles
produced per worker (Marukawa, 1995).

  Second, the industry was strongly sheltered from all kinds of competition.
This protection allowed inefficient domestic enterprises to survive despite
their high costs and poor quality. It also delayed the rationalisation of the
automotive industry necessary to become internationally competitive.
Although some imports were allowed, especially for special vehicles and

passenger cars, they were not a threat to domestic producers because they were tightly controlled and limited by the state plan that was administrated by the central government.

Third, the automotive parts industry was seriously underdeveloped, because the finished vehicle producers were involved in a large part of the upstream processes, e.g. parts and components. For instance, as much as 75% of the parts and components for the Jiefang truck were produced internally by FAW until the early 1980s (Marukawa, 1995). This so-called 'vertical division' was quite different from the global automotive industry, which tends to create horizontal relationships between component suppliers and final assemblers. A vertical and intra-firm supply system resulted in small-scale activities and rigid production systems of the Chinese automotive sector.

Fourth, there was a lack of sectoral policy to oblige companies to exploit economies of scale. Locational advantages were non-existent or limited, because the regional dispersion of the industrial capacity across the country had been carried out on the basis of political considerations rather than rational economic criteria. The spatially dispersed and segmented industrial structure – favoured by local governments and different ministries – impeded the diffusion of technological knowledge and contributed to low efficiency and sub-scale production.

Facing these structural problems, the Chinese government decided in the early 1980s to restructure the industry in order to make it into a real 'pillar' of the country's economy. The restructuring process consisted of several aspects, such as the re-organisation of the industry in terms of ownership and product diversification, the creation of enterprise groups to realise economies of scale, the development of horizontal linkages between vehicle manufacturers and assemblers, etc. The restructuring process would be largely based on the infusion of foreign technology and capital, especially in the passenger car segment.

In 1982, the China National Automotive Industry Corporation (CNAIC) was established to coordinate the activities of different planning bureaucracies (central ministries, provincial governments and municipalities) by providing industrial focus to the planning system and to organise the industrial restructuring in a more efficient way. In 1983, 8 subsidiary companies were brought under the control of CNAIC, based on the product lines rather than the traditional administrative functions. Five of these companies produced finished vehicles, i.e. each in one product segment, while the three others specialised in the production of parts, marketing services and foreign trade. CNAIC regrouped 291 enterprises that were previously controlled by 10 different ministries and 27 provinces and contributed about 80% of the industry's total output.

This restructuring process was driven by government initiatives, however, rather than by the economic aspirations of the enterprises themselves. With the ongoing decentralisation of the Chinese economic system and the expansion of the market mechanism, the control by CNAIC over the industry was not all that strong. In 1987, CNAIC was therefore reformed into a federation of nationwide automotive enterprises. In 1993, its monitoring and policy function was transferred to the newly created Automotive Industry Bureau (AIB) of the Ministry of Machinery Industry, which is responsible for supervising industry-related investment, project approval, production planning, and overall policy decision. Yet, the administration and management of the Chinese automobile industry is still under control of different ministries and different local governments. For instance, among the seven leading passenger car manufacturers in China – FAW, SAW, Beijing Automotive Industry Corp. (BAIC), Shanghai Automotive Industry Corp (SAIC), Tianjin Automotive Industry Corp. (TAIC), Changan Machinery Corp. (CMC), Guizhou Aero Industry Corp. (GAIC) – two are under the direct authority of the State Planning Commission (FAW and SAW), three belong to the jurisdictions of their respective municipalities (BAIC, SAIC and TAIC) and two are under the control of ministry-level entities, (China North Industries Corp. (CMC) and China National Aviation Industry Corp (GAIC)). Such a complicated organisational structure and dispersed industry, together with the strong regional and sectoral protectionism continue to be the key problems for restructuring China's automotive industry.

The most significant industrial restructuring occurred at the company level. Starting from the early 1980s, all large Chinese automotive enterprises began forming inter- and intra-firm linkages in order to extend their production scale and to establish horizontal supply chains. FSW, for instance, brought together ten automobile firms in 1982 by setting up an alliance structure (Jiefang United Automotive Industry Corporation). Thereafter the number of affiliated enterprises gradually increased and reached 149 in 1992. The creation and reorganisation of large enterprise groups resulted both in specialisation and concentration of the production activities. In 1995, the production of seven leading Chinese automotive groups accounted for 64% of the total output of the industry in terms of vehicle units, while 24 (20%) of the 122 vehicle manufacturers reached an annual output of 10 000 units. The proportion of enterprises with an annual production of less than 500 units decreased from 44% to 24% during the period 1980–1995 (AIB, 1996).

The ownership structure of Chinese automotive enterprises became more diversified as a result of the gradual development of the private sector and the establishment of joint ventures and strategic alliances between foreign and domestic enterprises, especially for automotive parts and components. By the end of 1995, state-owned enterprises (SOEs) represented 60% of the automobile sector in terms of number of firms, 77% in employment, 63% in industrial output and 57% in exports. Foreign equity joint ventures also became quite important and took up about a quarter of total output, sales,

Table 15.3 Characteristics of Chinese automotive industry by ownership and subsector (1995)

	No. of enterprises	No. of employees	Output (CNY mil.)	Growth rate (%)	Sales (CNY mil.).	Value added (CNY mil.)	Exports (CNY mil.)
Total	2479	1952542	221651	21.37	217514	54074	3967
Ownership (%)							
SOEs	59.70	77.21	62.89	21.57	63.03	63.03	56.83
Collective	28.20	10.05	7.17	23.93	6.62	7.93	11.89
EJVS	6.82	6.63	24.79	20.40	25.26	24.15	23.11
Others	5.28	6.10	5.14	16.24	5.09	4.89	8.16
Subsector (%)							
Vehicle production	4.92	32.35	51.12	19.74	51.72	47.71	33.38
Conversion	20.81	14.69	8.11	18.46	7.94	7.03	8.14
Motorcycles	4.40	7.59	18.09	19.76	18.42	16.44	18.32
Engines	2.46	5.95	4.70	24.72	4.63	5.51	5.38
Components	67.41	39.42	17.97	28.14	17.30	23.32	34.78

Note: * At the end of the period.
Source: AIB (1996).

value added and exports in this sector. Although the share of collective enterprises – often rural enterprises with mixed ownership – is relatively important in terms of the number of plants and employment, their industrial output and sales are quite small. This reflects their highly labour intensive technology and small scale of production (Table 15.3).

Product diversification in China's automotive sector consists of the establishment of greenfield passenger car plants and the restructuring of production in existing factories. Within the context of the government's new sectoral policy, which privileged the development of the car industry, several production lines were set up in the 1980s for assembling knocked-down (KD) kits through joint venture (Shanghai–Volkswagen) and licensing agreements (Tianjin–Daihatsu). In conjunction with these greenfield passenger car projects, two leading automotive enterprises (FAS and SAW), although they were originally conceived for, and for a long time completely concentrated on, the production of trucks also diversified into the manufacture of passenger cars. In the early 1990s, SAW established a joint venture with Citroën, while FSA started to produce passenger cars, firstly under license from Volkswagen (Audi) and later through a joint venture (FAW–Volkswagen), for producing the Jetta and Golf models. Although these two Sino-European joint ventures only accounted for about 14% of total passenger cars production in 1995, their full production capacity is much higher than the above mentioned greenfield plants in Shanghai and Tianjin.

Consolidation and Rationalisation (1994–)

In February 1994, the State Planning Commission adopted a new automotive policy with the ambitious objectives, on the one hand, to produce 90% of the domestic demand in China by the year 2000 and, on the other hand, to make the Chinese automotive industry internationally competitive both in terms of exports and size by 2010. For this purpose, the industrial restructuring process was accelerated through a set of regulatory measures, such as the introduction and implementation of industrial standards and technical regulations with a production certification system; the consolidation of the industry into large groups; the direct financial support of research and development activities and the encouragement of co-operative ventures with foreign companies; the protection of the domestic market by the imposition of annual import quotas; the restriction of automotive imports to enter via specific ports and the prohibition to import used cars and motorcycles; the promotion of the production of local components by prohibiting the importation of 'knocked down' kits for assembly and by granting preferential import duties and tax benefits to companies meeting local content requirements, etc.

Despite these efforts by the government, automobile production over the past three years in China has actually slowed down considerably: average annual growth rates dropped from 37% between 1990–1993 to 4.7% during the period 1993–1996. The decline of the automotive industry was likely caused by inappropriate credit policies[5] and tremendous inefficiencies resulting in prices that are too high to meet demand. On the other hand, the market for passenger cars in China is quite small by international standards, not only because of the limited purchasing power of Chinese households and the absence of an efficient credit system, but also because of China's government policy that discouraged the private use of passenger cars in the past. Yet, the proportion of cars purchased for private purposes increased from 15% in 1996 to 21% in 1997 (Pilmanis, 1998).

As a result of the high growth rate of passenger car investment in the mid-1980s and early 1990s, over-capacity occurred in the industry. By the end of 1997, the total production capacity of the leading car manufacturers reached 900 000 units, while the output for 1997 was only 450 000, i.e. only half of the existing capacity. Such disappointing figures have prompted the central government to reassess its ambitious growth plan for the automobile sector, and to promise that difficult measures will be taken to restructure the industry in the coming years. Since 1996, the automotive sector was no longer officially designated as a 'pillar' industry and in early 1997, the Chinese government announced that no new automobile plant projects would be approved until 2005, i.e. after the industry went through a serious consolidation and rationalisation process.

The main objective of the Chinese government in taking these consolidating and rationalising measures in the automotive industry is to achieve higher production efficiency on the basis of larger-scale operations and to gain the ability to develop product technology independently. By regrouping more than 100 existing car producers into 8 major manufacturers, known as 'The Big Three', 'The Little Three' and 'The Mini Two',[6] the government intends to limit passenger car production (Xing, 1997). This rationalisation process is likely to foster the clustering of automotive and component industries in certain regions, especially in Shanghai. Through the consolidation process, the Chinese government is also trying to develop the industry's capability in new product development and design, because the production of passenger cars in China has become dominated by leading MNEs.[7] With the tacit support of the Chinese government, China Automotive Industrial Corp. recently formed a consortium with several Italian design firms to develop a new car (Simonian, 1997).

FOREIGN AND EUROPEAN COMPANIES IN THE CHINESE AUTOMOTIVE INDUSTRY

One of the major forces that shaped the restructuring and development of the Chinese automotive industry during the last two decades was the

Table 15.4 Major foreign participation and alliances in Chinese passenger car production (1983–95)

Foreign parent company	Chinese partner	Location	Products	Annual output targets (units)	Output in 1995 (units)	As % of national output	Year of establish.	Form	Foreign equity share (%)	Total investment (US$ million)*
Volkswagen	First Auto Works	Changchun	Jetta, Golf	150 000	20 001	6.15	1990	JV	40.0	533.75
	First Auto Works	Changchun	Audi 100	30 000	19 717	6.06	1989	Licence	–	–
	SAIC	Shanghai	Santana	300 000	160 070	49.18	1985	JV	50.0	435.63
Peugeot**	Guangzhou Auto Industry Corp.	Guangzhou	Peugeot 505	30 000	6936	2.13	1985	JV	34.0	260.75
Citroën	Second Auto Works	Wuhan	Citroën ZX	150 000	3 797	1.17	1990	JV	30.0	981.00
Daihatsu	Tianjin Auto Industry Corp.	Tianjin	Charade	150 000	65 000	19.97	1986	Licence	–	–
Chrysler	Beijing Jeep Corp.	Beijing	Cherokee	80 000	25 127	7.72	1983	JV	31.4	152.33
Suzuki	Changan Machinery	Chongqing	Alto	150 000	7725	2.37	1988	Licence-JV	50.0	21.37
Fuji	Guizhou Aero Industry Corp.	Guiyang	Fuji Rex	10 000	7 105	2.18	–	Licence-JV (planned)	–	–
GM	SAIC	Shanghai	Buick	100 000	–	–	1997	JV		1 570
Honda	Guangzhou Auto Industry Corp.	Guangzhou	Accord	30 000	–	–	1997	JV	50.0	200

Notes:
* The amount of total investment was converted from Chinese Yuan (CNY) at the rate of 1 US$ = 8 CNY.
** Peugeot withdrew from the venture in February 1997.

expansion of FDI and its embodied technology. By the end of 1995, the number of foreign-invested automotive enterprises (including the production of automotive parts and components) in China had reached 382, while the amount of foreign-contracted investment was reported to be US$ 4872 million, of which US$ 2292 million was effectively invested. Yet, this represented only 1.7% of the total Chinese inward FDI. The most important source for Chinese inward FDI in the automotive industry is Hong Kong, with 162 enterprises and US$ 540 million of investment, followed by the US with US$ 308 million and Germany with US$ 275 million.

While reviewing data on FDI in the Chinese automotive industry, several characteristics can be identified. First, while FDI in the automotive sector in the 1980s was mainly concentrated in the assembly of complete vehicles, MNEs in the 1990s largely directed their investments into components and parts manufacturing. Between 1981 and 1990, foreign companies established 10 joint ventures for assembling passenger cars, trucks and motorcycles. The total investment in these enterprises reached US$ 2130 million, with a foreign contribution of US$ 320 million. Four leading MNEs engaged in joint ventures with Chinese companies for producing passenger cars, namely Chrysler in the Beijing Jeep Corporation (1983), Volkswagen in the Shanghai Automotive Corp. (1985) and in First Auto Works (1990), Peugeot in Guangzhou (1985), and Citroën in the Second Auto Works (1990) (Table 15.4). During the 1990s, the number of foreign-invested enterprises in the vehicle production sector amounted to 32, while foreign-contracted investment reached US$ 410 million. Yet, almost all of these projects were concentrated in truck and bus production in which the largest investments were made by Renault and Isuzu in medium-size trucks and Volvo and Daimler-Benz in luxury bus assembly. FDI in the automotive parts and component industry significantly increased in the 1990s, when the number of foreign-invested parts manufacturing companies reached 297 between 1991–1995, as compared to only 34 during the period 1981–1990.

Secondly, since the greenfield investment projects for complete vehicle production became strictly controlled by the Chinese government in the 1990s and the early movers had acquired dominant market positions, the entry barriers for latecomers became quite high. Therefore, leading automotive MNEs, especially those from Japan and the US, tried to take over existing local companies to establish a foothold in complete vehicle production. For instance, Ford took over 20% of the equity capital of Jianglin in 1995, and Isuzu and Itochu participated in the Beijing Travel Bus Corp. Yet, the acquisition of local companies by foreign investors through the purchase of shares was initially not encouraged by the Chinese government, because it was considered as a way for foreign companies to force their entry into restricted sectors.

Thirdly, with regard to the ownership structure of foreign-invested enterprises in the Chinese automotive industry, 324 (85%) are equity joint

ventures, 11 (2.9%) are wholly foreign-owned and 57 (12.1%) are contractual joint ventures. The total equity in most (56.3%) foreign-invested
enterprises are dominated by Chinese partners, while foreign-majority and
wholly owned enterprises account for 28%, and the equally owned joint
ventures account for 16%. Foreign investors in the Chinese automotive
industry are only allowed to form minority and equally owned joint ventures, especially in passenger car manufacturing. Although a limited number
of majority foreign-owned joint ventures have been set up in recent years,
this possibility has become restricted. The policy of the Chinese government
to restrain foreign participation reflects its intention to exert long-term
control over the development of the automotive industry. Yet, the ownership control in the component and motorcycle sectors is less strict: majority
and wholly foreign-owned enterprises account for 28.4% and 32.1% of all
foreign invested firms in these respective sectors.

Fourthly, FDI is highly concentrated in the regions that were the original
planned production bases of the Chinese automotive industry. One-fifth of
the total investment of foreign-invested enterprises was directed to the
Hubei province, which is the basis of SAW, 12% to Shanghai because of
the presence of Shanghai Automotive Industrial Corp., and 7% to Jilin
Province, the home of FAW. The geographic location of foreign automotive
enterprises in China has clearly been affected by the presence of existing
firms and has lead to the clustering of the Chinese component and car
industry in the home bases of these firms.

Compared to their overall weak FDI position in China, European MNEs,
which represents less than 4% of the total Chinese inward FDI, are well
established in the Chinese automotive industry, especially in passenger car
production, and since the 1990s also in luxury bus assembly activities.
European-invested joint ventures produced 65% of all passenger cars 'made'
in China in 1995, while the other third was taken up by American jeeps and
Japanese mini-cars (Table 15.4). The first step towards the strong market
position of European automotive MNEs in China was taken in 1985, when
Volkswagen established its first automotive joint venture in Shanghai.
European FDI in the Chinese automotive industries is mainly carried out by
German and French car producers and their domestic and European
suppliers. Companies from Italy, the UK and Austria also entered into the
Chinese automotive industry in the early 1980s, but they mainly concluded
licensing or co-production arrangements and concentrated on, for example,
dump trucks (Terex, 1987) and light trucks (Iveco, 1986). Table 15.5 presents
a more complete list of foreign and European manufacturing firms in the
Chinese automotive sector.

The investment patterns of European MNEs in the Chinese automotive
industry have been quite different from their Japanese and American rivals.[8]
First, European car manufacturers, notably Volkswagen, Peugeot and
Citroën, adopted a long-term strategy with regard to their investment

Table 15.5 Major foreign participations and alliances in Chinese truck and bus production (1997)

Foreign MNEs	Major Chinese partner	Product/model	Form	Foreign share	Target capacity (units)
European					
Iveco (Italy)	Nan Jin Auto Plant (Yuejin Group)	Mini van (Daily)	JV	50.0	60 000
Mercedes Benz (Germany)	South China Motor	Mini van	JV (planned)	45.0	60 000
	Yangzhou Motor Coach	Touring coach	JV	n.a.	7 000
Kogel (Germany)	Jinan Hongqi Refitting Truck Works	Trucks	JV	n.a.	4 100
Renault (France)	China Sanjiang Space Industry Group	Mini van (Trafic, Espace)	JV	33.7	40 000
	Second Inner Mongolia Machinery	Heavy truck	JV	n.a.	300
Terex (UK)	Shanghai Automotive Industry Group	Coach	JV (planned)	n.a.	500
Volvo (Sweden)	Xi'an Aircraft Corp.	Touring bus	JV	n.a.	1 000
US					
Ford	Jiangling Motors Corp.	Transit van	JV (through stock purchase)	20.0	60 000
	Jinbei Automobile Corp.	Pickup truck (S-10)	JV (through stock purchase)	30.0	n.a.
Freightliner Corp.	Shanghai Zehai	Heavy-duty truck	JV	n.a.	4 000
GM	FAW	Pick-up truck	JV	n.a.	30 000

Japan

Company	Partner	Product	Type		Volume
Daihatsu	Tianjin Automotive Industry Group	Mini van	Tech. transfer	n.a.	150 000
Isuzu	Jiangling Motors Corp.	Truck	Tech. transfer	n.a.	30 000
	Chongqing Auto Corp.	Truck	Tech. transfer	n.a.	50 000
	Beijing Automotive Industry Group	Light truck	JV	n.a.	50 000
Itochu	Beijing Automotive Industry Group	Light vehicle	JV (through stock purchase)	n.a.	60 000
Mazda (Japan)	Hainan Provincial Development & Construction	Touring bus	JV	17.5	50 000
Mitsubishi	Fuzhou Auto Works	Delica van	JV	n.a.	10 000
Nissan	Zhengzhou Light Truck Factory	Pick-up truck	JV	n.a.	20 000
	SAW	Bus	JV	n.a.	5 000
Suzuki	Harbib Aircraft	Suisuki Carry	Licence	n.a.	n.a.
	Jiangxi Changhe Machinery	Suisuki Carry	Licence	n.a.	n.a.
Toyota	Sichuan Tourist Coach Factory	Touring bus	JV	n.a.	20 000

Note:
n.a. = not available.
Source: China Auto International Information Co., Ltd.

operations in China. Volkswagen, for instance, from the very beginning considered its Chinese operation as part of its global strategy to build up an industrial and commercial base in Asia in order to compete with its Japanese and American competitors in the region. Its investments in China were not only focussed on acquiring an important share in the Chinese automobile market, but also to extend its activities to neighbouring countries (Wang, 1996). By contrast, most firms from Japan and the US – except AMC – Chrysler limited their Chinese operations to the licensing of production when they tapped the initially inaccessible market (e.g. Suzuki). Because of these short-term strategic considerations, these companies seemed to have missed the opportunities that were present in the early 1980s to invest in the growing Chinese passenger car industry. Yet, the initially weak position of Japanese and American car makers in China was somewhat improved by their late decision to move into light trucks (e.g. Isuzu), medium-sized buses (e.g. Toyota and Mazda) and components (e.g. GM-Delphi and Ford). Yet, the entry costs were high for these latecomers. When GM, for instance, finally recognised the strategic importance of China as the highest growth market for passenger cars in the world and was ready to invest in complete car production, it was obliged by the Chinese government to firstly invest in parts manufacturing and a technology institute before it could be accepted as a joint venture partner for vehicle assembly[9] in 1997.

EUROPEAN MNEs AND THE RESTRUCTURING OF THE CHINESE AUTOMOTIVE INDUSTRY

The early European entrants have changed the market and industrial structure in the Chinese automotive sector. They clearly contributed to the passenger car and component industry agglomeration and shaped the future development of the industry. First, the large-scale investment by European MNEs allowed them quickly to acquire a dominant position in the Chinese car market. The proportion of European car models, such as the Santana, Audi, Peugeot, Jetta and Citroën, in the total Chinese car fleet rose from less than 7% in 1989 to 62.4% in 1993 (World Bank, 1993; National Information Centre, 1996). In 1997, Shanghai Volkswagen sold 200 000 Santana cars, accounting for 52% of total passenger car sales in China, while the market share for its Jetta was 10%.

Secondly, European car manufacturers in China actively participate in the local content programme and have entered into cooperation agreements with local suppliers and the Chinese government (De Bruijn and Jia, 1994). They often provide technical assistance and development funds to local suppliers. Between 1988 and 1994, for instance, Shanghai Volkswagen contributed 5 billion Chinese Yuan (CNY) to the 'Localisation Funds' of Santana, i.e. CNY 28 000 per car, which was used for the technological upgrading of local suppliers. The German parent company also actively supported the Chinese localisation programme by funding and organising training programmes and by helping to identify foreign partners for the Chinese suppliers in the automotive industry (see below). As far as the co-operation with the government is concerned, Shanghai Volkswagen as well as Guangzhou Peugeot formed a localisation commission with local suppliers, auto industry research institutions and government agencies in order to better support and monitor their localisation programmes. The improvement of local supply capabilities and the increase of local value-added allowed these enterprises to lower their costs of production and to benefit from the government's tariff and tax incentives. By the end of 1995, the local content rate of the Volkswagen Santana and Peugeot cars reached 88.6% and 84% respectively, while that for the Volkswagen Jetta increased from 7% to 62% only three years after having been introduced in China in 1992 (Figure 15.2). Because of the implementation of a strict local content programme by the Chinese government, the proportion of assembled CKD cars in the total Chinese car production decreased from 66% to 32% between 1988 and 1995. Imported cars took up only 8% of the domestic market in 1995, compared with 67% in 1988.

Thirdly, European car manufacturers have actively participated in market and product development in order to maintain their early entrants' advantages and become market leaders. When Volkswagen established its first subsidiary in Shanghai, it introduced a rather outdated model, the Santana, in order to extend the 'life cycle' of this model in China and to

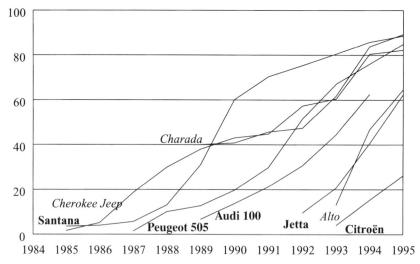

Figure 15.2 Local content of major foreign models produced in China (1984–95).
Source: AIB and CNAIC (1995) and AIB (1996)

compensate for its huge development costs. Although this model was not successful in the European market, it was regarded as potentially competitive to imported Toyota and Nissan cars in the Chinese market (De Bruijn and Jia, 1993). However, with the entry of other car manufacturers, Volkswagen quickly moved into a more luxurious and sophisticated product range by licensing the Audi 100 (1989) and re-launching the production of 'Red Flag' (1994) – the most prestigious model of the Chinese indigenous automobile sector – with an Audi chassis and a Chrysler engine. In 1991, VW introduced the Jetta and Golf cars in its newly-built joint venture with FSW in Changchun. At the same time, Shanghai Volkswagen successfully introduced its own designed and developed model – the Santana 2000 – in 1994.

In order to meet both local content regulations and quality requirements, vehicle producers have tried to convince component suppliers from Europe to establish JVs with selected Chinese partners, often offering financial guarantees and future contracts as an inducement (Table 15.6). For instance, 27 German parts and accessories firms have already launched 45

Table 15.6 Major European automotive parts manufacturers with production activities in China (end of 1995)

	Company headquarters	Year of entry	Supplier for
Aling Klinger	Germany	n.a.	Santana, Cherokee, Peugeot, Citroën
Autoliv	Sweden	1990	Audi, Jetta, Golf, Santana, Citroën, Peugeot
BASCN	Germany	1994	
BCS	France	n.a.	Alto, Citroën, Peugeot
Bosch	Germany	1995	Santana, Audi, etc
Codan Gummi	Denmark	1987	Santana, Audi, Alto
Freudenberg	Germany	n.a.	Audi, Santana
GKN	Germany	1988	Santana, Audi, Citroën, Peugeot, Cherokee
Hella	France	n.a.	Audi
Hülsbeck & Fürst	Germany	n.a.	Jetta, Audi, Opel, Ford, Passat
IAO	Italy	n.a.	Alto, Iveco
Lucas	UK	1994	Audi, Jetta
OKU	Germany	1994	
Philips	Netherlands	1995	Santana, Peugeot,
Pilkington	UK	n.a.	Citroën, Renault
Plantack	Germany	n.a.	Audi, Jetta
Procal	France	1992	Citroën, Renault
Valeo	France	1994	Audi, Alto
VDU	Germany	1995	
ZF	Germany	1994	Santana

Note:
n.a. = not available.
Source: CNAIC (1996).

joint ventures with Chinese partners, with the German management being strongly intent on keeping a grip on this highly promising market (Department of Foreign Affairs and International Trade of Canada, 1996). On the other hand, the latecomers in passenger car manufacturing have to invest in the local production of parts as a condition for being acceptable as partners in future car assembling joint ventures.

The recent consolidation process in the passenger car sector has presented both challenges and opportunities for foreign MNEs. First, the early entrants in car manufacturing in China have been able to reinforce their market position as a result of the limited access of the sector to newcomers. Secondly, with the slowdown of the growth of the market and the over-capacity of production, several car makers lost their confidence and abandoned their initial investment plan, Mercedes Benz for instance, which proposed to invest US$ 1.29 billion in two projects for manufacturing family cars (1994) and mini vans (1995) slowed down its activities in the Chinese market (The Economist, 1998), while Peugeot withdrew from its joint venture in Guangzhou after 12 years of cooperation (Harwit, 1997; Wong, 1997).

CONCLUSION

The restructuring of the Chinese automotive industry since the 1980s has been strongly influenced by the European automotive multinationals. At the early stage of their entry, European vehicle manufacturers engaged in the transfer of technology for passenger car production in China by establishing CKD assembly facilities. As compared to their triad rivals, who relied more on production and technology licensing for tapping into a still very limited market, European producers moved quickly into local production that allowed them to build up a dominant market position and provided them with an early mover's advantage. With the high resource commitment in market and product development, especially by continuously introducing new products, European automotive producers also succeeded in creating and sustaining a leading market position and in mapping the industrial structure.

In the 1990s, the continued infusion of product and production technology has gradually shifted towards the component sector as a result of the increasing intention of the Chinese government to upgrade the local sourcing capabilities. European vehicle manufacturers have actively cooperated in the government's local content programme and exercised pressure on their suppliers to invest in China to increase their cost-based efficiency. The entry of these European component producers has not only changed the technological level of the Chinese automotive industry, but also forged the Chinese component sector into a new 'supply-assembly' relationship that is also changing the automotive industry worldwide.

The successful development of the Chinese automotive industry during the last two decades showed that the dynamic interaction between host government policy and strategic setting of MNEs is crucial for the restructuring of the indigenous industry. Yet, the future development of the Chinese automotive industry and its determination to achieve a strong global competitive position relies not only on the infusion of foreign assembly and production technology, but also on its ability to develop product technology.

Notes

1. Although the automotive parts sector is increasingly considered as an important separate industry in the industrial countries, since the 1980s (OECD, 1992), it is still treated as a subsector of the automobile industry in China.
2. This technology was itself derived from the blueprints for American trucks in the 1920s (World Bank, 1993).
3. From 1964 to the late 1970s, the Chinese government started and relocated a large number of industrial enterprises into inland regions to protect them against possible nuclear attacks from the US and the former Soviet Union. This period was known as the construction of the 'third front'.
4. The spatial dispersion of subscale plants went to such an extreme that by 1979, for example, 405 establishments were producing engines, while the size of the market was hardly large enough for even a single efficient plant.
5. In 1997, the Chinese government decided to postpone the application of the consumer credit service for the purchase of cars. Given the current emphasis on the reforn of the state-owned enterprises, the development of consumer credit will focus on housing.
6. The 'Big Three' are Shanghai Auto Industry Corp. (Volkswagen Santana, GM Buick), FAW (Volkswagen Jetta and Audi) and SAW (Citroën ZX, Honda Accord), while the 'Little Three' are Beijing Auto Industry Corp. (Chrysler Cherokee), Tianjing Automotive Industry Corp. (Daihatsu Charade) and Guangzhou Auto Industry Corp. (Peugeot SW). The 'Mini Two' are Chongqing Changan (Suzuki Alto) and Guizhou Aerospace (Fuji Rex).
7. The Charade car is an exception and is produced by the Tianjin Automobile Industrial Corporation on the basis of a licensing arrangment with Daihatsu.
8. The non-Japanese Asian investors, mostly from Hong Kong, Taiwan, South Korea and Malaysia, are not comparable to the Triad MNEs, as they are operating in a lower-tech segment of the industry. These companies are mostly concentrated in motorcycle assembly and low-tech components production, such as electrical and electronic systems and decorative textiles.
9. In 1997, GM was finally selected by the Chinese government as a partner in a joint venture with SAIC for producing its Buick Salon. The total capacity wil be 300 000 per year.

References

Aggarwal, R. and Agmon, T. (1990) 'The international success of developing country firms: role of government-directed comparative advantage', *Management International Review*, 30(2): 163–180.

AIB (1996) *China Automotive Industry Yearbook* (Beijing: AIB, Ministry of Machinery Industry).

AIB and CNAIC (1995) *Policies about China Automotive Industry* (Beijing: AIB, Ministry of Machinery Industry).

Cantwell, J.A. (1991) 'The technological competence theory of international production and its implications', in D. McFetridge (ed.) *Foreign Investment, Technology and Economic Growth* (Toronto: University of Toronto Press).

CNAIC (1996) *Directory of Parts Suppliers for Chinese Introduced Vehicle* (Beijing: Auto Information Service, CNAIC).

De Bruijn, E.J. and Jia, X. (1993) 'Managing Sino-Western joint ventures: product selection strategy', *Management International Review*, 33(4): 335–360 (Greenwich, Connecticut).

De Bruijn, E.J. and Jia, X. (1994) 'Managing Sino-Western joint ventures: localisation of content', in S. Stewart (ed.) *Joint Ventures in the PRC, Advances in Chinese Industrial Studies*, 4, 233–254 (JAI Press).

Department of Foreign Affairs and International Trade of Canada (1996) *German Automotive Industry Outlook, 1995* (Munich: Canadian Consulate).

Dunning, J.H. (1997) 'Reconciling some paradoxes of global economy', Paper presented at Round Table and Workshop on Globalisation and the Small Open Economy, May, 29, University of Antwerp, Antwerp.

Economist (The) (1998) 'Daimler-Benz: Stalling in China', *The Economist*, April 18: 74.

Harwit, E. (1997) 'Guangzhou Peugeot: portrait of a commercial divorce', *China Business Review*, November–December: 10–11.

Lall, S. (1985) 'Multinationals and technology development in host countries', in S. Lall (ed.) *Multinationals, Technology and Exports* (London: Macmillan).

Marukawa, T. (1995) 'Industrial groups and division of labour in China's automobile industry', *The Development Economies*, 33(3): 300–355.

National Information Centre (1994) *The Perspective of Chinese Automobile Market in 1995* (Beijing: National Information Centre and Chinese Automobile Trade Corp.).

OECD (1992) *Globalisation of Industrial Activities, Four Case Studies: Auto Parts, Chemicals, Construction and Semiconductors* (Paris: OECD).

Simonian, H. (1997) 'China looks to Italians to develop car industry', *Financial Times*, November 26.

Pilmanis, K. (1998) *Automotive Industry* (Beijing: US Commercial Service).

Tolentino, E.E. (1993) *Technological Innovation and Third World Multinationals* (London and New York: Routledge).

Wang, Z. (1996) *Investment of Transnational Corporations* (Beijing: Chinese Economy Edition) (in Chinese).

Wong, L. (1997) 'Honda wins Guangzhou base', *South China Morning Post*, November 14, 1997.

World Bank (1993) *China Industrial Organisation and Efficiently Case Study: The Automotive Sector*, Report No. 12134-CHA (New York).

Xing, W. J. (1997) 'Shifting gears', *The China Business Review*, November–December: 8–18.

Index